S0-AYB-201

Milton and the Rabbis

Milton and the Rabbis

Hebraism, Hellenism, & Christianity

Jeffrey S. Shoulson

COLUMBIA UNIVERSITY PRESS   NEW YORK

Columbia University Press
Publishers Since 1893
New York   Chichester, West Sussex
Copyright © 2001 Columbia University Press
All rights reserved
Library of Congress Cataloging-in-Publication Data
Shoulson, Jeffrey S.
Milton and the rabbis : Hebraism, Hellenism, and Christianity / Jeffrey S. Shoulson.
p. cm.
Includes bibliographical references and index.
ISBN 0-231-12328-0 (cloth : alk. paper) — ISBN 0-231-12329-9 (pbk. : alk. paper)
1. Milton, John, 1608–1674—Knowledge—Judaism. 2. Christianity and other
religions—Judaism—History—17th century. 3. Jewish learning and
scholarship—England—History—17th century. 4.
Judaism—Relations—Christianity—History—17th century. 5. Jewish learning and
scholarship in literature. 6. Hebrew literature—Appreciation—England. 7. Milton, John,
1608–1674—Religion. 8. Hellenism—History—17th century. 9. Judaism in literature. I.
Title.
PR3592.R4 S45 2001
821'.4—dc21
2001032330

Casebound editions of Columbia University Press books
are printed on permanent and durable acid-free paper.
Printed in the United States of America
Designed by Lisa Hamm
c 10 9 8 7 6 5 4 3 2 1
p 10 9 8 7 6 5 4 3 2 1

For Margery

'Love, sweetness, goodness, in her person shine'

Contents

Acknowledgments

I SHOULD BEGIN by acknowledging the many caring teachers with whom I have had the privilege of studying, far too many to name individually. I do want specifically to thank Rabbi Jay Miller, who gave me an early appreciation of the challenges and delights that attend the study of rabbinic literature. In his personal example, Rav Yehuda Amital offered me a glimpse of the very best synthesis of Torah and *derekh eretz*, intellectual rigor and social commitment.

My interest in the relationship between Milton and rabbinic literature began while I was an undergraduate at Princeton University, where I studied Milton with Victoria Kahn and wrote an undergraduate thesis under the guidance of John Fleming. Without their early encouragement—along with support from other members of the faculty there—I have a strong suspicion that I might have opted for law school. A wonderful year at Jesus College, Cambridge, gave me the privilege of studying with Lisa Jardine, the late Jeremy Maule, and early modern bibliographer par excellence Elizabeth Leedham-Green. It was at Cambridge that I also met Bill Sherman, whose intelligence and drive have had a lasting impact on me. As a graduate student at Yale University, I learned what it means to read poetry from Leslie Brisman,

Paul Fry, and John Hollander. Geoffrey Hartman's guidance as I wrote my dissertation was exemplary in its generosity and wisdom; his extraordinary range of interests continues to serve as a model for my own endeavors. Thoughtful comments from Annabel Patterson, David Quint, and John Rogers were essential to the extensive revisions and expansions I undertook as I turned a graduate dissertation into a first book. None of my work at Yale would have been as meaningful to me were it not for the lasting friendships I developed with Ian Baucom, Kevis Goodman, Lee Oser, Nikhil Singh, and Cliff Spargo, each of whom has contributed to this project in visible and invisible ways.

The rabbinic term for friend, *chaver*, also means teacher or scholar, and I consider the following people to be *chaverim* in the fullest sense of the word. Dwight McBride's valued friendship has been emotionally sustaining and intellectually challenging. My colleagues at the University of Miami, among them Joe Alkana, Peter Bellis, Shari Benstock, Zack Bowen, and Henry Green, provided encouragement and support. Members of the UM Humanities Colloquium were instrumental in fostering a fertile intellectual atmosphere. David Glimp, Tassie Gwilliam, and John Paul Russo gave helpful comments on various parts of the book. Outside of Miami, William Flesch, Achsah Guibbory, Richard Halpern, Michael Lieb, and John Shawcross have offered incisive and useful suggestions. An extraordinary group of scholars assembled by David Ruderman at the University of Pennsylvania's Center for Advanced Judaic Studies to study early modern Christian Hebraism helped me to see my project from a new perspective: Elisheva Baumgarten, Sylvia Berti, Allison Coudert, Yaacov Deutsch, Matt Goldish, Anthony Grafton, Joseph Hacker, Chaim Hames, Michael Heyd, Moshe Idel, Aaron Katchen, Fabrizio Lelli, Ora Limor, Nils Roemer, Wilhelm Schmidt-Biggemann, Peter Stallybrass, Guy Stroumsa, Piet van Boxl, Joanna Weinberg, and Yisrael Yuval. Joseph Wittreich read the entire manuscript and was especially helpful in the development of the epilogue.

James Shapiro generously served as the *shadchan* (matchmaker) between Columbia University Press and me; Jennifer Crewe has been supportive of the project since it first crossed her desk. Susan Pensak helped polish the project not only through her skills as a copyeditor but also with her knowledge of the rabbinic tradition.

Among all my intellectual debts, I must single out those to Jason Rosenblatt. In all the years that I have known him, he has been gracious and eager to help me. It has been a delight to engage in work that I can share with such a wise and caring mentor.

I remain forever grateful for the unstinting love and support of my parents, Robyn and Bruce Shoulson. Sophia Elizabeth and Oliver Hart continue to remind me of what really matters. This book is dedicated to my partner, my lover, my companion, my friend, Margery Sokoloff. Her mark appears indelibly on every page of my life, which would otherwise have lots of empty spaces.

THIS PROJECT has been generously supported by a variety of sources. A Fulbright Scholarship for study in Cambridge gave me an opportunity to explore some aspects of early modern English Hebraism. A Mellon Fellowship for graduate study in the humanities helped to fund my time at Yale, where I completed a dissertation that formed the basis for this book. Two Max Orovitz Summer Research Grants and a General Research Grant, all administered by the University of Miami, allowed me to devote my summers to further research, writing, and revision. I benefited greatly from a Short-Term Fellowship at the William Andrews Clark Memorial Library. Finally, a significant portion of this book was completed while I enjoyed a year-long fellowship at the University of Pennsylvania's Center for Advanced Judaic Studies.

A portion of chapter 3 first appeared in *Milton Studies* and portion of chapter 4 was originally published in *English Literary History.* I would like to thank the University of Pittsburgh Press and the Johns Hopkins University Press respectively for permission to reprint the material here.

A Note on the Texts

MY DISCUSSIONS OF RABBINIC LITERATURE are based upon the original Hebrew and Aramaic texts. While quotations in English occasionally draw upon the modern translations listed in the selected bibliography, I have made considerable changes based upon my own readings of the original; often, I have retranslated the passage entirely. Because the rabbinic approach depends so heavily on the manipulation of the language of Scripture—puns, anagrams, homophones, etc.—I have included a transliteration where it helps to expose some of these wordplays. Portions of Genesis Rabbah are cited by chapter and section in the body of the text. Passages from the Babylonian Talmud are designated as BT followed by the tractate and the page. Passages from the Palestinian Talmud are cited as PT followed by the tractate, chapter, and section. All other rabbinic texts are designated by name, edition (when appropriate), chapter, and section.

Except where an alternative translation is crucial to the argument, passages from the Bible appear in the King James (Authorized) Version. Unless otherwise noted, translations from the Latin are by the author.

All quotations from Milton's poetry are taken from *John Milton: Complete Poems and Major Prose*, ed. Merritt Y. Hughes (New York: Macmillan, 1957). Selections of Milton's prose, unless otherwise attributed, are taken from *Complete Prose Works of John Milton*, ed. Don M. Wolfe (New Haven: Yale University Press, 1953–1982), and designated as YP, followed by volume and page number.

Milton and the Rabbis

Introduction: Hebraism and Literary History

> We may regard this energy driving at practice, this paramount sense
> of the obligation of duty, self control, and work, this earnestness in
> going manfully with the best light we have, as one force. And we may
> regard the intelligence driving at those ideas which are, after all, the
> basis of right practice, the ardent sense for all the new and changing
> combinations of them which man's development brings with it, the
> indomitable impulse to know and adjust them perfectly, as another
> force.
>
> —*Matthew Arnold*, Culture and Anarchy

CREDITED BY most recent discussions on the university as one of the
central figures in the origins of the academic study of English,
Matthew Arnold has helped to contribute and define many of the key terms
still used in the analysis of literature. Arnold's identification of the two distinctive forces behind Western culture's continuing development in his seminal *Culture and Anarchy* has had the ongoing effect of rendering even contemporary discussions of literary history in terms of a tension between
Hebraism, the first "energy" described above by Arnold, and Hellenism, the
second "force." Arnold famously asserts in the fourth part of *Culture and Anarchy*, itself titled "Hebraism and Hellenism," the key features that distinguish these two forces: "The uppermost idea with Hellenism is to see things
as they really are," writes Arnold, and "the uppermost idea with Hebraism is
conduct and obedience."[1] Though much of Arnold's essay is devoted to forging something like a reconciliation between these two modes of thought,
they nevertheless remain distinct forces working in dialectical relationship to
one another.[2] As an account of the history of culture, *Culture and Anarchy* tells
a story of great swings back and forth between the values of Hebraism and
Hellenism. In so doing, it accounts for Christianity not so much as a third

historical force, a qualitative change from Hebraism, but as a quantitative revision of that moral force. In Arnold's view Christianity may have substituted a larger devotion for Hebraism's narrow ethnic parameters—he calls Christianity's devotion "boundless"—but it still sought the same Hebraic ideal of self-conquest. Arnold continues:

> As the great movement of Christianity was a triumph of Hebraism and man's moral impulses, so the great movement which goes by the name of the Renascence was an uprising and re-instatement of man's intellectual impulses and of Hellenism. . . . The Reformation has often been called a Hebraising revival, a return to the ardour and sincereness of primitive Christianity. No one, however, can study the development of Protestant Churches without feeling that into the Reformation too,—Hebraising child of the Renascence and offspring of its fervour, rather than its intelligence, as it undoubtedly was,—the subtle Hellenic leaven of the Renascence found its way, and that the exact respective parts, in the Reformation, of Hebraism and of Hellenism, are not easy to separate.[3]

ALTHOUGH THERE IS much of which to be critical in Arnold's sweepingly general account of literary and cultural history, this final observation concerning the difficulty of separating Hellenism and Hebraism offers an astute, and often disregarded, qualification to everything that has preceded it. It also serves as the starting point for this book.

For at least a century critics who have wanted to find an early foothold for Hebraic thinking in the English literary tradition have looked to the writings of the seventeenth-century poet and polemicist, John Milton. In the story that is often told about trends in early modern English literature—a story that owes its contours to Matthew Arnold—Milton's writings stand out as something apparently new. After the writers most commonly associated with the English Renaissance—Spenser, Sidney, Shakespeare—seemed to have embraced the classical values of Hellenism, along comes John Milton with all the zealotry of a Puritan preacher thundering forth on God's justice and Christian moral and religious duty. Hebraism, specifically the Hebraism of a Protestant Christian, finds its most eloquent advocate in the poet of *Paradise Lost, Paradise Regained,* and *Samson Agonistes.*

The Hebraic and Judaic aspects of Milton's writings have been the subject of numerous studies, some cursory, plagued by shoddy scholarship, and filled with undisguised antagonism for anything that smacks of Judaism,

others characterized by impressive learning, nuanced readings, and more generous sympathies for the subject.[4] Most recently, two book-length studies
have appeared in which the Judaic features of Milton's writings have been
linked through painstaking research to specific early modern Hebraists. In
his brilliant *Torah and Law in "Paradise Lost,"* Jason Rosenblatt has argued—
quite convincingly—that Milton's extensive knowledge of rabbinic marriage
law, as evidenced especially in his writings on divorce, comes from reading
the works of the great seventeenth-century English legal and rabbinic scholar, John Selden. Rosenblatt shows how Milton's sympathies with Jewish
views on human relationships manifest themselves especially in the middle
books of *Paradise Lost*, where a decisively monist view of the continuity between body and soul inflects virtually all the poetry of prelapsarian Eden.[5] In
her own recent study, Golda Werman has offered an admirable account of
the central rabbinic source for all of Milton's knowledge of rabbinic legends
suggested by their appearance, in however modified form, in *Paradise Lost*.
Werman argues that the 1644 Latin translation of the rabbinic collection
Pirke de R. Eliezer by the Dutch Christian Hebraist Guglielmus Vorstius
(Willem Voorst) is the likeliest candidate, both because it offers a sequential
narrative account of the creation of the universe and because its Latin translator shared the same Arminian viewpoint held by Milton.[6] In an effort to
show the extent of Milton's use of midrash, Werman's study includes a sev-
enty-page appendix in which she offers a line-by-line gloss to Milton's epic
that indicates parallels with rabbinic material. As Werman explicitly acknowledges, however, she makes no attempt to address Christian sources for
Paradise Lost, and she cites the original Jewish source "even when the aggadic
material is readily found in Christian secondary sources."[7] Therein lies the
real crux of the matter. I remain unconvinced of any direct link between a
specific collection of rabbinic midrashim—in either their original Hebrew
and Aramaic or in translation—and Milton's inventions. Without a proverbial "smoking gun" like a book annotated in Milton's hand or some unimpeachable testimony by one of his contemporaries, such links are virtually
unverifiable; in this volume I make no effort to do so. Many of the poetic
ideas one finds in Milton that parallel midrash may indeed have had rabbinic
origins, but they are likely to have entered Christian discourse through any
number of direct and indirect means, not just the works of early modern
Christian Hebraists like Selden and Vorstius but also Protestant writers and
preachers without special knowledge of Hebrew (themselves consumers of
early modern Christian Hebraica) or even the writings of the early Church

fathers who were sometimes in direct dialogue with the first producers of rabbinic literature. Given the diverse ways that so-called Hebraic and Judaic ideas enter into Christian thought, the question finally becomes a definitional one: when is an idea, a theme, an emphasis distinctively Judaic or Hebraic and when is it Christian? It is this precise difficulty—the fluid interaction between ostensibly Jewish, Hellenistic, and Christian modes of thought, not only during the early modern period but at the very origins of rabbinic Judaism and Christianity—that is at the heart of my approach to the question of Milton and the rabbis.

What virtually all prior studies of the relation between the writings of Milton and the rabbis have in common is a tendency to polarize Hebraic, Hellenic, and Christian perspectives or influences. These distinctions fail to acknowledge that the category of Hebraic, or Judaic, is not only constituted by multiple, often conflicting, voices but also dynamically engaged with Hellenic and Christian sensibilities. To construe Milton's poetry as a literary, cultural, or religious agon of Hellenism and Hebraism, Pauline Christianity and rabbinic Judaism, or even orthodox (Calvinist) Puritanism and radical sectarianism, demands a consideration of related conflicts in the rabbinic texts themselves. In the pages that follow I work to break down many of the time-honored divisions critics have distilled out of Milton's writings. Indeed, the recent debate within the community of Milton scholars concerning the provenance of the *De Doctrina Christiana* may be understood as, in part, a result of this impulse toward polarization and rigid classification. Those scholars who have challenged Milton's authorship of the text have done so on the basis of the treatise's incompatibility with traditional Christianity as defined by Calvin and his followers.[8] In their view, Milton was just such an orthodox Protestant and thus could never have written so heterodox an account of Christian beliefs. William Hunter insists that the heresies thought to be a part of *Paradise Lost* "are not evident to the objective reader who limits himself to the poem and ignores the interpretations of it derived from ideas in the treatise."[9] Setting aside the tautological nature of this argument, it should be clear that it also depends upon an inflexible view of the cultural and religious contours of Christianity. If we regard early modern Christianity, as formulated by Milton or by any other writer of the period, as an ongoing negotiation of a variety of inherited and invented attitudes, I think we will be less inclined to insist on a Milton either specifically orthodox or heretical.[10]

This volume explores the fuller implications of the critical tendency to

characterize John Milton as a Hebraic poet by probing the limits of the relationship between Milton and his Jewish antecedents. The rabbis and Milton
both shaped their identities in relation to the religious and political forces to
which they had evidently lost out. Elements of Milton's poem that have
come to be regarded by modern critics as Hebraic (or Judaic) were, in their
earlier formulations during the rabbinic period, already fraught with tensions
between biblical, Hellenic, and Christian impulses. Similarly, the so-called
classical and Pauline aspects of Milton's poem are profoundly implicated in
the question of *Paradise Lost*'s Hebraism. The Hebraic elements of the epic
function to preserve a crucial dialogic textuality. With the revision of these
cultural genealogies, I suggest that the rabbis' radical reformulation of postbiblical Judaism finds its own uncanny recapitulation in Milton's innovative
refashioning of post-Reformation Christianity. My study explores these homologous negotiations of national and religious identity, giving fuller expression to theoretical and literary analogies between midrashic aggadah and
Milton's epic.[11]

ℒℴ

MY FIRST CHAPTER attends to the historical parallels between the rabbinic
view of post-Temple Judaism and the Miltonic view of post–Civil War England. The midrashim to which I compare *Paradise Lost* in the latter portion of
this study emerged during a period of crisis precipitated by the destruction
of the Temple in Jerusalem and the ascendancy of Christianity in the Roman
Empire. Milton's biblical epic was finished during a similar period of religious and political crisis in the wake of the abject failure of parliamentary
rule and the ensuing Restoration of the English monarchy with its attendant
High Church Anglicanism. Deep-seated dissatisfaction with their respective
historical predicaments conditioned both the rabbis' midrashic hermeneutic
and Milton's justification of God's ways to man. The parallels between Milton and the rabbis were already anticipated within the context of a dramatic
rise in English discussions of Hebrew, Judaism, and Jews during the seventeenth century. In addition to the aforementioned studies that have sought to
connect Milton to Hebraic and Judaic learning, the many important discussions of portions of Milton's writings against the backdrop of millenarian
and radical Protestant trends in the middle of the seventeenth century constitute an essential aspect of this study. So do the several sophisticated scholarly analyses of the debates surrounding Jews and their readmission to En-

gland in the 1640s and 1650s. So far as I know, there has been little effort to combine these three lines of inquiry. By bringing aspects of all these elements together, along with the recent innovative study of classic rabbinic literature, I seek to understand Milton's so-called Hebraic writings in light of the cultural forces at work in the contemporary legacy of this Hebraic tradition in living Jews. Textual formulations of English national identity depend upon an incipient religio-ethnic discourse that posits "the Jew" as a liminal figure on the English landscape. The Jew—especially as constructed by the Christian imagination—appeared uncannily close to Milton's evolving self-perception while at the same time resisting full assimilation to his Protestant English identity. Yet the "real" Jew of Milton's time was already heir to a parallel struggle between identity and difference in the fourth through sixth centuries of the Common Era, which dictated the terms of rabbinic self-fashioning in opposition to Judaism's prodigal son, Christianity.

In chapter 2 I explore further aspects of seventeenth-century English perceptions of this analogy through a reading of Milton's prose writings. The inconsistent nature of Milton's invocation of Jewish precedent throughout his writings reveals how ambivalently the poet's Hebraicisms function in *Paradise Lost*. In his polemics against the prelacy, divorce tracts, and writings on monarchy and regicide, Milton turned time and again to Hebraic and rabbinic precedent, but in a remarkably conflicted manner. Throughout his career, Milton situated his writings at the center of many key religious and political debates; yet he increasingly marginalized himself even as he participated in these controversies. Milton's work thus affords an especially rich opportunity to examine the evolving and politically charged use of Hebraica during this period of "a world turned upside down." Rosenblatt's study has shown the prevalence of Judaic thought in Milton's writings on divorce. In these texts one finds Milton at his most explicitly generous with respect to the Jewish tradition. My analysis in this chapter focuses, instead, primarily on the tracts that constituted Milton's first foray into the vituperative world of prose polemics, i.e., his writings against the hierarchical English prelacy. Unlike the divorce tracts, when the antiprelatical tracts cite Jewish precedent they nearly always do so in what looks to be a derogatory fashion. And yet, I shall argue that even—or precisely—in those moments of Milton's greatest antagonism toward Jewish precedent he reveals the complex interrelations of the Hebraic and the Hellenic, the Jewish and the Christian.

Chapters 3 through 5 explore epistemological, ontological, and phenomenological aspects of Milton's epic alongside portions of midrash. Throughout each chapter I move back and forth between Milton's writings and those of the rabbis, showing how Milton's text can inform a more nuanced reading of midrash as much as midrash can offer new insights into *Paradise Lost*.

Chapter 3 compares Milton's rendition of the Celestial Dialogue between the Father and the Son in book 3 to the rabbinic reliance on anthropomorphic depictions of God. I am concerned here with the philosophical and theological questions of epistemology. By discerning various forms of knowledge—their contours and limitations—the rabbis and Milton confront crucial theological questions. "Man's first disobedience," recounted in Genesis 3, occasioned profound thought and sometimes debilitating anxiety about the status of knowledge after the consumption of the fruit of the Tree of Knowledge. But the historical circumstances of both the rabbis and Milton, each experiencing catastrophic political and ideological defeat, were just as instrumental in provoking prolonged meditation on the possibility of knowing and understanding the world where nothing seemed to be going as expected. Epistemological concerns go hand in hand with theological questions, in particular those that pertain to theodicy, as the rabbis and Milton each attempt to "assert Eternal Providence / And justify the ways of God to men." In this epistemological confrontation with God—from επι ιϲταμαι, to stand before or confront—both the rabbis and Milton articulate an ethics of engagement that reinvigorates the dynamics of human-divine encounters, and especially encounters within the human, social universe. I argue that both the rabbis and Milton enlist God's readability—above all, God's excessively human traits—in their respective theodical projects. In both midrash and *Paradise Lost* unflattering anthropomorphic depictions of God as earthly tyrant are exploited for their value in shifting the responsibility of interpretation (and, by extension, human agency) to the reader.

The fourth chapter examines the poem's three narratives of creation: Eve's in book 4, Raphael's in book 7, and Adam's in book 8. I specifically address the parallels and differences between divine and human creativity taken up by Milton's writings and the midrash on the first three chapters of Genesis. The affirmation of sexuality in both texts is balanced by an intense ambivalence about the corrupting potential of human desire and imagination. This ambivalence can be seen especially in the way that both Milton and the rabbis negotiate the presence of Hellenic or classical literary models in their respective writings. Crucial to this parallel between the rabbis and Milton is their shared ontological monism, which gives rise to distinctive psychologies and anthropologies. Largely in response to the rise of a politically empowered Christianity, the rabbis sought to distinguish themselves from a Pauline dualist ontology that posited a radical disjunction between body and soul by emphasizing a monist view of sexuality. Similarly, Milton's unorthodox view of sexuality was based upon a monism that distinguished him not only from High Church Protestants and Catholics but also from most followers of Calvin. The monism of Milton and the rabbis served not only to recuperate a potentially more positive view of the body and sexuality, it yielded implications for the ethical nature of human imagination and desire as well.

In the fifth chapter I argue that Milton's version of proleptic history functions in much the same way as the rabbinical replacement of prophecy with interpretation. After the destruction of the Temple, midrash stands in for prophecy as the proper mode of consolation and access to divine truths. The events of the past, both distant and more recent, that make themselves felt in the writings of the rabbis and Milton pose a special challenge. With few exceptions, these events mark painful losses. Yet if these texts purport to serve as theodicy—for the rabbis implicitly, for Milton explicitly—part of "this great argument" must offer some form of consolation by suggesting the possibility of redeeming this history of loss. In this chapter I revisit many of the historical analogies I identified in my first chapters, this time offering a more detailed account of the manner in which the rabbis and Milton negotiate their respective predicaments. I examine references to the history of loss in midrash and *Paradise Lost*, arguing that these moments of mourning constitute distinctive phenomenologies of history, implying, in turn, a rabbinic and Miltonic politics. The rabbis replace the "false surmise" of historical narration with a nonlinear folding together of the biblical past, the rabbinical present, and the hoped-for future of redemption. Similarly, Michael's visitation to the fallen couple at the end of Milton's epic posits a paradoxically cyclical teleology to the (future) history of humankind, the "Ages of endless date." Historical phenomena—from φαινεσθαι, to appear—become interpretive fantasies. Rabbinic literature and *Paradise Lost* lament the death and loss they uncover in commemorating the past; yet they seek consolation in a sublation of that past, producing a kind of synthetic history with direct implications for the renewal of political agency.

Finally, although my analysis of Milton's poetry focuses primarily on *Paradise Lost*, I conclude with an epilogue that summarizes the preceding arguments by way of a brief prospective discussion of *Samson Agonistes*. Perhaps more so than anything else he wrote, Milton's closet drama has been read by generations of critics specifically in light of its relationship to the so-called

Hebraic tradition. Drawing on my readings of interactions and parallels between Miltonic and rabbinic epistemologies, ontologies, phenomenologies, I shall suggest an alternative approach to this age-old question. The Samson of both Milton and the rabbis embodies a range of contradictory impulses, from faithfulness to heretical obstinance, from productive to destructive sexuality, from violence to passivity. It is in what most regard as Milton's final poetic achievement that we may finally recognize just how inextricably intertwined are the discourses of Hebraism, Hellenism, and Christianity.

I

Diaspora and Restoration

And yet while we detest *Judaism*, we know our selves commanded by
St. *Paul, Rom.* 11. to respect the *Jews,* and by all means to endeavor thir
conversion.

—*John Milton, "Observations Upon the Articles of Peace"*

I BEGIN WITH a few working definitions.[1] Midrash, from which most of
my examples of rabbinic literature will be drawn, takes as its organizing
principle the sequence of verses, portions, and books of the Hebrew Bible.
Though its individual comments and observations can, and usually do, range
widely within the biblical canon, its sequence of homilies, narratives, or legal
pronouncements inevitably follows the main biblical text to which it has been
appended.[2] In terms of the historical development of rabbinic interpretive
genres, the midrashic mode seems to have predated the Mishnaic (Talmudic)
mode. The midrashic approach, firmly anchored in biblical prooftexts, justified itself by virtue of its perceived adherence to Scripture. The intervening
Mishnaic mode, which David Weiss Halivni and others have characterized as
an aberration, lacked the programmatic scriptural relevance of its precursor
in midrash and thus required various means of justification, including the
ideology of divine origin of the Oral Torah and abstract hermeneutical rules.
When the midrashic prooftext mode reasserted itself (within and without
the developing Talmudic corpus), the Mishnaic justification of divine origin
lingered and soon became associated with midrash as well.[3]

Aggadah, as opposed to halakhah, consists of longer and shorter narratives and textual amplifications that do not have a direct bearing on the expected normative behavior (as codified by the halakhah) of the audience to which it has been directed. This is not to say that the aggadah has no worldly or contemporary application. On the contrary, aggadah is everywhere and always concerned with finding ways to apply the lessons and stories of Scripture to its contemporary situation. But such application takes a form other than, say, a halakhic pronouncement on dietary laws. Both halakhah and aggadah are occasioned by difficulties arising from a reading of Scripture; whereas halakhah will pose the problem, present differing opinions on the matter, and propose a resolution to be instituted in the daily praxis of the Jewish community, aggadah will allow for a greater play of possibilities, contradictions, and fancies in an effort to provoke its audience to a more active engagement with the text and all its implications. We might recall as a starting point the observation of the early twentieth-century Hebrew poet and philologist Hayim Nahman Bialik on the distinction between these two rabbinic modes: "Halakah wears an angry frown; Aggada, a broad smile."[4] A halakhic midrash seeks to create a bridge between normative praxis and the biblical verse. Halakhah must ultimately have one definable application, even when more than one interpretation is raised. Not so for midrash aggadah, where the multiplication of interpretations and exemplary illustrations—even those that seem to contradict each other—is welcomed as a means of revealing ever more facets of Scripture.

Although most midrashic collections have been classified by modern scholars as either halakhic or aggadic—a third category, homiletic, is also used—there does not exist a midrashic collection that is either purely halakhic or purely aggadic. The rabbis were always illustrating their halakhic arguments with narrative asides and drawing halakhic implications from their literary embellishments of biblical narratives. The simultaneous presence of aggadic and halakhic concerns inevitably led to certain conflicts between the two interpretive modes, and already in the Tannaitic centuries there was a discernible tension between these two sides of midrashic hermeneutics.[5] The results of this tension were far-reaching—they continue to be felt in some Jewish circles to this day—and it has been argued by Judah Goldin that the conflict between halakhah and aggadah describes a permanent human agon between restraint and freedom as the best way to get closer to God.[6] I would add further that this agon between restraint and freedom is the *most essential el-*

ement in the constitution of the methods of midrash aggadah and not only manifested in the clash between halakhah (as the restrained approach) and aggadah (as the free approach).

Despite numerous attempts to develop an all-encompassing theoretical description of rabbinic hermeneutics in general and midrash aggadah in particular, there has yet to appear a satisfying formulation. Even if we could forget that the texts that constitute the vast corpus of classical rabbinical writings were accumulated over the course of at least six centuries, even if we did not have to consider that there were at least two major centers of Jewish learning during this period, Palestine and Babylonia, each of which produced its own set of rabbinic texts, even if we were able to set aside any ideas about the ever changing sociopolitical climates in each location, even if it were possible to isolate one text out of the hundreds in existence as *the* paradigm for all analyses of rabbinic hermeneutics, even if all this (and more) were possible, we would still be left with the remarkable lack of systematizing by the rabbinic writers themselves. The rabbis were wary—almost obsessively so— of any attempt to establish a universal set of guidelines for interpreting the Bible and making its rules of behavior applicable to their own times. Given the choice between abstraction and particularization, the rabbis favored the latter, subjecting generalities to careful scrutiny of detail and variation. There are, to be sure, several exceptions: the seven *middot*, or rules, ascribed to the great early sage Hillel in Tosefta Sanhedrin 7:11,[7] the thirteen middot ascribed to Rabbi Ishmael at the beginning of the Sifra,[8] and, finally, the thirty-two middot named after Eliezer ben Yose ha-Gelili in the Mishnat R. Eliezer.[9] But these lists are of little use in trying to determine a general modus operandi for rabbinic readers of the Bible. First, they apply to halakhic discourse much more so than to aggadic readings; second, the rules are often more descriptive than prescriptive, with their applications to individual textual cruxes appearing strangely arbitrary at best. Generally speaking, rabbinic hermeneutics makes use of certain logical categories, like inference, deduction, and analogy; it places great emphasis on the context of words, phrases, or verses and, based on the conviction that every jot and tittle of Scripture is charged with significance, it takes notice of irregularities or oddities of grammar and syntax. First and foremost, though, rabbinic interpretive techniques are *occasional* rather than universal or systematic. The given interpretive dilemma, occasioned by the close reading of Scripture, gives rise to the method used for its resolution, and thus even rules of logic are not particularly useful to describe the midrashic hermeneutic. The best we can hope to do in looking for an aggadic method is to try to isolate certain tradition-al forms of midrash aggadah, always bearing in mind that exceptions and combinations are inevitable.

The aggadoth that have been preserved take one of three broad forms. They are either narrative, descriptive, or reported speech. Within the first category of narrative we may enumerate a number of different kinds: exten-sion or amplification of biblical narrative, historical anecdote, biographical note, biographical narrative, miracle narrative, narrative with moral, narrative in first person, divine intervention, fable, legend, and so on. A description may be geographical, ethnological, medical, or even astronomical. Speeches often offer explicit ethical guidance.[10] To a modern reader the aggadic form may seem abruptly discontinuous, even random. But the organizing principle was always the Bible itself and the pursuit of interpretation according to the sequence of words and verses; continuity was considered to be *the* property of Scripture, and the rabbis never felt any need to reproduce it in their own dis-cursive practices. I say *the* property because scriptural continuity was a matter of historical relevance as much as it was one of narrative coherence. The rab-bis completely depended on the assumption of contemporary application, and it was the nature of this application that usually provided the occasion for an aggadic assertion: "Midrash came into being the very moment a cer-tain text was treated as Scripture; Midrash is the shadow of Scripture."[11]

Once the biblical texts were canonized and ceded divine authority—ei-ther because they were presumed to be divinely authored or because the hu-man authors were held to be divinely inspired—any and all gaps, anomalies, and contradictions within those texts became fully overdetermined. Within this framework everything in Scripture has meaning, and everything that *is not* in Scripture also has meaning. Midrashic analysis seeks to solve contra-dictions based on an assumed unity of view in the text; it gives new meanings by juxtaposing nonadjacent units within the text; it fills in the background with which the scriptural narrative is so fraught, rounding out biblical figures and better identifying names. The Bible elicits the most marvelous specula-tions by the rabbis, and within these speculations they achieve the same flights of fancy, the same profundities of thought, that their surrounding contemporaries reached in epic, lyric, or dramatic poetry. The rabbis were perhaps the first to read the Bible as literature. By assuming a divine author, they had little trouble identifying the same heteroglossia, the same plurivo-cality, the same richness literary critics discern in any novel or poem. There would be no concern about the fear of diminishment or belittlement by reading the Bible in this way since their own response to this literary reading of the Bible was to generate a voluminous library of literary responses which themselves reproduce much of the richness and heterogeneity of the biblical text. Recently there has been a great deal of speculation about how we might use the traces of earlier (perhaps premonotheistic) texts in a literary analysis of the Hebrew Bible in its present form.[12] In many respects this approach was anticipated nearly two thousand years ago by the rabbis, who sought to "restore" the full impact of extrabiblical stories whose traces they had themselves located in Scripture. Often this restoration transpired under the aegis of literal interpretation. The rabbis would not hesitate to characterize inventive interpretations that seemed to extend far beyond the simple explanation of confusing words—what has been labeled *p'shat*, the simple meaning—as *k'mashma'o*, "like it sounds."

Genesis Rabbah, the source of many of my midrashic citations, is considered to be the oldest extant aggadic midrash compilation. It was redacted in Palestine in the fourth or fifth century *c.e.*, and its language is a hybrid of biblical Hebrew and Galilean Aramaic. In the classical Judaism that found its first full expression in the Mishnah (around 200 *c.e.*) and culminated in the Babylonian Talmud (ca. 600 *c.e.*), Genesis Rabbah assumes an important position. It is considered by scholars to provide one of the first comprehensive accounts of how rabbinic Judaism proposed to read and make sense of the first book of the Hebrew Scriptures.[13] Structured as a sequential investigation, verse by verse, into the material of the book of Genesis, Genesis Rabbah uses each verse as an occasion to explore aspects of the rest of the Torah. Many of these investigations begin with a midrashic proem, or *petihtah*. There are 246 *petihtot* divided among the 100 sections of Genesis Rabbah. The homilist begins a petihtah with a verse from somewhere else in the Bible that seems to have little to do with the base verse that has occasioned the homily. Most of these proems draw their initial verses from the Writings; some are taken from the Prophets; a few come from another part of the Pentateuch. The successful proem capitalizes on the initial suspense generated by this apparently irrelevant intersecting text; the reader (or audience, since most of these homilies were originally delivered orally) wonders how the proem will find its way back to the base text and what will be discovered in the process. The formal structure of this midrashic technique, its rhetoricity, thus shifts into the foreground. Indeed, the complexity of the route by which the homilist finds his way back to the base text suggests that the skill required by the petihtah for successful execution was at a premium among the rabbis. Often, having been introduced for one purpose, the intersecting text will provide the occasion for additional comments, and if the midrashist can unite the diverse observations into a fuller illumination of the base text, then the proem stands as a more remarkable tour de force. Though it may be somewhat premature to regard the rabbis as aiming at "things unattempted yet," we would do well to note that Milton's poetic ambitions find parallels in the goals of the rabbinic homilist.

In his crucial study Isaac Heinemann describes midrash aggadah in terms of the twin tasks of creative philology and creative historiography.[14] Like the fantasies of literary romance, the parables and homilies of the midrash transcend the mundane and the literal, exhorting the audience to deeper understanding of the past and present and to greater expectations for the future. Like the allegories suggested by historical fictions and implied in poetic anachronisms, midrash looks to explain the biblical past with the help of the present and the present as a fulfillment or image of the biblical past. Like the densely filled epics and lyrics that reward expert and novice readers, midrash has the uncanny ability to appeal equally to scholar and nonscholar. Like *Paradise Lost*, laden with Milton's erudition, constructed out of the building blocks of a literary heritage the poet lived and breathed, midrash is often most effective quoting biblical verses, one after the other, and generating thoughts and images out of their unanticipated juxtapositions.

Most aggadoth originated with Palestinian Jewry; even those rabbinic texts edited in Babylonia that contain aggadic material probably drew on earlier Palestinian texts in their composition. The Palestinian origins of midrash aggadah are a result of the constant external pressures from other cultures and religions—especially the early Christians—the Jews in Palestine had to face to a much greater degree than did the Jews in Babylonia, who lived in relative peace and isolation. From the end of the first century *c.e.* until the Arab conquests around 640 *c.e.*, Jews in Palestine suffered through a succession of oppressive regimes, which must have produced a large portion of the aggadic homilies that have as either their implicit or explicit goal the renunciation of foreign beliefs and values. If Jews living under pagan Rome were able from time to time to reach a peaceful understanding with the authorities,[15] as Rome became increasingly Christianized, the possibility for Jewish accommodation quickly disappeared.[16] As historians of rabbinic Judaism have observed, there are five events of fundamental importance for occidental Judaism in the fourth and fifth centuries (as distinct from the Babylonian Jewish communities, which would face their own oppressive regimes several centuries later): (1) Constantine's conversion to Christianity, (2) the subsequent "apostasy" of Emperor Julian and his plan to rebuild the Temple in Jerusalem (ca. 360), which produced an inevitable Christian backlash upon his death, (3) the Christinization of Rome following the accession of Theodosius II (383), (4) the conversion to Christianity of a majority of population of Palestine, (5) the creation of the Palestinian Talmud and its related midrashim.

Although Christianity, as a belief system distinct from its Jewish roots, had its origins in the late first and second centuries, and though Judaism's origins reach centuries further back into biblical history, it was not until the spectacular growth of Christianity and its political embrace by the Roman Empire, as manifested in Constantine's conversion, that these two kindred religious worldviews took on the distinguishing characteristics with which we associate them today. The Church fathers of the fourth and fifth centuries, among them Chrysostom, Eusebius, Jerome, and Augustine, wrote for a community of Christian faithful that was enjoying only recently achieved political power. The system of beliefs and practices that they sought to develop had to cohere within this newfound worldly success, a task made all the more challenging given that the earliest Christian writings, including most of what had become the Christian Scriptures, were addressed to a distinctly disempowered and disenfranchised readership for whom Christ's mission held specifically apocalyptic and otherworldly significance. To give just one example of how this shift of political fortunes produced a significant shift in hermeneutics, we can cite Augustine's deliberately allegorical reading of the book of Revelation. Whereas prior to Christianity's political successes, John's eschatological visions bespoke a cataclysmic and abrupt (near) future change in world history, for Augustine Revelation depicted a heavenly Jerusalem to be achieved spiritually by each Christian believer. The political sea change had obviated the need for a literal millenarian reign, since Christ already ruled through the Roman Empire and the Bishop of Rome.[17]

That this period was also seminal for the origins of Christianity is clearly no coincidence. Indeed, the path rabbinic Judaism followed was partly determined by what its prodigal son claimed as its own "Jewish" legacy. As Christianity took upon itself the project of proselytizing the pagan world, a task that, before the advent of Christianity, had been part of Judaism's worldly mission, rabbinic Judaism reformulated its relation to the non-Jewish world in terms of a respect for particularism and difference, values rejected by Pauline Christianity's favoring of "universal" salvation.[18] Between 70 and 429 the Jewish community in Palestine (and elsewhere) experienced one political disappointment after another, and, as a result, during this period rabbinic thinking had to adapt to these new circumstances. While Christianity was changing from a faith of the have-nots to a faith of the haves, Judaism was coming to develop a systematic set of responses to its political and religious losses.[19] The years around Constantine's reign would also become a period rife with controversy as early modern reformers attempted to locate the origins of the "true" Christianity to which they sought to return. The importance of this period for the development of Diaspora rabbinic Judaism would not be lost on these reformers, either.[20]

Genesis Rabbah is an especially useful text for this study because of its redaction in the late fourth or early fifth century *c.e.*, placing it at a crucial moment of transition, from a Judaism accustomed to dealing with a radically other pagan Rome to a Judaism having to face an increasingly and disturbingly familiar Christian Rome. The redactors inherited a tradition that had taken to acknowledging Others and Difference in ways no longer fully adequate to the complex sameness and difference manifest in a Christianized Rome. Wherever one looks in the rabbinic literature of this period, regardless of the overriding theme or the ostensible occasion, one discovers how difficult it is to distill a distinctly Hebraic or Jewish or rabbinic view from the text. All the materials that I examine in this study reveal in one way or another a dynamic interaction with the surrounding culture, Hellenistic, Christian, or otherwise.[21] The following example from Genesis Rabbah will begin to demonstrate the political and cultural, not to mention religious, stakes in midrash.

Central to the rabbinic assumption that their rhetorical and interpretive flourishes were licensed by the text itself was the implicit belief that the Torah provides the means for its own interpretation and restoration. Reading the creation account in the context of an increasingly loud Christian insistence on the plurality of the Godhead in the form of the Trinity, the rabbis were especially sensitive to any plural terms in the Torah that might suggest more than one divine agent. In response to the notoriously challenging "let *us* make man in *our* image, in *our* likeness" of Genesis 1:26, R. Simlai said, "In every place [in the text] that you find a challenge that the heretics [*minim*][22] may use, you find alongside it its remedy [*r'fuatah*]" (Genesis Rabbah 8:9). Literally, the scriptural antidote to heretical interpretations is embedded in the text. The remedy the rabbis draw upon in this particular instance comes from an attention to the grammar of the Bible that challenges the specificity of the insistence on the plural "let *us* make." R. Simlai points out that the actual act of creation occurs in the third person *singular*: "'And God*s* made man [in *their* image]' is not written; rather, [the text says] 'And God made man [in *his* image].'" The reply is deceiving in its simplicity. R. Simlai figures his interpretation as an act of preservation, as a saving of the text. In fact, one might just as well characterize it as a struggle with the text.[23] The scriptural language itself does not absolutely affirm that the singular reading is the appropriate one. R. Simlai's answer to the heretics still does not account for the strange use of the plural form in the declaration of divine intention. Indeed, the midrash seems sensitive to this interpretive aporia and describes the reaction of R. Simlai's students when the heretics have left the room: "'You dismissed them with a paltry reply,' his students said. 'How will you answer the challenge for us?' He said to them, 'At first Man was created from the earth, and Eve was created from Adam. From then on [men were created] in our image and in our likeness [that is, the image and likeness of Adam and Eve].'" The final resolution R. Simlai gives to this challenge depends on a rather extreme refashioning of the biblical text, so that the plural verbs project forward into the future when all humanity will be the products of two parents. To preserve the integrity of the text, to adduce its internal antidote, R. Simlai radically alters the words on the page. The dual nature of this reading—its characteristic innovations for the sake of a particular kind of devotion—is emblematic of the rabbinic approach to scriptural interpretation. The text is understood to be self-sufficient, but only insofar as the human community of readers fulfills the interpretive imperative embedded everywhere in the Bible. The primary concern in this midrash is for the satisfaction of R. Simlai's students and the Jewish audience of the midrash. The heretical challengers are dismissed with little effort to convince them. Under the circumstances in which this midrash is likely to have been composed, such an extended disputation would have been politically ill-advised and would have given too much "text time" to a group from which the rabbis were seeking to distance themselves in every way possible.

What began in these first few centuries of the Common Era as a struggle for the right to claim Scripture for one's own group reemerged in a variety of contexts over the next thousand years. It was not until the early modern period, however, that Christian scholars began systematically to examine Hebraic and rabbinic traditions, returning as it were to their origins.

HEBRAICA VERITAS: JEWS IN EARLY MODERN EUROPE

Non sunt Autores, qui Lectorem magis terrent et torquent; et non sunt tamen, qui magis alliciunt et delectant. Apud nullos major est, aut aequa nugacitas; et vix tamen apud ullos major, aut aequa utilitas. Acriores hostes, quam istos, non habet doctrina Evangelica; et tamen planiores interpretes, quam istos, non habet textus Evangelii. Verbo omnia. *Judaeis* suis nihil nisi nugas propinant, et perniciem, et venenum: at *Christiani*, arte et industia suam, eos sibi reddere possunt studiis suis utilissime famulantes, atque inservientes commodissime interpretationi Novi Testamenti.

There are no Authors who more frighten and torment the Reader, and yet there are none who more attract and delight him. In none is greater or equal nonsense, and yet in none is greater or equal utility. Evangelical Doctrine has no more bitter enemies than they, and yet the Evangelical Text has no clearer interpreters. In a word: To their fellow *Jews* they recommend nothing but trifles and destruction and poison; but with skill and industry, *Christians* may render them most usefully serviceable to their studies, and especially in aiding to the interpretation of the New Testament.[24]

CONSIDERED BY MANY to be the greatest English scholar of Jewish literature of his time, John Lightfoot was skilled not only in biblical Hebrew but also in Mishnaic Hebrew and Talmudic Aramaic. He became master of St. Catharine's Hall, Cambridge, in 1643, and vice-chancellor of Cambridge University in 1654. As a member of Parliament, Lightfoot was entrusted with overseeing and administering a large purchase of texts in several Semitic languages for Cambridge in 1647–48. Perhaps his most significant scholarly achievement, *Horae Hebricae et Talmudicae*, from which this extended quotation has been taken, drew extensively on Talmudic literature, the writings of Josephus, and other classical sources, offering a detailed geography of all the locations in the Land of Israel mentioned in the Gospels and showing the Talmudic parallels and rabbinic background to the four Gospels, Acts, 1 Corinthians, and parts of Romans. This complex characterization of Jews and Jewish learning by Lightfoot reveals how fraught the early modern discourse of Hebraism and Judaism was. In his study of seventeenth-century Dutch Hebraists, Peter van Rooden notes the tendency among Christian scholars to portray Judaism as a creed-based religion rather than one based primarily on practice. In so doing, van Rooden observes that these Hebraists collectively rendered Judaism as a mirror image of Christianity: just as Christianity was first and foremost a religious system rooted in foundational beliefs, so, too, Judaism was construed as a "system of propositions concerning God and his relation to the world."[25] In accounting for this tendency, van Rooden speculates that Dutch Hebraists may have found validation for their view within the Jewish community in seventeenth-century Holland itself. Since this community was largely comprised of Sephardic Jews who had come to the Netherlands in the period surrounding the expulsion of Iberian Jewry in the late fifteenth century, there is reason to believe that their perspective on Judaism was heavily influenced by the writings of Maimonides, who was among the first Jewish thinkers to consider Judaism in terms of a core set of beliefs. In response to ideological and theological attacks from the Christians of Spain, Jewish leaders were obliged to adopt the Maimonidean approach to Judaism as a means of defending themselves. What is more, the seventeenth-century Sephardi community in Amsterdam was continually absorbing many Conversos fleeing the ongoing Inquisition (some of whom were several generations removed from their openly Jewish ancestors), who had come to think of religion—be it Christianity, Judaism, or even Islam—from a Christian perspective, as a system of beliefs based on revelation.[26] Presumably, since many of the Jews with whom late sixteenth- and seventeenth-century Englishmen would have had contact were also from this Sephardic background, and especially given that Menasseh ben Israel, the self-appointed spokesman of the Jewish community to Cromwell, was himself a Sephardic Jew who adopted this creed-based approach to Judaism, van Rooden's argument bears some relevance to England as well as to Holland.

If one examines English writers from the mid seventeenth century, however, a much more diverse set of perspectives seems to characterize the references to Judaism and Jewish practice. As has been noted by a number of important recent historical studies, among the most dramatic sites of Protestant interest in Jews and Judaism were England and Sweden. Since both locations were home to virtually no visible, identifiable Jews, Jews could be constructed as the Christians wished them to be.[27] The diversity of opinions one finds in England stems from the diverse and deep-rooted religious and doctrinal disputes, and serves as an initial index of the extensive reliance on some form of Jewish precedent—both positively and negatively expressed—among religious disputants of all stripes and orientations.

The English construction of the Jew as Other took on a number of different forms, with diverse and often contradictory results. James Shapiro's analysis of this dynamics of otherness in his recent study offers a useful entry point into the matter.[28] Much of Shapiro's analysis engages with those writings that sought, with varying degrees of success, to distinguish between the English and the Jews, in order to give greater definition to both religio-ethnic classifications. This approach offers a functional model for the discussion of Judaism as van Rooden's mirror image of Christianity. Within such a representational field Judaism is both different from and similar to Christianity. From a doctrinal standpoint Judaism serves as a cautionary tale, marking the false path true Christianity should vigilantly guard against. At the same time, Judaism functions as an essentially positive precursor to English Protestantism, serving as paradigm for the "new" Israel finding its full expression on English soil. Thomas Luxon links this tension to a crisis in representation during the seventeenth century. On the one hand, the Reformation shifted attention from symbol and sacrament to the Scriptural, linguistic fulfillment of faith. On the other hand, Protestantism pursued the desire to be one with Christ, i.e., God incarnate. As such it was a system of beliefs that both rejected and embraced the body. Similarly, English Protestants "oscillate between identifying themselves with the ancient Israelite of the 'Old Testament' and regarding 'the Jew' as the quintessential misbeliever, Christianity's constitutive other."[29] Thomas Calvert's infamous treatise on the evils of Judaism illustrates this final point most dramatically:

> Out of the Jews, and taking part of Judaisme, sprung up divers of the worst sort of damnable Heresies, and sundry Sects, as the Samaritans, Sadduces, Gorthenians, Jebusaeans, Essenes, Dositheans, Scribes, Pharisees, Hemerobaptists, Hossinians, Nazaraeans, Herodians, Simonians, Ebionites, Valentinians, Cerinthians, Sethians, Melchisedechians, Arians, Hypsistarians, and Mahometans; which last religion was compiled, and abundance of Jewish matters thrust into it by some Jews that helped Mahomet to make up that confused Chaos of a strange Religion and Sect; so that Judaisme hath been the fruitfull Mother and Nurse, to give both Wombe and Pap to many monstrous Children.[30]

CREDITED AS THE originator of every single group seen to stand in opposition to English Protestantism, Judaism is quite explicitly the Mother of all Others, essential insofar as it allows Calvert to define his own beliefs in direct opposition to it.

While we might expect to find among the Presbyterians, and other more normative Calvinists, attitudes toward Jewish practice and belief parallel to those of the Dutch described by van Rooden, some within this group, like William Prynne, revived the myth of ritual murder as part of a larger litany of morally repugnant *acts* practiced by Jews.[31] Among the Independents, where we may identify both "philosemites" and "antisemites," there is an even wider diversity of opinion; some regarded Judaism as creed based, others, like John Selden, who compiled systematic analyses of Jewish practices in marriage and government, portrayed Judaism as deed based. Complicating this scheme further are two related matters. First, there is no consistent relationship between a writer's views concerning Jewish toleration, on the one hand, and his perspective of Judaism as a religion grounded in theory or praxis, on the other. Second, because early modern English perceptions and representations of Jews and Judaism had as much to do with English self-perceptions, we must also consider whether a writer's concern with Judaism stems from an implicit or explicit analogy he is drawing between Judaism and his own view or Judaism and his antagonist(s)'s view(s). Van Rooden's model does not allow for the tendency to construe Judaism as an accurate mirror image or adumbration of one's opponent's beliefs and practices rather than as a corrupted mirror image of one's own views.

The late sixteenth and early seventeenth centuries saw the "discovery" of a plurality of Judaisms by Christian Hebraists and humanists, especially scholars like the Jesuit professor of theology, Nicholas Serarius (1558–1609), the rabbinic scholar of Leiden and Franeker, Johannes Drusius (1550–1616), and the great Dutch classical scholar, Joseph Scaliger (1540–1609).[32] This is the period in which Christians first became aware of Karaites, Samaritans, Sadducees, and hellenized Jewry as distinctive strains of Judaism, to be differentiated from what, until then, had been assumed to be one single version of monolithic rabbinic Judaism. By the second half of the seventeenth century these divisions were used as a means to characterize confessional and doctrinal splits within Christianity. Richard Simon (1638–1712), the French translator of Leon da Modena's *Riti ebraici*, is a key figure in the polemical use of Karaism and rabbinism. Even given this rough historical progression, several caveats must be borne in mind. First, while from a later perspective it may appear that rabbinic Judaism is to Karaism as Catholicism is to Protestantism, because of the apparent disagreements over the value of tradition (i.e., the rabbis and Catholics credit tradition, whereas the Karaites and Protestants show exclusive favor for the unadorned biblical text), in reality, many Catholics were drawn to Karaites, just as many Protestant scholars made use of different elements of rabbinic scholarship. Differences and similarities were far less easily categorizable than they might first appear to be. Second, the Christian construction of these different Jewish groups was *never* the same thing as the groups themselves and always informed by specific doctrinal and ideological predispositions. When we speak about Christian Hebraism, we may mean a number of different formulations, each wielding its own attraction to diverse Christian viewpoints. Hence, we might wish to speak of Christian Rabbinism, Christian Kabbalism, Christian Karaism, Christian Sabbateanism, Christian Maimonideanism, and so on.

In this Christian inflection of Judaism there is an uncanny recapitulation of the dynamics that produced normative rabbinic Judaism in the period following the destruction of the Second Temple. In both explicit and implicit ways the rabbis produced a set of practices *and* beliefs meant to distinguish Judaism from the surrounding culture, especially from an ascendant Christianity. If one adopts the view of Jacob Neusner and regards the rabbis as systematic theologians whose worldview manifests itself in the particularities of halakhic praxis, then one may conclude, as Neusner himself repeatedly does, that this rabbinic system was an elaborate reply to Pauline and Patristic theology. If, however, one adopts the view of scholars like David Weiss Halivni and perceives rabbinic thinking as nonsystematic, occasional, text-oriented, then one may nevertheless conclude that rabbinic Judaism's aversion to totalizing theology and basic credos is a culturally defined reaction formation against Christianity. In either case, Judaism is changed irreversibly as it encounters Christianity. Similarly, in the early modern period Christianity infiltrates Judaism both through Conversos and through the effects of anti-Christian polemics. If Christianity regards Judaism as its perverted mirror image, there may be more than a little truth to that perception, both in the earliest history of the two religions and in their early modern manifestations.

As the major Protestant state during the mid seventeenth century, England was perceived by many Englishmen as the elect, chosen nation, destined by God to destroy Rome and precipitate the millennium. The cautious foreign policy of James I and Charles I, especially the refusal to enter into the Thirty Years War, seemed to contradict the English theory of election. When the Civil War began, its perception as the beginning of the end brought the prompt reappearance of the theory of the Elect Nation. Arguably the foundational text in this English nexus of national and religious election, John

Foxe's *Actes and Monuments* was primarily concerned with establishing an English tradition of church reform.[33] Foxe repeatedly championed the English monarchy in opposition to Roman Catholicism, certainly until the fourteenth century. Yet, Foxe's marriage of the English monarchy with the true Christian faith was a tenuous one, which he promulgated largely in support of his goal of maintaining Elizabeth I as a patron of his cause. Foxe depicted Constantine's role in the early church as prototype for the role he expected Elizabeth I to play in the English church. In his dedication to the queen in the 1563 edition of *Actes and Monuments*, Foxe explicitly likened Elizabeth to Constantine, expecting her to bring to an end an era of persecution and suffering for the true believers. Indeed, Foxe concluded the first book of his account by suggesting that Constantine's conversion was due in no small part to his purported British heritage.[34] With the crowning of James I, and certainly by the time his son Charles took the throne, this union of faith and crown shifted onto much shakier ground. If any notion of England's elect status was to persist, it needed to undergo a shift in meaning—if not in content, then at least in outward expression.[35] Though Archbishop Laud and other advocates of the episcopal hierarchy were part of a more explicitly national religious institution and enterprise in the Church of England, whose sovereign head was also the reigning monarch, it was the Presbyterian opposition and, perhaps more surprisingly, many Independents, who most often deployed nationalist rhetoric concerning Englishness and providential English history.[36] Remarking on this very phenomenon among those whom he and other supporters of the Church of England labeled "schismatics," Richard Carter wondered how they "compare Old *England* to *Egypt*, and themselves to the onely true *Israelites*; and they (forsooth) are holden in bondage under cruell Taske-masters. But our eyes are up to the hills, from whence our helpe commeth (Oh Lord) helpe us, and send us prosperity: and pray we all for the Lords annoynted, and with one heart say (helpe oh *King*, helpe oh *King*.)"[37] Carter suggests that these schismatics distinguish between "Old England" and the "true Israelites," but the claim to be the New Israel was far more frequently uttered in the same breath as the claim to be the true England.

This tendency to couple claims to English election with invocations of Israelite and Jewish precedent often yielded conflicting results.[38] The revolutionary preacher, John Goodwin, took his fellow countrymen to task for leaving the church reforms begun a century earlier incomplete.

Such a Reformation, as that whereby the Angel of darknesse, Satan is reformed, when he *is transformed into an Angel of light* (as the Apostle speaketh) is
no reformation of desires: open loosenesse and prophanenesse reformed
into Pharasaicall hypocrisie, brings in little to Religion. For what saith our
Saviour of such a Reformation as this? *Verily I say unto you, that Publicans and
Harlots go before you into the Kingdome of God*. If then such a Reformation as this
should take place, it is much to be feared, that when the Genealogie of it
shall be sought, it will be found to be of the house and linage of that Reformation, which the *Scribes* and *Pharisees* attempted into the world, when *they
compassed Sea and Land to make one Proselyte; and when he was made, they made him
twofold more a childe of hell*, then he was before; yea, *then they were themselves*.[39]

THE CURRENT REFORMATION threatens to repeat, because it may be the actual offspring of, the hypocritical reformation of postbiblical Jewry. Goodwin
adopts a historical model characteristic of many of his contemporaries (one,
I shall argue in the next chapter, resisted by Milton), regarding the present
moment as having been anticipated by Jewish history at the time of the destruction of the Temple in Jerusalem. In an anonymous treatise on contemporary religious debates in light of post-Temple Jewish history, the paradigm
precipitated by the destruction is said to apply equally to Jews and Christians.

The Hebrew Doctors say, That it was unlawful to make any house, either
synagogue, or any other private house, after the fashion of the Temple, or a
Porch thereof, of a Court-yard like the Court-yard thereof, or a Table like
the Table thereof, or a Candlestick like the Candlestick thereof, &c. *vid. Ainsw.*
in *Levit.* 19.30. Neither had the synagogues any thing to do with sacrifice, neither might they any more imitate *Aarons* attire, then they might sacrifice
there: and yet the Father of *Rome* doth counterfeit all, He will have a *Candlestick, Cope, Linen-Garments, Precious-Stones, Miter, Girdle,* &c. He will have *Sacrifice,
Priest, and Altar,* and *Iubilees,* &c. and yet it was death for any in *Israel* to med-
dle with *Levies* proper duty; and now seeing his Office is quite extinguished, it
is a most high contempt of God to revive it by imitation from mans brain;
and therefore such Reformed Churches as retain any of these Popish Jewish
Rites, ought speedily to repent and reforme, or else God will surely purge
them by sharp tryals, to provoke them to repentance and reformation.[40]

IN MOST RESPECTS, Christianity posits Christ's advent as *the* paradigm shift.

Here, the destruction, which was forty years after Christ's passion, and which was ostensibly of much greater significance to those who did not follow Christ, becomes the defining event for matters of ceremony and ritual. Of particular interest is the insight this treatise offers as it resembles Rosemary Ruether's observations concerning the split between rabbinic Judaism and Pauline Christianity.[41] In the hands of the anonymous author of this tract, the same doctrinal and practical differences serve to emphasize what re-formed Christianity regards as the failings of "Popish Jewish Rites."

It is one thing to note the widespread practice among preachers, pamphleteers, and polemicists of all religious or political views of paralleling the contemporary situation in England with that of the Jews as described throughout the Hebrew Bible. The hermeneutics of typology in its various modes made it possible to invoke the antitype of "Israel after the flesh," if only to render it fulfilled in Christ and the New Israel. It is quite another matter, however, to separate those references to a Jewish past found in the Hebrew Bible from discussions of intertestamental, New Testament, and Christian-era Jewish precedent.[42] Indeed, in many twentieth-century discussions of English Protestantisms' Hebraic aspects, the former definition of Hebraism has so overwhelmed the latter as to render it virtually nonexistent. When accounts do make the distinction, it is often as part of a far too seamless narrative that describes the lack of regard, held by Puritan and Anglican alike, for the unconverted postbiblical Jew. Bernard Glassman, for example, claims that the sermons "reveal a common bond of hate that both these groups shared."[43] Even in those discussions of more affirmative representations of contemporary Judaism, the emphasis usually falls either on the radical fringes of English Protestantism, figures like Thomas Tany (who took the name Theareau John and declared himself to be "King of the Jews"), or on the academic specialists, like John Selden, whose audience was so narrow as to have played a minimal role in the larger discursive network of Jewish images.[44] The aforementioned treatise on the post-Temple Jewish synagogue, clearly written by a figure with only secondhand knowledge of Jewish sources, posits a relationship between Judaism and Christianity that reveals the degree to which the complex citations of nonbiblical Jewish precedent contributed to competing notions of English religious, cultural and political self-definitions.

But when the Apostles and Disciples did evidently evince by the Scriptures that Christ must die and rise again, then it stirred up many Iews to envy, which caused persecution, and persecution caused the believing part of the synagogue to separate from the unbelieving and malignant part. This separation was not made because the beleeving part held the unbeleeving part no true Church, but because they could not be suffered to preach and teach those fundamental truths, and must endure great opposition and persecution if they did still abide with them.[45]

IN PARTICULAR, and especially in the case of Milton, the hermeneutics of suffering would play an increasingly significant role in the dialectical fashioning of English Christian identity in relation to its Jewish precedents.

Especially because this English negotiation of Jewish history was so fraught, in debates over religious theory and practice, the extraordinarily damaging accusation of "Judaizing" was effectively deployed by Catholics, Anglicans, Presbyterians, Independents, and radical sectarians. Catholics and Anglicans accused their opponents of Judaizing because of their seeming return to an Hebraic prehistory of Christianity, at the latter's expense. The Puritan focus on the word and the Word was vulnerable to the attack of "pharisaical" in a variety of contexts. Presbyterians and Independents, on the other hand, could accuse their antagonists (and each other, for that matter), of not reforming the Church enough and thereby staying too close to the Judaism from which Christianity needed to distinguish itself. Among the writings of the "ceremonialists,"[46] and even those more idiosyncratic Arminians who were otherwise opponents of the episcopal hierarchy, we often find an interest in Jewish practice for its own sake and not merely as an indication of underlying tenets of belief. This interest is frequently offset, however, by a rhetorical association of Jewish practice with the excessively precise attitudes of the Puritan opposition. Yet even as many opponents of the Roman and Anglican churches attacked their adversaries with the label *pharisaical* or *judaical*, thereby asserting a failure to reform Christianity's Jewish roots sufficiently, these same antagonists of the ceremonies and hierarchies associated with papists and prelates construed the rituals and sacraments as newfangled accretions. In such a context, paradoxically, the precedent of the Hebrew Bible took on a far more authentic cast. These ambivalent references to Christianity's Hebraic past were a function, in particular, of the newly available humanist scholarship that made it possible in more sophisticated ways than any earlier period to historicize Christ's Jewish milieu. With all its ideological predispositions and tacit theological polemics, the study of Jewish materials from the postbiblical period by Christian Hebraists of the sixteenth and seventeenth centuries nevertheless contributed to an increasingly complex and nuanced understanding of Jewish belief and practice. While most of the participants in the English debates concerning church doctrine and discipline and religious toleration were not themselves trained scholars of Hebrew and Judaism, they were necessarily influenced by the work of these Christian Hebraists, which entered into the discourse of the period by a variety of direct and indirect means.

It is tempting to clarify the confusing status of Jewish alterity in England by positing a consistent differentiation, among all the Christian writers and thinkers of the period, between Hebraism and Judaism. Such a distinction, specifically as it pertains to Milton, has been suggestively proposed by Samuel Stollman. Rejecting the all-inclusive category of Hebraic as being insufficiently discriminating, Stollman has argued that for Milton, who mediates Luther's consignment of the Hebrew Bible to the past (as being too Jewish) and Calvin's embrace of the Old Testament (as being wholly Christian), there was a crucial difference between Hebraic factors and Judaic factors:

> The "Judaic" connotes the "particular," the Jewish religion and race, Mosaic Law and people, practices and ethnic traits. The Law and the People both represent the "letter" of the Old Testament. The "Hebraic," on the other hand, refers to the "universal" ("applicable to all men") aspects of the Old Testament: the divine, the law of nature and of nations, and reason—that which, in effect, is independent of the Jewish people although shared by them, at one time, and to a degree.[47]

APPLYING THE PAULINE FORMULA, Stollman proposes that the Judaic is to the "Hebraic as the letter is to the spirit." This distinction might help to clarify the function of Jewish precedent in the religious and political debates of the period. According to this model, when Israel is cited in an affirmative fashion, we may be sure that the writer is invoking a Hebraic past as support for his position. When Jews stand in for offensive beliefs and behaviors, however, we may conclude that the writer is distinguishing his own opinions from a Judaic worldview. For example, Foxe's *Actes and Monuments* asserts the accuracy of the myth of Jewish ritual murder; Foxe is then cited as authoritative on this matter by Thomas Calvert and subsequently by William Prynne in his *Short Demurrer*. That Foxe is also one of the key figures in the proliferation of English chosenness, its status as the New Israel (an idea also echoed in Calvert and Prynne), seems worth noting in relation to his report of Jewish villainy. England's chosenness is a Hebraic concept. Jewish ritual murder is the result of Judaism's moral decrepitude.

As Stollman has observed, Milton appears to accept, with some modifications, the standard division of Mosaic law into *Ceremonialia, Judicialia,* and *Moralia.* He addresses these distinctions most explicitly in *The Reason of Church-Government,* as part of an extended discussion offered primarily in response to the publication of an extraordinarily influential collection of treatises aimed at validating episcopal practices and hierarchies, some reissued and some written for the volume, under the title *Certain briefe treatises: written by diverse learned men, concerning the ancient and moderne government of the church.*[48] One of these tracts, *The Originall of Bishops and Metropolitans* by James Ussher, archbishop of Armagh, presented the prelacy's identification of Hebraic—indeed, in Stollman's word, *Judaic*—precedent in no uncertain terms:

> The ground of *Episcopacy* is fetched partly from the patterne prescribed by God in the *Old* Testament: and partly from the imitation thereof brought in by the *Apostles* and confirmed by *Christ* himselfe in the time of the *New.* The government of the Church of the *Old* Testament was committed to the *Priests* and *Levits*: unto whom the minister of the *New* doe now succeed—that it might be fulfilled which was spoken by the Prophet, touching the vocation of the Gentiles. *I will take them for Priests, and for Levits, saith the Lord.*[49]

USSHER GIVES AN explicit demonstration of the way that arguments from a hermeneutics of Christian typology and historiography of Christian succession can be mutually supportive. An absolutely typological reading of the Old Testament would in principle need no historical link between ancient Israel and modern Christendom to validate itself. If Old Testament types serve to foreshadow their true fulfillment in Christ's life and, subsequently, in the body of Christ, i.e., the Church of believers, then even when the historicity of these Old Testament figures and events is maintained—and this is itself a matter of some dispute—any real or material lineage connecting those figures with the modern church should be largely irrelevant. Yet, Ussher maintains that the English Church not only fulfills Old Testament prophecy typologically; he asserts a continuity, as well. I think that the Hebraic *and the Judaic* partake of a much more ambivalent status than Stollman's dichotomy recognizes. Neither fully rejected nor wholly embraced, they function dialogically.

Further evidence of this complicated relationship can be seen in how frequently in this period discussions of Hebraic and Jewish precedent raised the questions of religious toleration and the readmission of Jews to England. The Fifth Monarchists, who advocated an adherence to the moral and judicial laws of the Pentateuch, but also to many of the so-called ceremonial laws, believed that the conversion of the Jews to Christianity was a necessary and imminent sign of the approaching millennium.[50] Participants in the religious controversies of the 1640s and fifties frequently cited the present status of the Jews in exile as both evidence of their fall from divine favor and indication of their continued special status, a status with which many compared England in good times and in bad. In a text not at all sympathetic to contemporary Jews, Thomas Calvert observed,

> For what ever they be, though a people that seem to be the Saltest Pillar of Gods wrath to all the world, yet we may look on them as a Book of our Saviours Passion, and when we see a bloodie Iew, remember bleeding Iesus. They may be to us the Looking-glasse of Divine vengeance, and better than a Crucifix. They are to be pitied by men, because there is a promise of mercy from God, there must be a blessed revocation, and an happy re-union of Jews and Gentiles. We should not utterly cast off, whom God has not utterly cast off.[51]

THE WRITER OF *An Endeavor* further observed that the scattering of the Jews to the "four winds of heaven" was not only a function of God's anger at their apostasy. Christ also remembered mercy, "For at last he gave them favour in the sight of all Nations, to have and build synagogues for the free exercise of their Religion."[52]

With very few exceptions, seventeenth-century Englishmen and women who called for the readmission and religious toleration of the Jews believed that this change in attitude and behavior was the most effective means of achieving their conversion.[53] Andrew Willett was the first English biblical scholar to have devoted an entire treatise to the calling of the Jews, *De Universali et Nouissima Judaeorum Vocatione* (Cambridge, 1590). Other crucial figures in the development of English theories concerning the calling and conversion of the Jews included Thomas Brightman, whose writings on the books of Daniel and Revelation placed crucial emphasis on the conversion of the Jews, Henry Finch, author of *The Worlds Great Restauration* (1621), and Joseph Mede, along with Brightman, one of the two central figures in all English apocalyptic thought. There was a large consensus among preacher and pamphleteers that the years 1650–56 were the crucial period in which the conversion would occur. As Katz, Hill, Shapiro, Matar and others have noted, conversion of the Jews in English writing was powerfully connected with the political and economic ambitions inherent in (1) the exploration and colonization of North America and (2) trade and other commerce with the "Turkish Empire." In his recent discussions of England and Islam, Nabil Matar has argued that in the context of this latter ambition, Jews took on a specifically military role in the unfolding of Christian history: "Having been fitted into the Protestant worldview, the Jews were to conquer and then convert: first, they would act like Davidic warriors and fight the 'Turkes': then, after overcoming them, they would become, like Paul, converts to the true faith."[54] To characterize the early modern English change in attitudes toward Jews as "philosemitic" thus begs a further question. Can one be said to accord Jews and Judaism a new respect, when the motivation for this new respect is ultimately the elimination of Jews and Judaism as such? Certainly, there is an important difference between the antisemitic views so prevalent in the medieval and early modern periods that rendered Jews as evil, deserving of punishment from God and man, and these more recently espoused views of the so-called philosemites. We would do well to recall, however, that until he was rebuffed by the German Jewish community, Martin Luther held similar views. When Jews resisted his attempts at reconciliation and conversion to Christianity, Luther authored some of the most venomous antisemitic prose in the history of Europe.

Advocates of Jewish readmission and toleration who believed it to be the most effective way to bring about the conversion of the Jews (in either an apocalyptic or nonapocalyptic context) tended to argue that while the Jewish failure to accept Christ stood at the root of the Jewish history of suffering and persecution, through greater tolerance the Jews would recognize their error and come to Christ. James Shapiro has observed that there persisted in England the firm belief that Jews were somehow racially unassimilable, which is attributable in part to the introduction and dissemination of the racist idea of *limpieza di sangre*, which originated during the early stages of the Inquisition but owes at least as much to the theological necessity perceived in Paul's apparent prophecy concerning the ultimate redemption of the Jews as an adumbration of the Second Coming.[55] That is, Jews needed to be identifiable as such so that when the time came they could embrace the Christian faith *as Jews*, thereby verifying what Christians of all ethnic, national and racial origins had believed for centuries. Here is Thomas Fuller's version of this idea:

The *Jews* ever since their exile from their own land, when the *Romans* sold their Countrey, . . . have continued many hundred years a distinct nation. As if they had learned from their River of *Jordan*, running through the *Galilean Sea*, and not mingling therewith, daily to pass through an Ocean of other nations, and remain an unmixt, and un-confounded people by themselves. A comfortable presumption (when in company with many other arguments) that they, once *Gods peculiar*, are still preserved *a peculiar people*, for some *token for good* in due time to be shewed upon them; and that these *materials* are thus carefully kept entire by themselves, because intended by Divine Providence, for some *beautifull building* to be made of them hereafter.[56]

WHEN ADVOCATES OF Jewish readmission and conversion found their larger political and religious views falling out of favor, it may have been especially tempting for them to posit a parallel between this perception of postbiblical Jewish history and English history (as it seems to fail to embrace the true path).[57]

"SOME WOND'ROUS CALL"

AS IN MANY other matters of doctrinal and theological importance, Milton's views on the nature and time of the apocalypse were idiosyncratic, bearing an ambivalent relationship to the English tradition that dates back at least as far as Thomas Brightman's apocalyptical commentaries.[58] Milton's first prose tract, *Of Reformation*, concludes with the famous "Hymns and Halleluiahs" passage, replete with the apocalyptic figures and passion characteristic of so many of his contemporaries who seemed genuinely to expect the Parousia at any moment (YP 1:614–17). Even in this early stage of his career, however, Milton is adhering to a set of generic conventions as much as he is fully embracing the millenarian and apocalyptic views depicted in the final paragraphs. By the time we come to his *Animadversions*, only a year later, Milton's discomfort with this mode of thought and writing is even more in evidence. It is true that in the spirited voice so characteristic of this response to Joseph Hall, Milton calls for a worldly messianic reign:

Come forth out of thy Royall Chambers, O Prince of all the Kings of the earth, put on the visible roabes of thy imperiall Majesty, take up that unlimited Scepter which thy Almighty Father hath bequeath'd thee; for now the voice of thy Bride calls thee, and all creatures sigh to bee renew'd. (YP 1:707)

YET THIS APOCALYPTIC fervor has already been tempered by what can only be called a Mosaic disputation with God, one that adopts a tone anticipating the Son's rejoinder to the Father in book 3 of *Paradise Lost*. Milton asserts that if God prevents English church reform from achieving its completion, it would be akin to the destruction of the Israelites following the Exodus, at the shore of the Red Sea. Whether or not England merits such treatment from God, Milton continues,

> yet thy great name would suffer in the rejoycing of thine enemies, and the deluded hope of all thy servants. When thou hast settl'd peace in the Church, and righteous judgement in the Kingdome, then shall all thy Saints addresse their voyces of joy, and triumph to thee, standing on the shoare of that red Sea into which our enemies had almost driven us. (YP 1:706)

IT WAS NOT uncommon for apocalyptic writers of the period to use the occasion to offer criticism—sometimes quite virulent—of contemporary English politics and religion. Indeed, social criticism of some form or another appears to be a constitutive element of apocalyptical writing. It is much more unusual for this critical tone to be turned on God. As we shall see below, the impulse to argue with God is one embraced by Milton repeatedly and bears a striking resemblance to rabbinical modes of exegesis.

Not unlike his millenarian contemporaries, Milton combines the language of apocalypse with the idea of English election. As is the case in his tempered apocalypticism, however, Milton's conception of English election begins with ambivalence and concludes, in his later years, with dismissal. *Animadversions* gives voice to some of the standard tropes of English national election, as in the following passage.

> For he being equally neere to his whole Creation of Mankind, and of free power to turne his benefick and fatherly regard to what Region or Kingdome he pleases, hath yet ever had this Iland under the speciall indulgent eye of his providence; and pittying us the first of all other Nations, after he had decreed to purifie and renew his Church that lay wallowing in Idolatrous pollutions, sent first to us a healing messenger to touch softly our sores, and carry

a gentle hand over our wounds: he knockt once and twice and came againe, opening our drousie eye-lids leasurely by that glimmering light which *Wicklef,* and his followers dispers't, and still talking off by degrees the inveterat scales from our nigh perisht sight, purg'd also our deaf eares, and prepar'd them to attend his second warning trumpet in our Grandsires dayes. (YP 1:704)

YET EVEN IN such passages, where the legacy of Wyclif stands for "the speciall indulgent eye" of God's providence, Milton positions the very arbitrary nature of English election in the foreground, where it occupies the primary syntactic position in his long periodic sentence. In *Of Reformation* the precedence of Wyclif functions as reason for condemnation and concern rather than promise of future glories for the Elect Nation:

> Yet me thinkes the *Precedencie* which God gave this *Iland,* to be the first *Restorer* of *buried Truth,* should have beene followed with more happy successe, and sooner attain'd Perfection; in which, as yet we are amongst the last: for, albeit in *purity* of *Doctrine* we agree with our Brethren; yet in Discipline, which is the *execution* and *applying* of *Doctrine* home . . . we are no better than a *Schisme,* from all the *Reformation,* and a sore scandall to them. (YP 1:526)

TURNING THE ACCUSATION of divisiveness so often voiced by supporters of the episcopacy on its head, Milton constructs the abortive English reformation as schism and scandal. As Janel Mueller has shown, Milton regarded schism as distinct from heresy, a term with which it was often connected following Paul in 1 Corinthians 11:18–19. Whereas, especially in his later prose, Milton recuperates heresy by returning to its Greek etymology, ηαιρεσις, which he defines in *A Treatise on Civil Power* (1659) as "the choise or following of any opinion good or bad in religion or any other learning," schism is taken to signify "division, and in the worst sense" (YP 7:247).[59] Rather than leading the vanguard in unifying the body of Christ, England threatens to fragment it further, repeating doctrinally the literal execution of Jesus ascribed to that other failed chosen people, the Jews.[60]

Of course, the idea of national election has its individualist corollary in the Calvinist doctrine of predestinarian salvation. Milton, whose embrace of the Arminian heterodoxy on the question of salvation renders the Celestial Dialogue in book 3 of *Paradise Lost* so notoriously complex, addresses the relationship between individual and national election explicitly in his *De Doctrina Christiana.* Seeking to distinguish his anti-Calvinist interpretation of predestination from the national election exemplified in God's selection of the Israelites, Milton goes on to argue that both national and individual election are resistible. That is, just as the biblical Israelites refused God's favor by turning from the true path, so too an individual called to salvation by God can choose to resist such a vocation (YP 6:171–74). Chosenness is for Milton—as it was for the rabbis—a two-way street demanding participation by both divine and human parties.

Stephen Fallon has recently argued that Milton's theological treatise deserves to be read autobiographically, reflecting Milton's personal concerns about his own elect status. Fallon offers as evidence the unusually extensive justification of usury in the *De Doctrina Christiana* (YP 6:776–77), noting that Milton depended for much of his life on income earned by loans his father had made.[61] There is another aspect of this defense of usury, however, one that has further implications for the self-representational qualities of Milton's writings. Shylock's bond with Antonio is only the most vivid example of the medieval and early modern association of usury with Jews; virtually without exception this association was offered to the detriment of European Jewry. Fallon's identification of Milton's own life circumstances peering through an otherwise abstract section of doctrinal argumentation suggests yet a further (nervous) acknowledgment of the parallel circumstances of the Jews with Milton, not only on a national level but also on a personal level.

As I shall argue in the next chapter, it is the nervous awareness of these parallels that determine the dynamics of Milton's citation of Jewish precedent in his writings on the prelacy. In other contexts Milton's statements about the Jews—biblical, but especially the Jews of more recent history—are notoriously elliptical and succinct. In *A Treatise on Civil Power*, a tract Milton wrote in 1659 on the eve of the Restoration, when the possibility of his falling out of religious and political favor was becoming more real by the day, Milton drew the following distinction between Jews and Christians: "To the Jewish law that nation, as a servant, was oblig'd; but to the gospel each person is left voluntarie, calld only, as a son, by the preaching of the word; not to be driven in by edicts and force of arms" (YP 7:268). Ostensibly in order to argue against the call voiced by both Presbyterians and supporters of the reviving episcopal hierarchy to institute prescribed religious belief and practice with civil laws, Milton dismisses any use of the Old Testament in order to prove the legitimacy of force in such matters. What Milton's argument fails to recognize in either this treatise or its companion piece, *Considerations Touching the Likeliest Means to Remove Hirelings* (1659), is the tradition of forced conversion practiced on Jews by Christianity, most notably in Spain and other Catholic countries but not uncommon in Protestant locations either. Some of Milton's religious and political allies, among them Henry Robinson and Roger Williams, directly referred to these attempts at forced conversion as failures of Christianity. Milton is unwilling to acknowledge this later reality of Jewish history because it threatens to render Diaspora Judaism as too much akin to his own religious and political identity. Indeed, when one considers the many factors converging in and around Milton from 1640 until his death in 1674, it is remarkable how little this famously verbose poet and polemicist had to say about the religious toleration of Jews (pro or contra), the question of officially readmitting Jews to England, the matter of the conversion of the Jews (in either a millenarian or nonmillenarian framework), or the restoration of the Jews to the Holy Land.[62]

Milton lived *precisely* during the period of time when these issues were most prominently debated in public. The Whitehall Conference of 1655–56 called by Cromwell, in whose cabinet Milton served, debated the question of readmission. Both the monarchy and the protectorate considered the restoration of the Jews to the Holy Land to be of strategic as well as religious importance in the fight against the Ottoman Empire. And we have already seen how prevalent was the hope of the imminent conversion of the Jews during the period. Furthermore, as Jason Rosenblatt has made clear, Milton was no stranger to Jewish learning, in however mediated a fashion; he admired a good deal of rabbinic thought. Finally, many of Milton's teachers, friends, and acquaintances took active part in the debates concerning the status of contemporary Jews, including Samuel Hartlib, John Dury, Moses Wall, and Joseph Mede. Thomas Goodwin, whose sermons Milton attended in Cambridge during the 1630s, advocated in 1639 the restoration of the Jews to the Holy Land and directly linked it to the advent of the messianic kingdom in England.[63]

In his various prose tracts Milton explicitly addresses the matter of Jewish toleration and conversion only twice. The first occurs in his *Observations Upon the Articles of Peace*, written in 1649, not long after Milton was named by the Council of State to be secretary of foreign tongues. His comment, which comprises a minute portion of an otherwise lengthy text,[64] has found its way into most recent attempts at identifying Milton's attitude toward Jews. Milton writes, "And yet while we detest *Judaism*, we know our selves commanded by St. *Paul, Rom.* 11. to respect the *Jews*, and by all means to endeavor thir conversion" (YP 3:326). On the face of it, Milton's succinct statement seems entirely consistent with the opinions expressed by many of the so-called philosemites who had begun to advocate for the readmission of the Jews so as to facilitate their conversion. Milton identifies a biblically commanded respect for Jews as not at all inconsistent with the requirement to eliminate Judaism through conversion.[65] Rarely, however, do modern accounts offer the full context of Milton's statement. *A Necessary Representation of the present evills, and eminent dangers to Religion, Lawes, and Liberties* (February 15, 1649 [YP 3:296–99]) was written by representatives of the Belfast Presbytery objecting to the peace imposed by Parliament on the warring Catholics and Puritans in Ireland. Attacking what they perceived as the abrogation of the religious settlements that had authorized a Presbyterian mode of church government, the Ulster Presbyters argued,

> Moreover; their great dis-affection to the Settlement of Religion, and so their future breach of Covenant doth more fully appeare by their strong oppositions to Persbyteriall Government (the hedge, and Bulwarke of Religion) whilest they express their hatred to it, more then to the worst of errours, by excluding it under the name of Compulsion; when they imbrace, even Paganisme, and Judaisme in the Armes of Toleration. Not to speake of their Aspersions upon it, and the Assertors thereof as Antichristian, and·Popish, though they have deeply sworn to maintaine the same Government in the first Article of the Covenant, as it is established in the Church of *Scotland*, which they now so despise, and fully blaspheme. (297)

MILTON'S RESPONSE TO this impeachment deserves to be read in a fuller context, for it brings together the matters of religious tolerance and oppression. Answering the claim that the Presbyterian government functions to preserve religion, Milton replies, "We hold it no more to be *the hedg and bulwark of Religion*, then the Popish and Prelaticall Courts, or the *Spanish Inquisition*" (326). Having equated Presbyterianism with the evils of the Spanish Inquisition, Milton turns immediately in the next brief paragraph to the accusation of Judaizing, claiming, "But we are told, *We imbrace Paganism and Judaism in the arms of toleration.* A most audacious calumny. And yet while we detest *Judaism*, we know our selves commanded by St. *Paul, Rom.* 11. to respect the *Jews*, and by all means to endeavor thir conversion." The transition from Spanish Inquisition to an ambivalent embrace of Jews (and not Judaism) captures much of Milton's anxiety concerning parallels between himself and the Jew. As soon as he has cast himself in a position analogous to that of the Diaspora Jew (i.e., he has suffered at the hands of the Presbytery in much the same way as the Jews have suffered at the hands of the Inquisition) Milton feels obliged to clarify his distance from the fuller implications of that Jewish analogy.[66]

The only other mention Milton gives to the future conversion of the Jews occurs in his theological treatise. There, Milton is distinctively noncommittal. In book 1, chapter 33, entitled "Of Complete Glorification, Also of Christ's Second Coming, the Resurrection of the Dead, and the Conflagration of This World," Milton cites various biblical indications of the signs portending the Parousia. Among them, he writes, "Some authorities think that a further portent will herald this event, namely, the calling of the entire nation not only of the Jews but also of the Israelites" (*De Doctrina Christiana*, YP 6:617).[67] Though his statement is followed by numerous biblical citations as evidence for this claim, it is significant that Milton does not give the calling of the Jews the same prominent position among the signs of the coming apocalypse that many of his contemporaries had given it. It is merely "a further portent," one deemed creditable by "some authorities." The distinct lack of enthusiasm in this passage links it to the most elaborate reference to the Restoration of the Jews in Milton's poetic corpus. When Satan tempts Jesus to assume his messianic role by embracing an earthly kingship, he presses the Son of God to collect the exiled tribes of Judah and Israel. Jesus replies that the time for such a calling has not yet come, adding that the exile experienced by the sons of Abraham is a necessary result of their sinfulness:

> but so died
> Impenitent, and left a race behind
> Like to themselves, distinguishable scarce
> From Gentiles but by Circumcision vain,
> And God with Idols in their worship join'd. (*Paradise Regained*, 3.422–26)

MILTON'S JESUS, good reader of Paul that he is, specifically targets the practice of circumcision as the embodiment of all that is misconceived and corrupted by the Jews, who will soon fail to acknowledge him as their promised messiah. This mark in the flesh functions both to distinguish Jews from pagans and to unite them in its inefficacy. The conflation of Gentile and Jew in this passage is clearly a function of their collective status as unredeemed. It is a combination entirely consistent with the rest of *Paradise Regained*, where all knowledge outside of pure faith is condemned as vain, "little else but dreams" (4.291). As I shall argue in the following chapter, in much of Milton's writing the association of Judaism with paganism, Hebraism with Hellenism, is far more complex. To return to Jesus's response to Satan at the end of book 3 of *Paradise Regained*, however, it is especially striking how unenthusiastic the Son of God is regarding the future Restoration of the Jews. He goes on,

> Yet [God] at length, time to himself best known,
> Rememb'ring *Abraham*, by some wond'rous call
> May bring them back repentant and sincere,
> And at their passing cleave the *Assyrian* flood,
> While to their native land with joy they haste,
> As the Red Sea and *Jordan* once he cleft,
> When to the promis'd land thir Fathers pass'd;
> To his due time and providence I leave them. (433–40)

TAKEN BY MANY modern critics as an indication of Milton's general support for the idea of the restoration of the Jews, this passage is notably subdued. The "wond'rous call" that will bring the children of Abraham back to their land is modified by the deliberately unspecific "some." Indeed, the miraculous return of the Jews to the promised land arises only as a possibility: "some wond'rous call / *May* bring them back repentant and sincere" (emphasis added). And the timing of this call? "To his due time and providence I leave them." The Son dismisses the Jews in a remarkably cursory fashion. While this dismissal may be read as a characteristic gesture of the ideology of Christian supersession, I want to suggest that Milton needs Jesus to drop the Jews of the Diaspora so that he may embrace their mirror image, i.e., a politically and religiously disenfranchised Restoration Milton.

PARADISE LOST AND MIDRASH

THROUGHOUT HIS WRITINGS, amidst volatile political and social realities, and torn between personal triumphs and tragedies, Milton constantly found himself in the situation of wanting to "enjoy the good" while trying to "cavil the conditions" (*Paradise Lost* 10.758–59). William Kerrigan has described this ongoing conflict in terms of an analogy with pre- and postlapsarian Adam: "As Adam discovers his happy state, and then in his second education prepares for a world negating his first happiness, so Milton relives through artistic invention his own agon with necessity."[68] As aspects of what Milton regarded as the providential plan failed, he looked to negotiate the crisis of faith precipitated by the Restoration. Add to these the ubiquitous complications posed by a cryptic and occasionally contradictory biblical text, and the historico-political crises take on even greater significance. Especially after 1660, Milton's position paralleled that of the rabbis. Having assumed a privileged status, a chosenness even, Milton and the rabbis were both faced with historical realities that directly contradicted their respective expectations of deliverance and communion with God. After a long and arduous conversion process, apparently beginning early in life when he was "church-outed by the Prelates," Milton undertook the completion of his midrashic poem, *Paradise Lost.*

In its representational and philosophical reach Milton's religious outlook differs rather profoundly from that of most Protestant theologians in early modern Europe. The Protestantism of Luther or Calvin was inimical to the very notion of theodicy. Although both Christian reformers insisted on the human capacity to interpret the Scriptures without being subject to the dictates of a central authority like Rome, both also acknowledged the profound epistemological shortcomings inherent in any human attempt to understand the nature and the ways of God. Luther, in his dispute with Erasmus, the *De servo arbitrio* (*Bondage of the Will*, December 1525), argued that the whole effort of theodicy, of holding God's justice to human standards, is a manifestation of the devil's ability to deceive humanity into believing in its complete freedom and independence. Humanity's vulnerability to this deception results in undeserved pride in the self:

> When therefore Reason praises God for saving the unworthy, but finds fault with him for damning the undeserving, she stands convicted of not praising God as God, but as serving her own interests. That is to say, what she seeks and praises in God is herself and the things of self, not God or the things of God.[69]

SIMILARLY, CALVIN INSISTED that to "be ignorant of things which it is neither possible nor lawful to know is to be learned," and he recommended a kind of learned ignorance on matters involving divine reason and the nature of God:[70]

> When, therefore, one asks why God has so done, we must reply: because he has willed it. But if you proceed further to ask why he so willed, you are

seeking something greater and higher than God's will, which cannot be found. Let men's rashness, then, restrain itself, and not seek what does not exist, lest perhaps it fail to find what does exist. This bridle, I say, will effectively restrain anyone who wants to ponder in reverence the secrets of God.[71]

CALVIN DID INSIST upon God's rationality, but he placed it beyond the reach of human understanding, effectively denying the possibility of a theodicy.[72] Maintaining a consistency with his conception of grace and predestination, Calvin did not cede intellectual or moral independence to humankind.

Milton's position is much closer to a version of Christian humanism, like that of Erasmus. His famous pronouncements on the shortcomings of "a fugitive and cloistered virtue, unexercised and unbreathed, that never sallies out and sees her adversary," demonstrate how much stock Milton places in mortal reason as essential to obtaining "that immortal garland."[73] Not only is it conceivable to attempt a theodical justification based upon this view of human epistemology, it is irresponsible *not* to attempt one. From this perspective the Bible presents God and the divine plan in the most effective way possible, and it is up to individual readers to make all that they can out of these scriptural traces. The rabbis and Milton understand the immediate currency of cosmology—its relevance to their respective historical circumstances—in similar terms: on the one hand, it liberates the text from its local context, giving it the freedom to be carried forward to the reading present; on the other hand, the dynamics of this interpretive translation restrict the kinds of speculations about origins that might otherwise have been invited by an account of beginnings.[74] In Genesis Rabbah R. Eliezer warns his audience, "Do not investigate that which is greater than you, do not interrogate that which is stronger than you, do not seek to know that which is more wondrous than you, do not ask about that which is hidden from you. Only seek to understand that which is permitted to you, for you have no business with hidden matters" (8:2). Raphael issues a similar warning to Adam, following his version of the hexameron:

> Heav'n is for thee too high
> To know what passes there; be lowly wise:
> Think only what concerns thee and thy being;
> Dream not of other Worlds, what creatures there
> Live, in what state, condition or degree,

Contented that thus far hath been reveal'd
Not of Earth only but of highest Heav'n. (8.172–78)

IN HIS MEDIATING ROLE Raphael presents to Adam his ontological vision in the form of a trade-off. There are certain matters that do not concern Adam and should therefore not be considered; nevertheless, the lowly wisdom Raphael offers to Adam instead functions like the bounded hermeneutics of R. Eliezer. The audience of Genesis Rabbah is meant to recognize in the text's homilies and narrative interpolations a revelation "not of earth only but of highest heaven." Adam's comprehension of this epistemological boundary resembles the rabbis' view of the fence, which it was their task to erect around Scripture: "to know / That which before us lies in daily life, / Is the prime wisdom" (8:192–94).

Inevitably, amidst the ongoing search for textual affirmation of Israel's chosenness and its glorious future, the rabbis find moments to express anticipatory praise and gratitude as part of their reinvention of Creation. Generic distinctions had little relevance for the rabbis; their interpretive homilies include varieties of formal structures and thematic concerns. Included among these is prayer:

> "And the Lord made the two great lights. . . ." "The day is thine, the night also is thine . . ." (Ps. 74:16). To you the day gives praise, to you the night gives praise. Just as the day is within your dominion, so too the night is within your dominion. In the hour that you perform miracles for us during the day, "The day is thine"; in the hour that you perform miracles for us during the night, "the night also is thine." In the hour that you perform miracles for us in the day, we sing a song of praise before you in the day; in the hour that you perform miracles for us in the night, we sing a song of praise before you in the night. You performed miracles for us in the day, and we sang a song of praise for you in the day: "Then sang Deborah and Barak the son of Abinoam on that day, etc." (Judges 5:1). You performed miracles for us in the night, and we sang a song of praise for you in the night: "Ye shall have a song, as in the night when a holy solemnity is kept" (Isa. 30:29). It is pleasing to sing you praises in the day and in the night. Why? "Thou has prepared the light and the sun" (Ps. 74:16), and you made the two great lights. (6:2)

THE LITURGICAL POEM that comprises the reading of this moment of creation draws additional power from the theme upon which it has been written:

prayer. That is, the exegesis takes the form of an enclosed prayer *about* prayer. The ritualistic anaphora act as the architectural support of this beautifully simple poem of praise. On the one hand, its theme is the exemplification of certain moments of Israel's praise of God; on the other hand, these prayers (in Judges and Isaiah) were responses to God's active participation in the salvific history of Israel. Thus, while the homily superficially functions as praise corresponding to the creation of the sun and moon, it strongly suggests the expectation of future divine intervention upon which any further poems of praise will depend. The narrative produces its own formulation of prayer, which itself functions as a homily on the verse in question. Similarly, in *Paradise Lost*, Milton takes his cue from the liturgical structure of Genesis 1 in formulating an epic that itself contains diverse prayer forms, including the magnificent coda to the book 7 hexameron:

> Great are thy works, *Jehovah*, infinite
> Thy power; what thought can measure thee or tongue
> Relate thee; greater now in thy return
> Than from the Giant Angels; thee that day
> Thy Thunders magnifi'd; but to create
> Is greater than created to destroy.
> Who can impair thee, mighty King, or bound
> Thy Empire? easily the proud attempt
> Of Spirits apostate and thir Counsels vain
> Thou has repell'd, while impiously they thought
> Thee to diminish, and from thee withdraw
> The number of thy worshippers. Who seeks
> To lessen thee, against his purpose serves
> To manifest the more thy might: his evil
> Thou usest, and from thence creat'st more good. (7.602–16)

MILTON FORMULATES THIS grand hymn of praise out of the very same consideration of adversity and the evidence of divine conquest that promises greater deliverance in the future. Like the rabbis, Milton views "the Book of God before [him] set" (8.67) as proof not only of God's hand in creation and past events but also as assurance of future triumph. Indeed, some recent critics have considered *Paradise Lost* on a large scale as a structural emulation of prayer,[75] which yields yet a further affinity between Milton's poem and Genesis Rabbah. The organization of the collections of midrashim into individual *parshioth* has suggested to some scholars that the text's final form stems from its ritual use as part of the weekly liturgy in early Jewish communities.[76]

Lacking anything as programmatic as an invocation, the rabbis never offer their audience the equivalent of Milton's pronouncement of his "great argument." It is possible, however, to locate midrashic statements that anticipate Milton's assertion of eternal providence. Taking the apparently extraneous letters and words in the final pronouncement on creation as an invitation for comment, R. Simeon b. Laqish offers the following observation:

> "Behold [*hineh*], it was very good [*me'od*]" (Gen. 1:31) refers to the kingdom of heaven. "*And* behold [*v'hineh*], it was very good" refers to the kingdom of earth. But is the kingdom of earth really very good? Rather, it [the earthly kingdom] demands justice [*diqyut*] from humanity, [as is suggested in the following verse,] "I made the earth and created man [*adam*] upon it" (Is. 45:12). (9:12)

IN ADDITION TO the more explicit Hebrew anagram of "very" [*me'od*] and "man" [*adam*], the midrash implicitly invokes a Hellenistic notion of justice, in its use of the term *diqyut*, which comes from the Greek δικη and also through a silent pun on *edom*, the rabbinic term for Rome. The homily thus works at least partly to affirm the legitimacy of Roman authority, the paradigmatic earthly kingdom, so long as it maintains some standards of justice, understood specifically in Hellenistic terms, i.e., δικαιον. The midrash also reverses the burden shouldered by Milton. Instead of seeking to justify God's ways to humanity, the rabbis seek to locate the ways of human justice, to underscore the imperative for a just society, even outside of a specifically Jewish realm. For this project, the encounter with the non-Hebraic is absolutely central. As we shall see in the next chapter, the cultural hybridities characteristic of midrashic literature are both parallel and familiar to John Milton.

2

"Taking Sanctuary Among the Jews":
Milton and the Form of Jewish Precedent

It is a sad thing to me to think that they which look on one another
as Saints, should behave themselves each to other as the Jewes had
wont to doe toward Heathens.
——*Henry Wilkinson,* Miranda, Stupenda: or the Wonderful Mercies
which the Lord hath Wrought for England

Of Reformation in England and the Cawses that Hitherto have Hindered it
(May 1641), the first of Milton's five pamphlets written against the
prelacy, the hierarchical clergy of the Church of England, begins with a protracted lament over the decline of the Church since the time of the apostles.
Charged with key terms from the debates over religious doctrine, not only
between the Roman church and Protestants, or among diverse Protestant
groupings, but also from the age-old debates between Judaism and Christianity, Milton's account of this decline describes

> how that Doctrine of the *Gospel*, planted by teachers Divinely inspir'd, and by
> them winnow'd, and sifted, from the chaffe of overdated Ceremonies, and re-
> fin'd to such a Spirituall height, and temper of purity, and knowledge of the
> Creator, that the body, with all the circumstances of time and place, were pu-
> rifi'd by the affections of the regenerat Soule, and nothing left impure, but
> sinne . . . should through the grossenesse, and blindnesse, of her Professors,
> and the fraud of deceivable traditions, drag so downwards. (YP 1:519–20)

AT STAKE HERE is the very question of the relationship between body and

spirit that had constituted such a crucial division between some of the earliest Church fathers and the rabbis of the fourth, fifth, and sixth centuries.
While I shall have a great deal more to say on this matter in chapter 4, it is
worth noticing that, even in such an early prose tract as this, Milton resists
a rigid distinction between the body and the spirit that many of his contemporaries avidly asserted. Anticipating what will become a far more explicit monism in the divorce tracts and the later poetry, Milton alters the
nature of the body rather than fully dispensing with it. The body was not
made irrelevant or unnecessary by these "Divinely inspir'd" teachers of the
early Church, rather, it was "purifi'd by the affections of the regenerate
Soule." Sin can and does find a habitation within the body—or, to use the
Pauline terms, the letter—but it is not equivalent to it.[1] Furthermore, unlike many of his Presbyterian contemporaries, who drew their arguments directly from Calvin, Milton depicts the earliest apostolic Church as the result
of a prolonged process of winnowing. While the core of this Church may
have been present even in the earliest formations of Hebrew and Jewish
practice, Milton does not regard the Church as absolutely coeval with the religion of the Hebrews. In the chronological frame posited in this passage,
Judaism holds the more senior position. Christianity's task was to refine this
ancient wisdom, thereby dispensing with its "overdated Ceremonies." Calvin
and his followers, on the other hand, regarded the entire Old Testament as
always already Christianized. For them, anything attributed to the Hebrew
Bible that was not consistent with Christian doctrine, even prior to the Incarnation of Christ, was necessarily a misreading.[2] The problem of the body
and the problem of Christianity's Jewish past are inextricably tied to one another. How any Christian hermeneutics defines its relation to a Hebraic past
detailed in the Hebrew Bible inevitably depends upon the status of that biblical history, which, even when read along purely typological lines, posits the
lived experiences of Jewish bodies as the ground for interpretation. Even
in the most nonliteral modes of reading, the body—of the letter and of
the Jew—constitutes an irreducible element of meaning. In an England
where few identifiably Jewish bodies had existed for three and a half centuries, these issues take on an even greater importance for Milton and his
contemporaries.

That Milton's resistance to the more normative Protestant attitude immediately precedes a curious invocation of Christianity's Jewish prehistory
makes it even more noteworthy. Milton's characteristically interminable periodic sentence continues by mourning how sad it is

that such [purified] Doctrine should . . . backslide one way into the Jewish beggery, of old cast rudiments, and stumble forward another way into the new-vomited Paganisme of sensuall Idolatry, attributing purity, or impurity, to things indifferent, that they might bring the inward acts of the *Spirit* to the outward, and customary ey-Service of the body.

MILTON CHARTS A COURSE for reform between the Scylla of Jewish beggary rejected long ago and the Charybdis of recently cast-off pagan rituals associated with the Roman church. The "new-vomited Paganisme of sensuall Idolatry" figures the advocates of the prelacy as the dog who perversely returns to his vomit in Proverbs 26:11 and 2 Peter 2:22, suggesting that any reformation that might have been achieved by the English church's break with Rome is abrogated by a return to the ceremonies and hierarchies of that rejected mode of Christian belief. 2 Peter's use of the Hebrew Bible's proverb is preceded by the observation that "it would have been better for them never to have known the way of righteousness than after knowing it to turn back from the holy commandment delivered to them." Within this expanded biblical context, though, Milton's seemingly simple contrast between the old Jewish ways and the new Idolatry becomes more complicated and tautological. What Milton depicts as "new-vomited" is anything but new; rather, it is yet another old mode, an analogue to the earlier cast-off Jewish beggary. Newness and oldness are not determined by the relative age of the practices that have been rejected but by the point in Church history when they were properly discarded.

Advocates and opponents of the prelacy often accused each other of similar forms of ignorance. From the supporters of the episcopal hierarchy, these attacks often smacked of an aristocratic elitism, part of the more systematic depiction of Puritans and Independents as boorish and uneducated. In his extended attack on what he construed as Puritanism's ignorant prejudices, Richard Carter described his antagonists as enemies of any "Orthodoxe Divine, because hee useth to speake sometimes in his Sermon, *Hebrew, Greeke,* and *Latine*; because these three were accursed on the *Crosse*: and *Latine* (forsooth) is the language of the whore of *Rome*."[3] I have not been able to determine whether Carter's account of these Puritan zealots is wholly a caricature or whether there actually were those who opposed the use of the three classical languages of antiquity because they were believed to have appeared on the cross. Either way, Carter's attack paints a rather ridiculous picture of ignorant and overeager reformers rushing to throw the baby out with the bathwater. It clearly conflicts with the historical data now available to us, which suggests that many of the most avid supporters of the study of these languages, especially Hebrew, were also deeply involved in efforts of radical reformation of the Church. Indeed, during the early modern period of religious reform and counterreform, the content of the biblical past, to which all participants in the controversies turned, became increasingly linked to its form, that is, to its language(s).

Perhaps one of the "Schizmatics" to whom Carter was referring, Milton could never have been rightly accused of such willful ignorance in matters of language. Indeed, he was wont to make similar attacks on those who supported the prelacy, complaining on one occasion, "In the Greek tongue most of them [are] unletter'd, or unenter'd to any sound proficiency in those *Attick* maisters of morall wisdome and eloquence. In the Hebrew text, which is so necessary to be understood except it be some few of them, their lips are utterly uncircumcis'd" (YP 1:934). As we have already seen from Milton's colorful depiction of new-vomited idolatry, the association of Hebraic traditions with pagan ones often serves to denigrate both in Milton's prose tracts. There are instances, however, where the humanist impulse makes itself felt through a more affirmative assertion concerning the value of these older traditions. In this passage Milton accuses his prelatical opponents of ignorance in two of the three pillars of early modern humanist scholarship, Greek and Hebrew; yet, despite his placement of these two forms of knowledge together, their differences remain evident. Milton does not complain of the ignorance of bishops in the Greek of the New Testament. Instead, he links Greek to the wisdom of the "*Attick* masters," which is of a moral and rhetorical order. From a distinctly pre-Christian classical Greece, Milton derives the values of philosophy and eloquence. Hebrew's importance, on the other hand, is purely scriptural in this passage; the uninitiated stumbles in the language with uncircumcised lips.

In his note to the Yale edition of Milton's prose writings, Frederick Lovett Taft cites the *New English Dictionary*, which in turn cites Acts 7:51, to define "uncircumcis'd" as "Not spiritually chastened or purified, irreligious, heathen." In this passage from Acts, a speech viewed by many scholars of early Christianity as one of the first total invalidations of the Temple and the Mosaic law, St. Stephen concludes his attack on the Jewish community that is about to stone him with the well-worn accusation of stubbornness, "Ye stiffnecked and uncircumcised [απεριτμοτοι] in heart and ears, ye do always resist the Holy Ghost: as your fathers did, so do ye." If we try to apply this definition to Milton's attack, we may conclude that it is precisely an *ignorance* of Hebrew that is tantamount to paganism. According to this reading, Milton appears to be equating the prelates with the un-Christianized Jewish community. Yet Taft's citation of the *New English Dictionary*'s definition via Acts is most curious. While Stephen describes his accusers as uncircumcised in *hearts* and *ears*, Milton describes *his* opponents' *lips* as uncircumcised. Stephen's ire is focused on those who hear—or in this case, fail to hear—whereas Milton aims his reprimands at those who speak the wrong message and thereby mislead. Presumably, what Milton means here is that the prelates' lack of skill in Hebrew is a contributing factor to their abusive leadership of the English church. Milton certainly also considers the episcopacy as irreligious, tantamount to paganism, but the relation between prelatical paganism and ignorance in the Hebrew language deserves further examination.

A better biblical reference for "uncircumcis'd" is Exodus 6:12. Following his initial frustrating encounter with the Israelites, Moses complains to God, "Behold, the children of Israel have not hearkened unto me; how then shall Pharaoh hear me, who am of uncircumcised lips [Hebrew, *'aral s'fatayim*]?"[4] If Milton echoes Moses at this moment, and associates the (mis)leadership of the prelacy with Moses's early failure, his attack takes on further implications. Though he cites Moses here as a means of attacking the episcopacy, in its larger context the biblical passage is just as critical of the audience who is deaf to Moses's pleas—not just Pharaoh but also the Israelites. Read within this context, Milton's complaint may be construed as a tacit criticism of the English population who passively accept the misguided leadership of the church hierarchy. Furthermore, if Moses's attribution of uncircumcised lips to himself functions as the paradigm for the prelates, then, by extension, Moses's role as leader of the Children of Israel may be read as pretext for the prelatical leadership of the Church of England. A figure who combines contradictory qualities for the Protestant reader, Moses's association with the prelates in this attack of the episcopacy calls into question Milton's view of the paradigmatic leader of the biblical nation of Israel even more so than it casts further aspersions on the corrupt religious leaders of mid seventeenth-century England.

To describe the prelatical ignorance of Hebrew in terms of circumcision is to plunge into an already overdetermined matter with a history as old as Christianity itself. The biblical command to circumcise every male child was, of course, an especially divisive issue in the early apostolic Church. Paul devoted a significant portion of his epistles to addressing the dispute over whether a Christian was expected to circumcise himself according to Jewish practice. In response to the so-called Judaizers among the followers of Jesus, Paul argued, "For in Jesus Christ neither circumcision availeth any thing, nor uncircumcision; but faith which worketh by love" (Galatians 5:6).[5] Indeed, in Pauline theology circumcision comes to epitomize the shortcomings of Israel after the flesh. The condemnation of being "uncircumcised," it would seem, has a much different weight for a Protestant Christian like Milton than it might have had for Moses or even for Stephen. Insofar as Milton uses it specifically to signify an ignorance in the Hebrew language, the term becomes especially fraught, since it complicates the value attached to the presumptive language of the Jewish people. Israel of the flesh, the first speakers of the Hebrew language, were precisely those people who consistently practiced circumcision and, perhaps more significantly, continued to practice the ritual during Milton's own time.

The very figurative use of the term in Milton's attack—lips, after all, cannot be literally circumcised—allows him to sever the otherwise literal relationship between Hebrew and Judaism. Such a figurative appropriation of the language is analogous to Taft's citation of the passage from Acts, which reenacts one of the central dynamics of Milton's use of Hebraic precedent. Instead of referring to the more directly appropriate verse from the *Hebrew Bible*, Taft looks to the New Testament's revision of what thereby becomes the *Old Testament*, assuming that Milton's contact with the earlier Hebraic tradition would have necessarily been mediated by a Christian intervention. Part of my goal in this chapter is to restore some elements of Milton's negotiations of Hebrew and Jewish learning while simultaneously acknowledging the complex intermingling of these influences with both pre-Christian, classical, and pagan thought on the one hand and Christianity's (primarily) typological rereading of the Old Testament on the other. The competition among religious and political antagonists of pre–Civil War and Interregnum England over proper claims to the title of "new" or "spiritual" Israel offers a rich terrain for the analysis of trends in early modern hermeneutics and historiography and allows us to revise our understanding of value attributed to the wisdom of the ancients, both pagan and Jewish, during the period. Most important for my purposes, the ensuing analysis gives fuller context to the argument of the second half of this book, i.e., that Milton's later poetry manifests a cultural agon parallel to that found within rabbinic writings of the fourth through sixth centuries and that this clash of cultures was appar-

ent in various ways to Milton and his contemporaries. Milton's attack on
prelatical linguistic ignorance and this modern editor's annotations neatly
encapsulate the core of my argument here. First, the passage shows Milton,
already at this relatively early stage in his polemical career, positioning himself in an ambiguous relation to any developing sense of English national
identity: the English people are partly accountable for the success of these
prelates with uncircumcised lips. As his career progresses, his role as both insider and outsider to English politics, religion, and culture—a role, I shall argue, that connects Milton with the situation of the Diaspora Jew—becomes
an even more prominent feature of his prose and poetry. Second, as Taft's
mistaken annotation suggests, at issue in the nature of Hebraic and Jewish
precedent during this period in England is a mode of reading that still depends on typology, even as the Reformation is said to have restored a more
"literal" biblical hermeneutic. Third, inasmuch as it is a figure that is anchored in the body, circumcision raises the very status of the body in Milton's writings, especially the historical status of Jewish bodies. And finally,
the charge of a failure in language brings together the learning of the pre-
Christian classics and ancient Judaism while at the same time maintaining
certain crucial distinctions between the two.

"UBICUNQUE EST BENE": ALTERITY AND ENGLISHNESS

WHILE IT MAY have been possible for someone of Milton's vast learning and
intelligence to present Hebrew scholarship as a means of breaking down a
monolithic religious orthodoxy, there were those within the radical camp
who were wary of a heavy reliance on the liberating powers of linguistic erudition. For these political and religious activists, advanced education was yet
another means of reestablishing a hierarchy they were working hard to level.[6]
William Walwyn complained that although the Bible had been translated
into English several times by the 1640s, there were still those ministers who
claimed that Scripture was not understandable to lay folk without the help
of linguistically trained clergy. "Let us argue a little with them," Walwyn
continues,

> either the Scriptures are not rightly Translated, or they are: If they are not,
> why have wee not beene told so all this while? why have wee beene cheated
> into errours? If they are rightly Translated, why should not Englishmen un-

derstand them? The Idiomes and properties of the Hebrew, and Greeke Languages, which some say, cannot word for word be exprest in English, might all this while have beene Translated into as many English words as will carry the sence thereof. There is nothing in the Hebrew or Greeke but may be exprest in English, though not just in so many words (which is not materiall) so that it must be confest, that either we have not beene fairly dealt withall hitherto in the conveyance of the Scripture (a thing which few dare suspect) or else the Scriptures are as well to be understood by us, as by any Linguist whatsoever.[7]

WALWYN'S CHARACTERISTICALLY ANTIELITIST view of translation differs markedly from our contemporary ideas about language and idiom. It also places him at odds with the opinions of many of his English contemporaries, who bestowed upon the Hebrew language certain properties that elude translation while at the same granting to English a peculiar affinity to the language of the Holy Scriptures, a language that was held by many to be the prelapsarian *Ursprach.*[8]

The view of Hebrew as possessing certain unique mystical qualities, manifesting unmediated relations between words and things, stands in rich tension with the Christian view of the Hebrew Bible as the typologically reconstituted Old Testament. In other words, if the Old Testament is only complete in light of the New Testament, then arguably the nexus between word and thing (in Hebrew, *davar* can mean either) is not so fully independent and unmediated. There remains a figurative or allegorical quality to Hebrew. Furthermore, when Hebrew moves from a biblical to a postbiblical language, what becomes of its special qualities? Milton's opinion is characteristically complex. *Of Reformation* offers an early version of the attack on prelatical linguistic ignorance:

> If these Doctors who had scarse half the light that we enjoy, who all except 2 or 3 were ignorant of the Hebrew tongue, and many of the Greek, blundring upon the dangerous, and suspectfull translations of the Apostat *Aquila*, the Heretical Theodotion; Judaïzed *Symmachus*; the erroneous *Origen*; if these could yet find the Bible so easie, why should we doubt, that have all the helps of Learning, and faithfull industry that man in this life can look for, and the assistance of *God* as neer now to us as ever. (YP 1:566—68)

MILTON'S ATTACK ON the authority of the Church fathers draws a distinction between the value of Hebrew scholarship from a philological standpoint and the corruption of the Judaic tradition. Aquila, Theodotion, and Symmachus have produced "dangerous, and suspectfull translations" out of their lack of authentic Hebrew knowledge, a lack that seems to be confirmed precisely because of what Milton characterizes as their Judaizing (and hence, heretical) tendencies. Thus, in a move that is characteristic of many Christian Hebraists from the early modern period, Milton asserts that genuine authority in matters of the Hebrew language belongs to the properly reformed Christian tradition and no longer rests in the hands of Jewish scholars. The transition from Israel of the flesh to the new Israel of the spirit was a linguistic one as well as a theological one.

The status of the Hebrew language, and, in particular, its relationship to English, was part of a broader trend in sixteenth- and seventeenth-century England to render questions of politics and religion in terms of England's status as God's elect nation. The explosion of Hebrew study during the early modern period had a very different dynamic in England than elsewhere. Because in England Jews were by and large an absent presence since the end of the thirteenth century, the first major impact of Hebrew and Jewish studies in England (outside of a small circle of specialists) coincided with the first open discussions concerning the possibility of an official return of Jews to English soil.[9] On the continent Hebrew studies often meant more intensive contact with Jews; in England the study of Hebrew was not only intellectually and religiously transformative, it brought with it—and was partly produced by—a political transformation. What had been idealized as a homogeneous body politic now stood open to intrusion by foreign Jewish bodies.

The religious and political disputes in France or Spain, or within the diverse German political entities of the period, were not necessarily disconnected to matters of nationalism and national identity; but, in England, as the single locus of English-speaking people in all of Europe, debates over church government, political formations, and marriage laws quickly became debates about what it meant to be English, especially in light of the widespread doctrine of national election documented by William Haller.[10] Given this tendency to construe religious controversies in terms of competing notions of Englishness, we may identify a curious paradox at the heart of Milton's prose tracts. Milton repeatedly portrays England as God's elect nation, providentially destined to lead the vanguard in the reform of the church.[11] Yet, like others who opposed an established English church, Milton advocates what amounts to a separation of Church and State.[12] He strenuously objects to the combination of civil authority with religious doctrine, repeatedly insisting that church discipline can only be enforced internally, through the operations of "Right Reason." In his first antiprelatical tract Milton articulates his position by citing the example of Constantine, who, as we saw in chapter 1, was depicted by many early English reformers as the paradigmatic Christian emperor. Milton's regard for Constantine could not be more different: "For there is nothing wanting but *Constantine* to reigne, and then Tyranny her selfe shall give up all her cittadels into your [the Bishops'] hands, and count ye thence forward her trustiest agents" (*Of Reformation*, YP 1:551). Looking back nostalgically on what he considers "the ancientest, and most virgin times between *Christ* and *Constantine*," Milton disputes the claims of earlier Church historians:

> I am not of the opinion to thinke the Church a *Vine* in this respect, because, as they take it, she cannot subsist without clasping about the Elme of worldly strength, and felicity, as if the heavenly City could not support it selfe without the props and buttresses of secular Authoritie. They extoll *Constantine* because he extol'd them; as our homebred Monks in their Histories blanch the Kings their Benefactors, and brand those that went about to be their Correctors. If he had curb'd the growing Pride, Avarice, and Luxury of the *Clergie*, then every Page of his Story should have sweld with his Faults. (YP 1:554)[13]

IN MILTON'S CHARACTERIZATION of Constantine's reign, Protestantism recovers its early roots in an oppositional and disenfranchised community, not unlike the post-Constantine *Jewish* community.[14] I am not suggesting that Milton was deliberately figuring his ideal Church in opposition to Constantine so as to align it with fourth-century rabbinic Judaism. It does seem productive, however, to recognize that Milton's idealized apostolic Church has more in common with this politically disempowered version of Judaism than it does with the spectacularly successful post-Constantine Church. "Church-outed by the prelates," as he described his own position, Milton depends upon this antithetical stance vis-à-vis entrenched political and religious power to give his writing a prophetic force.[15]

Within this historical context, an aspect of Milton's use of organic imagery becomes especially significant. The figure of the vine in the passage functions for Milton as a sign of weakness and dependence, subjecting the Church (invisible *and* visible) to the mortality of the natural world.[16] It also affords Milton the opportunity to proffer a critique in miniature of nearly all previous English church historiography, certainly that which proceeds from the venerable Bede and onward. Most intriguing, however, is that even as Milton fashions an antithetical Protestant identity, heir to rabbinic Judaism's own oppositional stance, his rejection of the figure of the vine denaturalizes Christianity's genealogy, connecting it to Judaism exclusively on a textual basis. Charging Parliament to eliminate the episcopacy with the famous "root and branch" petition of 1640, radical opponents of the prelacy simultaneously reasserted versions of the "new Israel" ideology.[17] Some of these London petitioners came very close, at one time or another, to asserting a Jewish ancestry as support for their claim to the status of Zion.[18] By contrast, Milton, who shared many of the same radical opinions in doctrinal matters, almost never acknowledges the existence of a "real," contemporary embodied Jew. His elision of living Jews has as much to do with his recognition of other deeper parallels between his own circumstances and that of the Diaspora Jew as it does with any insistence on abiding differences. The radically textual formulation of Jewish precedent allows Milton strategically to assert his own direct links to the early apostolic Church and to Judaism when it is severed from state power. Not an absolute refusal of a genealogical rendering, Milton's rejection of naturalizing metaphors is noteworthy in contrast to what I have already described as his monistic retention of the body. It suggests, I think, a nervous awareness of the ongoing presence of Jewish bodies, who threaten to disrupt the typological sense of Christianity's fulfillment of its Hebraic past.

For further evidence of this fraught encounter with natural images of relation and lineage, we can contrast Milton's refusal of the image of the vine to his opponent's embrace of the same figure. Responding to the onslaught of antiprelatical tracts condemning the episcopacy as corrupt, James Ussher wonders,

> With what shew of reason then can any man imagin, that what was instituted by *God* in the *Law*, for meer matter of government and preservation of good order (without all respect of type or ceremony:) should now be rejected in the *Gospel*, as a device of *Antichrist?* what was by the Lord once *planted a noble vine, wholly a right seed,* should now be so *turned into the degenerate plant of a strange vine;* that no purging or pruning of it will serve the turne, but it must be cut down root and branch, as *a plant which our heavenly Father had never planted?*[19]

IN THE HANDS of defenders of the episcopacy, the organic image functions as a sign of strength, vitality, and, above all, authenticity. By asserting a continuity between the biblical law instituted by God and the Church of England, Ussher and others were laying claim to the same argument that had been made in previous generations during the earliest breaks from Rome. The debate over church government, as a version of the Reformation itself, was a debate over authenticity and originality. Yet the authenticity to which Anglicans (and Catholics) lay claim stands in uneasy tension with the "type" and "ceremony" that make a nervous appearance in Ussher's parenthetical aside. The laws of church government authorized by the Old Testament function to preserve "good order" and are thus not made irrelevant by the New Dispensation under the Gospel. Yet they also wield a ceremonial and typological significance that potentially throws into doubt the validity of the old forms. On all sides of the questions, Catholic and Protestant, Anglican and Puritan, Presbyterian and Independent, appeals to authenticity open the doors to an unwieldy return of the Jewish repressed, as the body of the type or the body of the law/tradition.

Milton was one of many opponents of episcopacy, and, later, of those who opposed the Presbyterians, in simultaneously asserting a version of Hebraic precedent and opposing a church government in possession of civil powers as a means of enforcement. As the disputes ceased to be between Anglicans and an undifferentiated body of church reformers, that is, as the matter became less a question of English Erastianism and shifted to the nature of religious authority as distinct from state authority, Presbyterians and Independents found support for their respective positions in the "Jewish Church," biblical and postbiblical. In 1644, George Gillespie, a Presbyterian minister who became a vocal opponent of Parliament's increasing impulses toward religious toleration, offered the following distinction:

> Though the Jewish Church and Commonwealth were for the most part not different materially, the same men being members of both, even as in all Christian Republikes, yet they were formally different one from another, in regard of distinct Acts, Lawes, Courts, Officers, Censure, and Administrations. For, 1. The Ceremoniall law given was given to them as a Church, the Judiciall law given to them as a State. 2. They did not worship, doe sacrifice, pray, praise, &c. as a State; nor did they kill malefactors with the sword of the Church. 3. As the Lords matters and the Kings matters were distinguished, so there were two different Courts for judging of the one, and the

other, 2. *Chron.* 19.8.11. *Fourthly*, when the *Romans* took away the Jewish State and Civill government, yet their Church did remain. 5. The government of the State and the constitution thereof was not the same under the Judges, under the Kings, and after the captivity: shall we therefore say that the Church was altered and new moulded, as oft as the Civill government was changed.[20]

ANTICIPATING THE MAJOR political shifts of the next several years, and perhaps even the arrest and execution of Charles I, Gillespie offers a model of church government, linked directly to *post*biblical Jewry, that is inured to even the most dramatic of civil disruptions, the loss of state authority. Separation of Church and State, then, need not signify the loss of the pragmatic means of maintaining proper church discipline, which would include, though not be limited to, the power of excommunication, an issue that, more than many others, tended to function as a lightning rod for controversies among Presbyterians, Independents, and radical sectarians of the mid 1640s.

The tension in Milton's position between his embrace of some version of English election (especially in these early years of his career as polemicist) and his opposition to tying church worship or government to an institutionalized, established, and distinctively English church, suggests a provocative distinction between a nascent form of national/ethnic identity and a different formulation of civil/political allegiance. Susanne Woods has argued, in a specifically Italian context, that Milton's identification of English nationalism with Protestantism (of his own formulation) functioned rhetorically to oppose the tyrannical papacy tied to Rome, which, in *The Reason of Church Government* and *Areopagitica*, became inextricably bound up with the Stuart monarchy and its prelacy. This is noteworthy because Milton did not opt for the stance taken by many of his fellow dissenters, who set themselves explicitly against contemporary English self-definition. Instead, Milton constructed a kind of virtual Englishness, one that valued freedom and religious toleration.[21] Contrary to all empirical historical evidence, Milton seemed to be suggesting that the episcopal, and later, Presbyterian, forms of church discipline were the aberrations. What is more, at this stage in early modern history, Milton's position suggests either that burgeoning forms of national identity had not yet converged with the newly evolving imagined community of the political state or that this convergence encounters modes of resistance.

Throughout his career, for reasons that are no doubt psychological and personal as much as sociological and political, Milton characteristically constructs his identity as balanced between insider and outsider.[22] The Romantic identification—to which we are still heir—of Milton as the paradigmatic poet-prophet, addressing a "fit audience . . . though few," may be partly a function of the personal impositions of Blake, or Wordsworth, or Shelley, seeking to find precedent for their own hyperindividualized stances. But it owes at least as much to Milton's own antithetical self-fashioning. In the notoriously prolonged autobiographical preface to the second part of *The Reason of Church-Government*, he announces his intention, "That what the greatest and choycest wits of *Athens, Rome,* or modern *Italy,* and those Hebrews of old did for their country, I in my proportion with this over and above of being a Christian, might doe for mine: not caring to be once nam'd abroad, though perhaps I could attaine to that, but content with these British Ilands as my world" (YP 1:812). Milton projects a poetry that will place England in the company of the great cultural centers of the past and present, but which will make it distinctive, "with this over and above [his] being a Christian." Similarly, while his ostensible goal is to bring respect and fame to England, the secondary and no less important effect his writing will have will be to distinguish *himself* from the ordinary Englishman. That is, Milton's gesture of literary patriotism is also an act of individuation and isolation. This poetic impulse, like others we have already seen, has its parallel in writings about the dynamics of church reform. John Goodwin observes,

> Yea, most of those revelations of himselfe, which he was graciously pleas'd to impart to his ancient Church of the *Jewes*, were not imparted unto them by their Synedrion or Great Councell, but by particular men; who likewise usually (if not alwayes) received their inspirations from God, in their greatest privacie and sequestration; yea, and that (if the observations of the Rabbins will hold in that behalfe) whilst they were yong. That light of Evangelicall truth, wherein the Reformed Churches rejoyce at this day, yea, and triumph over Antichristian darkness, did not break out of the clouds of Councels and Synods unto them, but God caused it to shine upon them, from scattered and single starres, as *Luther, Calvin, Zuinglius, Martyr,* &c.[23]

THROUGHOUT THE HISTORY of Christendom, which begins for Goodwin as for may others with the "Church of the *Jewes,*" reform has come at the hands of the individual who, while he may seek to bring glory to the faithful, also brings glory to himself. Goodwin's embrace of the rabbinical view on this matter suggests an additional aspect of the dynamics of the outsider whose role it is to offer criticism of the world in relation to which he stands at some odds. Since the political ascendancy of Christianity in the West, Jews, both as individuals and as a community, have stood in uneasy relation to the society in which they live. One does not have be Jewish to serve as a social or cultural critic; but the position occupied by that critic has, especially in modern times, been associated with the Jew, for better, and more often, for worse. England in the middle of the seventeenth century is filled with an astonishing and growing number of cultural critics, self-identified outsiders like Milton, from nearly all ideological and religious perspectives. It is also the period in which England faces more concretely than it ever had before its relation to the paradigmatic outsider, the Jew.[24]

Outsiders and opponents of hierarchy were not the only ones thinking about culture in terms of the Jewish question. Indeed, the parallel and yet strikingly distinct association of poetry and Jews in the writings of a staunch Anglican like Abraham Cowley confirms the use to which a "Jewish" stance might be put in mid seventeenth-century England. In the preface to his 1656 volume of poems, Cowley writes that of all human gifts none had been "so long usurpt [by the Devil] as *Poetry*. It is time to *Baptize* it in *Jordan*, for it will never become clean by bathing in the *Waters* of *Damascus*. There wants, methinks, but the Conversion of *That* and the *Jews*, for the accomplishing of the *Kingdom* of *Christ*." Sixteen hundred and fifty-six was, of course, the year of the Whitehall Conference to determine the question of Jewish readmission. Cowley, who was undoubtedly dissatisfied with the state of English culture and politics during the height of the Cromwellian Protectorate, combines, almost as an afterthought, the Christianization of poetry with the conversion of the Jews, revealing an anxiety that connects an attack on the old order of the English church and crown with the role of the Jew.

English writing of the period repeatedly makes reference to the "Jewish Nation"; this despite the absence of one of the defining elements in the developing discourse of nationalism: a homeland. Shapiro writes that "the failure of the Jews to conform to acceptable notions of nationhood rendered equally unsatisfactory the alternatives of assimilating these vagabonds into Christian commonwealths or providing them with their own land so that they could rule their own nation once more."[25] But if the Jew could be both the prototypical landless wanderer and part of a nation, then this had both troubling and liberating implications for the meaning of nation as it applied to the English, especially those who felt alienated politically and religiously from the dominant modes of thought and expression. Consistent with his

Arminian divergence from mainstream Calvinism, Milton regards glorification as something an individual or people must achieve through merit and
not by virtue of election. Mueller concludes her discussion of *Of Reformation*
by distinguishing Milton's notion of a "meritorious nation" from the "prov-
identially-steered 'elect nation' that begins to figure conspicuously after
Foxe."[26] About a quarter of a century after his avid engagement in the controversies over church government, at a very different point in English history as well as Milton's life (he was probably putting the finishing touches on
the first edition of *Paradise Lost*), Milton wrote to his friend Peter Heimbach,
an elector of Brandenburg, about his own sense of Englishness. In an earlier
letter Heimbach had complimented Milton on his synthesis of different
virtues, "the measure of gravity . . . with the most serene kindness, . . .
charity with prudence, . . . piety with political ability." Deflecting Heimbach's praise in characteristically Miltonic fashion, the blind and politically
enfeebled poet and polemicist replied that the virtue Heimbach had called
political, "which I should prefer you to call devotion to my country, almost
drove me from my country . . . after I had been charmed by her pretty
name." He concludes with his famously pithy observation, which might just
as well have been applied to Diaspora Jewry, "Patria est, ubicunque est
bene."[27] A far cry from the heady days of 1640–42, locating one's homeland
in terms of one's well-being follows as an outgrowth of Milton's self-fashioning as the insider/outsider, and it is consistent with the view Milton had
taken from very early on concerning the state, national election, and religious
integrity.

CHILD AND TUDOR: TYPOLOGY AND/OR
JEWISH PRECEDENT

IN THE FIRST of his series of tracts in support of the church hierarchy,
Joseph Hall asserts a complex relationship between the Church of England
and Jewish precedent. To prove the validity of clerical titles, Bishop Hall
refers to the examples of Paul and Barnabas, who

> ordained Presbyters in all the Churches of *Lystra, Antioch, Iconium*: . . . And
> vvhat els, I beseech you, vvould the rigid exacters of the over-severe and Ju-
> daicall observation of the Lords day, as an Evangelicall Sabbath, seem to

plead for their vvarant (vvere they able to make it good any vvay), but the guise and practice of the Apostles.[28]

PURITANICAL CONCERN WITH the exact manner of practice is construed negatively as "Judaicall," suggesting that for Hall this kind of precedent is less important, perhaps even irrelevant. Yet, as Hall delves further into the scriptural authority for episcopacy, he has extensive recourse to a different kind of Jewish precedent: "What are the twelve Tribes of Israel, but the whole Church of God? For, whereof did the first Christian Church consist, but of converted Iewes? And whither did our Saviour bend all his allusions but to them?"[29] Hall argues that his contemporary English church needs to take seriously its Jewish legacy, not merely in terms of a scriptural tradition, or even in terms of typological adumbration and fulfillment (i.e., following the Augustinian model of the earthly and heavenly Jerusalems), but also as the incarnate progenitors of the first Christian Church. This embrace of Christianity's Jewish roots—which stands in direct contrast to what I have described as Milton's denaturalized genealogy—is what sets the stage for Hall's subsequent claims, which are repeated throughout the dispute over the prelacy by supporters of the church hierarchy:

> They had their twelve Princes of the Tribes of their Fathers, heads of the thousands of Israel. They had their seventy Elders to bear the burden of the people.
>
> The Son of God affects to imitate his former Polity, and therefore chooses his twelve Apostles, and 70 Disciples otgather [*sic*] and saw his Evangelicall Church: The twelve Tribes then are the Church: The twelve Apostles must be their Iudges and governours: Their sitting showes authoritie: Their sitting on Thrones, eminence of power: their sitting on twelve Thrones, equalitie of their Rule: their sitting to judge, power and exercise of Iurisdiction: their sitting to judge the twelve Tribes of Israel, the universalitie of their power and jurisdiction: And what Iudgement could this be but Ecclesiasticall and Spiritual (for civill rule they challenged not) and what Thrones but Apostolicall, and by their derivation, Episcopall?[30]

THROUGH A METICULOUS parsing of the details of apostolic leadership in the earliest Church, especially as they "imitate"—and this is Hall's own term—

the ecclesio-political structure of the ancient Israelites, Hall defends the current hierarchical establishment of the Church of England, asserting an absolute continuity, historically, typologically, even genealogically, between the Jews of the Old Testament and the England of the mid seventeenth century.

Citing Jewish custom as acceptable authority for Christian practice was tricky business, however, and no matter how carefully Hall or any other Anglican writer might try to distinguish between good biblical precedent and bad pharisaical accretion, the historical and theological connections between the two opened the door for antagonists like the irrepressible William Prynne to construe all episcopal practices as having their roots in the habits of the Pharisees. In one of his many tracts against the prelacy, Prynne writes that if the bishop did not have ceremonies

> to garnish his *worship of God* (as he calls it) the *world* could not see how *right* his *heart stands*, nor yet see *his good works*; because instead of *good works* (*perverting Christs word*) he puts his *Devotion*, and his *Devotion* stands in his *Ceremonies*; which he saith must not be *too few*, for *then they leave his Service naked*, and therefore to avoyd that he must have both a *Surplice*, and *Hood*, and *Cope*, to cover that *nakednesse*. So as all his *light* is in his *Externall worship shining forth* in his brave Garbe of *Ceremonies*, as that of the *Pharises* in their broad *Philacteries*.[31]

HALL MAY HAVE embraced the association of the surplice, hood, and cope with the Temple priests that Prynne offers to condemn the prelates; indeed, other advocates of the episcopal hierarchy make this analogy explicitly, though it held little persuasive power for those who read the Levitical passages in the Hebrew Bible as having purely typological import. Prynne makes no effort here to offer such an argument, choosing instead to overleap the biblical priests so as to compare his prelatical targets with the Pharisees. While there is nothing especially new about attempts to establish links between ancient Israel and the modern Church, what is of interest for the present study is the anxious contours of this invocation of Jewish precedent.

It is often difficult to determine whether the Jewish Synagogue stands for a system of *practices* utterly alien to Christian faith or for a system of *beliefs* uncorrected by Christ's Incarnation. Responding to accusations by Presbyterians, the Independent, Henry Burton, drew comparisons between the English reformation and the earliest stages of Christianity's break from Judaism. Just as that "Gospell-Reformation" was a gathering of such churches out of that of the Jewes, as acknowledged Christ to be their onely King and Law-giver, to govern consciences and churches by his Word, when the rest of that church, even the main body of it, did reject Christ, and renounce him for their King, this being the very Title set over him on his crosse, for which they crucified him: So the preaching up of Christs Kingdome in these dayes, is that which calleth and gathereth those unto Christ; who acknowledge him alone for their King to govern them; and this out of those, that doe not, or will not submit unto his Kingly government, but depend upon the sole determination of men, what kind of church-government they will set up in the Land, which you tell us must be *sutable to the lawes and customes of the Realme, and manners of the people.*[32]

THE PARALLELS ASSERTED by Burton between the early apostolic Church and the Independent churches of England may stem from a homology of the unreconstructed nature of the Jewish synagogue and the unreformed nature of the Anglican church. But these similarities do not suggest whether the synagogue and the Anglican church are regarded as wholly Other, placing their respective emphases on deed rather than creed, or as perversions of the true faith.

A Judaism regarded as having been founded primarily on works, and only secondarily on faith, is far more consistent with the Pauline and Augustinian polemics of the formative periods of Christianity. It comes as some surprise, in fact, to discover that this was not consistently the approach adopted by early modern writers on Judaism, since Paul's depiction of an "Israel after the flesh" forms such a foundational element of Christianity's self-definition. When Judaism is perceived as bad faith, change is not necessarily alien to Jewish historical development; that is, Judaism may have indeed evolved since the time of Christ, but it has changed to its detriment. When Judaism is condemned for its improper emphasis on ritualized behavior, true Christian faith takes its definition from a systematic differentiation from and subordination of Jewish practice. This formulation of Judaism's otherness does not completely sever the ties between the two religions, but it renders Judaism as frozen in time, having failed to make the proper evolutionary leap precipitated by Christ's Incarnation and Passion. Given the Christian argument of typological supersession, Judaism, even contemporary Judaism, remains a fossilized record of the errors of the past. Through this view, one can begin to see how it might be possible for Christian writers to draw so many connections between Judaism and the practices (and beliefs) of the pagan world.

A corollary of the view of "Israel after the flesh" is the construction of Jews as constituting a racially distinct, and necessarily stigmatized, alien nation/ethnicity mistakenly attending to deed instead of creed. This version of Jewish alterity poses some potential tensions in Christian typology. It offers to Christianity the opportunity to retain some aspect of a literal physical genealogy while at the same time embracing Paul's assertion in Romans 4:16, which would appear to reject the value of fleshly genealogy in favor of a more faith-based lineage: "Therefore it is of faith, that it might be by grace; to the end the promise might be sure to all the seed; not to that only which is of the law, but that also which of the faith of Abraham; *who is the father of us all.*"[33] What is especially noteworthy about this version of Jewish alterity is that it is only functional when Abraham's seed means biological progeny, a meaning made available precisely through the kind of literalizing interpretations attributed to Judaism and condemned by Paul and his followers. In other words, Jews as a racial category become the repository for a hermeneutics that in turn produces a rejection of racial categorizations. Judaism is the source *and* the primary victim of this mode of alterity.[34]

Milton shared the commonly held view that Christians should work to achieve the conversion of the Jews but, as we saw in chapter 1, he had very little more to say on this matter than his few statements to that effect. He certainly does not appear to have been among those whose eschatological expectations included an imminent mass conversion. Much of this may be attributable to Milton's rejection of millenarian apocalypticism in favor of a "native apocalypticism" so richly discussed by Janel Mueller. Yet if a key aspect of Milton's apocalyptic vision is, according to Mueller, the flesh and blood bodies of his contemporary Englishmen, it is all the more noteworthy that Milton devotes whatever energies he does on the question of Christianity's Jewish lineage to the systematic denaturalization of such a genealogy.[35] As we have already seen, Milton mitigates some of the more troubling aspects of Jewish-Christian lineage by denaturalizing any notion of genealogy. Illustrating his argument against episcopal privilege in *The Reason of Church-Government* through a reductio ad absurdam, Milton points out that the priests and Levites held their offices as a result of their paternal inheritance. "Therefore," he concludes, "unlesse we shall choose our Prelats only out of the Nobility, and let them runne in a blood, there can be no possible imitation of Lording over their brethren in regard of their persons altogether unlike" (YP 1:767). In place of this mode of naturalized inheritance, Milton posits a very different model for transmission through ordination: "Verily neither the nature, nor the example of ordination doth any way require an imparity betweene the ordainer and the ordained. For what more naturall then every like to produce his like, man to beget man, fire to propagate fire" (YP 1:768). The means may be that of artifice, of the language of ordination, but the effect is rendered as a begetting, supplanting the natural mode of procreation.[36] Bodies do indeed matter for Milton, but only, it would seem, English Protestant bodies.

For an opponent of the episcopacy like Milton, especially as he moved further and further toward the position of the Independents, there was a ready-made stance available regarding the question of biblical, Hebraic precedents in matters of church government. Inasmuch as Christ's Incarnation and Passion functioned as the completion of the Old Covenant, including its ceremonial laws and rituals, it made perfect sense for Milton to regard these ceremonies and rituals surrounding the tabernacle and Temple, the laws concerning Aaron and the priests, as antiquated, superseded, no longer valid. And indeed, we do find him giving voice to this view, casting his opponents in his antiprelatical tracts as excessively Judaic, still operating under the dispensation of the old law. Milton asserts,

> that the Gospell is the end and fulfilling of the Law, our liberty also from
> the bondage of the Law I plainly reade. How then the ripe age of the
> Gospell should be put to schoole againe, and learn to governe her selfe from
> the infancy of the Law, the stronger to imitate the weaker, the freeman to
> follow the captive, the learned to be lesson'd by the rude, will be a hard un-
> dertaking to evince from any of those principles which either art or inspira-
> tion hath written. (YP 1:763)

GIVEN THE HOMOLOGIES between Milton's circumstances and those of the diaspora Jew, it is of particular interest that Milton adopts to his own use a well-established tradition of stock images to portray Judaism's subordination to Christianity. The law's immaturity, weakness, bondage, and ignorance are contrasted to the Gospel's maturity, strength, freedom, and wisdom. What is more, Milton asserts a typological hermeneutic so extreme that it threatens entirely to elide the reality of the Hebrew Bible. He argues that "the imperfect and obscure institution of the Law, which the Apostles themselves doubt not oft-times to vilifie, cannot give rules to the compleat and glorious ministration of the Gospel, which lookes on the Law, as on a childe, not as on a tutor" (YP 1:762). Though he is clearly alluding to Paul, Milton's contrast of the child and the tutor revises the argument offered in the apostle's letter to the Galatians. Putting forward a strong argument for the legitimacy of Christianity's Jewish heritage, Paul wrote,

> Now I say, That the heir, as long as he is a child, differeth nothing from a servant, though he be lord of all. But is under tutors and governors until the time appointed of the father. Even so we, when we were children, were in bondage under the elements of the world: But when the fulness of the time was come, God sent forth his Son, made of a woman, made under the law, To redeem them that were under the law, that we might receive the adoption of sons. And because ye are sons, God hath sent forth the Spirit of his Son into your hearts, crying, Abba, Father. Wherefore thou art no more a servant, but a son; and if a son, then heir of God through Christ. (Galatians 4:1–7)

PAUL HAD EARLIER depicted the law as a tutor [παιδαγωγος], neutrally positing the necessary, if temporary, function of the law. Instead of denaturalizing the status of the new Christian through the figure of adoption, Paul posits an alternative notion of natural paternity: the newly baptized believer claims his birthright—which was his all along—by virtue of his newfound recognition of his true father.[37] Milton reverses the images completely, suggesting that the Gospel serves as the tutor of the law, which plays the role of child. The effect is twofold. First, by casting the law as the child, Milton resists any aspect of the naturalizing figure of paternity. Second, in a historical reorientation akin to the one we saw earlier, Milton makes the law (and therefore, the Jews) into the younger, more recent system, thereby inverting the chronological order in which Judaism and Christianity came into being.

The contrast is ready-made for an argument against the complex rituals and hierarchies of either the Catholic or the Anglican church. Asserting his own version of the Christian division of the Mosaic law, Milton writes,

> The whole Judaick law is either politicall, and to take pattern by that, no Christian nation ever thought it selfe oblig'd in conscience; or morall, which containes in it the observation of whatsoever is substantially, and perpetually true and good, either in religion, or course of life.

CONTENT WITH NEITHER Aquinas's identification of moral, ceremonial, and judicial laws nor Augustine's bipartite distinction between moral and ceremonial biblical precepts, Milton divides Jewish law into its typical practices, what he calls political, and its moral guidance.[38] In the former category Milton includes the ritual and ceremonial practices associated with the Temple and the Levites and those so-called judicial laws that, for him, have no grounding in a nonjuridical morality. In the latter category, "besides what we fetch from those unwritten lawes and Ideas which nature hath ingraven in us," he places the Gospel, which "lectures to us from her own authentick hand-writing and command, [instead of copying] out from the borrow'd manuscript of a subservient scrowl, by way of imitating" (YP 1:764). This departure from Aquinas and Augustine has made it notoriously difficult to determine whether or not Milton should be considered an antinomian. Sounding very much like Luther, he comes close to suggesting that the Christian Scriptures not only fulfill the Old Testament, they make it irrelevant. Hardly the opinion of what Don M. Wolfe once described as "an Old Testament Christian,"[39] the characterization of the Hebrew Bible as "the borrow'd manuscript of a subservient scrowl" seems to refuse *any* value to the earlier Hebrew tradition. What begins as Hebraic precedent very quickly becomes yet another formulation of Christianity, inseparable from that which initially distinguished it. When this occurs, the question of Milton's (or anyone's) status as an Hebraic writer returns. Insofar as Hebraicisms are really Christian elements, we may well ask how it remains possible to characterize a given writer as more "Hebraic" than any of his contemporaries.

Those who wished to argue for a material continuity between the priestly hierarchy of the Israelites and the episcopacy of the Church of England sought to distinguish between biblical phenomena that functioned exclusively as types and those that had more unmediated application. Calling it "the *Anabaptists* only shift," Lancelot Andrewes responded with noticeable exasperation to the argument made by his antiprelatical opponents that Aaron and the priests were all types, no longer meaningful with the advent of Christ, the true priest.[40] Even more conservative opponents of the prelacy perceived a danger in the desire to typologize everything. The defender of Scottish Presbyterianism, George Gillespie, is equally adamant concerning the power of excommunication, which, he argues, still belongs to the Church (albeit a different church than Andrewes'!):

> To me it is plaine, that these things doe as much concerne us now, as the Jewes of old, which whosoever denieth, must shew, that either we may take no rules nor patternes from the Old Testament: or that the foresaid Lawes and practises were not intended by the holy Ghost to binde us, (as other things in

the Old Testament doe) but were cermoniall and typicall, intended to bind the Jewes onely. Mr. *Williams* in his *bloody Tenant* . . . perceiving that such arguments from the Old Testament can not be taken off without this answer, that all these were typicall and figurative: he therefore goeth much upon that ground, and so deviseth more types and figures in the Old Testament then ever any body did before him, and pleaseth himselfe with such fancies and conjectures therein, as I dare say, will satsifie no indifferent Reader: and in effect making void by his principles all arguments from the Old Testament, so that we may not from the examples of the godly Kings of *Judah*, teach Christian Magistrates what their duty is.[41]

GILLESPIE REGARDS THE radical protestantism exemplified by Roger Williams as the reductio ad absurdam of typology, dangerously anarchic and without structure. Far from an esoteric matter of concern only to biblical scholars and theologians, typology was at the heart of all the political debates of the mid seventeenth century. In reading how the debates over English church government and ritual wrestle with the question and value of Jewish precedent, one is struck by an odd common ground on which typologists and literalists found themselves standing. Those traditionalists who read the Levitical passages as typological models for Christian clergy and sacraments (Anglicans and Catholics) were making use of the same historicizing tools as the radicals who took an interest in the cultic details of Jewish worship for their value in contextualizing biblical faith and anticipating Christ's imminent kingdom on earth.

Just how fraught the use of Judaic precedent is can be seen in the following anonymous response to Henry Burton's important early manifesto of English Independency, *The Protestation Protested*:

> What if you should finde the Decalogue, and the Lords Prayer (as you have already the Creed) to be Popish, must not all the Principles of our Religion, for your pleasure, be drawne within the verge of a thundring abjuration? nor is this feare in vaine: your precisest Gospellers already deny the Law, as only suteable to the Climate of the *Jewes*, and some of your best Rabbies make it a case of conscience not to say the Lords Prayer, that *Magicum canticum* (as they tearme it) *Pontificorum*.[42]

THE ATTACK ON Independency's perceived antinomianism and its concomitant political lawlessness revealingly combines an embrace of Jewish heritage with a vilification of Christianity's age-old opponents. The pamphleteer is disturbed by the thought that the Decalogue, the Lord's prayer, and the law have been construed as antiquated relics of a Jewish past. Yet his condemnation of those who consign such central features of Christianity to "the Climate of the *Jewes*" is targeted at "your best Rabbies." Jews are both the same as and different than the English church.

In the hands of some advocates of the episcopacy, this historical/typological nexus afforded yet another means to claim special status for the Church of England. Invoking the reverence Anglican liturgy had traditionally been accorded, Bishop Hall observes that besides its historic confirmation by martyrs, princes, and parliamentary acts, it had lately been translated for use by "forraigne Divines and Churches." Now, however, the liturgy

> begins to complain of scorn at home: The matter is quarrelled by some, the Forme by others, the Vse of it by both: That which was never before heard of in the Church of God, whether Iewish or Christian, the very prescription of the most holy devotion offendeth. Surely, our blessed Saviour, and his gracious Fore-runner; were so farre from this new Divinity, as that they plainly taught that, vvhich these men gain-say; a direct forme of prayer; and such, as that part of the frame prescribed by our Saviour, vvas composed of those formed of devotion which have been since usuall with the Iewes; And indeed Gods people ever since *Moses* his dayes constantly practised a set forme; and put it over unto the times of the Gospell, under w^ch, whiles it is said that *Peter* and *Iohn* went up to the Temple at the ninth houre of prayer, wee know the prayer wherewith they joyned, was not of an extemporary, and sudden conception, but of a regular prescription.[43]

In arguments like this we can see how essential is the uninterrupted continuity between biblical Judaism and English Christianity. The pre-Christian practices associated with Jewish worship are regarded not only as wholly authentic but of central relevance to the reformed Church of England.

Opponents of the prelacy had their own responses to these claims of continuity and they often took the form of historical revision, parallel to the chronological realignment we have seen in Milton's writings. Attacks on the claims of liturgical authenticity took two forms. First, recalling Bishop Andrewes's attempts to translate Jewish prayers for use in English church services, the cadre of Smectymnuan writers noted that it was soon discovered these prayers had been formulated "long after the Jewes ceased to be the

Church of God."[44] Insofar as the prayers are authentically Jewish, they are precisely inauthentic. Second, accounting for the various parallels between Christian and Jewish liturgy, the Smectymnuans note, "Wee have read that the *Rabbines* since the dayes of our Saviour have borrowed some expressions from [Christ's prayer in the Gospels], and from other *Evangelicall passages*."[45] Biblical Judaism may have a longer history than Christianity, but anything worth valuing from contemporary Judaism becomes, according to this version of Hebraica Veritas, the legacy of Christianity.

If we follow the train of this dispute over liturgical authenticity, we will discover a further terminological refinement that has implications for a reading of typology and Jewish precedent. In his attack on Hall in *Animadversions*, Milton claims, "'Tis not the goodnesse of matter therefore which is not, nor can be ow'd to the *Liturgie*, that will beare it out, if the form, which is the essence of it, be fantastick, and superstitious, the end sinister, and the imposition violent" (YP 1:688). The content of the prayer, what we might expect Milton to regard as its essential aspect, is of less relevance than the form, which, quite surprisingly, he regards as the essence. Hall's reply is equally remarkable.

> Phantastick? like enough they might think so, that saw or heard you read them; *Sed male dum recitas, &c.* But then the fault was not in the Prayers, but in your officiating. If ever you were present at a Synagogue in Amsterdam, and saw how the Jewes wth voice and gesture read a Section of the Law, or one of the *Davids* Psalmes, you might justly say the men were phantastick, yet the matter was good.[46]

BETWEEN MILTON'S ACCUSATION and Hall's response we can identify a slippage from "form" to "men." That is, Hall accepts Milton's characterization insofar as it applies to the Jewish bodies performing the prayer; they are, indeed, fantastic. But such a condemnation has no bearing, for Hall, on the value of the matter of their prayer, which may be quite good. Milton cannot admit this distinction. The form of the prayer is the same as the Jewish bodies who utter it; neither is acceptable because they bridge a gap between Judaism and his sense of Christianity that Milton has every reason to want to preserve.

The importance of Jewish authenticity and continuity is not solely an aspect of episcopal arguments, however. Milton himself offers an argument from the same basis in *Of Reformation*. Significantly, however, the parallels between Judaism (biblical and postbiblical) and English Protestantism point toward an anti-Erastian and antiestablishment view of the church.

> The ancient Republick of the Jews is evident to have run through all the changes of civil estate, if we survey the Story from the giving of the Law to the *Herods*, yet did one manner of Priestly government serve without inconvenience to all these temporal mutations: it serv'd the mild Aristocracy of elective Dukes, and heads of Tribes joyn'd with them; the dictatorship of the Judges, the easie, or hard-handed Monarchy's, the domestick, or forrain tyrannies, Lastly the Roman Senat from without, the Jewish Senat at home with the Galilean Tetrach, yet the Levites had some right to deal in civil affairs. (YP 1:574–75)

THIS IS AN exceptional passage in the context of Milton's larger antiprelatical project. Throughout much of his attacks on the bishops and episcopacy Milton primarily adduces Jewish precedent in the form of counterexample. The system of priests and Levites associated with the Temple cannot be used as evidence for a church government based on hierarchy for one of at least three reasons: (1) because it was made obsolete by the Gospel and the so-called completion of the law by Christ's Incarnation, (2) because the Old Testament typically formulated such a system of priests to adumbrate a spiritualized version of church government to be understood on an individualized and internalized basis, or (3) because it was presented in the Bible as a cautionary tale, warning the Christian reader not to follow the example of the Jews, who have suffered ever since for taking the path described in the text. Indeed, earlier in the same paragraph, Milton offers just such an account of a road not to take:

> Must Church government that is appointed in the Gospel, and has chief respect of the soul, be conformable, and pliant to civil, that is arbitrary, and chiefly conversant about the visible and external part of man? this is the very maxim that moulded the Calvs of *Bethel* and of *Dan*, this was the quintessence of *Jeroboams* policy, he made Religion conform to his politick interests, & this was the sin that watcht over the Israelites till their final captivity. (YP 1:573–74)

AS JEROBOAM'S EXAMPLE illustrates, a hierarchical system of priests and other church officers, especially when it depends upon systematic and structural connections to any form of civil government, may be easily abused both for political ends and with dire religious results. It is all the more remarkable then, that only several sentences later, Milton should refer to the "ancient Republick of the Jews" as an example of the viability of religious system distinct from any specific form of civil government. The Levites, ordinarily for Milton models for the corrupt and bloated English clergy and prelacy, are here given credit for having served "without incovenience" the diverse forms of Jewish temporal governments, while at the same time retaining "some right to deal in civil affairs." Now it is true that Milton immediately goes on to remind his readers that "the Evangelical precept forbids Churchmen to intermeddle with worldly imployments." Yet this makes Milton's apparently positive invocation of Jewish precedent all the more remarkable. If the point of this portion of *Of Reformation* is to counter the claim that the elimination of church hierarchy would have a deleterious effect on civil authority, that is, if Milton is here responding to the cry of "No bishop, no King,"[47] then the example of the Levites' flexibility within the changing "Republick of the Jews" would appear to be at best irrelevant, at worst, counterproductive. Why bother showing the possibility of a hierarchical church government when the larger point Milton is trying to make is that the Gospel forecloses the need for such a structure?

The Reason of Church-Government provides one of the most detailed examples of Milton's Christian hermeneutics, what at the end of *Paradise Lost* he would call the movement "from shadowy Types to Truth." As Jason Rosenblatt has made clear, Milton's monist ontology, which has its roots in the Hebrew and rabbinic thinking made available to Milton by the great English Hebraist, John Selden, has directly hermeneutical implications.[48] At first blush, the inseparability of body and soul, letter and spirit, seem to stand in conflict with the overtly typological mode Milton deploys in most of his antiprelatical tracts. He offers as his interpretive model the prophecies of Ezekiel, which, appearing in the Hebrew Scriptures as they do, establish a mode of understanding the Temple to be taken up by the Gospels and subsequent Christian readers. Noting the apparent disjunction between the extensive descriptions of the Temple in Ezekiel 40–48 and the destruction of the first Temple, which was thought to have occurred in Ezekiel's time, Milton argues that

God by his Prophet seeking to weane the hearts of the Jewes from their old

law to expect a new and more perfect reformation under Christ, sets out before their eyes the stately fabrick & constitution of his Church, with al the
ecclesiasticall functions appertaining; indeed the description is as sorted best
to the apprehension of those times, typicall and shadowie, but in such manner as never yet came to passe, nor never must literally, unlesse we mean to
annihilat the Gospel. But so exquisit and lively the description is in portraying the new state of the Church, and especially in those points where government seems to be most active, that both Jewes and Gentiles might have
good cause to be assur'd, that God when ever he meant to reforme his
Church, never intended to leave the governement thereof delineated here in
such curious architecture, to be patch't afterwards, and varnish't over with the
devices and imbellishings of mans imagination. (YP 1:757)

THE EARLY 1640S, both in England and in the Netherlands, were witness to
an increased interest in the structure of the Jewish Temple. Not only did the
Hebrew Scriptures provide extensive details of Solomon's temple in 1 Kings
5–6 and 2 Chronicles 2–5 and of the construction of the Second Temple in
Ezra and Nehemiah, but the writings of Josephus Flavius, which enjoyed
enormous popularity during the early modern period, devoted pages to
minute descriptions of the Temple in Jerusalem.[49] Even more tangible, the
Dutch Jew, Jacob Jehuda Leon, composed a detailed treatise on the Temple,
Afbeeldinge vanden Tempel Salomonis, and constructed a scale model of the entire
structure, which apparently attracted a stream of tourists, mostly Christian,
interested in catching a glimpse of the site of ancient Jewish worship. So
successful was this undertaking, that Leon took the name Templo.[50] It is not
hard to understand why advocates of the maintenance of ritual and ceremony, with its attendant hierarchy (whether Catholic or Anglican), might have
shown interest in the physical Temple. What is more noteworthy, numerous
figures associated with a far more radical Protestantism were attracted to
the project of reconstructing the Temple, as an aspect of their millenarian
expectations.[51]

As widespread as this interest was in early modern Europe (England, as
well as the Continent), Milton refuses any reading of the Temple that takes
its historicity—its material existence—as having a value to the Christian
reader. In a typically Miltonic counterintuitive argument by assertion, he offers the very liveliness of Ezekiel's vision as proof of its *unreality*. That he
cites Ezekiel's prophetic vision of the future Temple, rather than any other
biblical account, speaks volumes in itself. Perhaps Ezekiel's vision is best read

eschatologically, and even metaphorically. Yet Milton elides the intervening Second Temple! Milton offers a typological reading of Ezekiel's prophecy, *not* of the Temple in 2 Kings that served as a model for Ezekiel.

> Did God take such delight in measuring out the pillars, arches, and doores of a materiall Temple, was he so punctuall and circumspect in lavers, altars, and sacrifices soone after to be abrogated, lest any of these should have beene made contrary to his minde? is not a farre more perfect worke more agreeable to his perfection in the most perfect state of the Church militant, the new alliance of God to man? should not he rather now by his owne prescribed discipline have cast his line and levell upon the soule of man which is his rationall temple, and by the divine square and compasse thereof forme and regenerate in us the lovely shapes of vertues and graces, the sooner to edifie and accomplish that immortal stature of Christs body which is his Church, in all her glorious lineaments and proportions. And that this indeed God hath done for us in the Gospel we shall see with open eyes, not under a vaile. (YP 1:757–58)

REPLETE WITH CORPORAL FIGURES—indeed, virtually in spite of them— Milton's reading asserts a thoroughly typological reading of the Temple and its worship.

Reformation hermeneutics is credited for having refocused the reading experience of the Bible on the literal and the personal. Numerous critics have attempted to show how the emphasis by Luther and Calvin on the individual's encounter with Scripture encouraged Protestants to attend to the historical realities, the psychological dynamics, the other textual details of the biblical narrative as a means of discovering the text's application to the contemporary moment.[52] Yet even from this more personalized perspective, the biblical text is only functional insofar as it is translatable. What is more, allegorical and typological modes of reading possessed a remarkable resilience in seventeenth-century English Protestant hermeneutics, within a community that is considered to have restored the literal reading of Scripture to a more prominent role than it had played prior to the Reformation. Even when Reformation readers seemed to be reading the Hebrew Scriptures for historical information, any such reading relied upon a view of this world as a mere shadow of the divine realm, for the sake of the achievement of which any such readings were ever undertaken. In his analysis of reformation typology Thomas Luxon has shown that all history before the Parousia constitutes nothing but a train of preliminary types pointing to that final moment, the second coming of Christ, which would mean the *end* of history: "This event would combine being and meaning in a manner never known before, for it would literally signify nothing; rather, it would be the 'thing' signified by everything that ever was."[53]

Observing that Protestantism's literalism always sits uncomfortably in relation to the "insistently allegorical metaphysics of Christianity," Luxon draws a critical connection between Reformation typology, with its emphasis on locating meaning dialectically in relation to the shadow or type, and Christianity's Jewish antecedents. The name for the other against which the real is defined, "whether it be the old self, the other of the past, or the other of the present (as viewed from eternity), are the Jew, the Synagogue, the 'carnal' Jerusalem, the whore, the flesh, and the world."[54] If contemporary history is to have any "reality" associated with it for the early modern Protestant, then the history narrated in the Old Testament demands the same "realism." If, on the other hand, the biblical history that Protestant literalists had recently redeemed as "true" is nevertheless typological and figurative, then so must contemporary lived experience be. The history of the biblical Hebraic past and the modern English present both have as their fulfillment the truth of Christian eschatology. Given this tension, the Jew not only functions as the constitutive Other of the English Protestant, the Jew also functions as "the self in history."[55]

Milton's citation of Ezekiel's vision, his prophetic mediation of the Jewish Temple, is a version of Luxon's endless deferral and emptying out of lived history in the service of Protestantism's apocalyptic Christian truth. Citing the epistles to Timothy and Titus, Milton insists,

> Where the spirituall eye may discerne more goodly and gracefully erected then all the magnificence of Temple or Tabernacle, such a heavenly structure of evangelick discipline so diffusive of knowledge and charity to the prosperous increase and growth of the Church, that it cannot be wonder'd if that elegant and artfull symmetry of the promised new temple in Ezechiel, and all those sumptuous things under the Law were made to signifie the inward beauty and splendor of the Christian Church thus govern'd. (YP 1:758)

THE RELATIONSHIP BETWEEN Ezekiel and the epistles is the same as the relationship between the Jewish Temple and the Christian Soul. Milton insists that with the coming of Christ's Priesthood, "both law and Priesthood fades away of it selfe, and *passes into aire like a transitory vision"* (YP 1:770, emphasis added). Justifying the retention of church hierarchy and the preservation of ceremonies and rituals through reference to an literal and historical reading of the Hebrew Scriptures shows that the Prelates are "driven to take sanctuary amongst the Jewes" (YP 1:775).

"PERPETUAL LIVING PROOF": THE MEANING OF
JEWISH BODIES

NEVERTHELESS, AS HIS OWN repeated forays in the field of historiography attest,[56] and as I shall argue below in my discussion of the final books of *Paradise Lost*, Milton never fully defers history or even its meaning. As such, the moment Milton's history reasserts a reality principle, the body of the Jew returns, or threatens to do so. No matter how much Milton asserts otherwise, the Jew is an unspoken presence in his reading of Scripture and of history. From a typological perspective, the Jew's body represents that element of the text, that element of lived experience, which is necessarily unassimilable, which resists an exhaustive reading. Neither Scripture nor history are self-consuming artifacts, and it is precisely at those moments when the world seems unreadable even within a thoroughly providential framework that the "Jewish" aspect of Milton's writings emerges.

Let me put the matter somewhat differently. For those English Protestants who embrace a version of Jewish precedent, the following difficulty arises. The biblical and postbiblical accounts of Israel hardly describe the history of a triumphant nation passing from strength to strength until its final glory had been reached.[57] There does not seem to be any historical advantage in identifying oneself as part of the new Israel if the old Israel's history has transpired so inauspiciously. It is certainly true that preachers, prophets, and poets of the seventeenth century used the biblical moments of Israel's defeat to great effect in their castigations of contemporary events or trends. One particular biblical example enjoyed extraordinary popularity in the late 1630s and 1640s among "root and branch" reformers, that of Achan's sinful plundering of Jericho and Israel's subsequent defeat at the city of Ai in Joshua 7–8. John Goodwin, for instance, drew a comparison at England's expense:

My Brethren, the case of the Children of *Israel* upon their losse neere unto the Citie of *Ai*, is our condition and case at this day; save onely that the hand of God hath been laid heavier upon us, then it was upon them, in that breach.[58]

YET, EVEN WHEN Israel was cited as an affirmative precedent—God's graciousness to his people, his repeatedly available salvation, etc.—there necessarily lay behind this positive model, often not far behind at all, the potential for disaster and condemnation. The beautifully hopeful words of Psalm 126, "They that sow in tears shall reap in joy," are concluded with yet further tears. The seeds of Israel's decline and fall, and by extension England's as well, are to be found even when the very fruits of election are harvested. When Milton reads Israel's biblical story as a closed book, preliminary to Christian salvation, it is in light of the necessarily and eternally unregenerate character of man and the physical world in the absence of Christ's sacrifice and "prevenient grace." Christianity's placement of this preeminent deus ex machina at the core of its belief works to abrogate the meaning and value of the Hebrew Bible.

The covenant theology outlined most powerfully within the corpus of the Deuteronomist asserts that election is conditional, tied to certain obligations. Milton regards the episcopal reassertion of law and ceremony as a restoration of a conditional covenant that can never be fully satisfied and inevitably results in human failure and consequent suffering.

> Now to breed, and bring up the children of the promise, the heirs of liberty and grace under such a kinde of government as is profest to be but an imitation of that ministery which engender'd to bondage the sons of Agar, how can this be but a foul injury and derogation, if not a cancelling of that birthright and immunity which Christ hath purchas'd for us with his blood. For the ministration of the law consisting of carnall things, drew to it such a ministery as consisted of carnall respects, dignity, precedence, and the like. And such a ministery establish't in the Gospell, as is founded upon the points and termes of superiority, and nests it selfe in worldly honours, will draw to it, and we see it doth, such a religion as runnes back againe to the old pompe and glory of the flesh. (YP 1:765–66)

IN GALATIANS 4:21–31 Paul famously deracinates the category of "children of the promise," fully allegorizing the story of Isaac and Ishmael. The account in Genesis ties Isaac's status as the favored child to the promise made to

Abraham in his old age that he would produce a great nation. Abraham's descendants enjoy a special relationship with God—for better and for worse—precisely because of their physical paternity. Paul's reading starkly reverses this genealogical account, positing instead that these fleshly ties are precisely *not* what guarantee the ongoing status of "children of the promise." Indeed, for Paul, the ability to distinguish oneself physically as a descendant of Abraham is contrary to the salvation offered by Christ. As Boyarin has observed, "while Galatians is not an anti-Judaic text, its theory of the Jews nevertheless is one that is inimical to Jewish difference, indeed to all difference as such."[59] A primary danger inherent in the prelatical assertion of Old Testament precedent for church government is that it threatens to reinstall a naturalized lineage between the Jews and English Protestants, which would in turn subject Christians not only to the covenantal theology that inevitably results in their damnation but also the exile and alienation depicted in the story of Hagar and Ishmael and repeated generation after generation by Jews everywhere.

If all that finally matters is Christ's Incarnation and Passion, and the believer's utter acceptance of this salvation, then what value do these preliminary stories of God's tumultuous relationship with a relatively minor group of people have anyway? To what extent is it useful or accurate to consider Milton an "Old Testament Christian" or a Hebraic writer?

Milton's notorious ambivalence regarding Christ's Passion—stretching from his youthful inability to complete a poem on the subject, to his displacement of the crucifixion story with the wilderness story of Christ's temptation in *Paradise Regained*—suggests one approach to this question, since it seems to stem from his ongoing belief in human agency and his view of redemption as cooperatively achieved by God and man. While it is possible to assert Milton's Arminianism here as indicative of his retention of some aspect of the conditional covenant, I think the answer depends as much upon a return of the Jewish repressed even when the typological hermeneutic is in full force.[60] Milton's apparent elimination of the historicity of the Hebrew Bible (and thereby the Jews) is incomplete. The Jews' bodies are necessary specifically because of their history of suffering and the promise of salvation that accompanies that history. Henry Robinson, with whom Milton had much in common concerning matters of religious toleration and free press, and who searches for meaning in suffering and loss, justifies the ways of God to men in his political tract by arguing that if those responsible for religious persecution understood

that to be persecuted, is a mark and signe of the true Church, and conse-
quently to persecute, and infallible character of unsound Christians and the
Church malignant, in charity we ought to thinke they might likely be re-
claimed, I shall therefore intreat them for their owne direction to call to
minde, what St. *Paul* saith to the Galatians, *viz.*, Now *we, Brethren as Isaac was,*
are the children of promise, but *as then he that was borne after the flesh persecuted him that*
was borne after the Spirit, even so it is now. This text declares how the true Church
and true Beleevers are children of the promise, figured out in *Abel, Isaac* and
Jacob, persecuted by *Cain, Ismael, Esau,* and their posterity, children of the
bond-woman, teaching us in expresse words, that as those which persecuted
in the Old Testament were not the Elect or children of the promise, so now
the best servants of God were persecuted under the Gospel.[61]

THAT ROBINSON WOULD CITE the portion of Paul's theology found in Galatians 4 to explain the value of suffering is of note, as it produces a tension
between the fully allegorical/typological Pauline hermeneutic and the attention given and value ascribed to the details of lived history. At an earlier
point in Robinson's argument for liberty of conscience, he specifically identifies the persecution experienced by the Jews during the Expulsion and Inquisition as counterproductive, a failure of Christianity. Significantly, however, he does not offer any connection between this history of persecution and
his theology of suffering.[62] The further implications of the homologies and
relations between Jews and Englishmen are too threatening to allow for such
a connection.

In his *De Doctrina Christiana* Milton offers an analogous assertion. In order
to establish the existence of a providential, omnipotent God, without which
everything that follows in his theological treatise is meaningless, Milton argues that not only does the whole of Scripture prove the truth of such a
principle, what is more,

> The fact that the Jews, an extremely ancient nation, are now dispersed all
> over the world, demonstrates the same thing. God often warned them that
> this would be the outcome of their sins. Amidst the constant flux of history
> they have been preserved in this state, scattered among the other nations,
> right up to the present day. This has been done not only to make them pay
> the penalty of their sins but much rather to give the whole world a perpetu-
> al living proof of the existence of God and the truth of scriptures. (1.2; YP
> 6:132)

Presumably, Milton might have chosen any one of a number of historical verifications of God's existence. It is striking that he has singled out the dispersion and suffering of the Jews. Jewish presence guarantees a meaning to Christian salvation. It is precisely as a disempowered and suffering people that Milton allows himself to acknowledge the presence of Jewish bodies and thereby, I suggest, identifies himself with them.

"TURNING CHRISTIANS INTO JEWS AND PAGANS"

WRITING TO A highly educated and diverse readership, Robert Burton categorized the follower of the pope as only one of many "superstitious Gentiles, Pagans, Idolators, and Jews; their blind zeal and idolatrous superstition in all kinds is much at one; little or no difference, and it is hard to say which is to the greatest, which is the grossest."[63] Following an extended discussion of the erroneous beliefs to be found in the Greek and Roman pantheons, Burton turns his attention specifically to the Jews.

> In this superstitious row, Jews for antiquity may go next to Gentiles; what of old they have done, what idolatries they have committed in their groves and high places, what their Pharisees, Sadducees, Scribes, Essei, and such sectaries have maintained, I will not so much as mention.

THAT THESE VARIOUS Jewish sects were no longer in evidence in 1621, when Burton published *The Anatomy of Melancholy,* may have suggested to him a parallel with the defunct practitioners of the cults of Zeus or Minerva. Burton moves very quickly, however, from these antiquated Jewish groups to a present that continues to see Jewish practice, if not in reality, at least in the English imagination, populated by the likes of Barabbas and Shylock:

> I presume no nation under heaven can be more sottish, ignorant, blind, superstitious, wilful, obstinate, and peevish, tiring themselves with vain ceremonies to no purpose; he that shall but read their rabbins' ridiculous comments, their strange interpretation of Scriptures, their absurd ceremonies, fables, childish tales, which they steadfastly believe, will think they be scarce rational creatures; their foolish customs, when they rise in the morning, and how they prepare themselves to prayer, to meat, with what superstitious washings, how to their Sabbath, to their other feasts, weddings, burials, &c.[64]

Last of all, the expectation of their Messiah, and those figments, miracles, vain pomp that shall attend him, as how he shall terrify the Gentiles, and overcome them by new diseases; how Michael the archangel shall sound his trumpet, how he shall gather all the scattered Jews in the Holy Land, and there make them a great banquet. . . . With an infinite number of such lies and forgeries, which they verily believe, feed themselves with vain hope, and in the mean time will by no persuasions be diverted, but still crucify their souls with a company of idle ceremonies, live like slaves and vagabonds, will not be relieved or reconciled.[65]

FAR FROM UNIQUE, Burton's condemnation of Jewish belief and practice is rather typical in its characterizations: "ignorant," "blind," "superstitious," "obstinate," "childish," and "foolish" are all adjectives with a long-standing Christian tradition of association with Judaism. Neither is Burton's association of Judaism with other forms of paganism and idolatry especially unique, and it is this connection to which I now turn. Throughout the medieval and early modern period—and indeed, well into the Enlightenment and beyond—Judaism suffered at the hands of Christianity not only because it epitomized the contemporary refusal to embrace Christ by those to whom his coming had initially been addressed. Judaism was also the object of opprobrium as one of many versions of paganism that Christianity condemned as corrupt, decadent, and antiquated. That is, even as the Hebrew prophets bemoaned Israelite participation in idolatrous cults, Christianity tended to portray the religion of the Jews as yet one more version of those idolatrous cults. Condemned from both sides, Judaism was attacked on the one hand for being too similar to Christianity, and on the other hand for being too different.

We may add to this early modern tendency the effect that New World encounters had on seventeenth-century theories of Jewish Diaspora. David Katz and Elliot Horowitz have both demonstrated the prevalence of the view in England that many or most of the native inhabitants encountered in the early modern expeditions to North and South America and the Caribbean were descendants of the Ten Lost Tribes.[66] Indeed, in his plea to Parliament for official readmission of the Jews to England, Menasseh Ben Israel did everything he could to encourage this view (for reasons elaborated by Katz in his study on the readmission question) by citing as authoritative the reports of Antonio de Montezinus (Aaron Levy) who claimed that while traveling in South America he met a tribe of natives in the Cordilleras who recited the Shema, performed other Jewish rituals, and claimed to be descendants of the tribe of Reuben.[67] For some Englishmen who entertained the possibility of a genealogical connection between the "savages" of the New World and the Jews, the result was a further denigration of Jewish tradition and learning. These claims were likely to have contributed to the association of Judaism with paganism and may have confirmed in the eyes of many English Protestants the view of Judaism as yet another mode of idol worshipping. An early seventeenth-century edition of Vincenzio Cartari's enormously popular mythology manual, *Images of the Gods*, included as an appendix a discourse on the Mexican and Japanese pantheons, thereby bringing together under one cover the gods of the Old World and the gods of the New.[68]

Even for those so-called philosemites who greeted this news with delight as an indication of the approaching millennial fulfillment of the prophecies regarding the ingathering of the Jews (including the Lost Tribes), the possibility that these newly encountered natives were Jews would not necessarily have been taken as indicative of the presence of anything valuable to be salvaged from their traditions. What is more, according to Horowitz, even among those enlightened Europeans who responded to the age of discovery and exploration with a new relativism concerning non-Western cultures, or by regarding these natives as prelapsarian "noble savages," the Jew, "was still held largely in contempt, and [his] culture was still generally identified with barbarism."[69]

But there is another side to this repeated linkage of Judaism with paganism, one where ideas and beliefs attributed to both do not suffer through guilt by association but rather help to recuperate one another. I want to suggest that one means of accounting for the resilience and importance of both classical/pagan lore and Hebraic/Judaic learning is by recognizing a symbiotic relationship between these two manifestations of the wisdom of the ancients. Where the values of classicism are regarded as dangerously corrupting because of their roots in pagan, atheistic, polytheistic, heathen, and/or anti-Christian practices and beliefs, Judaism's biblical status as the prefiguration of Christianity, coupled with its historical associations with classical learning within the context of the earliest stages of Christianity—Paul's addresses to the Hellenists and Judaizers in his letter to the Romans, those patristic writings that invoke a pre-Christian classical tradition to supplement Christianity's Jewish heritage, and so on—served to restore some of the esteem in which pagan learning was held.

Where the Jewish tradition was threatened by a Pauline rejection of carnal Israel and what it literally embodied, and by a thorough allegorization of the Scriptures, the humanistic respect accorded to the ancients from philological, historiographical, and philosophical perspectives was commuted to a renovated respect for Jewish learning. The acknowledgement of Hebrew scholarship as the third foundational pillar of Western thought had the dramatic effect of shielding the study of Hebrew and Judaism from the total dismissal of having been superseded by the New Covenant. This was not a foolproof partnership, as Burton's wholesale condemnation suggests, and, inevitably in the hands of Christian readers, even those of a distinctly humanist persuasion, these ancient traditions were regarded as useful supplements to Christian wisdom, to be read with particular interpretive tools (often, though not always, typological and allegorical in orientation). Indeed, even as allegory and typology dictated the terms under which the Old Testament was often read by medieval and early modern Christianity, they provided a similar framework for the preservation and incorporation of classical and mythological material into a Christian framework.[70] Yet even when the early modern, characteristically Protestant attention to biblical literalism overshadowed allegorical and typological readings, it did not necessarily abrogate an interest in pagan mythologies. The humanist revival of euhemerism as a means of historicizing the classical pantheons paralleled the renewed interest in the history and philology of the Hebrew Scriptures. In 1531 the reformer Huldreich Zwingli wrote to Francis I, "Shouldst thou follow in the footsteps of David, thou wilt one day see God Himself; and near to Him thou mayest hope to see Adam, Abel, Enoch, Paul, Hercules, Theseus, Socrates, the Catos, the Scipios."[71]

During the medieval period, thanks in part to the early Church fathers' unwillingness to dispose of the classical training from which they continued to derive benefit and pleasure, the culture of pagan Greece and Rome was turned into a system of moral philosophy. Egyptian gold retained its value, despite its origins in an idolatrous world, because of the use to which it could be put.[72] Christian humanists of the early modern period inherited this tradition and continued, in more complex and subtle ways, to lend authority to the writings of classical Greece and Rome by seeing in them allusions to scriptural truths and, in particular, the coming of Christ. One of the more obvious but by no means unique examples of this tradition is the christological reading of Virgil's Fourth Eclogue. The *prisca sapientia*, an imaginative tradition of a primitive wisdom (moral, theological, scientific) of the Gentiles formulated by the

Neoplatonists of fifteenth-century Florence, most notably Marsilio Ficino, looked on Hermes Trismegistus as the "first author of a theology" which, merging with Zoroastrianism, was inherited by Orpheus and Pythagoras among others, to find its way into the books of Plato.[73] Profane wisdom became intimately linked to biblical wisdom. Homer, Socrates, and Plato were regarded as beneficiaries of Moses, David, and Solomon.

Milton's Christian humanism has been the subject of critical discussion for many years. His irrepressible delight in the cultural achievements of classical Greece and Rome is often regarded as being at odds with what has been called his "Old Testament Christianity." The sometimes tense coexistence of Hellenism and Hebraism in Milton's writings, both prose and poetry, is far more complex than has hitherto been acknowledged. Like many of his contemporaries, Milton does use his knowledge of pre-Christian Jewish practice and belief, not to mention the core elements of apostolic Christianity, to dismiss the pagan world of Hellenism. Yet, when he writes with his left hand, as much as when he expresses himself more dexterously in poetry, Milton also counterbalances the retention of Hebraic and Judaic knowledge with a programmatic construction of Judaism as a form of paganism.

Milton's association of Judaism with paganism begins in his very earliest writings against the prelacy. From the outset, though, it is possible to discern a tension produced by his adoption of this somewhat commonplace characterization. *Of Reformation* describes how in the days following Constantine, the Church

> began to draw downe all the Divine intercours, betwixt *God*, and the Soule, yea, the very shape of *God* himselfe, into an exterior, and bodily forme, urgently pretending necessity, and obligement of joyning the body in a formall reverence, and *Worship* circumscrib'd, they hallow'd it, they fum'd it, they sprincl'd it, they be deck't it, not in robes of pure innocency, but of pure Linnen, with other deformed, and fantastick dresses in Palls, and Miters, gold, and guegaw's fetcht from *Arons* old wardrope, or the *Flamins vestry*. (YP 1:520–21)

WHEREAS THE PAGAN practices of classical Greece and Rome were never divine in nature, never appropriate modes of worship, the rituals associated with the biblical tabernacle and Temple *were* understood to be divinely mandated elements of the service of God, however limited they may have been to an historical period or group of people. Yet Milton aligns these outmoded Jewish ceremonies, embodied in *"Arons* old wordrope," with the pagan practices figured by the fifteen *flamines* in ancient Rome, sacrificial priests of the patrician and plebeian classes charged with the service of the gods. Like other Puritan opponents of Catholic and Anglican rituals, Milton condemns all external modes of worship, because they necessitate an "exterior, and bodily form." Iconoclasm and the rejection of Judaism and paganism are not only related but inextricably bound up with one another, indeed, identical.

That apparent condemnation of all physical forms becomes, in his far more animated response to Bishop Hall, an attack on bodies and their attendant sexuality. Characterizing the Church of England's desire to win converts from Catholicism as "Pharisaicall," "vain-glorious," "a greedy desire," Milton compares it to

> the desire of *Tamar*, who to raise up seed to her Husband sate in the common road drest like a Curtezan, and he that came to her committed incest with her. This was that which made the old Christians Paganize, while by their scandalous and base conforming to heathenisme they did no more, when they had done thir utmost, but to bring some Pagans to Christianize; for true Christians they neither were themselves, nor could make others such in this fashion. (*Animadversions*, YP 1:688–89)

TAMAR, AS A FIGURE of carnality and excessive sexuality, embodies the dangers of the ritual seductions of the ceremonialists, who combine the traits of the Pharisees and the heathens. As with most biblical examples, this apparent condemnation of Anglicans through the example of Tamar is far more complicated than it might seem at first blush. Milton only gives us half the story, the half that would seem to cast sexuality and the body in the most negative light. Yet if we recall the entire episode in Genesis 38, that notorious interruption in an otherwise coherent narrative of Joseph and his brothers, we may observe that Tamar is finally vindicated for her behavior. When she was brought before Judah, ostensibly to be burned for her harlotry,

> she sent to her father in law, saying, By the man, whose these are, am I with child: and she said, Discern, I pray thee, whose are these, the signets, and bracelets, and staff. And Judah acknowledged them, and said, She hath been more righteous than I, because that I gave her not to Shelah my son. (25–26)

WHILE MILTON OFFERS his circumcised citation as a condemnation of the body, the larger story serves precisely to recuperate the body, to reveal the irreducible value of sexuality. Indeed, Tamar's justification is magnified immeasurably within the Christian framework, for as the genealogy that begins the Gospel of Matthew makes absolutely clear, Jesus's Davidic lineage—essential to his role as Messiah—reaches directly back to Paretz, one of the two children produced by Tamar's seduction of Judah. Try as he might, then, Milton cannot simply dispense with the Jewish (in this case, notably female) body, which provides the necessary genealogical link. Yet the story does not end there, either, for the moment we have restored the absent presence of the Jewish body to Milton's account, we must further acknowledge that Matthew's Davidic genealogy is much ado about nothing. Jesus is not, after all, the son of Joseph, whose patrimony is Davidic. He is the son of Mary and the Holy Spirit. Thus the Jewish (female) body serves as a receptacle, the status of which remains in doubt.

Milton picks up the theme of Jewish and pagan apostasy and its relation to divine and human generation several pages later in his *Animadversions*, where he addresses Hall's objection that the episcopacy has never until now faced opposition.

> What an over-worne and bedrid Argument is this, the last refuge ever of old falshood, and therefore a good signe I trust that your Castle cannot hold out long. This was the plea of *Judaisme*, and Idolatry against *Christ* and his *Apostles*, of *Papacie* against Reformation: and perhaps to the frailty of flesh and blood in a man destitute of better enlight'ning, may for some while bee pardonable; for what has fleshly apprehension other to subsist by then Succession, Custome, and Visibility, which onely hold if in his weaknesse and blindnesse he be loath to lose, who can blame? but in a *Protestant* Nation that should have throwne off these tatter'd Rudiments long agoe, after the many strivings of Gods Spirit, and our fourscore yeares vexation of him in this our wildernesse since Reformation began, to urge these rotten Principles, and twit us with the present age, which is to us an age of ages wherein God is manifestly come downe among us, to doe some remarkable good to our Church or state, is as if a man should taxe the renovating and re-ingendring Spirit of God with innovation, and that new creature for an upstart noveltie; yea the new Jerusalem, which without your admired linke of succession descends from Heaven, could not scape some such like censure. (YP 1:703)

JUDAISM AND PAGANISM, indistinguishable in this passage, both objected to

Christianity's advent because of its newness. And if Jews and idolaters resisted Christ's mission in the earliest stages of the Church, followers of the pope have expressed similar resistance to the reform movements. Milton offers an orientation to Church history that posits a cycle of repetitive reforms and resistance, thereby eliding any differences between each instance of resistance. In each case the conflict amounts to the assertion of competing modes of procreation. For if Judaism, Paganism, and Catholicism all depend upon "fleshly apprehension" to validate their "Succession, Custome, and Visibility," the true Spirit of God, the motivating force behind Christianity's initial advent and each successive reform, renovates the body of Christ, that is, the Church of the faithful, through a "re-ingendring." That this restoration comes at the hand of such an overtly sexual figure of procreation suggests that the tension between the preservation and elision of the body I described in Tamar's example is reiterated here in the very dynamics of Milton's church reforms.

Milton's erstwhile allies in the antiprelatical tracts, the Smectymnuans, offer further insight into the status of Judaism as a "Canaanitish doctrine." Their *Answer to a Book Entitvled an Humble Remonstrance* offers a response to Bishop Hall's claim for the value of the fifteen-hundred-year legacy of Church hierarchy by positing a relationship between Judaism's historical attacks on the Church and paganism's parallel antagonisms. Smectymnuus writes, "For thus the Jewes might have pleaded against Christ the Antiquitie of more then so many hundred yeares; and thus the Heathens did plead against the Christian Religion, which *Justin Martyr* in his Apologie Answers. And by this argument the Pope sits as fast rivetted in his chayre at Rome, as ours in theirs: whose plea for Antiquitie runs paralell with theirs."[74] These Presbyterian authors regarded all resistances to change as rhetorically parallel; thus the Jews, Heathens, and Papists have all historically rooted their objections to church reform in the same basic argument founded on tradition. Unlike Milton, however, the Smectymnuan association of Judaism and paganism is much more haphazard and occasional. The convenience of relating Judaism to paganism and thereby vilifying both as adumbrations of the prelacy is exploited without much apparent thought regarding the further implications of this potentially disruptive tie. More to the point, for most of the Presbyterian opponents of the prelacy—indeed, for many of the more radical Independents and sectarians with whom Milton would later ally himself—the wisdom of the ancients was of little acknowledged value. They may have been heirs to a humanist tradition that dictated some of the structures of their attacks, but they did not make extensive use of the classical tradition.[75]

In Milton's case, of course, the classical tradition held a much more prominent, albeit ambivalent, position. In his poetry Milton's assertions of some kind of Christian purity, whether it be in the early lyrical expressions of "On the Morning of the Christ's Nativity," *Lycidas*, *Comus* or in the later epic form of *Paradise Lost*, are disrupted time and again by the reemergence of what have been called "Hebraisms," on the one hand, and the poet's notoriously erudite and complex uses of classical, pre-Christian literary, historical, and philosophical antecedents, on the other. This tension is related, I think, to the tension between literary imagination, what we may call Miltonic poesis, and the drive toward a Puritan iconoclasm. In developing his own understanding of Protestantism's theology of the Word, defined as Scripture, as Christ, and as Christ as Scripture, Milton progressively refined the nature of scriptural authority. Thomas Kranidas has shown that many of Milton's polemics against the prelacy contain within them a tacit attack on the power of the spoken over the written word. Milton repeatedly insists that "truth is printed, not spoken."[76] Hence, Milton often construes the printed word as an organic body, alive independent of its author. The most memorable instance of this figure appears in *Areopagitica*, where Truth is described as having come into the world in the company of Christ. When Christ reascended, though,

> then strait arose a wicked race of deceivers, who as that story goes of the *Aegyptian Typhon* with his conspirators, how they dealt with good *Osiris*, took the virgin Truth, hewd her lovely form into a thousand peeces, and scatter'd them to the four winds. From that time ever since, the sad friends of Truth, such as durst appear, imitating the carefull search that *Isis* made for the mangl'd body of *Osiris*, went up and down gathering up limb by limb still as they could find them. (YP 2:549)

A STRIKING IMAGE for the search to recover something like a Platonic notion of Truth, the story of Osiris and Isis marks a rich instance of the conflation of pagan forms with Christian thought. Indeed, for the moment at least, Milton casts the Christian "friends of Truth" in the role of imitators of the pagan goddess. The poetic impulse, one that draws its power from a complex mimesis, stands in direct tension with Milton's call to break the forms—be they ceremony, icon, or even language—that prevent access to the truth of Christian salvation.[77] Writing a prose tract advocating free publication in the service of truth, Milton embraces the myth of Osiris and Isis for what it allows him to render vivid and compelling. Writing poetry, that epitome of creative achievement, Milton is far less inclined to sympathize with this pagan myth. In one of his earliest poems, the Nativity Ode, lines 211–23, and one of his last, *Paradise Lost*, 1.475–82, Milton consigns these Egyptian deities to the infernal company of Satan. This ambivalence toward the Egyptian myth is a mirror image of Milton's more general tendencies in his prose and poetry. As a polemicist, he roundly condemns the deceptive nature of fiction and storytelling; it is, after all, the legends of the early saints and martyrs that contributes significantly to the early Church's fall away from true Christian doctrine. As a poet, however, he invents, sometimes as it seems from whole cloth, stories to embellish, expand, and interpret the truths contained in Scripture.[78] Perhaps even more problematic, when his poetic embellishments are not original inventions, their genealogies lead us right back into the pagan classical world or, perhaps more indirectly, the postbiblical Jewish tradition. Milton's Hebraisms and classicisms are the various—occasionally conflicting—forms his imaginative work takes in the larger service of the breaking of these images and the final rejection of these traditions. Christian truth and the wisdom of the ancients are not mutually exclusive for Milton; the latter often facilitates a better appreciation of the former. But their relationship is a fraught one, much like—I would say, as a version of—Milton's anxiously ambivalent embrace of Hebrew and Jewish precedent. The forms of pagan wisdom and Hebrew learning threaten always to bring with them the bodies.[79]

Let us examine one final example, taken from a very different period in Milton's career, when any of the optimism he may have been feeling during the early 1640s was surely diminished by the fiasco of the Commonwealth and Cromwellian Protectorate, to which Milton had leant his pen and reputation. In 1659, a year before the Restoration of Charles II to the throne, Milton dictated (for by then he was totally blind) a plea against the institution of tithing, which was an essential aspect of any state-established church, Anglican, Presbyterian, or otherwise. Depending heavily on John Selden's extensive rabbinical learning, as demonstrated in his *History of Tithes* (1618), Milton asserts that there is no evidence in the earliest apostolic church for the acceptance of the practice of tithing. Thus, the defenders of tithes,

after along pomp and tedious preparation out of Heathen authors, telling us that tithes were paid to *Hercules* and *Apollo*, which perhaps was imitated from the *Jewes*, and as it were bespeaking our expectation, that they will abound much more with autorities out of Christian storie, have nothing of general approbation to beginn with from the first three or four ages, but that which abundantly serves to the confutation of thir tithes. (*Considerations touching the Likeliest Means to Remove Hirelings*, YP 7:290–91)

IN ADDRESSING THE possibility that tithes in Hellenistic religions imitated the tithing practices during the period of the Jewish Temple, Milton acknowledges the commonly held opinion, partly stemming from view that Hebrew was the original Adamic language from which all other languages were derived, that the myths and practices of pagan cultures were only corrupted derivatives of the original biblical revelation.[80]

Thus far hath the church bin alwaies, whether in her prime, or in her ancientest reformation, from the approving of tithes: nor without reason; for they might easily perceive that tithes were fitted to the *Jewes* only, a national church of many incomplete synagogues; uniting the accomplishment of divine worship in one temple; and the Levites there had thir tithes paid where they did thir bodilie work; to which a particular tribe was set apart by divine appointment, not by the peoples election: but the Christian church is universal; not ti'd to nation, dioces or parish, but consisting of many particular churches complete in themselves; gatherd not by compulsion or the accident of dwelling nigh together, but by free consent chusing both thir particular church and thir church-officers. Whereas if tithes be set up, all these Christian privileges will be disturbd and soone lost, and with them Christian libertie. (YP 7:292)

THOUGH HE ALWAYS regards the Church as universal, in the heady days of 1640–42 Milton was far more inclined to underscore the distinctive qualities of English church reform. Always opposed to an established state church, Milton nevertheless was wont in the early days to wax rhapsodic about his "noble and puissant Nation rousing herself like a strong man after sleep, and shaking her invincible locks" (*Areopagitica*, YP 2:558). In 1659 any national pride he might have felt is replaced by a focus on a universal Christian Church "not ti'd to any nation." What is especially remarkable about this passage is the way in which Milton fashions his own religio-political identity specifically in contrast to the pre-Christian *Jewish* church, yet parallel to the post-Temple Jewish communities.

And yet the *Jewes* ever since thir temple was destroid, though they have Rabbies and teachers of thir law, yet pay no tithes, as having no Levites to whom, no temple where to pay them, no altar wheron to hallow them; which argues that the *Jewes* themselves never thought tithes moral, but ceremonial only. That Christians therefor should take them up, when *Jewes* have laid them down, must needs be very absurd and preposterous. (YP 7:282)

READERS OF MILTON'S poetry will recognize in the word *preposterous* an example of the poet's suggestive use of etymologies. The idea of Christianity following Judaism's lead is "preposterous" specifically because it reverses the true order of things, placing the last before the first. As I suggested at the beginning of this chapter, this is the case only because Milton has already placed the last before the first, asserting Christianity's priority against history as it was commonly read. Jesus's messianic role may have been precisely counter to the messianic expectations of the Jewish prophetic tradition, which seemed to call for a worldly king as much as a spiritual deliverer. The Jews who rejected Jesus because of his failure to take up the worldly crown of his ostensible Davidic ancestor misunderstood the true nature of the Christ. The earliest stages of the apostolic Church, idealized by Milton, revealed a Kingdom of God wholly distinct from any kind of earthly sovereignty. It is the case, nevertheless, that by the fourth century the Church, in Milton's view, had lost sight of this redefinition of the Messiah. That true understanding was preserved in the few just souls who resisted, Christlike, the temptations of earthly power and reward. *And*, it was preserved in a newly revised Jewish view of messianic expectations that were explicitly apolitical and unworldly. The last had become first again.

While Milton never explicitly acknowledges this fundamental reversal, I want to suggest that he and his English contemporaries were aware of it, which further deepens the seventeenth-century English interest in Jews and Judaism. Dismissing the evidence of tithes from the early Church and its support in the writings of Church fathers like Ambrose and Augustine (both of whom flourished during the first period of Christian political ascendancy) as irrelevant and "without pertinent scripture," Milton insists that

what they vouch, is founded on the law of *Moses*, with which, every where pitifully mistaken, they again incorporate the gospel; as did the rest also of those titular fathers, perhaps an age or two before them, by many rights and ceremonies, both Jewish and Heathenish introduc'd; whereby thinking to gain all, they lost all: and instead of winning Jewes and Pagans to be Christians, by too much condescending they turnd Christians into Jewes and Pagans. (YP 7:293)

MILTON HAS TO construe Jews as pagan so as to recover a definition of Christianity that, for all intents and purposes, has been preserved for the last thirteen centuries within the world of Diaspora Jewry through its ongoing antithetical engagement with Hellenism, Christianity, and the innumerable hybrids thereof.

3

The Poetics of Accommodation: Theodicy and the Language of Kingship

WHEN CRITICS refer to Milton as a Hebraic writer, they frequently cite the God of *Paradise Lost* as a prime example of the poet's ongoing fascination with the Jewish tradition. The depiction of the Father in relation to the Son dramatizes the poet's interest in the connection between the Hebraic and the Christian, between the Old Covenant and its reformulation, especially by Paul, in the New Covenant. Milton, so the critical view goes, was more reluctant than some of his contemporaries to relinquish the legacy of Christianity's Jewish heritage, a legacy to which he and many others lay claim in light of the continuity they identified between pre-Christian Judaism and post-Reformation Christianity.[1]

A frequent corollary to this Hebraic Father–Christian Son dichotomy has been an alignment of the figure of the Father with the divine perspective and that of Christ with the human perspective. That is, not only does Christ serve to balance the divine justice expressed by the Father with divine mercy, but he achieves this balance by standing in for humanity in its confrontation with the distant and often inscrutable world of God. Of course, this alignment of Christ with humanity follows directly from the economy of guilt, sacrifice, and redemption that forms the core of Christian theology. Christ's suffering and crucifixion can only achieve the salvation of humanity if it is preceded by the Incarnation, at which time Christ becomes human, and therefore humanity. The Celestial Dialogue in book 3 of *Paradise Lost*, which has been read by many critics as a version of the medieval tradition of morality plays, replaces the allegorical figures of Justice and Mercy with the "real" personae of the Father and the Son.[2] The Hebraic Father demands justice; the humanized Son argues for Christian mercy.[3]

In the pages that follow I argue for a more complex relation between the poem's Hebraic and Pauline aspects, on the one hand, and its textual formulations of the Father and the Son, on the other. By writing through the personae of the godhead, Milton has imagined an alternative mode of human-divine interrogation that bears a striking resemblance to rabbinical forms of biblical interpretation, many of which predate the medieval allegorical mode by at least a millennium. These analogies become important especially when they offer competing characterizations both of God and of humanity's role in its ongoing dialogue with the divine.

MATCHING "HEAV'N'S MATCHLESS KING"

THE FIRST *parashah* (chapter) of Genesis Rabbah concerns itself generally with the nature and validity of human inquiry into the details of the creation. Much of its commentary takes the form of the midrashic proem, or petih-tah; the homilist begins with a verse from somewhere else in the Bible, which seems to have little to do with the base verse that has occasioned the homily.[4] Rav Huna, in the name of Bar Qappara, introduces an intersecting verse from the book of Psalms (a favorite source for interrogating the Pentateuch) as the beginning of a petihtah: "Let the lying lips be put to silence; which speak grievous things proudly and contemptuously against the righteous" (31:19). The midrash asks (as a rhetorical effect, since the expectation was that any listener would be well-versed in the Psalms or, for that matter, in any other biblical text), What verse follows this statement from Psalms?

> "How great is thy goodness, which thou hast laid up for them that fear thee" (31:20).

> Rav said, "Let he [who has revealed the mysteries of creation] not receive your great goodness. As it happens in this world, when a king of flesh and

blood builds his palace in a place of sewers, garbage, and rancidity, if anyone comes and says, 'This palace was built in a place of sewers, garbage, and rancidity,' will he not offend? Similarly, anyone who comes and says that this world was created out of formlessness, emptiness [*tohu va-vohu*], and darkness, will he not offend?"

Rav Huna in the name of Bar Qappara: "Were it not explicitly written so, it would not be permitted to say so. 'God created heaven and earth . . .' from where? 'And the earth was formless, etc.' " (1:5).

BY SUGGESTING AN equivalence between the sewers, garbage, and rancidity that preceded the palace and the formlessness, emptiness, and darkness that preceded the created universe, Rav's *mashal*, or rabbinic parable, commits the very act it is intended to warn against. What motivates this parable seems to be Rav's anticipation of an ontological attack with significant theodical questions: the world was created out of garbage, and hence it is garbage as well. Rav Huna's coda, which stands as a modification of Rav's position, displays a concern that the biblical text has revealed too much by describing the initial state of creation. His inclination would have been to prohibit the articulation of the very details contained within Scripture! Just as in Milton's attempt to "justify the ways of God to men" though, these potentially embarrassing or incriminating details are given voice.

There is another aspect of this midrash that bears an important resemblance to Milton's epic; it is a similarity made more apparent as the midrash returns to consider the proper definition of *tohu va-vohu* in the second parashah, approaching the issue via another series of *meshalim*:

"And the earth was formless [*tohu va-vohu*] . . ." R. Abahu and R. Yehuda the son of R. Simon: R. Abahu said, "It is like a king who bought two servants on one bill of sale and for the same price. He then decreed that one should be fed by the public treasury, and the other would have to work to eat. The latter sat utterly confused [*tohe u-vohe*], and said, 'We were bought for the same price, yet why is this [other] one fed by the public treasury, while I have to work for my food?' Similarly, the land sat utterly confused [*tohe u-vohe*], saying, 'The upper world and the lower world were created simultaneously, yet the upper world is nourished by the splendor of God's presence, while the lower creatures will not eat unless they work.' "

R. Yehudah the son of R. Simon said, "It is like a king who purchased two maidservants on the same bill of sale and for the same price. He decreed that one never leave the palace, while he banished the other. The latter one sat utterly confused [*tohe u-vohe*], saying, 'We were bought by the same bill of sale and for the same price, yet this [other] one never has to leave the palace while I have been banished.' Similarly, the earth sat utterly confused [*tohe u-vohe*], saying, 'The upper world and lower world were created simultaneously. Why does the upper world live forever, while the [creatures of the] lower world die?' Hence it is written, 'The earth was formless, etc.'" (2:2)

THE PARABLES LAY an astonishing amount of blame on the initial state of the created world. The philological impetus for this homily serves to exaggerate the interpretive problems that occasioned the meshalim. In this respect we may observe a dramatic instance of what David Stern has identified as the continuity between the mashal and the biblical narrative. They both make use of gaps in their respective narrative poetics, relying on disparities between text and interpretation, unexplained motives, improbable and excessive acts, gaps in plot, and other violations of norms to elicit the active participation of the audience.[5]

The homilists of this series of midrashim deploy one of their favorite forms of the mashal, the king-parable. As Ignaz Ziegler's study has shown, confirmed by Stern's recent work on rabbinic parables, the king-parable was a dominant mode of rabbinic narrative exegesis.[6] Ziegler's survey of the king-mashal suggests, further, that the king in these parables, situated in a world replete with material details of the Greco-Roman period, was specifically based upon the rabbis' own lived experience with the Roman emperor and his proxies, the procurators and proconsuls. Noting that "nothing was more characteristic of the Roman emperorship than the imperial cult, a fact that did not escape the Rabbis," Stern goes on to describe how the rabbis "enthusiastically exploited the emperor as a symbolic figure for God; they did not even hesitate to borrow from the imperial cult some of its most singularly idolatrous features in order to use them as symbols for various subjects."[7] The paradox raised by this conflation of the sacred (Hebraic) and the profane (pagan) is a crucial one. Why did the rabbis not hesitate to deploy these pagan symbols in their biblical exegesis, especially when they turned their attention to things divine in nature? Stern provides an answer, one that resonates profoundly with the response many Milton critics have given to a similar difficulty raised by the imagery of *Paradise Lost*. He explains this conflict of interests by comparing it to early Christianity's use of the iconography and stylistic conventions of classical Greco-Roman art: "The imagery and regalia of the cult, once removed from their lived context, lost their transgressive character."[8]

Given what we know about the vehemence of Milton's antimonarchist views, his extensive prose writings against the royalist cause, and the personal dangers he encountered following the Restoration, "fall'n on evil days, / On evil days though fall'n, and evil tongues; / In darkness, and with dangers compast round, / And solitude" (*PL* 7.25–28), how can we make sense of the kingly fashion in which he constructs his representations of God and of the Son? As Robert Fallon concludes, "There is, in the end, no way to avoid the impression that Milton's God is an absolute monarch who governs in ways that the poet roundly condemned in earthly kings. He is treated like a king. . . . He sounds like a king. . . . He acts like a king."[9] Of course, Milton, like the rabbis before him, might have justified his monarchical images of God by pointing to their biblical precedent. The Hebrew Bible and the New Testament both deploy images of kingship, as well as the name of *King*, in their depictions of God. On its own, however, the biblical precedent does not offer a satisfying explanation for the specific details, the local color, that midrash and *Paradise Lost* invoke. It is one thing to speak of God as "King of all the earth" (Psalms 47:7). It is yet another matter entirely to describe how the assembly of angels,

> Innumerable before th'Almighty's Throne
> Forthwith from all the ends of Heav'n appear'd
> Under thir Hierarchs in orders bright;
> Ten thousand thousand Ensigns high advanc'd,
> Standards and Gonfalons, twixt Van and Rear
> Stream in the Air, and for distinction serve
> Of Hierarchies, of Orders, and Degrees. (5.585–91)

AS RECENT CRITICS have noted, it is largely this paradox that has impelled previous generations of Miltonists to some of their most outlandish interpretations. Malcolm Mackenzie Ross perversely concluded that Milton must have been a closet royalist who fully endorsed these hierarchies in human society as well.[10] Empson famously characterized Milton's God as Joseph Stalin, insisting that Milton's poem was written to reveal the wickedness of Christianity and its God.[11]

In recent years a more measured response has been forthcoming. Invoking Milton's theory of divine accommodation, Leland Ryken has argued that "when human qualities are attributed to God they must be divested of some of their usual connotations. . . . We are free to see that Milton could without contradiction use the royalist symbol to represent true spiritual perfection, despite the fact that he was hostile to the royalist images as it existed in the political situation in England."[12] Stevie Davies has suggested that Milton distinguished four modes of kingship; the first two, the absolute monarch and the Turkish sultan, are wholly negative and associated with Satan; the third, the Roman emperor, offered benign and malevolent versions to be associated to God and Satan (or Charles I) respectively; the fourth, the feudal lord, stood as the primary model for God's kingship as first among equals.[13] Joan Bennett sees Milton's God-as-King as distinct from earthly kings in his voluntary acceptance of his own laws, yet she does not consider how just these laws may have been in and of themselves.[14] Fallon's view is that by showing how God rules, Milton "drew a picture of government truly sublime and warned temporal rulers not to reach for it."[15]

As useful as each of these solutions is, they all seek to diminish the transgressive nature of Milton's images of kingship in the much the same way that Stern's explanation of the rabbinic king-parable does. In both cases critics are determined to avoid the possibility that "Heav'n's matchless King" (4.41) might have suffered in comparison. I propose a different approach, one that acknowledges the potential for paradox and contradiction that inheres in both the rabbis' and Milton's comparison of God to an earthly (and distinctively flawed) monarch. Midrash and *Paradise Lost* offer themselves as theodicy, an understanding of the world that posits God as just, merciful, and good. Yet, there is no escaping the implication of the consecutive meshalim with which I began: the earth was created in a state of lack, a potentially catastrophic flaw that resembles the menacing rift in the world present in Milton's poem *prior* to the creation of the earth, the result of Satan's rebellion. The accusatory mode of this midrash does not operate in isolation, however. As a narrative, itself demanding an act of interpretation, the mashal stresses the insufficiency of meaning by resisting closure. It appears near the beginning of Genesis Rabbah's prolonged meditation on the biblical hexameron, describing a problem (i.e., the very real sense of a flawed world experienced by the rabbis and their community) that demands a variety of responses we have yet to encounter fully in the midrashic collection.[16] This specific midrash functions as an initial statement of theme, in much the same way that Milton's Celestial Dialogue operates. Neither this midrash nor book 3 of *Paradise Lost* stands independently as a fully satisfying theodicy. "High Thron'd above all highth" (58), God insists that man was created "Sufficient to have stood, though free to fall" (99), an essential element of Milton's Arminian defense of free will; as poetry, however, the speech in which this line appears is far from comforting or assuring.

Interpretation, in midrash and in Milton's poem, is formulated as an ethical imperative. The audience is enjoined to fulfill its responsibility to the text(s). Having been conveyed to the text through its narrative poetics, the reader must shoulder the burden, carrying the text back with him or her to the present (historical and personal) moment of encounter. Textual application, not simply from a normative stance but also from a philosophical one, motivates the midrashic hermeneutic, lending it a fully ethical purview. The rabbis and Milton share an interpretive stance vis-à-vis the biblical pretext. There can be no doubt that crucial disagreement exists between the rabbis and Milton on certain key elements of doctrine and biblical interpretation. Yet these culturally and religiously distinct readers interpreted and recreated the biblical text with a similarly dynamic combination of devotion and innovation, itself parallel to a view of human-divine communication fraught with anxiety and misapprehension. To that end, both the rabbis and Milton, enlist God's unreadability—or, what often amounts to the same thing, God's excessively human traits—in their respective theodical projects. The depiction of God serves as the opaque center, resisting a full understanding and representation but insisting in this inadequate form on the justice of his ways.

IN THE IMAGE OF GOD

IF THE FIRST two books of Milton's poem introduce the reader to the power and attraction of Satan and the fallen angels in all their rhetorical and poetical sublimity, and books 4 and 5 begin the process of representing the charm of prelapsarian Adam and Eve, their beauty and innocence, and even the beginnings of their seductive mortality, then, from a structural point of view at least, it would make sense for the poet to look for some means of making the transition from the sheer power of hell to the attractive innocence of Eden. *Paradise Lost* achieves this transition structurally and thematically through the Celestial Dialogue of book 3. This intervening episode in the narrative produces a dissonance that ruptures the reader's expectations, collapsing the pattern of meaning established in the first two books and preparing a new representational strategy for the next several books. The visual orientation of the first two books must be exchanged for a dependence on words and abstractions in the Celestial Dialogue, anticipated by the third book's invocation to "holy Light" (1), as distinct from the piercing ray that does not revisit the eyes of the poet. Despite being bathed in the light of divine truth, book 3 "sings darkling" (39) about a realm described as "Dark with excessive bright" (380).

In his posthumously published theological treatise Milton addresses the biblical practice of attributing to God human characteristics (both physical and emotional).

> However you may try to tone down these and similar texts about God by an elaborate show of interpretive glosses, it comes to the same thing in the end. After all, if *God is said to have created man in his own image, after his own likeness,* Gen. i. 26 . . . and if God attributes to himself again and again a human shape and form, why should we be afraid of assigning to him something he assigns to himself. (*De doctrina Christiana,* 1.ii; YP 6:135–36)

REJECTING THE RHETORICAL figure of anthropopathy invoked by theologians who were uncomfortable with the idea of divine passibility, Milton insists that the scriptural depictions of an angry, indignant, repentant, or rejoicing God are deliberate and precise representations of divine character.[17] This seemingly human conceptualization of God is in fact an elaboration of what it means for humanity to have been created in the image of God: it is through these affective human characteristics (and *only* through them) that we can come to understand the image of God.[18] Milton's departure from a more standard Calvinist view of anthropopathy—and return to the Augustinian assertion that the Bible would never have represented God in a form that might be the source of theological scandal—has an important unstated implication, one that speaks to the ongoing critical debate over the relationship between the *De Doctrina Christiana* and *Paradise Lost.* Milton insists that Scripture is self-sufficient, providing all the information necessary to construe divine nature and intention:

> It is safest for us to form an image of God in our minds which corresponds to his representation and description of himself in the sacred writings. . . .

We ought to form just such a mental image of him as he, in bringing himself within the limits of our understanding, wishes us to form. Indeed, he has brought himself down to our level expressly to prevent our being carried beyond the reach of human comprehension, and outside the written authority of scripture, into vague subtleties of speculation. (YP 6:133–34)

WE MAY RECOGNIZE in this passage not simply the themes to which Milton turns in his epic but also some of the images to be found there. In the phrase "carried beyond the reach of human comprehension" (*elati supra captum humanum*) we hear the same concern over uncontrollable exaltation and ascendancy expressed in the invocations to book 3 and book 7. The epic narrator worries aloud to the "holy Light,"

> Thee I revisit now with bolder wing,
> Escap't from the *Stygian* Pool, though long detain'd
> Through utter and through middle darkness borne
> With other notes than th'*Orphean* Lyre
> I sung of *Chaos* and *Eternal Night*,
> Taught by the heav'nly Muse to venture down
> The dark descent, and up to reascend,
> Though hard and rare. (3.13–21)

THOUGH THIS REASCENSION is a matter of much concern in book 3, the control of his—perhaps overly successful—exaltation and elevation becomes the concern of the epic poet at the beginning of book 7:

> . . . above th'*Olympian* Hill I soar,
> Above the flight of *Pegasean* wing.
> . . . .
> . . . Up led by thee
> Into the Heav'n of Heav'ns I have presum'd,
> An Earthly Guest, and drawn Empyreal Air,
> Thy temp'ring; with like safety guided down
> Return me to my Native Element:
> Lest from this flying Steed unrein'd, (as once
> *Bellerophon*, though from a lower Clime)
> Dismounted, on th'*Aleian* field I fall
> Erroneous there to wander and forlorn. (7.3–4, 12–20)

THE DANGER OF verticality conditions the focus of this invocation and captures precisely the concerns expressed earlier in *De Doctrina*. The doctrine of accommodation (or condescension) serves as an essential antidote to this danger of uncontrollable ascension. The poet describes this danger as one that has the potential to result in an "erroneous" fall, but it is essential to see this possibility of falling as arising specifically out of the "bolder wing" sought in book 3.[19]

For Milton the accommodated representation of God is the very limit of human understanding; the reader of the Bible must rest content with its formulation and not try to transcend this conception for something beyond that which is contained in Scripture. Heraclitus's famous dictum, ηθος ανθροπου δαιμων, may be said to hold true for Milton's reading of the creation of humanity in the divine image. The syntactical symmetry in the Greek allows the phrase to be read in both directions—"the character of man is divine" *and* "the divine in man is his character."[20] Similarly, humankind was created in the image of God, but it is only through the qualities of humankind that we can know the image of God. Scripture reveals that God wishes to be thought of as having an affective existence, comprehensible to us only through our own human passions, which are necessarily *outside* Scripture. It thus becomes impossible to sustain a view that both insists on scriptural sufficiency and rejects anthropopathy. This conflict in Milton's scriptural epistemology is likely to have provided a major impulse to write a biblical epic that repeats and reformulates the narrative of Scripture and, in the process, interrogates divine passibility in a way that would have been out of place in the poet's theological treatise.

Accommodation, in Milton's terms, works through two complementary and inseparable thrusts: first, it brings the divine system of truths down to earth by reducing or modifying the formulation of these transcendental truths, and, second, it raises the earthly mind to heaven through its vision of a higher or next level.[21] The figure of the Son serves as a typological paradigm for all work of scriptural accommodation. That is, just as the Son must descend to the realm of flesh so as to effect the redemption and translation of all fallen humanity back to its divine originary substance, so, too, accommodated language condescends to the fleshly realm, insisting on its materiality precisely so that it may point to a spiritual conception of the godhead. But if the redemption of humankind cannot work in the discourse of book 3 without the Incarnation and suffering of the Son, neither can accommodative language function unless its materiality is retained. This materiality or literariness contains within it the idea of literalism, but is not coterminous with that concept. Milton's literal notion of divine representation does indeed refuse—or anticipate and seek to eliminate—the gap implied between the form of representation and the content of the thing being represented. But the refusal of this gap does not suggest a transparency to language, the availability of an unmediated vision. Rather, the literariness of accommodative language maintains that the ideas represented by such language are also formulated in and confined by it. Milton's poetry, in other words, is *not* a self-consuming artifact, a vessel to be discarded once its contents have been drained. The meaning of the theodical epic does not exist without the form and phenomenological experience of the poem.

Hugh MacCallum has described the difference between Milton's understanding of accommodation and that of most other English Reformation theologians, most of whom followed Calvin either explicitly of implicitly. While other Reformation interpretations of accommodation usually implied a form of *social* accommodation, Milton's accommodation, must be called *epistemological*, in that it "defines the limits of man's comprehension." Yet, Milton's claim stands in tension with—and threatens to countermand—the suggestion throughout Milton's writings that the forms of expression contained within the Bible should be the locus of human investigation into the divine mysteries and apparent contradictions.[22] Milton's representation of the satanic mode in books 1 and 2 stands as one possible path: a rejection of epistemological and ontological limits in favor of intellectual and political activity, a resistance to perceived confinement and subordination in favor of a willed self-authorship. Indeed, it is this impulse upon which Satan, in the guise of the serpent, plays in his seduction of Eve: "and wherein lies / Th'offense, that Man should thus attain to know? / What can your knowledge hurt him, or this Tree / Impart against his will if all be his?" (9.725–28). The attraction of this alternative was great enough to account for many of the oft-noted parallels between Satan, Eve, and the epic narrator. The conflict between language as the limit of human knowledge and language as the locus of human investigation energizes Milton's poem, giving his great argument its celebrated two-part description, "To assert Eternal Providence"—this is the poetry of accommodation—"and justify the ways of God to men"—this is the doctrine of theodicy. The argument consists of two distinct yet inseparable aspects that arise from the reading of the biblical text, which is itself defined by its reliance upon accommodative language. There can be no discarding of images and metaphors once the kernel of meaning has been extracted, according to this approach to scriptural interpretation.[23] The only epistemologically available meaning resides in the operations of biblical language, in its literary existence. Milton does not read the "Bible as literature" in any contemporary academic sense, but he does insist on a conceptualization of the function of Scripture that can be understood as literary, if by this term we mean an approach that sustains the language and structure of narrative and that manifests a faith in the availability of meaning to the reader. Within this literary framework man (i.e., Milton) creates God in his own image.

THE HAMMER AND THE STONE

AN ANALOGOUS SET of tensions characterizes the work of midrash. As a hermeneutical vehicle, midrash transports the reader back to the text and its particular and general (intertextual) contexts, but it also brings the text forward to the historical circumstances of a given reading and interpretation. In serving this dual role it raises similar questions regarding the limits and capacities of human understanding. Stephen Benin has argued that early rabbinic Judaism worked very hard to maintain the chasm between the divine and human, a chasm that Christianity claimed to bridge through Christ's Incarnation. He adds, "In endeavoring to depict the abyss between God and the world and to stress his 'otherness' attempts were made to cleanse the scriptural understanding of anthropomorphisms and anthropopathisms."[24] Benin is certainly correct to underscore the rabbis' awareness of God's "otherness"; I am not convinced, however, that the rabbis did not seek to bridge that gap in their own distinctive ways. Rather than closing the abyss in the body of Christ, the rabbis built their bridges out of the very language of Scripture. Indeed, what Benin characterizes as a cleansing of anthropomorphisms and anthropopathisms seems to me on more than one occasion to be a deliberate muddying of the waters.

The Babylonian Talmud records the following statement by the second-generation tannah R. Ishmael:

[Is not my word like fire, saith the Lord?] and like a hammer that shatters stone? [Jeremiah 23:29] Just as this hammer gives off many sparks [when it hits a rock], so too every single word uttered by the Holy One Blessed be He is divided into seventy versions.[25]

AS I HAVE already indicated, the method of analogy or parable, the mashal, is one of the favorite techniques of rabbinic interpretation. In this case, however, the rabbinic use of analogy is secondary to the comparison described in the scriptural verse. The statement thus offers an instance, first and foremost, of the rabbinic method finding its precedent in the very text that it seeks to interpret. However, since the mashal functions at a remove from what is figured *already in scripture* as an epistemological problem—the word of God can only be appreciated by the use of analogy—what R. Ishmael poses as an apparently direct analogy between a natural phenomenon and the interpretive process is by no means clear. Exactly what is being compared to what? If we first take the verse from Jeremiah by itself, then the prophet seeks to compare God's word to the hammer that breaks the stone (the analog of which is not apparent, even in the larger scriptural context of the passage) into pieces. But when R. Ishmael gets his hands on this analogy, he shifts the terms. The *hammer* is that which gives off sparks, or, is shattered into splinters, as an alternative translation might render it. Read with any grammatical coherence, the form of the Hebrew verb *nitchaleq*, "is divided," cannot have as its subject anything but the hammer. Yet this revision of the analogy seems to suggest that it is the word of God (having been compared to the hammer) that divides into seventy versions or linguistic fragments.[26] What, then, is the stone? What splinters the words of Scripture into the multiplicity of voices that R. Ishmael seeks to locate within the text? Though no explicit resolution is offered by the redacted text of the Talmud, it seems to me that one possible explanation of this fascinating misreading of the biblical analogy would be as an audacious self-justification of the rabbinic method of interpretation.[27] The stone serves as figure for the midrashic hermeneutic, which, when it is struck by the words of the Bible, causes those words to refract and splinter, revealing a multiplicity of possible interpretations. The outlandishness of this revision of the biblical analogy should not be minimized: it forces the naturalized language of Jeremiah into an awkward reconfiguration, so that the active figure (the hammer) becomes passive and the passive figure (the stone) becomes active. The reversal cannily authorizes rabbinic interpretation by reifying it—the active, changeable term in this reconfigured relationship is the *biblical text* rather than the midrashic hermeneutic. It is because of its audacity, its own splintering of the text, that this statement serves as so marvelous an emblem for the rabbinic approach to interpretation. The rabbis are eminently creative and inventive. But the building blocks for their inventions are always taken from Scripture. Indeed, there may also be a latent wordplay at work here, since the term for hammer, *patish*, and the term for simple meaning, *peshat*, are anagrams of one another. If I am right in finding this paronomasia, then this description of the midrashic method is made even richer by a manifestation of one of its more innovative techniques in the very scriptural justification for such a technique. The hammer (*patish*), as the ostensibly simple or literal meaning of Scripture's language (*peshat*), splinters itself into seventy possibilities when it encounters the midrashic hermeneutic.[28] In this way the rabbis assume a posture with respect to the Bible that is at once devout and heretical. Indeed, it is often at precisely their most devoted moment when the rabbis also betray their ongoing struggle to free themselves from the strictures of a literalist or fundamentalist stance toward the text. Susan Handelman has observed something like this phenomenon in the implicit self-canonization in rabbinic texts: "When commentary crosses the line and itself becomes text we are simultaneously at the point of greatest piety and greatest impiety."[29] I suggest further that even as commentary, that is, even when it identifies itself as textual facilitator and scriptural mediator, midrash threatens to overwhelm its fidelity to the text with innovation. The rabbis were often of the Devil's party, and I think they knew it.

The rabbinic resistance to closure does not mean radical indeterminacy and contingency. It is always balanced by an implicit belief in the authority of Scripture. Indeed, keeping the text open was seen as the most effective way to guarantee the continued renewal of biblical authority. The first-generation Babylonian amorah Rab insisted that a rabbi had to prove his abilities as a legal scholar and biblical reader by arguing convincingly for the ritual purity of a biblically unclean reptile (Babylonian Tractate Sanhedrin 17a). The only way to prove oneself worthy of interpreting the Bible, in his view, was by demonstrating an ability to contradict it, to disprove it with its own words and arguments. But what would stop this rabbi, having apparently proved himself a master of the text, from insisting that this interpretation was correct *in practice*, thereby permitting the consumption and use of a creature expressly prohibited in Scripture? The Talmud does not even address this concern, but statements like Rab's serve to illustrate the dynamic tension produced by the posture the rabbis took in their tasks as biblical mediators. Readers of *Paradise Lost* have posed a similar question to Milton's text: if the poet has so successfully represented the fallen, rebellious perspective of a defeated Satan in the first two books of the poem, how can we possibly trust the subsequent rendition of the Celestial Dialogue, the encounters between Raphael and the first couple, and the attempts at comfort by various heavenly visitors after the Fall? How can Milton play both parts, arguing for the purity of the unclean serpent out of one side of his mouth, and for its impurity out of the other?

The tension between freedom and restraint in midrash, this agon of invention and textual fidelity, anticipates the conflict of free will and responsibility that Milton thematizes in the Celestial Dialogue. Milton allows the contradictions suggested in the Father's proleptic account of the Fall to rankle the reader. It is the very literariness of the poet's presentation of this problem and its resolution in a grand *imitatio Dei* (which itself refers back to an anthropomorphic *imitatio hominis*) that makes a case for a creative approach to the faithful reading of biblical (and divine) authority. Midrashic creativity is a version of this antifundamentalist approach to the text, where responsibility to the text is always balanced by an interpretive freedom. Midrash provides a model for the *ethics* of interpretation that I seek to discover in Milton's text as well.

While Milton's theory of divine accommodation insists that the anthropomorphisms and anthropopathisms of the Bible are not simply images that need to be understood symbolically or metaphorically, it is nevertheless also true that Milton is aware of the inadequacies of human language and human thought fully to perceive the Divine nature. Drawing on the work of the twentieth-century theologian Austin Farrer, Margarita Stocker has shown how language is both the instrument and limitation of human knowledge. But this similarity between theodicy and literary creation also suggests that imagination and control in literature are analogies for their combination in theodicy itself.[30] Each textual transition, change of course, or narrative shift functions to instruct the reader by temporarily undermining her or his confidence in translating landscape into character, character into concept, action into statement, and so on. The kind of theodicy produced in this heterogeneous discursive mode is predicated on a narrative didacticism that does not yield a set of theological principles so much as an act of reading that is itself an enactment of the text's theology.

THE DIVINE PROTAGONISTS

AS MILTON DESCRIBES the scene in heaven, the reader becomes aware of the drastic change in diction and rhetoric from the previous books, a change first noticeable in what the epic voice does not do rather than in what it does. Almost immediately following the invocation, the narrator presents himself with the opportunity to launch into one of his epic similes, so brilliantly accomplished earlier in the poem: "About him all the Sanctities of Heaven / Stood thick as . . ." (60–61). But, instead of surrounding the Father with a cluster of similes and metaphors, the narratives in miniature that we had come to expect, the poet virtually inverts the master trope with the single-word comparison "Stars." Here, a transcendental phenomenon has been naturalized, whereas in book 1, for instance, the physicality of Satan's shield had been famously abstracted by its comparison to the dynamics of vision embodied in Galileo's telescope. Indeed, one might say that the "optic glass" of 1.288 has now finally "descr[ied]" the heavenly bodies it sought as they orbit around God. The secondary layer of narrative implicit in the epic similes is replaced by a network of significations that operate thematically. The sanctities of heaven—itself a metonymic term whereby the angelic host is represented by its quality of holiness—stand as thick as the natural presence of stars in the sky. The operation of this simile on the one hand suggests a physicality to an otherwise completely abstract conception of the angels, and on the other hand attributes at least the potential for a metaphysical rendition of the stars. Put another way, this first simile of book 3 exemplifies an essential aspect of Milton's cosmology (and theology), i.e., his monism.

After a grand tableau of the entire universe—the two first parents in blissful solitude, Satan coasting the wall of heaven—God, "from his prospect high / Wherein past, present, future he beholds" (3.77–78), speaks for the first time in the epic, with unimpeachable foresight. Readers have found the ensuing speech objectionable because, by leaving no room for the possibility of a different outcome, God necessarily vitiates his attempt to justify his condemnation of humankind for falling. Man and woman may have been created "Sufficient to have stood, though free to fall" (99), but de facto their sufficiency was (or will be, in the time frame of the speech) *insufficient*, since God already predicts the Fall. Taken on its own, this speech does beg these theological questions, but, as Helen Gardner has remarked, "There is a fundamental absurdity in making God a theologian."[31] It is a mistake to judge Milton's (or God's) success in justifying his ways based solely on this speech.

What bothers many readers of God's first speech is its tone, even more, perhaps, than its arguably conflicted theology.[32] Stanley Fish's characterization of this speech's "calm tonelessness" or "unobtrusive" style is strangely inappropriate to an exclamation like "whose fault? / Whose bit his own? ingrate, he had of mee / All he could have" (96–98).[33] Indeed, the abundance of rhetorical questions in this first speech rings with resentment and accusation.[34] If we discover pain and anguish in the tone of the Father, we need not explain away these apparently inappropriate feelings by attributing them to a fallen readership. Rather, we should investigate the anger *as it has been represented* by a poet also interrogating a view of God wherein a convincing theodicy seems quite unobtainable. The accommodated representation of God necessarily implies an epic character upon whom struggle and anguish will always threaten to encroach. God is hardly "playing to the gallery of his auditors, the Son and the unfallen angels," as one critic has put it.[35] By writing through God, Milton seeks to convince not only his readers but also himself; and if we assume that there is an element of the poet in each of his characters, then there will be times when it appears to the reader that God is trying to convince himself![36]

God begins by wresting the argument of necessity from those who would claim the incommensurability of foreknowledge and free choice: "what praise could they receive? . . . had serv'd necessity, / Not mee" (3.106, 110–11). That is, rather than God's foreknowledge necessitating the Fall, man must be free of the necessity of obedience so that he may be credited with obeying of his own will. This co-optation of the rhetoric of necessity can be effective, but it also poses the danger of slippage, of being controlled by that language (and its deterministic implications) rather than having control over it. The threat of determinism raised in the argument finds its parallel in the potential determinism in the medium of language itself—a kind of theological nominalism. This rhetorical slippage corresponds to a temporal peculiarity in the collapse of tenses several lines later:

> So without least impulse or shadow of Fate,
> Or aught by me immutably foreseen,
> They trespass, Authors to themselves in all
> Both what they judge and what they choose; for so
> I form'd them free, and free they must remain,
> Till they enthrall themselves: I else must change
> Thir nature, and revoke the high Decree
> Unchangeable, Eternal, which ordain'd
> Thir freedom: they themselves ordain'd thir fall. (3.120–28)

THE FATHER FIRST speaks of the Fall as an event in the process of occurring:

"They trespass . . . Both what they judge and what they choose." Next, he projects it into the future, "free they must remain, / Till they enthrall themselves." Most abruptly, by the end of the passage, God portrays the Fall as an event of the past, a foregone conclusion: "they themselves ordain'd thir fall." The prevalent reading of this temporal elision argues that Milton herein grammatically represents the synchronic omniscience of divine perspective.[37] We know from the introduction to this speech, after all, that God speaks "from his prospect high, / Wherein past, present, future he beholds" (77–78). I suggest, however, that the necessary (grammatical) temporality of Milton's chosen narrative form conflicts with the eternal present of God's plan not in any direct attempt to represent the experience of foreknowledge but rather as a rhetorical mimesis of the very conflict experienced by the poet in his struggle with the apparent contradictions between the potential determinism of divine foreknowledge and the essential voluntarism of human free will. What may have been felt initially by the poet as a potential weakness in a vignette that is meant to transcend time—the grammatical necessity of verb tenses—is turned into an opportunity to explore and express the poetic impossibility of fully achieving that transcendence. Do we go too far in calling this a grammatical *felix culpa?* Perhaps. Yet if we sense a divine anxiety in these lines, it does have the same contours as the anxiety felt by Milton, who may be worrying that the traditional scholastic modes of explanation for this difficult matter are not wholly satisfying.

A DIALOGUE "NOT IN HEAVEN"

FURTHER TO INFLECT our reading of the doctrinal agon that motivates these opening speeches, I turn back to the rabbis. The struggle with (and for) the divinely authorized text is figured in a notorious story of the debate between R. Eliezer and the sages over the ritual purity of the oven of Akhnai.[38] R. Eliezer claimed that it was pure, and the sages insisted that it was impure:

> On the day [that he heard the sages' decision] R. Eliezer replied with every possible refutation in the world, but the sages did not accept them from him. He said to them, "If the law is as I say, this carob tree will prove it." The carob tree was uprooted from its place [and replaced] one hundred cubits [away]. Some say it was four hundred cubits. They responded to him, "One does not bring proof from a carob tree." He retorted, "If the law is as I say,

the water channel will prove it." The water channel reversed its direction [and began to flow the other way]. They said, "One does not bring proof from a water channel." Again he replied, "If the law is as I say, the walls of the study house will prove it." The walls of the house of study tilted to fall, and R. Yehoshua prevented them by saying, "If wise students are opposing each other in the name of the law, what good is it to you [to meddle]?" They did not fall out of honor for R. Yehoshua, and they did not straighten out of honor for R. Eliezer. And they continued to balance precariously [to this day]. Once more he responded, "If the law is as I say, the heavens will prove it." A voice went out from heaven and said, "How can you compete with R. Eliezer, whom the rules follow in all cases." R. Yehoshua rose to his feet and said, "It is not in heaven" (Deut. 30:12). What does "it is not in heaven" mean? R. Yermiah said, "Now that the Torah has been given from Sinai, we do not rule according to heavenly voices, since you wrote at Sinai, 'Follow majority opinion' (Exod. 23:2)." R. Natan found Elijah [the prophet] and asked him, "What was the Holy One Blessed be He doing at that moment?" He replied, "[God was] laughing and saying, 'My children have defeated me, my children have defeated me.'"[39]

WHILE IT DOES NOT serve as evidence for the absolute license the rabbis might have claimed for their interpretive methods, and while it by no means justifies free play as the midrashic mode, the legend is noteworthy as yet another example of Scripture being used to defeat, as it were, a divine pronouncement. Just as R. Ishmael's revision of the hammer and stone analogy in Jeremiah seemed to reverse the terms, thereby asserting midrashic authority in the very process of its enactment, so, too, here R. Yehoshua's citation of the biblical statement "It is not in heaven" functions as a means to undermine heavenly authority in favor of the authority of the rabbinic interpretive community, understood as the rule of the majority—which is *also* a principle authorized by scriptural prooftext. In its original context the statement "It is not in heaven" speaks to the theme of accessibility:

> For this commandment which I command to you today is not hidden from you, nor is it far. It is not in heaven, so that you will say, Who will go up to the heavens and take it for us so that we might hear it and perform it. Nor is it over the sea, so that you will say, Who will cross the sea and take it for us so that we might hear it and perform it. For this matter is close to you, in your mouth and in your heart, that you might perform it. (Deuteronomy 30:11–14)

BY CITING THIS PASSAGE, R. Yehoshua represents the accessibility of God's ways in terms of its *in*accessibility to the divine author. When midrash makes Scripture meaningful, fragmenting and reassembling its basic components, it must usurp divine intention. But it can only claim to do so within the framework of an appeal to a community of interpreters. This rabbinic legend dramatically stages a conflict between fundamental literalism (R. Eliezer's position, which, ironically, is the more lenient one in this particular instance) and an ever renewing standard of community relevance (grounded in the principle of majority rule). By situating *this* counsel, whose immediate application is rather narrow but whose larger implications reach to the very limits of human-divine relations, very deliberately "not in heaven" yet necessarily for the sake of heaven, the rabbinic text has enjoined its community of readers to engage in a fully ethical relationship among themselves and with the biblical text.

The object of midrash following the destruction of the Temple, and the accompanying sense of absolute alienation from the divine as it had been felt by the descendants of the Temple cult, was to engage the text and make *it* speak to Israel in the same way that God and the prophets had spoken before. This struggle for interpretation sought a textual malleability rather than a referentless indeterminacy.[40] Whatever authority had resided in the pronouncements issuing from the Temple and prophets was now taken over by the community of rabbinic interpreters. The possibility of multiple interpretations of Scripture became desirable specifically to justify that transfer of authority. Different views were tolerated, even encouraged, because authority did not reside in individual pronouncements but rather in the rabbis generally as mediators of the text, forever bringing their interpretations and applications up to date. Daniel Boyarin has called this phenomenon "canonized dissensus."[41]

In Milton's interpretive agon this dissensus is dramatized by an interlocutor to the Father's stern warnings, his only begotten Son, whose presence embellishes this notion of discursive struggle. It has been argued, by those who wish to see the Father as a coercive hypocrite, that Milton has provided an excessively negative portrayal of the Father in order to heighten the sense of compassion and grace attributed to the Son.[42] Indeed, this impression is partly attributable to the Son's first statement, "O Father, gracious was that word which clos'd / Thy sovran sentence, that Man should find grace" (144–45). The Son avers that the Father's graciousness resides only in the word that "closed" his long self-defense, suggesting that everything preceding it was not at all gracious. The too clever play on "gracious" and "grace" heightens the quick-witted quality of the Son's diction, in direct contrast to the agonistic grandiloquence of the Father. But does the Son's first speech operate "at his Father's expense, [tending] to confirm our incipient hostility towards God"? It seems to me that God's "brooding petulance" does not merely cast the Father in a negative oppositional light.[43] Rather, his brooding is also that of a reader troubled by the struggle for interpretation, of formulating a coherent theodical argument that does not ignore the potentially paralyzing conflict of freedom and foreknowledge.

In his capacity as interlocutor, the Son may in fact serve to mitigate the sense of anguish permitted to enter Milton's poem through the loud protestations of the Father. The Son warns that, through the success of Satan and the destruction of mankind, God's goodness and greatness "Be question'd and blasphem'd without defense" (166), but he has already anticipated and deflected this challenge with the celebrated chiasmus, "That be from thee far, / That far be from thee" (153–54). The Son's mediating role in presenting divine doctrine—he is called God's "dearest mediation" at line 226—corresponds to his own self-sacrificing accommodation into human corporeality to effect the redemption of humankind: on the one hand, the Son accommodates the doctrinal issues with which book 3 struggles by posing the theodical questions that Milton was working through in the composition of the epic; on the other hand, the central tenet of the literary theodicy—the redemption after the Fall—is achieved by the Son's physical self-accommodation and sacrifice.[44]

Moreover, in the roles that I am ascribing to the Father and the Son in book 3 we may actually discover an astonishing deviation. Although the Son (as the Mercy figure in traditional morality plays) assumes the role of advocate and intermediary for humankind, modifying the harsh judgments articulated by a transcendent Father (as the figure for Justice), in the dynamics of their representations here in book 3 they exchange places. The anguish in the Father's speech transforms him into a figure for the torment experienced by the poet, thereby narrowing the distance between the Father and fallen humanity. Similarly, the imperturbable faith expressed by the Son raises his position to a transcendent, superhuman height that inevitably eludes the reader.[45]

BAD WINE OR SOUR GRAPES?

MILTON LOOKED TO three biblical precedents for his representation of divine disputation over the fate of humankind: in Genesis 18 Abraham tries to convince God not to destroy Sodom; in Exodus 32 Moses seeks to appease God following Israel's sin of the Golden Calf; and in Numbers 14 Moses also works to defend Israel from divine destruction after the people have sinned by heeding the words of the ten spies. The presence of this "scriptural substratum," rather than vindicating the theology and style of the Celestial Dialogue,[46] functions as an interrogation of those biblical subtexts, opening up difficulties and inconsistencies within them. Milton, and the rabbis before him, saw in these moments the opportunity for a powerful questioning of God's just nature. Pesiqta de Rab Kahana, a midrashic collection that probably dates from the early sixth century *c.e.*, reports several homilies that grow out of the dialogue between Moses and God in Exodus 32. Like Milton, the rabbis were greatly intrigued by what seems to be a biblically condoned theomachy: God begins the conversation with the expressed intent of destroying the Israelites. It is only Moses's intervention that saves the Israelites from total destruction: in verse 32, where Moses remarkably demands that if God does not pardon the Israelites, "blot me . . . out of thy book which thou hast written." The rabbis turn to the king-parable for an explication of this episode:

R. Berakhiah, in the name of R. Levi, [told the following parable]: A king had a vineyard that he leased to a tenant. When the vineyard produced good wine, [the king] would say, "How excellent is the wine of my vineyard!" But when it produced poor wine [the king] would say, "How terrible is my tenant's wine!" The tenant said to him, "My Lord, the king, when the vineyard produces good wine you call it the wine of your vineyard, but when it produces poor wine you call it my tenant's wine. Yet, whether it is good or bad, the wine is yours!" In a like manner, God originally said to Moses, "Come now therefore, and I will send thee unto Pharaoh, that thou mayest bring forth *My* people, the children of Israel, out of Egypt" (Exod. 3:10). But when [the Israelites] performed this act [i.e., the sin of the Golden Calf], what did God say? "Go, get thee down; for *thy* people have dealt corruptly" (Exod. 32:7). Moses replied to the Holy One Blessed be He, "Master of the universe, when [the Israelites] sin, they are mine, but when they are innocent they are yours! Do they not belong to you, whether they are sinful or innocent? As it is written, 'They are *Thy* people, and *Thine* inheritance' (Deut. 9:29), 'Do not destroy *Thy* people, and *Thine* inheritance' (Deut. 9:26), 'Lord, why doth Thy wrath wax hot against *Thy* people?' (Exod. 32:11). Why would you destroy *your* people?"

R. Simon added, "Moses did not stop speaking affectionately of [the Is-raelites] until [God] called them 'My people': "And the Lord repented of the evil which He said He would do unto *His* people" (Exod. 32:14)." (Nahamu 9, emphasis added)

THE RABBIS READ Moses's deliberate choice of possessive pronouns—to whom do the Children of Israel really belong?—as a contentious reminder that *God's* sour grapes have produced the bad wine. What I find most re-markable about this midrash, and what it helps me to see in Milton's poem, is the stance the rabbis give to Moses vis-à-vis divine authority and, in turn, the stance the rabbis assume vis-à-vis the biblical text. The midrash fore-grounds the two related matters of dialogue and accountability by represent-ing Moses as playing an essential role in God's acknowledgment of his own responsibilities toward the Israelites. Any possible sense of divine mercy as inscrutable mystery is eliminated by this very human representation of God being cajoled into meeting his obligations. The use of the king-parable may function alternatively to lend some dignity to an analysis that otherwise threatens to characterize God as a rash figurehead, or precisely to stress that rashness, as the contemporary audience would have undoubtedly compared this example to their experiences with non-Jewish political authorities. In ei-ther case, the rabbis seem to be aware of their representation of God as un-reasonable, in need of a human rejoinder. The biblical text that occasioned the homily already contained that suggestion, but, rather than seeking out ways to cast God in a more equitable light, the rabbis exaggerate God's im-petuousness and, in so doing, emphasize the ethical importance of human-divine dialogue.

The delicate balance between reverence and opposition that Moses main-tains in this homiletic supplement to the narrative is analogous to the stance the rabbis take toward the Bible. Just as Moses calls attention to God's knee-jerk decision to destroy the Israelites, so too the rabbis draw our attention to their embellishment of a trait that we might not wish to associate with an omnipotent, omniscient, and most of all, just God. This is an ethical con-frontation with the Bible, a stance of human engagement, a dialogue with the divine realm for the sake of human community. Milton makes use of the same strategy in his epic depiction of God. How can we not read God's cry of "ingrate" as Milton's own version of sour grapes? By representing the Fa-ther as initially unreasonable, the poet gives himself room to explore the full ethical and interpretive implications of his literary theodicy. In both midrash and *Paradise Lost* unflattering depictions of God as earthly tyrant are exploited for their value in shifting the responsibility of interpretation (and by extension, human agency) to the reader.[47]

Traditional readings of these biblical debates understand them as elements in the ongoing training and testing of the paradigmatic leaders of Israel. These didactic disputations apply directly to the accommodative role played by the Son in the Celestial Dialogue: the poet's presence in the character of the Son undergoes a similar kind of instruction in the complementary association between the justice for which the Father stands—"Die hee or Justice must"—and the mercy for which the Son argues. The propaedeutics described in the biblical source texts, which are in turn revised in the Celestial Dialogue, necessitate an accommodative encounter between God and Abraham, Moses, and the Son. Given the association that the poem implicitly draws between Abraham and Moses and the Son, the strange deviation that I described earlier, in which the Father became allied with the human audience and the Son was thrust out of epistemological reach, is now remedied, at least for the time being. The reader may now compare his or her interpretive experience with that of the Son, who serves as anagogic mediator between fallen humanity and transcendent divinity.

A further interpretive dynamic is at work here, as well, and is evident in Milton's chronological usurpations of the three biblical episodes alluded to in book 3. Milton posits a typological relationship between the biblical patriarchs and the Son. Yet this typology reverses the Christian trope that had transformed the Hebrew Bible into the Old Testament. The standard typological relation between the Old and the New Testaments envisions the various Old Testament characters—Adam, Abraham, Joseph, Moses, Elijah, the suffering servant—as types for the true divine antitype, Christ, the Son of God. In Milton's presentation of the Celestial Dialogue, however, the Son prefigures the subsequent mortal interlocutors, Abraham and Moses; book 3's dialogue, after all, is supposed to have occurred long before either Abraham or Moses had their debates with God. This reversal serves at least two purposes: first, it inserts Milton, the poetic narrator of this discussion between the Father and the Son, prior to the biblical intertexts, thereby claiming the authority of precedence. Second, it retroactively characterizes the behavior of Abraham and Moses as an imitatio Christi, in which these two leaders of Israel have learned to deal with God from their divine precedent. The Son functions as both the type and the antitype: he prefigures Abraham's and Moses' behavior, serving as type. But he only plays this role because he is the fulfillment of Abraham's and Moses' Old Testament example. This typological indeterminacy is precisely what allows the poet to insert himself into its otherwise closed economy. Milton and his fit audience are charged to perform the imitatio Christi, which is itself only understandable as an imitation of fallen human behavior.

"ACCOUNT MEE MAN"

THOUGH THE FATHER insists upon his fatal view of human culpability, he leaves some room for the reassertion of human agency:

> Man shall not quite be lost, but sav'd who will,
> Yet not of will in him, but grace in me
> Freely voutsaf't; once more I will renew
> His lapsed powers, though forfeit and enthrall'd
> By sin to foul exorbitant desires;
> Upheld by me, yet once more he shall stand
> On even ground against his mortal foe,
> By me upheld, that he may know how frail
> His fall'n condition is, and to me owe
> All his deliv'rance, and to none but me. (3.173–82)

AS IN THE EARLIER conflation of verb tenses, this statement suggests further divine anxiety in the contradiction between the assertion of human agency by the relative pronoun as subject—"but sav'd who will"—and the ongoing references to human dependency through the indirect objective pronoun— "not of will in him, but grace in me." A potential resolution to this contradiction is to read the freedom to choose described by the Father as contingent upon man's obedience to the *godly* inclinations instilled within him: by fulfilling that potential man becomes free and creative. The Father's statement actually provides the initial motivation for the imitation of humanity's innate divinity by formulating the rhetorical terms in which it must transpire. This rhetorical formulation offers yet another parallel between midrash and Milton's poem; both texts offer a blueprint for a *human* resolution formulated as an imitatio dei. Just as the rabbis developed their imagined dialogue between Moses and God out of the seemingly innocuous shift in possessive pronouns, so too God's heavy repetition of the objective pronoun *me* within the larger sentence in which he appears as the subjective *I* initiates a developing understanding of freedom and responsibility elaborated by the poem. The subjective *I*'s ability to perceive itself as the objective *me*, the ego's sense of itself as object as well as subject, marks the necessary condition for a full awareness of the interrelation between freedom and responsibility.[48] Indeed, Milton's notorious use of Latinate syntax allows for even further precision in our reading of these pronouns. The Father articulates the proper interdependence of freedom and responsibility through his chiastic use of the objective pronoun as an ablative of agent: "Upheld by me . . . By me upheld." Even in his acknowledgment of objective responsibility the Father avers his freedom and agency.

When the Son utters his speech of voluntary self-sacrifice, he deliberately echoes the Father's insistent use of the word *me*, as if to emphasize his awareness of the importance of this rhetorical scheme:

> Behold mee, then, mee for him, life for life
> I offer, on mee let thine anger fall;
> Account mee man; I for his sake will leave
> Thy bosom, and this glory next to thee
> Freely put off, and for him lastly die
> Well pleas'd, on me let Death wreck all his rage;
> Under his gloomy power I shall not long
> Lie vanquisht; thou has giv'n me to possess
> Life in myself for ever, by thee I live,
> Though now to Death I yield. (236–45)

THE SON HEARS the concept of freely undertaken responsibility in his Father's repetition of *me* and imitates it as he assumes that responsibility. By presenting himself as the grammatical object of sacrifice and redemption— "Behold mee" and "on mee let thine anger fall"—the Son accommodates the complementary elements of freedom and responsibility in the deceptively simple language by which Milton accommodates the great argument of his poem. Just as subject and object interact in these graceful lines—"Account mee man; I for his sake will leave / Thy bosom"—the freedom associated with subjectivity and the responsibility inherent in seeing oneself as object intertwine.

In these canny grammatical distinctions and, more specifically, in his resistance to immediate resolution of the clash between a subjective and an objective perspective, Milton anticipates elements of the twentieth-century discourse in ethics and moral philosophy. Thomas Nagel emphasizes the need to recognize an intrinsic contradiction within basic terms of ethical argument:

> At the moment when we see ourselves from outside as bits of the world, two things happen: we are no longer satisfied in action with anything less than intervention in the world from outside; and we see clearly that this makes no sense. The very capacity that is the source of the trouble—our capacity to view ourselves from outside—encourages our aspirations of autonomy by giving us the sense that we ought to be able to encompass ourselves completely, and thus become the absolute source of what we do.[49]

NAGEL OFFERS AS A working solution to this contradiction what he calls the blind spot, an "*essentially incomplete objective view*, or *incomplete view* for short."[50] In other words, in order to achieve any semblance of agency in the world, one must act as a free subject who is at all times aware of imperceptible—because internal—limitations conditioned by one's position as object.[51] Nagel offers this analysis not as a *solution* to the problem but rather as an *acknowledgment* of it. Milton's version of this acknowledgment occurs within the dialogue between the Father and the Son, where the relation between human agency and "eternal providence" is raised interrogatively. Rather than figuring the Son's self-sacrifice as an impenetrable theological mystery, Milton represents it as the ethical outcome of dialogue and engagement. The Son will "freely put off" his Father's glory and "lie vanquisht" under the "gloomy power" of death, temporarily acceding to the incomplete view of human mortality. But it is precisely through his willing acceptance of this limitation that he gains for himself—and grants to humanity—the power of divinely authorized agency. The Son serves as the Father's interlocutor, and his stance with respect to the Father's initial statement of human responsibility enhances the poem's sense of accountability: "Account mee man." This sacrifice through the assertion of personal responsibility not only ensures the existence of God's created universe. It also establishes the subsequent pattern for human behavior—in the poem, but also for the reader—in which imitation of this self-sacrifice confirms man's "human face divine" (3.44). The Son is indeed central to Milton's theology, but ultimately the poem is about humanity and its salvation. The Son's behavior is important primarily as an ethical model for human activity and agency, a model that combines the freedom of subjectivity and the responsibility of objectivity.

In the next several books of the epic there follow a number of intermediary instances of the assumption of responsibility via this preestablished rhetorical scheme. Each case participates in the poetic development of Milton's theodicy, stressing especially the necessity of engagement. In 6.810–823 the Son addresses the armies of loyal angels as he readies himself to defeat Lucifer's followers:

> . . . stand only and behold
> God's indignation on these Godless pour'd
> By mee, not you but mee they have despis'd,
> Yet envied; against mee is all thir rage,
> Because the Father, t'whom in Heav'n supreme
> Kingdom and Power and Glory appertains,
> Hath honour'd me according to his will.
> Therefore to mee thir doom he hath assign'd;
> That they may have thir wish, to try with mee
> In Battle which the stronger proves, they all,
> Or I alone against them, since by strength
> They measure all, of other excellence
> Not emulous, nor care who them excels;
> Nor other strife with them do I voutsafe.

THE SON FORMULATES his active role in terms of his Father's ablative of agent, "behold / God's indignation on these godless poured / By mee." The assumption of responsibility reaches in two directions here. First, the Son relieves the loyal angels of their battle duties, insisting "not you but mee [the rebel angels] have despised." Second, he takes on the burden of the Father's role by arguing that, since the rebellion was prompted by his elevation into prominence, it falls to him to deal with those angels who were unhappy that the Father "Hath honour'd me according to his will." The rhetorical pattern first established in the earlier books now becomes charged with an economy of substitution that complements the earlier exchange offered by the Son when he volunteered his life for humankind's. This new economy stipulates that the Son's active role in the defeat of sinful rebellion—not simply angelic, but also human—stems from the earliest articulation of the divine blueprints in which the Son was initially held forth as the supreme manifestation of God's will. Milton's monism fully resides within the first person singular objective pronoun, directly contradicting the chaotic plurality of the Satanic worldview: "Number to this day's work is not ordain'd/ Nor multitude" (809–10).

In addition to offering intermediate instances of the evolution of the "me, me, me" *ploce* (the repetition of a word whose meaning evolves with each subsequent repetition), the poem provides counterexamples that deploy the trope of singularity and the responsibility of freedom. Satan's temptation of Eve proposes more than one compelling argument to the reader, as well as to Milton's Eve, for disobeying the divine decree in order to gain greater knowledge. His temptation's power to compel is never fully mitigated by what must be a constant awareness on the part of the reader that Satan misleads. The serpent addresses precisely the human aspiration for greatness that stems from humanity's resemblance to the divine. For a poet such as Milton, attempting to emulate the divine acts of creation and self-revelation, the arguments offered by Satan must have had more than a little force to them. The point of the balanced claim "sufficient to have stood, / Though free to fall" is that there be approximately equivalent weight of argument and persuasion given to the rhetoric for obeying and the rhetoric for disobeying. One way that Milton manages to maintain something like the fiction of a balance is through a satanic deployment of the topos whose trajectory we have been following. As Eve converses with the serpent in front of the forbidden tree, he slyly remarks:

> Queen of the Universe, do not believe
> Those rigid threats of Death; ye shall not Die:
> How should ye? by the Fruit? it gives you Life
> To Knowledge: By the Threat'ner? look on mee,
> Mee who have touch'd and tasted, yet both live,
> And life more perfet have attain'd than Fate
> Meant mee, by vent'ring higher than my Lot. (9.684–90)

SATAN INVOKES ARGUMENTS concerning necessity ("Fate") and chance ("my Lot") to encourage Eve to conceive of herself as having absolute freedom, that is, freedom from any sense of responsibility or accountability to divine precepts or even to Adam. Satan ingeniously incorporates the rhetoric of the freedom and responsibility topos, repeating the "mee" of objective responsibility several times and imparting to it his own fallen Satanic spin. The difference between Satan's use of this rhetorical scheme and that of the Son is slight but essential. When Satan says "look on mee, / Mee who have touch'd and tasted," he replaces the personal nominative *I* with the relative nominative *who*, severing the subject-object connection established by the Father and the Son. This seemingly minor modification helps to undermine the ongoing association between freedom and responsibility that depends on the complementarity of *I* and *me* and fully enables the temptation that succeeds in convincing Eve to abdicate her responsibilities to Adam, to God, and to herself. In Nagel's terms, Satan covers the blind spot, convincing Eve that she *can* act with complete autonomy and without any sense of the incompleteness of her subjective view.

What this blind spot hides, and, more important, what it reveals, becomes the subject of poem's recriminating vision of Adam and Eve the morning after their Fall:

> Soon as the force of that fallacious Fruit,
> That with exhilirating vapor bland
> About thir spirits had play'd, and inmost powers
> Made err, was now exhal'd, and grosser sleep
> Bred of unkindly fumes, with conscious dreams
> Encumber'd, now had left them, up they rose
> As from unrest, and each the other viewing,
> *Soon found thir Eyes how op'n'd, and thir minds*
> *How dark'n'd; innocence, that as a veil*
> *Had shadow'd them from knowing ill, was gone,*
> Just confidence, and native righteousness,
> And honor from about them, naked left
> To guilty shame: hee cover'd, but his Robe
> Uncover'd more. (9.1046–59, emphasis added)

MILTON COMPARES THE lost innocence to a "veil" that protected them from knowing evil, blinding them precisely to allow them to interact with each other and with God. Now that this blind spot has been removed, the first two humans find themselves at a loss. Rather than revealing a newly acquired ability to act, independent of divine will, the first hours following the Fall are characterized by a distinctive *loss* of agency on the part of Adam and Eve. Whereas yesterday Eve and Adam both awoke eager to tend to the garden, this morning finds neither of them willing to take any action, let alone confer with each other as to what to do. The recuperative process that must begin involves a resumption of agency made more difficult by the lifting of the veil, the removal of the blind spot.

The poem turns to investigate the satanic degradation of agency in book 10. As Satan recounts to his fallen companions the initial divine repercussions of the Fall, he tells of the curse that was uttered on the head of the serpent for having participated in humanity's corruption:

> True is, mee also he hath judg'd, or rather
> Mee not, but the brute Serpent in whose shape
> Man I deceiv'd: that which to mee belongs,
> Is enmity, which he will put between
> Mee and Mankind. (494–98)

TYPICALLY CONVOLUTED IN satanic syntax, the statement begins with what looks to be a full assumption of the blame and its punishment by Satan. By the time we reach the second line, however, Satan completely reverses the statement's implication—"Mee not, but the brute serpent." Indeed, Satan's words seem simultaneously to conflate and to distinguish between himself and the serpent form that he assumed, and it thereby becomes almost impossible to identify the locus of personal responsibility in the single epic figure of Satan. This impossibility is especially noteworthy as it contradicts Satan's main purpose in narrating his adventure: self-promotion. The narrative itself produces a fitting conclusion to this satanic inversion of the literary representation of freedom and responsibility. Immediately following Satan's speech he hears, "On all sides, from innumerable tongues / A dismal universal hiss, the sound / Of public scorn" (507–9), as all the fallen angels, and Satan himself, are turned into a mass of serpents, "in the shape he sinn'd, / According to his doom" (516–17). Since Satan confuses the boundaries between himself and the instrument of corruption, thereby muddying the issue of responsibility through the "me, me, me" topos, the form of his punishment, a Miltonic version of Dante's *contrappasso*, resolves that confusion.[52] Compelled to resume the shape in which he sinned, Satan physically contradicts his "mee not, but the brute Serpent"; what is more, his inability to articulate language functions as just recompense for his corruption of language in the seduction of Eve. All that Satan can utter is an incomprehensible, animalistic hiss.

The culmination of the thematic elaboration of this object/subject trope transpires within the gradual coming to awareness of the postlapsarian couple. As Adam and Eve each work through the full implications of their fall, they also invoke the rhetoric of freedom and responsibility set forth in book 3. Adam's first real complaint occurs near the end of book 10.

> Who of all Ages to succeed, but feeling
> The evil on him brought by me, will curse
> My Head; Ill fare our Ancestor impure,
> For this we may thank *Adam*; but his thanks
> Shall be the execration; so besides
> Mine own that bide upon me, all from mee
> Shall with a fierce reflux on mee redound,
> On mee as on thir natural centre light
> Heavy, though in thir place. O fleeting joys
> Of Paradise, dear bought with lasting woes!
> Did I request thee, Maker, from my Clay
> To mould me Man, did I solicit thee
> From darkness to promote me, or here place
> In this delicious Garden? as my Will
> Concurr'd not to my being, it were but right
> And equal to reduce me to my dust,
> Desirous to resign, and render back
> All I receiv'd, unable to perform
> Thy terms too hard, by which I was to hold
> The good I sought not. (10.733–52)

RESORTING TO THE SAME *diaphora* of *me* that constituted the Son's assumption of the responsibility for human fallibility, Adam talks himself through a series of positions essential to a theodical resolution of the issues he is now forced to confront. To Adam's newly fallen mind, God's justice indeed appears inexplicable. The future seems pointless, life useless. Adam's incorporation of first-person pronouns indicates that at this early stage he is capable only of seeing himself as object, as something created without his consent, acted upon against his will, scorned by future generations. Like the Father in book 3, Adam describes his responsibility with the ablative of agent: "The evil on him brought by me." The difference for Adam is that he understands his agency as capable only of evil. When he does refer to himself by the first person subjective pronoun, it is either to reject agency and independence:

"Did I request thee, Maker, from my Clay / To mould me Man, did I solicit thee / From darkness to promote me"; or it is to describe a debt owed: "Desirous to resign, and render back / All I receiv'd, unable to perform / Thy terms too hard, by which I was to hold / The good I sought not." Adam has learned a sense of responsibility, but it is still a limited one, negatively defined, unmitigated by the subjectivity of freedom. This speech, characterized by relentless self-examination, would not have been possible in a prelapsarian world, where Adam's thoughts in their most abstract turned to the movement and purpose of the heavenly bodies or the sexual practices of angels. Here, for the first time, Adam takes a long hard look at his own position in a created world, with rules instituted externally by a supreme deity; and Milton takes full advantage of this moment to formulate questions of responsibility and freedom that have been implicit from the very first lines of the poem.

As powerful and compelling as Satan may have been earlier in the epic, none of his speeches match this long lament in its honest and relentless pathos. Satan moves us because of the sheer power of his willful antagonism, even when it completely blinds him: "We know no time when we were not as now." (5.859). Adam moves us because his plight sounds so familiar, so contemporary. His speech works through the desire for death, as Adam sounds like Hamlet, longing to "sleep secure," perchance to dream.

> But say
> That Death be not one stroke, as I suppos'd,
> Bereaving sense, but endless misery
> From this day onward, which I feel begun
> Both in me, and without me, and so last
> To perpetuity. (10.808–13)

AYE, THERE'S THE RUB! Concern over the perpetuity of death and the multi-generational impact of the Fall directly connects Adam's lament to the Son's speech in book 3. Adam feels at the very core of his being the hopelessness that, merely *in potentia*, prompted the Son to take on the sins of humanity.

> all my evasions vain
> And reasonings, though through Mazes, lead me still
> But to my own conviction: first and last

On mee, mee only, as the source and spring
Of all corruption, all the blame lights due;
So might the wrath. (10.808–34)

ADAM REPEATS the Son's refrain, echoing his "Behold mee then, mee for him, life for life," but without the triumphant salvation that accompanied the Son's self-sacrifice. Adam's vain evasions "through Mazes" recall the fallen angels "wand'ring mazes lost" (2.561) as they reasoned through "Fix'd Fate, Free will, Foreknowledge absolute" (2.560). Adam feels only despair—akin to, but not the same as, the "final misery" (2.563) of the fallen angels—because he has not heard the theodical patterning achieved by the narrative thus far and has lacked access to the full implications of this topos that lends structure and coherence to the poem. Even more crucial to the poem's theodicy, Adam has yet to reengage in dialogue with Eve. Perceiving himself as object, he has only begun to understand himself as subject.

The critical juncture of this theme rests in Eve's own version of the topos. The following speech at 10.924–36 serves as the key passage in Milton's narrative theodicy because Adam must *hear* Eve say this and recognize it as part of a larger pattern in which he participates.

While yet we live, scarce one short hour perhaps,
Between us two let there be peace, both joining,
As join'd in injuries, one enmity
Against a Foe by doom express assign'd us,
That cruel Serpent: On me exercise not
Thy hatred for this misery befall'n,
On me already lost, mee than thyself
More miserable; both have sinn'd, but thou
Against God only, I against God and thee,
And to the place of judgment will return,
There with my cries importune Heaven, that all
The sentence from this head remov'd may light
On me, sole cause to thee of all this woe,
Mee mee only just object of his ire.

DEPLOYING THE SAME structure of personal pronouns, Eve wrests Adam from the clutches of despair, reminding him of his responsibility to her and, even more powerfully, her responsibility to him, by accepting the full blame for the first transgression. Her self-incrimination, "mee than thy self / More miserable; both have sinn'd, but thou / Against God only, I against God and thee," powerfully combines subjectivity's freedom and objectivity's responsibility: her version of *me* serves as the object of comparison but also hides an unstated subjectivity that adumbrates Nagel's "incomplete view." "My misery," she reminds Adam, "takes on its deeper implications only in the context of my relations to you and to God." Eve's statement revises the notoriously masculinist description of the First Couple, "Hee for God only, shee for God in him" (4.299). Instead of rejecting this initial hierarchy outright, Eve uses it as an occasion to instruct Adam in the fuller implications of the ethics of dialogue, the engaged and embattled stance of theodicy. Indeed, her final acceptance of guilt, "Mee mee only just object of his ire," serves as the human revision of the Father's assertion in book 3 that man owes his deliverance "to none but me." Eve has assumed a stance of agency that dramatically appropriates and recreates in her own image God's terms of redemption. And Adam hears the linguistic pattern, finally recognizing the overall structure to the events and the nascent theodicy proposed in the poem. None of this patterning would have been possible had Milton not assumed the theomachic stance (the dialogic stance I am attributing to midrash, as well) in the Celestial Dialogue.[53]

"HUMAN FACE DIVINE"

THE RABBIS IMAGINED their own version of the heavenly counsel and meditated on the dynamics of engagement—human, angelic, and divine—in ways that further illuminate a reading of *Paradise Lost*:

"And the Lord said, 'Let us make man, etc.'" With whom did he consult? R. Yehoshua b. Levi said, "He consulted with the works of heaven and earth. It may be compared to a king who had two senators without whose approval he would do nothing." R. Samuel b. Nahman said, "He consulted with the creations of each day. It may be compared to a king who had a vice-regent without whose approval he would do nothing." R. Ami said, "He consulted with his own heart. It may be compared to a king who built a palace with the help of an architect. When he saw it, it did not please him. To whom could he complain beside the architect? Similarly, 'and it grieved him at his heart' (Gen. 6:6)." R. Yose said, "It is like a king who had business done through a middleman, and lost money. To whom could he complain except the middle-man? Similarly, 'and it grieved him at his heart.'" (8:3)

THE MIDRASH BEGINS with a more "Gnostic" (and therefore less normative) understanding of the plural verb form "let us make"; R. Yehoshua b. Levi and R. Samuel b. Nahman each try to locate a possible external interlocutor for this verb of apparent consultation. The rabbis cannot make the complete leap to a second (even lesser) divinity, as is the case in the Gnostic source texts.[54] Yet neither can they resist the notion that God discussed his plans for the creation of humanity with an outside agent. They begin the process of taming this potentially disruptive notion of external consultation by describing God's interlocutors as created entities, created, that is, by God—either "the works of heaven and earth" or "the creations of each day." This taming process, in which cosmologically challenging ideas are gradually mitigated, transpires within the finely crafted organization of the homily. The next two rabbis, R. Ami and R. Yose, have moved the heavenly dialogue entirely inward. God no longer seeks the advice of outside counsel; rather, he consults his own heart.

The midrash cannot fully contain and diffuse the more extreme interpretive energies of opposition suggested by the first two rabbis, however; what follows seems to be a rupturing of the theological containment by R. Ami and R. Yose:

> R. Berakhiah said, "When the Holy One Blessed be He came to create Adam, he foresaw that both the righteous and the wicked would come from him. He said, 'If I create him, the wicked will come from him. If I do not create him, how will the righteous come from him?' What did the Holy One Blessed be He do? He hid the ways of the wicked from his face, and became partners with his merciful attribute [*midath ha-rahamim*], and created him. As it is written, 'For the Lord knoweth the way of the righteous: but the way of the ungodly shall perish [*t'oved*]' (Ps. 1:6). What does perish [*t'oved*] mean? He hid [*ivdah*] it [the way of the ungodly] from before his face, and became partners with his merciful attribute, and created Adam." (8:4)

THE IDEA OF divine self-deception, itself a rather stunning rabbinic innovation, a version of Nagel's blind spot, demands to be understood in terms of the opposition and dialogic mediation portrayed in the earlier portion of the midrash. R. Berakhiah's imaginative account of God's willful self-blinding draws much of its homiletic power from the very fact that it reveals to the human audience precisely what God had to hide from himself. David Stern speculates that the image of a self-deceiving king in many rabbinic parables mirrors the rabbis'"own feelings of insecurity, their own self-conscious powerlessness in the world, and their anger and resentment at the earthly powers who controlled their thisworldly existence."[55] I suggest further that this interpretive paradox, which opposes humanity's full awareness of the potential for evil within itself to God's selective awareness of only the righteous, places the largest weight of responsibility squarely on the shoulders of the human community, created out of God's mercy. We have become the other party in this rabbinic version of the Celestial Dialogue, fully aware of our future (indeed, present) potential for evil and thus accepting of the burden of responsibility.

The final shift in this remarkable series of cosmogonical speculations occurs when the midrash turns the tables on any presumed interpretive imperative, i.e., the all-too-present sense of evil and the possible reasons for its existence. Instead of formulating a defense of God (theodicy), the midrash represents God as having to defend humanity from the angels' accusations (anthropodicy?):

> He created man with great deliberation, since he first created his nutritional needs, and then created him. The ministering angels said to the Holy One Blessed be He, "Master of the Universe, 'what is man, that thou art mindful of him? and the son of man, that thou visitest him?' (Ps. 8:5). Why did you go to all this trouble to create him?" He replied, "If so, 'All sheep and oxen' (Ps. 8:8), why were they created, 'the fowl of the air and the fish of the sea' (Ps. 8:9), why were they created? If a tower is filled with all kinds of good things, and there are no guests in it, what pleasure does the owner who filled it have?" They replied, "Master of the Universe, 'O Lord our Lord, how excellent is thy name in all the land' (Ps. 8:10). Do what pleases you!" (8:6)

WHEN READ ON its own, Psalm 8, which provides the intersecting verses for this aggadah, functions as a celebration of God's majesty, his divine royalty, *at the expense of humanity.* "What is man, that thou art mindful of him" can hardly be said to justify humanity's continued existence in the world. And yet, the rabbis chose precisely this psalm to formulate their self-justification; furthermore, they placed that justification in the mouth of the heavenly king. Just as Milton's representation of the Son's self-sacrifice achieves its fullest meaning not as a theological mystery but rather as an ethical imperative, this rich aggadah suggests that the rabbis were arguing for a similar mode of interlocution. God puts himself on the line, justifying the ways of the world to the angels. His agonistic stance, embattled with the angels, serves as a model to be emulated by the rabbis and, in turn, by the community to whom they addressed their homilies. In the end, humanity takes its place alongside God, as guests created to enjoy the fruits of creation. God's kingship is not erased but is complemented by a human community charged with assuming a similarly royal position in the universe. In Milton's poem, too, the kingship of God, which resonates so menacingly within the historical context of Milton's antiroyalism, has the potential to be mitigated, perhaps even erased in a "New Heav'n and Earth": "Then thou thy regal Sceptre shalt lay by, / For regal Sceptre then no more shall need, / God shall be All in All" (3.335, 339–41).

Adam demonstrates the fuller implications of *Paradise Lost*'s engaged theodicy by his own powerful imitatio Christi. It is here that we are given greater insight into the necessity of dialogue and community.

> I to that place
> Would speed before thee, and be louder heard,
> That on my head all might be visited,
> Thy frailty and infirmer Sex forgiv'n,
> To me committed and by me expos'd. (10.953–57)

BY OFFERING TO assume the full burden of divine punishment, by displaying a willingness to stand in for Eve, Adam shows that he has learned the lesson begun in book 3. He has finally understood the connection between freedom and responsibility first articulated by the Father, harshly and defensively, in his decrees. And he has fulfilled the rhetorical patterning begun by those first speeches of the Son, in which one's awareness of oneself as subject and as object necessarily—and paradoxically—intertwine. One of the many truly remarkable aspects of this truly remarkable poem is that Adam and Eve can eventually talk themselves through so many desperate extremes until they reach the sense of hope at the end of book 10 *without* the aid of an angel or the Son. Indeed, their postlapsarian behavior eventually provides a model for precisely the ethical activity of Milton's poem: coming to terms with fallen existence. Milton's theodicy, which depends so much on human acceptance of responsibility in an imitation of the divine assumption of accountability, finds fullest expression in its poetic development through the stance of engagement and dialogue.

The Son's speech just before Michael's arrival (11.30–44) elaborates the final aspects of Milton's literary theodicy. In this speech the Son reminds the Father of the initiating version of the topos I have been following:

> Now therefore bend thine ear
> To supplication, hear his sighs though mute;
> Unskillful with what words to pray, let mee
> Interpret for him, mee his Advocate
> And propitiation, all his works on mee
> Good or not good ingraft, my Merit those
> Shall perfet, and for these my Death shall pay.
> Accept me, and in mee from these receive
> The smell of peace toward Mankind, let him live
> Before thee reconcil'd, at least his days
> Number'd, though sad, till Death, his doom (which I
> To mitigate thus plead, not to reverse)
> To better life shall yield him, where with mee
> All my redeem'd may dwell in joy and bliss,
> Made one with me as I with thee am one.

THE THEME, in its full development, recurs here one last time. The Son's mediatory role, which complements the condescending role articulated in book 3, serves to elevate earthly things to the divine realm. Through the accommodative mode it becomes possible for humanity to raise itself up, to fulfill potential implicit in the divine mold in which it was created, to realize the significance of "the human face divine." The final lines of this passage, which compare the relationship between humanity and Christ to that between Christ and God, leave open the question of priority. It is essential, after all, that from the poem's accommodative standpoint—the stance I have identified in midrash as well—human interrelations serve as models for human-divine relations, and relations within the godhead, as much as the latter functions as the "Truth" figured in humanity's "shadowy Types."

IN GENESIS RABBAH the relationship between the behavior of God and humanity, the rabbinic understanding of the idea of a "human face divine," is taken up in a remarkable sequence of parables about the fall and the creation of sexual difference:

> R. Hoshiah said, "When the Holy One Blessed be He created Adam, the ministering angels mistook him [for God] and wanted to say the prayer of divine sanctification. To what may the matter be likened? To a king and his governor who were traveling in the state carriage. The men of the region wished to greet the king properly [lit. to say, 'Our lord!'], but they did not know which was the king. What did the king do? He ejected the governor from the state carriage, and they then knew which was the king. Similarly, when the Holy One Blessed be He created Adam, the angels mistook him. What did the Holy One Blessed be He do? He cast a deep sleep upon him, and they all knew that he was a man, as it is written, 'Cease ye from man'" (Isa. 2:22). (8:10)

THE *nimshal* (the internal rabbinic solution to the parable) actually diminishes the audacity of the mashal, which on its own seems to suggest that the *expulsion from Eden*, and not the fact of human sleep, is what was necessary for the angels to distinguish man from God. The technique of the mashal is particularly powerful in its penchant actively to elicit an interpretive stance from its audience. In this case the stance the audience assumes will shift dramatically between the mashal and the nimshal. The implication of the mashal is that the man's first disobedience was something God needed all along so as to protect his unique status! According to Stern, in most (if not all) cases, when a midrash includes a nimshal it does so to provide a now absent contextualization to the mashal:

> For a mashal preserved within a narrative context, that narrative supplies the information that makes it possible to understand the mashal's allusive meaning. In the absence of a narrative context, as in most midrashic literature, the normative presence of the nimshal as part of the mashal is to be understood as a device of compensation for the missing narrative: instead of a narrative frame, there is now an exegetical context, which is provided through the invention of the nimshal.[56]

STERN RIGHTLY CALLS attention to the midrash's dependence on discontinuities within the mashal and between the mashal and the nimshal for its hermeneutical effect. In this mashal, more so than many others, the discontinuity between mashal and nimshal is so great as to be potentially irresolvable. Daniel Boyarin's rejoinder to Stern may give us some help; he argues that the relationship between the two elements—and the third, the biblical verse—relies on an ongoing exchange between all three rather than an application of one to the other. According to Boyarin, the mashal and nimshal are related not as signifier and signified but as signifier and signifier, and their interaction determines the structures of meaning.[57] In our mashal the mitigating effect of the nimshal functions as a red flag, calling our attention to the theodically offensive implications of the mashal's reading of the biblical text. The nimshal fails to convince the reader that the hermeneutical equivalent of the king removing the governor from the carriage is God putting Adam to sleep. The prooftext brought from Isaiah 2, which in its larger context speaks of man's breath as proof of the ineffectiveness of man-made idols, itself does not seem to correspond to the sleep into which man is cast in order to construct woman (cf. Gen. 2, 22). We may account, at least partially, for the connection drawn between Adam's threatening resemblance to God and the sleep necessary to create woman by the abrupt parataxis of Gen. 1, 27, "So God created man in his own image, in the image of God created he him; male and female created he them." The rabbis were struck by the verse's implicit suggestion that humanity was created in God's image *and also* that humanity was created as male and female. Does this mean that God also has male and female forms? Or, are humanity's male and female forms a distinction from God's image? The midrash seems to have understood the latter to be the case. Man's creation in God's image threatened to position him as equal to God. In response to the angelic desire to worship this new divine image, God had to do something to dramatize the difference between himself and humanity. He put man to sleep *in order to create woman*, and the difference between humanity and God became clear to the angels.

Because the mashal so powerfully suggests that the exile from Eden was the result of God's need to make clear the difference between himself and humanity, and because the nimshal argues implicitly that the creation of the two sexes resulted from this very same need, an interpretive or corrective need (since the angels had misinterpreted the status of humanity), the interaction between the two suggests a hermeneutic association between the creation of the two sexes and the exile from Eden *exclusive* of humanity's transgression of the prohibition against the Tree of Knowledge. There is no agreed upon rabbinic view on the origins of death and its relation to the first couple's transgression in Genesis 3. As A. P. Hayman has observed, there is a noticeable tendency in later rabbinic sources to avoid the earlier view that Adam brought the sentence of death upon all men and to take a rather light view of this first sin.[58] On the one hand, this move away from full human culpability may be seen as a reaction to the developing Christian doctrine of Original Sin. On the other hand, it is important not merely to view the rabbinic approach as reactive. Rather, the network of mistaken identities, the exile from Eden, and the presence of a human community in the form of two sexes that I have described above takes shape as a positive and *interpretive* one. The rabbis locate within the story of the exile from Eden the very origins of the midrashic hermeneutic and interpretive stance that depends on an engagement with and a battle for the text. As I shall argue in the next chapter, the dialogism of this interpretive dynamic finds expression also in Milton's rendition of the competing narratives of human origin.

4

Imagining Desire:
Divine and Human Creativity

Genesis rabbah recounts a disputation between two of the most important schools of rabbinic thought, the house of Shammai and the house of Hillel. The midrash asks: What was created first, the heavens (the response given by the house of Shammai) or the earth (the house of Hillel's response)? The debate continues:

> According to the House of Shammai, it is like a king who built a throne for himself, and then made a footstool to go with it, as it is written, "The heaven is My throne and the earth is My footstool" (Isa. 66:1). According to the House of Hillel, it is like a king who built a palace; after he built the ground floor, he built the upper stories, as it is written, "on the day when the Lord God made earth and heaven" (Gen. 2:4). (1:15)

IN KEEPING WITH the rabbinic desire to interpret *torah mitokh torah*—the Bible from the Bible—both schools of thought invoke biblical passages as evidence for their respective positions. The rabbis rarely give more than a few words of explanation or elaboration on the thinking that went into their interpretations. Each position introduces a new narrative to supplement and investigate the biblical narrative of creation. Both sides of the debate use the king-parable, a frequently employed topos in rabbinic aggadoth, some important aspects of which I have already addressed in the previous chapter.

Both parties seemingly ignore the more explicit biblical pronouncements on the very issue they debate. The house of Hillel's opinion directly contradicts the chronology implied by the first verse of Genesis, "In the beginning God created the Heavens and the Earth." First the Heavens, then the Earth. The house of Shammai ignores the fact that the Bible speaks of the earth—albeit without form and void—on the very first day, whereas the description of the *creation* of the Heavens does not occur until the second day. Why do both schools ignore the scriptural evidence that would seem to be most compelling?

The two illustrations initially seem very simple, primarily descriptive of two alternative orders of creation. But it should be clear that the question of priority implies much more than a primordial chicken or egg. The parables suggest two different conceptions of the nature of the universe and of God's relationship to the cosmos: for the house of Shammai, the earth is God's footstool; for the house of Hillel, it is his palace. Moreover, this issue of priority relates to the very purpose of creation. According to the house of Shammai, the earth was created entirely for instrumental reasons. Serving as the footstool to the Heavens, the earth exists to provide a means of divine (and ultimately human) access to the celestial or godly realm; all of creation has as its ultimate purpose the transcendence of the earthly footstool in favor of the heavenly throne. Implied within this king-parable is a kind of imitatio Dei; that is, just as God perceives the earth only instrumentally, so too human beings should understand their existence on earth essentially as a means to achieving greater unity with the divine world in Heaven. The house of Shammai's view may even be said to contain the idea of a prelapsarian felix culpa; that is, the physical world was created as a necessary, but lower, form of existence that would eventually provide the means to ascend to the higher realm of the heavens. According to this view, God participates, at least temporarily, in the fallen world; he, too, descends from the higher realm to his footstool. In the opinion of the house of Hillel, however, we find no such notion of a fall into creation. The physical world is posited as part of God's palace, indeed as its essential foundation and first story. The heavens are relegated to a secondary role, part of the divine plan but resting firmly on the steady structure of the created world. God's position in the universe and his relationship to the created world—especially to humanity—is understood very differently by the house of Hillel. Indeed, according to the house of Hillel, God's own position in Heaven is not at all independent of the physical universe.

After observations by several other sages, the midrash concludes its description of this discussion with the following statement by R. Simeon:

> I am puzzled by this debate between the fathers of the world. Were not both the heavens and the earth created together, as a pot and its lid? As it is written, "[My hand established the earth, and my right hand spread out the heaven;] I call to them and they stand together" (Isa. 48:13).

THE APPARENTLY CONCILIATORY position taken by R. Simeon—also based on a scriptural prooftext—is actually more radical than the opinion of either the house of Hillel or the house of Shammai. By insisting on their equivalent value, R. Simeon leaves no room for a prioritizing of heaven or of earth. They both matter equally; in any situation that might demand the preference of one over the other, the rabbis need only recall R. Simeon's statement to remind them always to balance the two. The rabbis were quite familiar with a particular form of the temptation to upset this balance. It presented itself to them always and everywhere in the necessarily creative task of interpreting the biblical text. The midrashic project of interpretation is precisely about coming to terms with its status as a lid to the biblical pot. The metaphor of containment and limitation is particularly apt. The rabbis understood themselves to be placing a boundary around the Torah: "The members of the Great Knesset said three things: be deliberate in judgment, raise up many students, and establish a fence (*s'yag*) around the Torah."[1] Rabbinic commentary claims value for itself comparable to that of Scripture, but its status is always understood relationally to the textual cruxes that give rise to its production.

In this chapter I shall argue that Milton and the rabbis regarded divine creativity as dynamically intertwined with the human imagination. The originary power may have rested with God, but creation could only be completed by the participation of humanity. In the beginning was the spirit of God, but the beginning already anticipated the means and end of creation: the participation of the human community.

Paradise Lost OFFERS A detailed account of the transition from a divinely ahistorical world prior to Lucifer's rebellion, the creation of the world and humanity, and the subsequent fall into history, and can therefore be said to mirror the biblical creation narrative's concern with God as the God of history. The epic also follows the lead of the biblical text in presenting its version of the creation so as to capture the liturgical nature of such a secondary (indeed, tertiary!) rendition. Human prayer fills the poem from beginning to end. The framing invocations uttered by the epic narrator complement the periodic songs of praise, thanksgiving, and repentance uttered by Adam and Eve. Raphael's hexameral account in book 7 begins only after the poet's invocation, and after Adam's request for more knowledge, which is itself described as a desire to praise God more fully:

> Deign to descend now lower, and relate
> What may no less perhaps avail us known,
> How first began this Heav'n which we behold . . .
> . . . .
>   . . . what cause
> Mov'd the Creator in his holy Rest
> Through all Eternity so late to build
> In *Chaos*, and the work begun, how soon
> Absolv'd, if unforbid thou mayst unfold
> What wee, not to explore the secrets ask
> Of his Eternal Empire, but the more
> To magnify his works, the more we know. (8.84–86, 90–97)

BESIDES ITS POINTED USE of one of the technical terms for accommodation—"descend" or condescension—to characterize this *pre*lapsarian request for knowledge of the divine realm (thus, in a word, refuting those who would argue that the accommodative mode is appropriate only to the fallen world), Adam's address to Raphael combines the two key elements of biblical and Miltonic depictions of the creation, history and liturgy. Adam wants to know why God created the universe when he did—"so late"—and how long it took him to complete it—"how soon absolved." Adam asks for this information so as to be able to praise God, "to magnify his works." Regina Schwartz has suggested that Adam's desire to praise stands as *the* factor that keeps this request from overstepping the divinely prescribed limitations of human knowledge: "A quest that is in the service of praise cannot aspire too high, cannot inquire too far."[2] But what of the peculiar use of "absolved"? Though it was sometimes used as a synonym for "accomplished" or "finished" in the mid seventeenth century, the far more common usage pertained to acquittal or deliverance. Could Milton have been suggesting a latent purpose to the creation of the universe, i.e., as a means of acquitting the transcendent world sullied by Satan's rebellion and damnation? To this possible reading I shall add another. Looking more closely at the final lines of the above quotation, we may discern the curious location of the verb "ask," curious because it has been separated from its subject, "we," and because it refers to two separate infinitive phrases, "not to explore the secrets" and "the more to magnify his works." In rhetorical terms, *ask* serves as a *mezozeugma*, i.e., a common verb placed in the middle of a construction on which two or more words or clauses depend. Adam's interest in God's rate of completion, or, more generally, the relationship between time and the creative task, has thus become caught in the middle and is yoked (from the Greek *zeugma*, a yoking) to two distinct tasks. On the one hand, creation operates as response. Within a world requiring correction or mediation, a world that needs to be saved, creation absolves or acquits as a function of its role as praise, commemoration, sacred song. In this sense the creation story plays the same role it is assumed to have played in its earliest forms, i.e., preserving the world and giving security to life. Claus Westermann writes that it was not "the philosopher inquiring about his origins that spoke in the Creation narratives; it was man threatened by his surroundings. The background was an existential, not an intellectual problem."[3] On the other hand, the creative task serves to complete, to supplement what is already present. This function of the creative task involves a recognition of abstract principles, essential formulations of divine truths, which are then realized more literally, and often materially. When Milton depicts Adam asking about the cause and purpose of creation, he positions himself between these two tasks, yoking his poetic project to the complementary charges of interpreting the old and creating the new.

An analogy between God's creative endeavor in fashioning the universe and Milton's composition of *Paradise Lost* has been suggested by numerous critics and is further substantiated by the function of the invocations. As representations of the process of poetic invention, the result of which is in turn a poem about creation, the invocations also function as prayer. But the hexameral narrative of book 7 that describes the process of creation is itself both structured as liturgy (following its biblical pretext, Genesis 1) and framed by prayer: as soon as the Son begins his task of creation, "Great triumph and rejoicing was in Heav'n / When such was heard declar'd the Almighty's will; / Glory they sung to the most High . . . to him / Glory

and praise" (180–82, 186–87), and, of course, when he returns to his heavenly seat to celebrate the first Sabbath, "Creation and the six days' acts [the angelic host] sung" (601). If the silence that precedes the creation—"Silence, ye
troubl'd waves, and thou Deep, peace, / . . . your discord end" (216–17)—
makes the initial inroads into the timeless void of Chaos, the song that succeeds creation sanctifies the establishment of time. The poetic structures of
the invocations and the hexameral narrative suggest a deep affinity between
the creation of the universe and the composition of the poem.

CREATIO EX MATERIA

WHEN GEORGE PUTTENHAM called poets "creating gods," he was not presenting a particularly new idea about literary makers, but his words aptly sum-
marized a common view of poets that continued to hold sway through Milton's lifetime. *Paradise Lost* offers diverse instances of the comparison of God's
and the poet's creativity, but perhaps the most compelling evidence of a cor-
respondence between the two stems from the verbal basis for both. Milton
takes the refiguring of the first words of Genesis 1 in John 1 at *its* word: "And
thou my Word, begotten Son, by thee / This I perform, speak thou, and be
it done" (163–64). The literal collapse of the Word as the Son into the word
as the creative act—the very speech act constitutes the creation—is suggested by the partially buried rhyme of "Son" and "done" and becomes more
explicit in Milton's characteristically Latinate usage of "fate": the only fate
that Milton's universe admits is *fatum*, or the words of God having been spoken and thereby enacted. The fact of creation—the *factus*, the effect, that
which has been made—stands as evidence of God's invulnerability to fate:
"what I will is Fate. / So spake th'Almighty, and to what he spake / His
Word, the Filial Godhead, gave effect" (173–75). The associations with poetic artistry are unavoidable, and are always working in Milton's mind. Though
he recognizes an insurmountable difference between the effects of his verbal
poesis and the effect of God's word, Milton's theological definition of divine
creation maintains a certain consistency with his own poetic activities.

Milton's well-documented disagreement with the doctrine of *creatio ex nihilo*, his insistence that God created the world out of preexistent material—as
suggested in his reading of the Hebrew word *bara* used in Genesis 1 to mean
"to create"—is methodologically analogous to the creation that Milton un-
dertakes in the poem, generally, and in books 7 and 8, in particular. In an oft-

quoted passage from his posthumously published theological treatise Milton writes:

> Primum autem constat, neque Hebraeo verbo [*bara*] neque Graeco κτιζειν neque Latino creare, idem quod ex nihilo facere significari, immo vero unum quodque horum idem quod ex materia facere passim significat.

> [In the first place, it is certain that neither the Hebrew verb [*bara*], nor the Greek κτιζειν, nor the Latin *creare* means "to make out of nothing." On the contrary, each of them always means "to make out of something."][4]

IN OTHER WORDS, just as God selects, distinguishes, defines, and distills pre-existent matter to form the different aspects of the world, congealing diverse essences out of one uniform and continuous substance, so too Milton selects, refines, reprocesses the preexistent material of the biblical narrative (as well as any classical precursors) into his own augmented account of creation. Milton depicts God's creation of the world—*both* the process of creation and its worldly results—as having a materiality that can never be discarded but is the necessary vessel for the transcendence of God's presence. Raphael tells Adam, "Immediate are the Acts of God, more swift / Than time or motion, but to human ears / Cannot without process of speech be told, / So told as earthly notion can receive" (176–79). But the ensuing narrative does not depict the time-bound nature of this account for human ears with any reluctance or hesitation. The joyous indulgence in progressive, paratactic poesis, in which one creative triumph succeeds the next, demonstrates the centrality of this temporality. As to the worldly results of this process, Raphael has already repeated for Adam's and our benefit the Creator's explicit purpose:

> in a moment [I] will create
> Another World, out of one man a Race
> Of men innumerable, there to dwell,
> Not here, till by degrees of merit rais'd
> They open to themselves at length the way
> Up hither, under long obedience tri'd,
> And Earth be changed to Heav'n, and Heav'n to Earth,
> One Kingdom, Joy, and Union without end. (154–61)

THE DEVELOPMENTAL NARRATIVE depicted by the Father makes absolutely clear the necessity of human participation. Humanity completes the creation initiated by God, taking the material already in existence (in this case their own selves) and translating it "up hither." Just as the house of Shammai proposed that the earth functions as an instrumental footstool, leading to God's heavenly throne, Raphael tells Adam that by "degrees of merit . . . under long obedience tried" humanity will open a path to the divine realm. Yet, in a way that suggests greater affinity with the position of the house of Hillel, this is not a path that assumes the role of the created world to be merely instrumental, a self-consuming artifact; at the end of this path "Earth [will] be changed to Heav'n, and Heav'n to Earth." The chiasmus of this statement has the force of maintaining both sides of its structure in equipoise. Earth and heaven exist along the same monistic continuum. Chiasmus is one of Milton's favorite rhetorical techniques, uniquely suited to the monism embodied in the epic, and it is a form to which I shall return at the end of this chapter.

Satan may in fact claim as his ultimate achievement "the making of discontinuity, points in time where something completely new can be born of itself, without cause, without dependent relation to any past."[5] This analogy of poetic and divine creations is indeed Satanic, Romantic, Freudian; the imagination (Romantically understood) is the power renounced in exchange for a different kind of poetic authority. But Milton's creation is never completely self-begotten, autochthonous. The imagination that Guillory equates with Satan stands in opposition to pure mimesis, but I am proposing a different version of the imaginative mode, one that is perhaps less anachronistic than that of Guillory. It is true that Milton's ongoing characterizations of the poetic process suggest his denial of the possibility of pure mimesis; however, Milton's accommodative mode never pretends to be capable of pure mimesis. It is a mode especially appropriate to Milton's project because it allows for (indeed, demands) imaginative augmentation in the context of an adherence to the spirit of inspiration embodied in the biblical pretexts. The connection between poetry and prophecy to which Joseph Wittreich and William Kerrigan have referred is worth recalling, for a prophet's task is also to create out of preexistent matter. The prophet represents himself as having been privy to divine communication, which he is now at pains to convey in a form at least partly accessible to a human audience. Furthermore, the biblical prophets are conspicuously aware of the prophetic tradition into which they work to insert themselves: "Whichever pairing of prophecies is studied, the comprehension of the new prophecy is dependent upon first comprehending the old one."[6]

There can be little doubt that artistic imagination tempts as well as empowers Milton. His representations of Satan, especially in the first half of the poem, draw much of their strength from the poet's sensitivity to these temptations. By the time we reach book 7, however, Milton has managed to put aside some of these concerns in exchange for other worries about the limits of imitation and language. Perhaps the war in heaven in book 6 gave the poet the occasion to overcome some of these earlier issues, riding triumphantly in the chariot of the Son, dutifully taking down the chain of events leading to the expulsion of the rebellious hoards to hell. Perhaps his increasingly intriguing development of Adam and Eve helped to distract his attention from the self-begotten world of Satan's imagination. Or, perhaps his awareness of the impending challenge of mediating the creative act par excellence finally wrested his poetic fascination away from Satan to the central matter of the world's first seven days. Whatever the cause, in book 7 anxiety about the propriety of autotelic imagination has shifted to the relation between this kind of imagination and the overwhelming generative power of the world's creation, which the poet must somehow seek to describe at the same time that he imitates it.

THE SYNTAX OF CREATION

IN HIS STUDY of the first three chapters of Genesis, Kenneth Burke comments on some of the central differences between the two biblical creation accounts in Genesis 1 and 2:

> In the first chapter of Genesis, the stress is upon the creative fiat as a means of classification. . . . The second chapter's revised account of the Creation shifts the emphasis to matters of dominion. . . . The seventh day, which is placed at the beginning of the second chapter, has a special dialectical interest in its role as a transition between the two emphases.[7]

WITHOUT EXPLICIT MENTION of the documentary hypothesis, which was already well-established at the time, Burke succinctly captures some of the issues that had interested readers of Genesis for centuries. Though Milton preceded Julius Wellhausen by about 250 years (and though he would have certainly dismissed many of Wellhausen's conclusions about separate biblical documents as pure heresy), the poet was keenly attuned to the differences in structure, language, and thematic emphasis that later led Wellhausen and others to postulate the P, or Priestly, document as the source for Genesis 1–2:3 and the J, or Yahwist, document as the source for Genesis 2:4–3. A significant aspect of the interpretive project of *Paradise Lost* stems from Milton's determination to resolve apparent contradictions and seemingly needless repetitions in the Bible. To this extent Milton may indeed be "astonishingly like the modern practitioners of higher biblical criticism,"[8] but only insofar as he approaches the Bible from a perspective similar to those whom he *succeeds*: the patristic, medieval rabbinic, and Reformation commentators on Genesis. Milton's anticipation of biblical higher criticism, as evidenced by his inclusion of at least two different accounts of creation in book 7 and book 8—which largely, though not exclusively, correspond to Genesis 1 and 2, respectively—may be said to have itself been anticipated by earlier creative commentaries on the Bible. Repeated beginnings, as they appear in the Bible, may in fact constitute the divinely authorized precedent for retelling the story of creation in something like an epic poem. That is, if Genesis 2 is understood as an *interpretation* of Genesis 1 (though this would reverse the order of composition assumed by most biblical scholars—first J, then P), then the Bible itself may be said to offer a model for its subsequent extrabiblical readings and revisions. To borrow the term Michael Fishbane has coined to describe the earliest stages of Hebraic interpretation, Milton understands Genesis 2 to be an example of "inner-biblical exegesis" that in turn demands yet further levels of such exegesis.[9]

The phenomenon of biblical precedent, more so perhaps than any other characteristic, distinguishes the task (and the techniques) performed by the poet in book 7 from that of book 3. These two books have in common the principal problematic associated with any attempt at recounting the discourse and activities of the Godhead. As we saw in book 3, Milton partly breaks through this impasse by generating his own precedents, modeling his Celestial Dialogue after biblical accounts of debates between God and man. By suggesting a pattern of imitation that unfolds over the course of the epic, Milton establishes an accommodated paradigm in the conversation between the Father and the Son and the voluntary self-sacrifice of the Son (the "me, me, me" pattern resolving itself in Eve's and Adam's grand imitatio Christi). Here in book 7 the precedent of Genesis 1 poses the converse problem of retaining an authoritative authenticity without simply repeating verbatim the words of the Bible.

Many critics understand the contrast between divine and satanic discourse to be one of absolutes. If Satan speaks in excess, in a language with which a fallen audience can all too easily identify, then ipso facto, these critics argue, God must speak with a verbal economy with which the reader can never fully come to terms. Anthony Low insists that the reader becomes a listener during these moments of God talk rather than the interlocutor he or she plays during the rest of the epic.[10] Stanley Fish goes further:

> The reader's inability to simulate the mindlessness of innocence by reading passively (without implications) is especially noticeable in Book 7 where there are no narrative concerns to draw attention away from the operations of his own consciousness . . . . The creation scene is the most objective presentation in the poem of the cosmic harmony Milton celebrates; it is the reader's misfortune not to be able to imitate the joyous and spontaneous abandon God's other creatures display here. Instead he saddles them with his burden.[11]

I HAVE ALREADY begun to discuss some of the narrative concerns that the hexameral account addresses, and the ensuing analysis will provide further details in this matter. As to the fallen reader's incapacity to experience the joy expressed by God's others creatures, I can only respond that there are few moments in English poetry that compare in my mind to the exuberance and productive joy displayed by the fallen poet and experienced by the fallen audience of book 7. God's words of creation (and the successive descriptions of those creative moments) are performative in two senses. First, their very utterance (the *fatum*) produces the created world (the *factum*). Second, they produce in the reader an awareness of the centrality of creation (and the Creator) to the experience of the poem and the understanding of its production. That is, the words of creation perform the principles of creativity that are imitated in and analogous to the mediation of these words in the poem we know as *Paradise Lost*.

Since creation is inextricably bound to language, the *ex materia* principles of order and organization suggest the matter of syntax. This σύνταξις consists in ordering of the chaotic prime matter produced in God's retirement and its alienation from him: "Though I uncircumscrib'd myself retire, / And put not

forth my goodness" (170–71). And it extends to an ordering of chaotic, meaningless (or worse, potentially malevolent) language into the literary form and
style of creative act—God's and Milton's. The continuity between these two
senses of syntax manifests most profoundly in the kinds of metaphors or,
more broadly construed, the provenance of the images Milton deploys to describe the process of creation. Drawing especially on contrasting themes of
natural fecundity (biological birth, growth, and development), on the one
hand, and the supernatural realm, on the other, the poet generates an implicit
argument about the relation between language and creation.

The first creative act of the Word is to command peace: "Silence, ye troubl'd waves, and thou Deep, peace, / Said then th'Omnific Word, your discord
end" (216–17). Milton calls the Word (the Johannine trope for the Son)
"Omnific," all-creating, which appears to be a word of the poet's own invention.[12] In one audacious stroke of the pen, the Word is made into a new
word, which itself argues for the omnipotent making power of all words.
And this power is first deployed as a means of restoring order: "your discord
end." The circularity of this linguistic syllogism establishes the precedent for
the self-referentiality of all subsequent rhetorical tropes in the hexameral account. As literary constructs they gesture simultaneously toward a super-
mimesis of the creation (i.e., they are creative renditions of creation) and toward a fulfillment of the anagogic turn of the reader's interpretive encounter
with them.

Milton describes the first stages of creation almost exclusively through
images of limitation, separation, distinction, and synthesis. These figures
partly serve to incorporate the effects of the Son's triumph over the rebellious angels and, as a result, portray the necessary link between order and
creation:

> He took the golden Compasses, prepar'd
> In God's Eternal store, to circumscribe
> The Universe, and all created things:
> One foot he centered, and the other turn'd
> Round through the vast profundity obscure,
> And said, Thus far extend, thus far thy bounds,
> This be thy Circumference, O World. (225–31)

IN CONTRAST TO God's voluntary self-retirement (170), the Son mathematical-
ly describes the extent of the universe. Milton draws on the notoriously dif-

ficult passage in Proverbs 8:27, "When he prepared the heavens, I was there: when he set a compass upon the face of the depth." What the King James version translates as "when he set a compass," the Hebrew, *b'chuqo chug*, could be more literally translated as "when he established a boundary," although the boundary in question is indeed circular—the Vulgate uses the term *gyrus*. The root of the word for "set" or "establish" is *choq*, which more often than not translates into one of the many divine ordinances as they have been commanded to the Israelites. The limitations necessary for the creation of the universe thus bear an important resemblance to the limitations of God's self-revelation to humanity. This revelation necessarily occurs always under the aegis of accommodation. By drawing on the language of Proverbs—a Wisdom text whose central theme is the character of divine knowledge made available to humanity—Milton invokes a vocabulary that combines, as in earlier instances, the themes of creativity and interpretation. In other words, the circumscription is at once the initiatory creative act and also the precedent for mediatory interpretation characterized by accommodation. Indeed, the universal centrifuge that begins the separation of matter may be seen as an even further literalization of the interpretive task that I have been analyzing:

> Darkness profound
> Cover'd th'Abyss: but on the wat'ry calm
> His brooding wings the Spirit of God outspread,
> And vital virtue infus'd, and vital warmth
> Throughout the fluid Mass, but downward purg'd
> The black tartareous cold Infernal dregs
> Adverse to life; then founded, then conglob'd
> Like things to like, the rest to several place
> Disparted, and between spun out the Air,
> And Earth self-balanc't on her Centre hung. (233–42)

THE THEODICAL GOAL of Milton's poem makes itself felt most notably in moments like these when we would least expect an argument about the inherent moral qualities of the created universe. That is, Milton's accommodative mode, which itself is analogous to the selection process the poet attributes to God's creation of the universe, makes the case for God's justification by portraying a material world with the potential for good or evil, to be determined by choice—in this case, God's choice. As John Rumrich has shown, "chaos is the material basis of God's power—his infinite potency—which, though prior to creation, nevertheless exists as an essential attribute of the deity."[13] The analogy between the creation of the world and the creation of the poem would then work as follows: God's text-creation, the original invention, continues to be interpreted, given meaning, by each individual reader, including the poet of *Paradise Lost*. The literary text, reiterating the first verbal act whereby God created the world, is not in itself original or inherently meaningful. Instead, readers of the text create meaning out of it. Combined with the elevation of interpretive choices, the reader's (re)invention of the text wrests it away from any fixity or determination.

The creation of light that ensues exemplifies the marriage of discourses, material and transcendent, to which I have alluded. The initial divine pronouncement is taken word for word from the Bible, "Let there be light, God said," but the Miltonic augmentation takes the form of an *isocolon* in which pairings of adjective and noun follow the same pattern:

> . . . forthwith *Light*
> Ethereal, first of things, quintessence pure
> Sprung from the Deep, and from her Native East
> To journey through the airy gloom began,
> Spher'd in a radiant cloud, for yet the Sun
> Was not; shee in a cloudy Tabernacle
> Sojourned the while . . . (243–51)

EACH ADJECTIVE-NOUN PAIR combines an abstract term or image with one of greater concreteness. Because we are situated only within the first few moments of the world's creation, no image can represent full material reality; but even in the pairing of "light" and "ethereal" the contrast suggests a synthesis of something of this world, i.e., light, with something of the transcendent realm, ether. The pairs that follow all possess this same contrastive quality, which will in turn be made more distinct as the matter of the world is further separated into discreet elements and, later, living creatures.

After the next set of separations that produce the firmament (dividing the waters of heaven and the waters of earth), Raphael introduces a crucial set of images for his creation narrative:

> The earth was form'd, but in the Womb as yet
> Of Waters, Embryon immature involv'd,

Appear'd not: over all the face of Earth
Main Ocean flow'd, not idle, but with warm
Prolific humour soft'ning all her Globe,
Fermented the great Mother to conceive,
Satiate with genial moisture . . . (276–82)

MATERNAL, FEMININE PROCREATION dominates this description of earth's gestation. As a particular mode of creation, it stands in direct contrast to the method of division and distinction that has informed most of the initial stages of Raphael's account. God's creation by fiat, his forceful subjugation of the chaos of undifferentiated matter, stands as one side of the creative coin; on the other side stands the life-giving warmth of the "great Mother." In a stunningly original reading of this passage, John Rogers has recently shown how its "syntactical infelicities" are a "meaningful symptom of the poem's larger struggle with the subject of agency," specifically the female agency exemplified in procreation. For, Rogers argues, if we parse the active verbs and verbal adjectives we find that Raphael is actually describing a process whereby the "great Mother" earth "conceives and generates the very embryo that was her former self."[14] Milton further thematizes the conjunction of masculine and feminine modes of creation in the ensuing description of the emergence of dry land:

Immediately the Mountains huge appear
Emergent, and their broad bare backs upheave
Into the Clouds, thir tops ascend the Sky:
So high as heav'd the tumid Hills, so low
Down sunk a hollow bottom broad and deep,
Capacious bed of Waters . . . (285–90)

THE PHALLIC EMERGENCE of the mountains occurs within the fertile, maternal, neonatal landscape; the heights of the mountains are explicitly complemented by the depths of the oceans. Into this new and vital landscape Milton does not hesitate to place many of the images that, in postlapsarian perspective, resonate with sin and death. The waters gather like armies responding to the call of the trumpet (and Raphael reminds Adam in an aside that he is already familiar with the concept of army from the story of the Battle in Heaven). The torrents of water find their paths to the ocean "with Serpent error wand'ring" (302). The Fishian reading of these images tainted for the reader by a necessarily postlapsarian perspective is only partially adequate. It is true that we are always and everywhere reminded of our fallen status. And indeed, these reminders wield special force and poignancy at the moments of God's sublime creativity. But Milton's inclusion of these terms suggests the converse as well. The presence of now fallen images in the world of divine creation argues for the peculiar power of linguistic creation to wrest the tainted language away from its assumed connotations. That is, through a sheer act of creative will Raphael (and Milton) assert that the mode of creativity now described has the capacity to revitalize language, to take its preexistent formal matter, and to imbue it with new and re- (or in this case *pre-*) interpreted content.

If the feminized element of the hexameral narrative is largely implicit in the first few hundred lines, when Raphael comes to describe the growth of vegetation he provides Adam with a detailed picture of a woman clothing and adorning herself:

> . . . the bare Earth, till then
> Desert and bare, unsightly, unadorn'd,
> Brought forth the tender Grass whose verdure clad
> Her Universal Face with pleasant green,
> Then Herbs of every leaf, that sudden flow'r'd
> Op'ning thir various colors, and made gay
> Her bosom smelling sweet. (313–19)

IN LIGHT OF the intense scrutiny to which female generation was subjected in the seventeenth century, as documented by Rumrich and Rogers, Milton's persistance in representing creation according to the female model of reproduction is especially noteworthy.[15] Rumrich adds that Milton's extraconventional concern with feminine procreative power is a sign of the poet's "yearning for transcendence of limitations imposed by gender."[16] This conclusion is especially apt for passages such as this one, where the collapse of categories more generally is a notable effect of creation. The lush details that follow support Raphael's conclusion that "earth now / Seem'd like to Heav'n" (328–29). Recalling Raphael's earlier description of the accommodative mode as it pertained to the heavenly matters—"What surmounts the reach / Of human sense, I shall delineate so, / By lik'ning spiritual to corporeal forms" (5.571–73)—here in book 7 we have gained access to the other side of accommodation in which the earthly realm is raised to the transcendent. To say that the newly created world "seemed like to Heav'n" functions much more powerfully than as a hyperbolic adulation of the beauty of the earth covered with new vegetation. Rather, it draws on the poet's monism so as to display the nature of God's creation and how the poet's narration can tap into its power. The earth does not merely function as a metaphor, expressing events and concepts whose reality is abstract.[17] Like the language that describes it in such rich detail, the created world has a reality all its own, balancing the abstract principles of an idealized world of divine truths—it is not merely a footstool to the heavenly throne, it is the first floor of God's palace. The subtle interleaving of chapters 1 and 2 of Genesis in lines 331–38 confirm this newly developing aspect of accommodation.

The "dewy mist [that] went up and watered all the ground . . ." is an interpolation of Genesis 2:5–6 into what has been, till now, a hexameral narrative that has drawn all its details either from Genesis 1 or from the poet's own imagination. The mist, in Hebrew *eyd*, is the Yahwist's explanation of how the plants were watered before any rain had fallen on the earth. Milton chooses to include this detail here, in Raphael's ostensibly theocentric account, to complicate the possibility of pure theocentrism. To this point, knowledge (and its purpose) have streamed in one direction—downward. The condescendatory movement of accommodation finds its analogy in the rain that falls from heaven. We have reached a moment in the poem when the reciprocal motion of accommodation must be made more evident. Thus the dewy mist "went up," turning the tables of accommodated knowledge so that the earth would indeed "seem like to Heav'n."

Once movement of creation has shifted directions, that is, once creation proceeds upward as well as—or in place of—the "downward purg[e]" (237) of the first moments of divine fiat, the momentum in that direction can hardly be stopped. The creation of the birds on the fifth day is noteworthy not only for its quasi-evolutionary description, Raphael tells his human audience:

> Mean while the tepid Caves, and Fens and shores
> Thir Brood as numerous hatch, from th'Egg that soon
> Bursting with kindly rupture forth disclos'd
> Thir callow young, but feather'd soon and fledge
> They summ'd thir Pens, and soaring th'air sublime
> With clang despis'd the ground, under a cloud
> In prospect. (417–24)

THE EGGS ARE located in the "tepid Caves, and Fens and shores," right on the margin dividing land and sea. Once they hatch, however, the birds distinguish themselves from other creatures already formed in these surroundings by taking to the air, despising the ground. The biblical description from which Milton has taken this portion of the hexameron speaks of "foul that may fly above the earth in the open firmament of heaven" (Genesis 1:20). The conjunction of earth, firmament (which we know was formed out of water), and heaven in the Bible offers enough of an occasion for the poet to assert a process of development that is at once naturalized and transcendent.

THE ANXIETY OF INSPIRATION

THE INSTANCE OF CREATIVITY that reflects most comprehensively on God as Creator is, of course, the creation of humankind. So important to the central concerns of the poem is this moment of divine creativity that Milton includes no fewer than three separate episodes or installments of its enactment. It is, to be sure, something of a commonplace to observe that the separate versions of the creation of humanity detailed in books 7 and 8 reflect Milton's awareness of and struggle with the apparently distinct accounts reported in Genesis 1:26–31 and 2:7–9, 15–25. The difference between the two books appears to have more to do with perspective than theme—the eighth book concerns itself with forming a new human language based on the dominance of human consciousness that supplants the cosmological attitude of the seventh book. This difference is clearly an effort to incorporate the same strategy entailed in the Bible's duplicate narratives of creation. The first version, attributed to the P text, is normally aligned with Raphael's grand description within the sequence of the seven days of creation in 7:505–50; the second account, part of the J text, is said to parallel Adam's rendition of his own coming to consciousness in book 8, where his perspective is more fully privileged. This correlation of sources fails to account for a far more complicated splicing of the P and J texts in book 7 and, more important, for the third version of human creation, Eve's narration of her awakening, which *precedes* books 7 and 8. Clearly there is more to these varying accounts than a distinction between theocentric and anthropocentric perspectives. By including Eve's story, Milton draws a second distinction between the masculine and feminine perspectives on the coming to self-awareness. Indeed, the presence of Eve's story in book 4 inevitably confounds many recent attempts to recover Milton's alternatively misogynist and protofeminist sympathies.[18] Eve's version of her own creation depends, for biblical precedent, on the brief pronouncement in Genesis 2:22, "and [God] brought her unto the man."[19] Most of the narrative details grown out of the Greek and Roman classics, specifically Ovid's story of Narcissus in the *Metamorphoses*. A poem that constantly negotiates the relative value of its precursor texts, *Paradise Lost* always seems to find the classical sources wanting. As the corrective to these fallen pagan models Milton inevitably posits the Bible. Thus, any representations of characters or figures that draw on these classical sources will necessarily suggest some for of devaluation.[20] The absolute scale upon which Milton's poem seems to place the Bible and classical romance suggests that, even at the level of source text, *Paradise Lost* subordinates Eve—her creation, her sexuality—to Adam.[21]

Midrashim of the fourth and fifth centuries *c.e.* offer a similar dichotomy, meditating explicitly and, more often, implicitly on the differences between a nascent rabbinic ontology and a Hellenistic (Platonic) one. With notable frequency these rabbinic encounters between Hebraism and Hellenism occur over matters concerning the body, sexuality (especially, though not exclusively, female sexuality), and human imagination. These thematic parallels between *Paradise Lost* and midrash may account for an ongoing interest in Milton as a Hebraic poet, potentially influenced (directly or indirectly) by the writings of classical and medieval Jewish scholars. Yet, for neither Milton nor the rabbis, are the associations of sexuality with paganism or Hellenism entirely consistent. Both *Paradise Lost* and the midrash stage conflicts between the sacredness of female sexuality, as a version of human creativity and imagination, and its profanity. At the same time, these texts both pit nonbiblical Hellenic influences against Hebraic ones. Despite the temptation to map these tensions onto each other, in neither case do we find a simple textual marking of sexuality as inherently corrupt or a consistent association of sexuality with the nonbiblical or romance genre.

Many commentators on *Paradise Lost*, especially those who have been interested in the epic's so-called Hebraism, attribute some of Milton's less conventionally Christian views on sexuality to his familiarity and sympathy with Jewish thought. Indeed, the very notion of prelapsarian coitus, unique to Milton among his widely diverse Christian contemporaries and predecessors, is an idea that can be traced to numerous rabbinic sources, including Genesis Rabbah (18:6). I do not wish to argue for a rabbinic source to this poetic innovation; rather, I cite it to demonstrate that even in its critical reception the poem's Hebraisms may function to incorporate a more positive version of sexuality and not merely as an antidote to the corrupt sexuality of the poem's classical forerunners. In more general terms Milton's monistic refusal to reject the body can be seen as a "Hebraic" element of *Paradise Lost*.[22] The result is a poem that plays on two different kinds of conflicts. First, there is the conflict between sexual libertinism and the ascetic rejection of any form of sexuality documented by James Grantham Turner.[23] Second, there is the conflict between the license of classical (nonbiblical) sources and the restrictive control of the biblical source texts. Despite several attempts by critics of the last half-century to coordinate these two seemingly parallel conflicts, they continually resist any possible schematic alignment with one another. By reading both midrash and Milton's poem as dynamic dialogic texts, I suggest that *Paradise Lost* has as much to teach us about the development of rabbinic attitudes toward sexuality and creativity as midrash has to inform our understanding of Milton's struggle with these same concepts.

In a fascinating reexamination of Genesis 1–11 (the synthetic P-J prehistory of the Hebrews) Ilana Pardes has argued that Eve's presence in the story of the Tree of Knowledge demands to be read in light of her subsequent activity as mother and—more important—as namer.[24] Eve's first naming speech occurs immediately after her violation of the injunction against eating from the Tree of Knowledge. She calls her first son Cain (*qayin*) in Genesis 4:1, explaining the choice with the following phrase, *qaniti ish eth YHWH*, translated by the authorized version as "I have gotten a man from the Lord." Pardes insists that the Hebrew verb *qanah* be translated as "create," or "fashion," and not as it has been subdued by various translators into "gotten" or "bought" or "gained"; furthermore, she argues, this statement should be read as a challenge to God's exclusive control of the activity of creation. In Genesis 3 Eve sought to acquire the power of divinity by eating from the tree. With the birth of her first child she seeks again to define herself as (pro)creator, comparable to YHWH. What Eve is really saying—and Pardes argues that the naming is addressed to Adam as well as to YHWH—is "It is not you who created woman out of man (with divine help) . . . but it is I who created you—*ish*—together with Yahweh!" The *ish* ("man") refers both to Cain and to Adam: "Through the naming of Cain, Eve rewrites Genesis 2 as a subversive comment on Adam's displacement of the generative power of the female body [when he called her *ishah*, in 2.23, having come from *ish*]."[25]

Pardes's remarkable revision of Eve's role as creative subject, and not merely object (of desire, of temptation, of impregnation), recovers the biblical text's denial, in both the P and the J versions, of woman's role as mother

and creator. Both of these accounts work to confirm the validity of patriarchal monotheism, which has been textually formulated as a rejection of premonotheistic (often matriarchal) culture.[26] The Yahwistic account presents
the astonishing reversal of biological birth, in which woman issues forth
from man—the rib's physiological location there stands in for the womb. But
even the supposedly egalitarian Priestly version eventually writes woman out
of the process of procreation: the final words of P's creation in 2:4a, "These
are the generations of the heavens and of the earth when they were created,"
find their complement in P's later human genealogies in Genesis 5: "This is
the book of the generations of Adam." As the text goes on to list the ten
generations separating Adam and Noah *not a single mother or daughter is mentioned*:
"Procreation becomes primarily a male issue once the generic term *'adam* in
5:1—2 turns into the proper name Adam in 5:3, once the relentless listing of
ancestors begins."[27] Pardes's recovery of these narrative denials of woman's
far more substantive role in procreation is useful not only for its restitution
of female subjectivity to the biblical text; the tension between Eve's palpably
creative act of motherhood and the patriarchal deity's loud protestations to
the contrary underscore a textual anxiety about man's seemingly trivial participation in the most dramatic instance of human creativity.

From this biblical (male) anxiety to the Miltonic anxiety about creativity
with which I began this chapter would seem to be an easy step. It is made more
complicated, however, by the ambivalent representations of female creativity
that pervade the poem. Janet Adelman has characterized the connection between Eve and the female muse as a manifestation of Milton's "concern with
the source and end of his own creativity apparently felt as an expression of the
female in his own nature and presided over by a female muse."[28] If he were to
have responded to this concern in a similar fashion to the biblical accounts,
then we might expect Milton to make more of a concerted effort to denigrate
or even excise female (pro)creativity from the poem's midst. But the invocations, as well as Milton's other representations of the feminine aspects of creation, reveal a more complex connection between bearing a child and producing a poem. I have already discussed the degree to which Raphael's account of
the creation indulges in the fructifying joy of sexual generation, the periodic
birthing of new elements of the universe in an ever renewing "labor." Mother
Earth's womb, impregnated by the Word, produces the world as Adam and
Eve come to know it. Similarly, the female muse—mediatory and inspiring—
to whom Milton addresses his invocations plays much more than a figurative
or conventional role in the poem.

In his first invocation the poet calls to the Spirit who

>   . . . from the first
> Wast present, and with mighty wings outspread
> Dove-like satst brooding on the vast Abyss,
> And mad'st it pregnant . . . (1.19–22)

THE IMAGERY HERE suggests a masculine insemination of the "vast Abyss" by the Spirit or Muse, and by analogy seems to imply that in the quest for inspiration Milton is seeking his own impregnation by the Muse.[29] But this reading of the motif of inspiration positions Milton as a passive receptacle, which in turn guarantees that "the poem is not his own invention: in order to deny the possibility of satanic inspiration, Milton must deny his own authorship."[30] It should be clear by now, though, that in my view the poet's understanding of creation as an *active* ordering, selecting, and augmenting of preexistent material argues against the possibility of Milton wishing to disown his poem, attributing it, however archly or defensively, to divine inspiration. The marvelous suspension of referent and syntax in book 3's invocation serves as further indication of the poet's desire to be both passive and active in the production of his poem:

> Then feed on thoughts, that voluntary move
> Harmonious numbers; as the wakeful bird
> Sings darkling, and in shadiest Covert hid
> Tunes her nocturnal Note. (37–40)

THE MOMENTARY AMBIGUITY generated by the enjambment of "that voluntary move / Harmonious numbers" proposes first that "move" be read intransitively, suggesting an inner activity within the poet as he creates the poem. Coupled with the uncertainty of address in these lines—they are written in the imperative, without a subject—the possibility of noncommunion frozen in the end-stop "move" describes a powerful inclination on the part of the poet to turn away from the holy Light, and to compose the poem in isolation.[31] The invocations are neither exclusively requests for divine inspiration from some yet-to-be-defined Muse nor periodic declarations of poetic independence.

The invocation to book 7 attempts to name the Muse for the first time: "Descend from Heav'n *Urania.*" Here, finally, the Muse to whom Milton calls is gendered female and given a classical pedigree. Noam Flinker has argued that the poet here "approximates a psychic stance of a lover courting his beloved,"[32] in which case the passive and active roles we saw in the first two invocations have been reassigned. But Flinker's claim that "Milton's narrator courts Urania in order to transfer the powers of sublimated inspiration from her mythical sources into his poem"[33] fails to recognize the hardly disguised antagonism Milton expresses toward this classical Muse. Indeed, the second line of the invocation immediately challenges the propriety of the appellation: "by that name / If rightly thou art call'd." Rather than a wholesale embrace of the classical female Muse, what we find in this invocation is intense ambivalence and apprehension concerning the source of inspiration.

My reading of the presence of images of female (pro)creativity in *Paradise Lost*, then, has circled back around to the male anxiety that Pardes described in her analysis of Genesis 1–11, with an important difference. For if Eve, through the power of naming, retains some of the authority of creativity that had been textually denied to her by P and J, then Milton challenges female (pro)creativity and sexuality through this same task of naming, or, rather, through an unnaming. Pardes's reading of Eve's act of naming Cain seeks to locate (premonotheistic) precursors to the biblical text that celebrated the female power to produce.[34] Milton's collation of classical (polytheistic) sources with biblical ones works to reverse that celebration by associating the dangers he sees in female sexuality with the seductions of classical pretexts.[35] This association surfaces explicitly as the invocation reaches its climax:

> But drive far off the barbarous dissonance
> Of *Bacchus* and his Revellers, the Race
> Of that wild Rout that tore the *Thracian* Bard
> In *Rhodope*, where Woods and Rocks had Ears
> To rapture, till savage clamour drown'd
> Both Harp and Voice; nor could the Muse defend
> Her Son. So fail not thou, who thee implores:
> For thou art Heavn'ly, shee an empty dream. (32–39)

THE DANGERS OF female sexuality are embodied in the Bacchante, whose "barbarous dissonance" stands in direct conflict with the Orphic sounds of an inspired (male) poet singing the natural world into lyrical enchantment. Milton poses as Orpheus, whose power to tame the feminine world of nature with his song is eventually usurped as he is rent asunder by the "wild Rout."

Pronouncing the idea of a female Muse "an empty dream," Milton condemns the very classical sources from which she is drawn because of her associations with the violence and destruction of female sexuality; classicism
becomes the "savage clamour" that threatens to drown out the "Harp and
Voice"—which also alludes to David the psalmist, a distinctively Hebraic
image—of Milton's poem.

CLASSICAL ROMANCE

MILTON'S APPARENT ANXIETY concerning female sexuality would thus seem
to overlap with his hostile attitude toward his classical percursors. Nevertheless, despite its omnipresent biblical and Christian correctives, which are frequently associated with Milton's conception of masculine creativity and the
control of female sexuality, *Paradise Lost* is never able to excise the presence of
classicism from its midst.[36] As a poet, writing in the tradition of "Blind
Thamyris, and blind *Maeonides,* / And *Tiresias* and *Phineus* Prophets old"
(3.35–6), and not merely as the latest in the line of "That Shepherd, who first
taught the chosen Seed" (1.8), Milton positions himself between the world
of the classics and the world of the Hebrew Bible, just as he occupies a pre-
carious middle ground between the perceived excesses of female sexuality
and the strictures of Christian discipline and asceticism.

The poet's temptation by—despite his apparent fear of—female sexuality is matched by his troubled inclination toward self-authorship. Satan's audacious claim to independence remains the poem's most celebrated instance
of autogenesis: "We know no time when we were not as now: / Know none
before us, self-begot, self-rais'd / By our own quick'ning power" (5.859–61).
As courageous as these words may sound to our own post-Romantic ears,
there can be little doubt that the poem records them in order eventually to
condemn them. But this satanic moment has its prelude in Eve's own prelapsarian narrative of her origins. Adam may begin the description of his first
coming to consciousness with the disclaimer "For Man to tell how human
Life began / Is hard; for who himself beginning knew?" (8.250–51), but what
ensues is also poetically inferior to Eve's marvelous story. Unlike Adam, Eve
appears to have little difficulty remembering and recounting her beginnings:
"That day I *oft remember,* when from sleep / I first awak't, and found myself
repos'd" (4.449–50, emphasis added). Milton's image of Eve-as-Narcissus

admiring her newly discovered reflection in the pond is one of the most compelling—seductive?—in the poem. Occupying the same position as Satan, who overhears Eve tell her story to Adam, we stare with the eyes of a voyeur, looking at the looker, who simultaneously reflects (mirrors, ponders) and creates her image.[37]

It has become almost a critical reflex to juxtapose Adam's and Eve's first waking moments in *Paradise Lost* to contrast man's upward inclination with woman's downward instinct: Adam looks "Straight toward Heav'n" (8.257); Eve lays herself "down / On the green bank, to look into the clear / Smooth Lake" (4.456–9). Yet what this comparison neglects is Eve's *first* set of thoughts, "much wond'ring where / And what I was, whence thither brought, and how" (451–52). This terse catalogue of philosophical and theological inquiries constitutes as comprehensive a summary of Milton's own project in the opening proem as any other moment in the epic. If Eve's first musings concern her physical and existential location, her ontological status, and her relation to any motivating force or *primum mobile*, then surely they do so in concert with the most basic questions addressed by a poem beginning at "the highth of this great Argument." The much remarked upon "unexperienc't thought" with which Eve approaches the lake necessarily resonates with the poet's characterization of his epic as "unpremeditated Verse" in the invocation to book 9. There is a difference, of course. The fallen poet cannot be anything but experienced, especially in the very invocation that prepares the way for the Fall. This difference is key. Critics often condemn Eve for her "unexperienc't thought" even though she *is not yet* fallen, whereas we read Milton's "unpremeditated Verse" as a sign of its divine origin even though he *is* fallen. The parallels that Milton draws between his poetic voice and Eve's unself-conscious narrative are nevertheless unmistakable.

At an earlier stage in his public career, when he was more directly engaged with the doctrinal controversies of his age, Milton had occasion to meditate on the dynamics of human (pro)creation in a very different context. In his animated response to Bishop Joseph Hall's defense of the English episcopacy, Milton wrote,

> There is no imployment more honourable, more worthy to take up a great spirit, more requiring a generous and free nurture, then to be the messenger, and Herald of heavenly truth from God to man, and by faithfull worke of holy doctrine, to procreate a number of faithfull men, making a kind of cre-

ation like to Gods, by infusing his spirit and likenesse into them, to their salvation, as God did into him; arising to what climat so ever he turne him, like
that Sun of righteousnesse that sent him, with healing in his wings, and new
light to break in upon the chill and gloomy hearts of his hearers, raising out
of darksome barrennesse a delicious and fragrant Spring of saving knowledge, and good workes. Can a man thus imployed, find himselfe discontent-
ed? (YP 1:721)

STILL ALLIED WITH the presbyterian opposition to church hierarchy, Milton
asserted that ministers and preachers should be more than satisfied with their
task of bringing the "new light . . . of saving knowledge" to the world, for,
in so doing, their work makes them creators just like God. Yet even here this
creation is multifaceted and derivative: the procreation of "faithfull men" is
a function of the production of words that preach salvation, which are in
turn the creation of the one true Word, Christ and/as Scripture.

In light of Milton's apparent rejection of the romance of classicism, it is
tempting to posit Eve's ensuing narration of her creation as the epitome of
self-centeredness, verging on self-obsession, and thus as a manifestation of
the dangerous narcissistic sexuality of classical sources. According to this interpretation, the voice that eventually calls Eve away from her reflection is the
masculine voice of biblical authority, correcting the inwardness and self-sat-
isfaction inherent in female sexuality and the classical romance tradition.
Milton's continuing flirtation with female sexuality and its concomitant creativity, however, will not allow him wholly to dismiss Eve's behavior as inappropriate. Milton wrote with extraordinary power in books 1 and 2, when the
satanic impulse toward self-authorship was at its most compelling. Following
the valiant, if not fully successful, attempt at representing the divine point of
view on freedom and responsibility in book 3, however, Milton must reassert
a mode of poetic authority in book 4 that responds to the threat of being
overwhelmed by divine authority as it had been represented in the Celestial
Dialogue. The poet must temporarily return to the self-gratification of Lacan's mirror stage.[38] Milton's representation of Eve is a powerful, if temporary, wresting of creative (and legislative) powers from the godhead. The
poem's indulgence in Eve's sexuality, both when she first appears in book 4
and especially in the beautiful passage describing the joys of prelapsarian sex
at the end of this book, is necessarily tied to a version of the poetic imagination that Milton must preserve.[39]

THE CREATION OF DESIRE

IN ORDER BETTER TO understand the complex network of associations between classicism, sexuality (good and bad), and human creativity in Milton's
poem, I suggest that we look back to the earlier Jewish tradition that has frequently been offered as precedent for Milton's own views. This tradition itself was neither monolithic nor unresponsive to historical and cultural
change. One of the earliest Hebraic texts, the J narrative, is also the most distinctively monist in its ontology, characterizing the first man as a "living
soul" (*nefesh chayah*; Genesis 2:7).[40] By the last several centuries *b.c.e.*, however,
many Jewish sects, especially those in close contact with Hellenistic cultural
forces, had adopted a more dualist worldview. This dualism took a variety of
forms, but in nearly all cases it produced a hierarchy of spirit and body, con-
signing the body and its accompanying sexuality to a lower (that is, less perfect) realm of being. Some of the oldest postbiblical Jewish texts (from the
last two centuries before the Common Era), including the Book of Jubilees
(3:2–6) and the Second Book of Baruch (56:5–6), assumed that the first couple lived in Eden without sexual intercourse, implying that the purity of
prelapsarian Eden could not sustain the depravity of sexuality.[41] In opposition to an emerging Christian view, which considered all modes of sexuality
to be a consequence of Original Sin, however, the rabbis of the Amoraic period (from the end of the third to the beginning fo the sixth centuries of the
Common Era) began to assert the importance of prelapsarian sexuality. This
was an essential aspect of the ongoing efforts by the rabbis to distinguish
their Judaism from what they perceived to be its dangerous mutation by Paul
and his followers. In his provocative study of sex in talmudic culture, Daniel
Boyarin characterizes the advent of *rabbinic* monism as a direct response to
the "increasing threat to the corporeal integrity of the Jewish people from
. . . platonizing tendencies within Judaism" and Hellenic dualism's rejection
of the body in favor of the soul.[42] When it came to matters of human
agency, these Amoraic rabbis inherited a tradition that also posited an ethical
dualism, a split within the individual between the good inclination and the
evil inclination. In order to adjust this dualist anthropology to their incipient
monism, they sought to reformulate the notion of the evil inclination, the
yetzer ha-ra, as part of an internal (psychological) dialectic. Genesis Rabbah
reports the following rabbinic account of necessary evils:

Nahman in the name of R. Samuel: "Behold it was good," this is the good inclination (*yetzer ha-tov*). "And behold it was *very* good," this is the evil inclination (*yetzer ha-ra*). How can the evil inclination be very good? Without the evil inclination a man would not build a house, marry a woman, and have children. As Solomon says, "[Again I considered all travail, and every right work,] that for this a man is envied of his neighbor" (Ecc. 4:4). (9.7)

THIS OFT-QUOTED STATEMENT marks the beginning of an ongoing revision of an earlier, dualistic conceptualization of the evil inclination (as the force opposing the good inclination). The *yetzer ha-ra* gradually loses the modifier *ha-ra*, evil, and becomes simply the *yetzer*, desire, and as such neither essentially evil nor uncomplicatedly good.

Critics who have sought to establish real textual links between the rabbis and Milton have often pointed to this famous passage as a possible source for the celebrated view of vice and virtue put forth by Milton in the *Areopagitica*:

> Look how much we thus expell of sin so much we expell of vertue: for the matter of them both is the same; remove that, and ye remove them both alike. This justifies the high providence of God, who though he command us temperance, justice, continence, yet powrs out before us ev'n to a profuseness all desireable things, and gives us minds that can wander beyond all limit and satiety. (YP 2:527–28)

WHETHER THIS IDEA comes directly or indirectly from the rabbis is probably impossible to determine. Ernest Sirluck's footnote in the Yale prose edition, which cites Thomas Browne's *Religio Medici* as expressing a similar view, suggests that it was an opinion not at all unique to Milton or to those especially persuaded by an Hebraic perspective.[43]

Rather than offering it as a possible rabbinic source for Milton, I read the rabbinic statement on the benefits of the yetzer ha-ra in tandem with this excerpt from Milton's prose in light of *Areopagitica*'s complex adumbration of the concern with the relation between desire, power, and providence that dominates the epic poem. The word *yetzer* may indeed properly be translated as "inclination" or "desire." But *yetzer* is also at the root of one of the several biblical and rabbinic Hebrew words meaning creation, *yetzirah*. It is specifically this mode of creation—and not *b'riah* or *assiyah*, two other verbs used in the Genesis account—that is invoked in Genesis 2:7's rendition of the creation of Adam: "*Vayitzar YHWH elohim et ha-adam*, And the Lord God formed man of the dust of the ground." Commenting on the relation between God's creation and the human yetzer, the rabbis note that the use of this verb indicates that Adam was created *with* a *yetzer*, and did not obtain it only as a result of his first transgression. In other words, rabbinic monism's insistence on prelapsarian sexuality stems from its association of God's creativity with humanity's desire.

But human sexuality is also related to humanity's own ability to create, for there is yet another meaning for the word *yetzer*: "imagination." The Hebrew Bible uses the word *yezter* to refer to the imagination for the first time in the story of the Great Flood.[44] Genesis 6:5 describes the moral decline of humanity in the following terms: "And YHWH saw the extent of man's wickedness in the land, for all the imagination [yetzer] of his heart's thoughts was only evil all day." Following the flood, when we might expect this moral decline to have been remedied, the Bible reiterates the characterization: "and YHWH said to himself, 'I will no longer curse the earth on account of man, for the imagination [yetzer] of man's [*adam*] heart is evil from his youth" (Genesis 8:21). Puzzling over this repetition, Genesis Rabbah reports a conversation that explicitly pits Hebraism against Hellenism.

> Antoninus asked out Rabbi, "When is the evil inclination [*yetzer ha-ra*] placed within a man ['*adam*]?" He replied, "From the moment he is formed [*notzar*]." [Antoninus] said to him, "If this were so, the fetus would immediately dig through the womb and come out. Rather, [the evil inclination is placed in a man] from the moment he exits [the womb]." Rabbi agreed with him, since it concurred with the verse, "For the imagination of a man's heart is evil from his youth." R. Yudan added, "It is written 'from his youth [*mi-ne'urav*]' to suggest the moment he awakens [*ni'or*] to the world." [Antoninus] further asked, "When is the soul placed within a man? He [Rabbi] replied, "From the moment he leaves his mother's womb." [Antoninus] said to him, "If you leave unsalted flesh out for three days, will it not rot? Rather [the soul is place within a man] from the moment he is conceived [*niphqad*]."[45] Rabbi again agreed with him, since it concurred with the verses, "For all the while my soul is in me and the spirit of God is in my nostrils" (Job 27:3), and "Your providence [*ph'qudath'khah*] watched over my spirit" (Job 10:12). "When did You place my soul within me? From the moment your providence extended to me [*phaqad'thani*]." (34:10)

THESE TWO EXCHANGES are part of a string of accounts scattered throughout the midrash and the Palestinian and Babylonian Talmuds describing an intimate friendship between Rabbi—R. Judah haNasi, the celebrated Tannaitic patriarch and redactor of the Mishnah—and the Roman emperor Antoninus.[46] They offer several important clues about the nature of the encounter between Hellenism and Hebraism, especially as it contributes to the fitful and inconsistent transition by the rabbis from a dualist to a monist ontology. First, Rabbi expresses no discomfort in accepting the correction of a Roman on matters with such profound religious and philosophical implications; nor does the midrash seem troubled by it. While it would not be so surprising to find conversations between a Roman emperor and a Jewish rabbi in which the rabbi time and again taught the Roman a lesson, it is far more surprising to observe a rabbi graciously accepting the correction of a Roman.[47] These stories probably come from a period in Jewish-Roman relations when Jewish authorities did not perceive Rome's Hellenistic worldview as a religious and philosophical threat. Both perceptions would change dramatically, with the advent of a hellenized Christianity—rabbinic Judaism's prodigal son—as a national religion serving as the key factor in this shift.[48]

Second, it is not the Jewish reader who advocates a monistic vitalism in this discussion but the Hellenic emperor![49] This is a reversal that most rabbinic texts work very hard to deny or rewrite in light of the rise of Pauline Christianity's staunchly dualist vision, as can be seen in what I consider to be a later version of this same debate.[50] In the following account the possible moments for the advent of the soul are altered:

> Antoninus said to Rabbi, "When is the soul placed within a man, at the moment of conception [*ph'qidah*] or at the moment of formation [*yetzirah*]?" He replied, "At the moment of formation." [Antoninus] said to him, "If you leave unsalted flesh out for three days, will it not rot? Rather [the soul is placed within a man] from the moment he is conceived [*niphqad*]." Rabbi said, "Antoninus has taught me this matter and Scripture agrees with him, 'Your providence [*ph'qudath'khah*] watched over my spirit' (Job 10:12)."[51]

THE MOST RADICALLY dualist alternative first offered by Rabbi in Genesis Rabbah, i.e., that the soul is not placed in man until the moment of birth, is not even considered here. What is more, in their discussion of the yetzer hara, the question they debate is not when it is placed [*nathun*] within man, but when it begins its influence [*sholet*]. All these differences suggest that this second version bears the distinctive markings of a later period in Jewish history, at a time when monism had become a much more accepted aspect of rabbinic thinking.[52] With that cosmological monism also came an ethical dialecticism and a revision of the rabbinic understanding of the yetzer, the imagination.

THE EMBRACE OF THE FIG TREE

IT IS BY this meaning of yetzer as imagination that we come to a deeper parallel between Milton's collation of classical and biblical source texts in his creation accounts and the midrashic understanding of these events. For if the imagination of *Paradise Lost* resides at least partly in its *creatio ex materia*, in its reformation of preexistent textual matter, then a similar dynamic may be said to function for the rabbis. Among their many speculations concerning man's first disobedience, the rabbis wonder about the exact species of the Tree of Knowledge. Genesis Rabbah reports a debate between R. Meir, who said it was a stalk of wheat as tall as the cedars of Lebanon,[53] R. Judah b. Ilai, who said it was a grapevine,[54] R. Abba of Acre, who said it was the *etrog*, or citron tree,[55] and R. Yose, who said it was a fig tree. The midrash goes on to give R. Yose's reasoning:

> It may be compared to a prince who corrupted himself with one of his maidservants. When the king heard about it he threw him out of the palace. The prince tried to return to the doors of the maidservants, but they did not receive him. However, the one with whom he corrupted himself opened her door and received him. Similarly, when Adam ate from the Tree, he was thrown out of the Garden of Eden. When he approached each tree [for shelter] they did not receive him. . . . But since it was from the fruit of the fig tree that he ate, the tree opened her doors and embraced him, as it is written, "and they sewed fig leaves together" (Gen. 3:7). (15:7)

THE MASHAL ACTUALLY rearranges the order of the biblical narrative, in which the fig tree leaves are donned by Adam and Eve *before* they are exiled from the garden! As a revision of the Bible's own account, it functions much like Milton's insertion of Eve's creation before Raphael's hexameron and Adam's account. Not only do both examples constitute narrative reworkings of Scripture, they both deploy these revisions via the insertion of nonbiblical

Hellenistic material: in the case of *Paradise Lost* Ovid's Narcissus story, and in this midrash a story that scholars have traced to earlier Hellenistic sources.[56] What is more, the association of divine wisdom and the fig tree is probably Gnostic in origin.[57] Apparently, R. Yose could not resist the *seduction* of this secular romance in his reconstruction of the narrative of creation and fall. The mashal was so effective that R. Yose was willing to sacrifice the scriptural sequence to the parable's narrative trajectory. That this imaginative disruption of the biblical narrative via the use of a nonbiblical romance or fable occurs in a discussion of the precise nature of the Fall suggests an uncanny awareness of the fallen aspect of this homily, even as it develops its own powerful interpretation of Scripture.

A further parallel between Milton's Ovidian story of Eve and the midrashic insertion of a Hellenistic story can be seen in their shared interest in sexuality: the offense committed by the prince is specifically sexual. While the prince's self-corruption through sexuality prompts the king to expel his beloved son, that corruption is movingly restored by the embrace of the fig tree. The very site of corruption becomes the site of restitution and healing. If sexuality is the form in which the rabbinic fall occurs, then sexuality—specifically *female* sexuality as allegorized in the fig tree—is also the specific form in which we may look to "repair the ruins of our first parents."[58] I say female sexuality because the parable elides Eve's culpability in the Fall or subsumes it within the seduction of the tree itself. Now, while it is certainly possible to read this omission of Eve as evidence of the rabbinic dismissal of female agency—all that really matters is that *Adam* sinned and that *Adam* will be restored—it is equally important to see how this nonbiblical parable allows the rabbis to restore female sexuality without dwelling on it as a contributing factor in humanity's fall.

The midrashic "embrace of the fig tree" stands both as a figure for sexuality and as a figure for the interpolation of the secular romance into the reading of the biblical account of the Fall. As a way of gauging this phenomenon of rabbinic cultural response it is worth looking to an earlier Hebraic identification of the Tree of Knowledge with the fig tree. The apocryphal text, the Apocalypse of Moses, also known as the Greek version of the Life of Adam and Eve, was probably originally composed without the allegorization or symbolic treatment of biblical figures characteristic of Philo and his followers, which has led scholars to compare it with midrash: "The form is that of midrash and the theology is that of Pharisaic Judaism."[59] Yet, unlike later rabbinic texts, the Apocalypse of Moses is consistent in its dualism. The narrative describes Adam's soul being taken to the third heaven (chapter 37), while his body is buried in the ground (chapter 40); similarly, God first converses with Adam's soul in chapter 39, and not until chapter 41 does God call to Adam's body. Before it narrates the aftermath of Adam's death, however, it offers two versions of humanity's fall, the first told by Adam and the second told by Eve.[60] Eve's version addresses the matter of postlapsarian nakedness:

> And at that very moment my eyes were opened and I knew that I was naked of the righteousness with which I had been clothed. And I wept saying "Why have you done this to me, that I have been estranged from my glory with which I was clothed?" . . . But that one [the serpent] came down from the tree and vanished. I looked for leaves in my region so that I might cover my shame, but I did not find (any) from the trees of Paradise, since while I ate the leaves of all the trees of my portion fell,[61] except (those) of the fig tree only. And I took its leaves and made for myself skirts; *they were from the same plants of which I ate.*[62]

DESPITE THE BASIC structural affinities between this apocryphal narrative and the story told in the midrash—the abandonment of the other trees and the return to the source of corruption for rudimentary covering—there are two crucial variations that make all the difference in the world. First, unlike the midrash, the Apocalypse of Moses does not interpolate a secondary narrative in order to suggest the connection between the Tree of Knowledge and the fig tree. Rather than invoking the seductiveness of the charming romance fable to establish the identity of the tree, the apocryphal text relies on sheer assertion to make the point. Thus, although the accepted view of the Apocalypse of Moses assumes its basic resemblance to aggadic midrash, we have discovered one important divergence, a divergence that may in fact make this text more Hebraic in its narrative construction than the hellenistically inflected Genesis Rabbah.

Second, whereas in Genesis Rabbah, the mashal elides Eve's participation in the story of the Fall (both to her benefit and detriment), in this apocryphal account the entire story told by Eve occurs even *before* she has convinced Adam to eat of the fruit. If the mashal diminishes Eve's culpability—and by extension, the inherent corruption of sexuality, female or male—then the Apocalypse of Moses embellishes her role in the Fall, condemning it as explicitly sexual, having only further corrupting effects on any notion of sexuality. God's words of punishment to Eve in chapter 25 of the Apocalypse speak of the pains of childbirth and further imagine Eve's words during labor: "And you shall confess and say, 'Lord, Lord, save me and I will never again turn to the sin of the flesh.'"

These are differences that make sense historically. The assumed date of composition for the Apocalypse of Moses is the first century *c.e.*, whereas the material within Genesis Rabbah (redacted in the fourth or fifth century) may come from a later period in the cultural history of Palestinian Jewry. The years between the composition of the Apocalypse of Moses and the redaction of Genesis Rabbah marked a period of intense encounter between Jews and the hellenized Christian culture by which they found themselves increasingly surrounded and assaulted.[63] In their efforts to distinguish rabbinic Judaism from these outside cultural influences—perceived to be especially threatening in light of Christianity's claim to be the true or new Israel—many midrashists emphasized a different view of the body, of sexuality, and of gender. Yet if the rabbinic restitution of sexuality reflects a cultural response to the forces of Hellenistic dualism within Judaism, then how might we account for what looks to be, in this particular midrash, a Hellenistic inspiration for the regenerative possibilities of sexuality? If rabbinic Judaism presents a more positive version of the *yetzer*, of desire, in response to Hellenism's rejection of the body, how are we to understand the midrash's embrace of the hellenized fig tree?

"MOTHER OF THE HUMAN RACE"

TO ADDRESS THIS complexity, I turn again to Milton's poem, specifically the fraught relation between the poet and his textual formulation of Eve. That we first observe unfallen Adam and Eve in book 4 through Satan's eyes, that we hear Eve's version of her creation through Satan's ears, does not mitigate the audacity of Milton's assertion of the redemptive qualities of sexuality. Eve figures simultaneously the glory of self-reflection and the grace of authorial subordination. Indeed, the envy that Satan expresses as he observes the couple at 4.358–65 includes a surprising reference to their creator:

> O Hell! what do mine eyes with grief behold,
> Into our room of bliss thus high advanc't
> Creatures of other mould, earth-born perhaps,

Not Spirits, yet to heav'nly Spirits bright
Little inferior; whom my thoughts pursue
With wonder, and could love, so lively shines
In them Divine resemblance, and such grace
The hand that form'd them on their shape hath pour'd.

WE MIGHT EXPECT Satan to feel jealousy toward these new creatures who appear to have replaced him and his fallen compatriots. But the quality that seems to move Satan to wonderment and, almost, to love (that most divine of attributes), is the manner in which they display the grace that signifies their resemblance to their creator. Satan recognizes the image of the Author in Adam and Eve, which he has already denied in himself by claiming to be "self-begot."

Any critical attempt to align Satan's self-authorship with Eve's self-reflection founders on what Satan perceives to be the quintessential attribute of Adam and Eve: willing submission. The notorious description of the First Couple having been formed "Hee for God only, shee for God in him" (4.299), is of course an articulation of gender hierarchy, but one in which the two first humans *both* occupy positions of subordination. The warning voice—biblical, masculine—holds out to Eve, as a fit replacement for her reflected image, "hee / Whose image thou art" (471–72). The compensation offered within this economy of reflection can only make sense, can only be worthwhile to Eve—"what could I do, / But follow straight, invisibly thus led?" (475–76)—if she recognizes the value of resemblance despite, or even because of, its implicit subordination. That she initially flees the image, "Less winning soft, less amiably mild," suggests an analogous poetic disappointment that ever threatens to turn *Milton's* image, his poem, into one wholly dominated by masculine/biblical authority, in other words, into a mere repetition of the divinely authored creation narrative in Genesis 1–3.

Eve's scene in book 4, as delightful as it is, plays out the virtually irresolvable conflict between two divergent sides of Milton's creative and interpretive inclinations. As she reflects on her image in the pool, Eve stands as the figure for imagination and hence self-generated thought. But the warning voice, never fully identified,[64] represents divine inspiration reinscribing sexuality—specifically female sexuality—within a larger authoritative framework of biblical stricture. Milton has the opportunity to pose simultaneously as the playful imaginative spectator, having his origins in the feminized classical texts of Ovid, and as the authoritative inspired lawgiver, whose antecedents are to be found in the biblical text. It is the case, after all, that the only aspect of Eve's story that has a basis in the biblical narrative occurs in lines 467–83:

> . . . a voice thus warn'd me, What thou seest,
> What there thou seest fair Creature is thyself,
> With thee it came and goes: but follow me,
> And I will bring thee where no shadow stays
> Thy coming, and thy soft embraces, hee
> Whose image thou art, him thou shall enjoy
> Inseparably thine, to him shalt bear
> Multitudes like thyself, and thence be call'd
> Mother of the human Race: what could I do,
> But follow straight, invisibly thus led?
> Till I espi'd thee, fair indeed and tall,
> Under a Platan, yet methought less fair,
> Less winning soft, less amiably mild,
> Than that smooth wat'ry image; back I turn'd,
> Thou following cri'd'st aloud, Return fair *Eve*.

THESE LINES STAND as an expanded rendition of the terse biblical pronouncement in Genesis 2:22, "and brought her unto the man," along with an allusion to Adam's naming of Eve, which in the Bible occurs *after the Fall*: "And Adam called his wife's name Eve; because she was the mother of all living" (Genesis 3:20). Milton's staging of the conflict between female creativity and masculine creativity (as represented by divine edict) thus comprehends an early articulation of the conflict between the classics and the Bible, which in turn sets the stage for the proem to book 7. Alistair Fowler has suggested that the transposition of Eve's naming from postlapsarian time to this prelapsarian moment may serve as a typically Miltonic "correction of conventional chronology, to enhance the status of sexuality and motherhood."[65] Nevertheless, the connection between Eve's procreative powers and her name has been partially severed: the Warning Voice calls her "Mother of human race," while Adam calls her Eve.

John Leonard has argued that Adam's naming of Eve in book 4 confers on Eve an *identity*, "exactly what Eve had lacked when encountering her reflection in the pool." As a masculine conferral of female identity, however, it is hard to read it as a "free and spontaneous act which proves to be [Adam's] most persuasive argument in winning Eve's love."[66] Indeed, if, as Pardes has shown, the activity of naming in the Genesis account constitutes a reclaiming of (pro)creative powers, then this instance of naming serves to *dissociate* Eve's name from her power to create. The conflict between different forms of creativity represented in Eve's story—between female (pro)creativity and male pronouncement, between imagination and inspiration, between the Greek and Roman classics and the Bible—sets the terms for its subsequent representation in books 7 and 8. Adam's narration of his first day, and especially his "creation" of Eve through discussion with God, follows on the subtle but pointed denigration of Eve's (pro)creativity in the separation of her name and her role as mother.

Milton does not follow the opinion expressed by R. Yose that the Tree of Knowledge was a fig tree. Like the biblical text that serves as its source (Genesis 3:7) *Paradise Lost* only reports on the presence of the fig tree *after* the Fall. This later account of the fig tree portrays it as an alternative mother figure to the ambivalent maternity of Eve. When Adam and Eve become aware of their nakedness after their first experience with postlapsarian sexuality they seek some means by which to cover "The Parts of each other, that seem most / To shame obnoxious, and unseemliest seen" (9.1093–94):

> . . . both together went
> Into the thickest Wood, there soon they chose
> The Figtree, not that kind for Fruit renown'd,
> But such as at this day to *Indians* known
> In *Malabar* or *Decan* spreads her Arms
> Branching so broad and long, that in the ground
> The bended Twigs take root, and Daughters grow
> About the Mother Tree, a Pillar'd shade
> High overarch't, and echoing Walks between;
> There oft the *Indian* Herdsman shunning heat
> Shelters in cool, and tends his pasturing Herds
> At Loopholes, cut through thickest shade: Those Leaves
> They gather'd, broad as *Amazonian* Targe,
> And with what skill they had, together sew'd,
> To gird thir waist, vain Covering if to hide
> Thir guilt and dreaded shame; O how unlike
> To that first naked Glory. (1099–1115)

THE PROVENANCE OF this passage has been the subject of some discussion among Milton's editors and annotators. John Gerard's *Herball* is frequently offered as the most immediate source for some of Milton's images. Gerard describes the manner in which the arched Indian fig tree sends down branches that in turn reroot themselves

> by meanes whereof, it cometh to passe that one tree is made a great wood, or desart of trees, which the Indians do vse for couerture against the extreme heate of the sunne, wherewith they are greeuously vexed: some likewise vse them for pleasure, cutting downe by a direct line a long walke, or as it were a vault, through the thickest part, from which also they cut certaine loope holes . . . that they may see their cattle that feedeth . . . ; from which vault or close walke, doth rebound such an admirable eccho, or answering voice . . . that it doth resound, or answer againe fower or fiue times . . . ; the first or mother of this wood or desart of trees, is hard to be knowne from the children.[67]

MILTON'S DESCRIPTION OF the fig tree clearly echoes many of the details of Gerard's account. Yet Kester Svendsen provides a longer list of the possible sources for the Indian fig tree in his study of Milton and science, largely to demonstrate the impossibility of determining with any real certainty the most immediate influence on the poet. These possibilities include, in addition to Gerard, Ben Jonson's *Neptune's Triumph*, Terry's *Voyage to East India*, Duret's *Histoire des Planteset Herbes*, Bartholomew's *De Proprietatibus Rerum*, and Pliny's *Historia Naturalis*.[68]

Ralegh's *History of the World*, another source cited by Svendsen, is a candidate deserving of special consideration, however, for, in his discussion of the "the chiefe Trees in the Garden of Paradise," Ralegh raises the possible connection between the Tree of Knowledge and the fig tree of Genesis 3:7 in some detail. Ralegh cites the Jesuit theologian and exegete Martinus Becanus (1550–1624) and the Syrian Bishop Moses Bar Kepha (813–903)—from whom, Ralegh claims, Becanus shamelessly plagiarized[69]—as having identified the Tree of Knowledge as the *Ficus Indica*:

> When *Adam* and *Eue* found themselues naked, they made them breeches of Fig-leaues; which proueth (indeede) that either the tree it selfe was a Fig-tree, or that a Fig-tree grew neare it: because *Adam* being possest with shame did not runne vp and downe the garden to seeke out leaues to couer him, but found them in the place it selfe; and these leaues of all other were most

commodious by reason of their largeness, which *Plinie* auoweth in these words; *Latitudo foliorum peltae effigiem Amazoniae habet, The breadth of the leaues hath the shape of an Amazonian shield.*[70]

THE CONNECTION BETWEEN the two trees is one that Milton very deliberately eschews—he mostly relies on the generic "Fruit"; when he does become more specific, the fruit he names is, of course, the apple.[71] Ralegh himself goes on to minimize the significance of Becanus's identification of the Tree of Knowledge with the fig tree because he holds, like most of his contemporaries (and Milton) that the genus of the Tree of Knowledge was unimportant. What mattered was the fact of the prohibition; the tree was merely the site for the proving of Man's obedience or disobedience. Milton writes in *De Doctrina Christiana*,

> Adam was not required to perform any works; he was merely forbidden to do one thing. It was necessary that one thing at least should be either forbidden or commanded, and above all something which was in itself neither good nor evil, so that man's obedience might in this way be made evident.

> . . . The tree of knowledge of good and evil . . . was a kind of pledge or memorial of obedience. (YP 6:351–52)

C. A. PATRIDES HAS demonstrated the prevalence of this view of the Tree of Knowledge as a thing in itself "indifferent," identifying this perspective with Augustine.[72] This theological agreement seems to suggest an even stronger affinity between Ralegh and Milton than with Bartholomew or Gerard.

Ralegh goes on to cite with greater approbation Becanus's "*allegorizing of the Storie of his* Ficus Indica." What Ralegh admires here is how the growth of the tree—its bending downward—mirrors or adumbrates humanity's moral and physical decline after the fall, and how the lack of fruit is analogous to the rarity of virtue. Whether this is also a view shared by Milton remains to be seen. Ralegh's reading of Becanus seems to have exercised an important influence—wittingly or unwittingly—on Alastair Fowler's annotation of the Milton passage, since he reads it as a poignant contrast with the prelapsarian nuptual bower.

> The Indian hersdman is put in because he is primitive and pagan, and perhaps also because his work is connected with fallen man's non-vegetarian

diet. Similarly the Amazonian targe is carried over from Gerard because before the Fall man never thought of fighting, let alone woman. The proliferating tree is a tree of error: it is an objective correlative of the proliferating sin
that that will ramify through Adam's and Eve's descendants.[73]

AS THE LANGUAGE of simile suggests, Milton doubtless meant for some kind
of contrast to be drawn between the "primitive" Indians and the postlapsarian couple, but whether this contrast reveals more in the *similarities* between
the two or in their *differences* depends both on an extratextual view of the non-
Western shepherds *and* a theological view of the first couple in the first hours
after their fall. As we should know by the time we reach book 9, Milton's epic
similes very often fold back on themselves, undermining the very comparisons they offer. We should not necessarily assume—as Fowler seems to
imply—that the Indian herdsman embodies an uncivilized, even barbaric existence. Neither, however, should we regard this passage as purely condemnatory in its depiction of Adam and Eve. That is, Milton's fig tree may offer its
pastoral dalliance with a false surmise not exclusively to underscore the loss
experienced by Adam and Eve, but to combine that awareness with a resolute
(and hopeful) projection forward to a regaining of paradise, to a restitution
of the pastoral world now lost. Even at the moment when the first couple are
made most acutely aware of their loss of innocence by the need to invent the
institution of clothing, even at the moment when they recognize that the joyous sexuality they enjoyed before the Fall is no longer available to them, they
look to the "Loopholes" in God's—the Father's—judgment, to the mother
tree that offers the possibility of a restored and (re)generative sexuality.

Svendsen's reading of the passage suggests something like this possibility.
He sees the image of the fig tree as pulling in two directions. On the one
hand, the momentary glimpse into the pastoral world stands in contrast to
the "frantic distress of Adam and Eve." Though we are made momentarily
aware of the proximity of this protective mother tree, we are quickly dis-
tanced from it in space and time, implying a denial "that this protected pastoral life exists any longer for the human pair." On the other hand, the mother tree nevertheless offers hope in its fecundity and especially in its
embodiment of the teleology of the poem itself: "The twigs still bound to
their mother fall to earth, root themselves, and rise again as daughters, one
more among a hundred images of rhythmic fall and rise, rise and fall."[74] As
in the rabbinic legend of the fig tree, then, Milton's embrace of the fig tree

stands, for Svendsen, as the possibility—even the promise—of redemption, but a redemption specifically figured as female and generative.

More recently, several critics have identified further tensions in the Miltonic fig tree. John Guillory picks up on the contrast to which Svendsen alludes between pre- and postlapsarian existence in his own suggestive reading of this passage.

> All that is left of Eden is this tree, a mother tree to set against the father's tree of prohibition. That matrilineal proliferation of this tree makes a little world, or another world in which labor itself is leisure, a suspending of the consequences of the fall hinted by the passage's slight evocation of Renaissance pastoral.[75]

THE CONSEQUENCE OF the father's judgment was sexual difference as embodied in the institution of clothing. Guillory reads the fig tree as posing the possibility—one that finally proves to be "an empty dream"—of a loophole in the father's decree. The shields of the Amazons to which the fig leaves are compared rehearses the ambivalence toward the mother in book 7's invocation. The mother (tree) is thus necessarily a version of the savage Amazon: "The mother's care is implicitly repudiated as an illusion, a fantasy," Guillory concludes. "There never was a mother."[76]

The rabbinic fig tree, while revealing the cultural tensions between a distinctly Hebraic perspective and one inflected by Hellenism, presents a view of (female) sexuality as regenerative and positive. Milton's fig tree embodies the various tensions concerning female procreativity and sexuality we have encountered thus far, associating them with the specifically pagan worlds of the East and the New World. We would be mistaken to take this difference between the midrash and *Paradise Lost* as an indication of the rabbis' greater ease with the nexus of sexuality and female creativity. I have noted that the second chapter of Genesis, with its more anthropocentric narration of the creation, describes God's creation of Adam with the verb *vayitzar*, thereby occasioning in the midrash an associative chain connecting God's creativity, Adam's sexual desire, and human imagination. If we look to this same chapter's notorious depiction of Eve's creation from Adam's *tzela*, usually translated as "rib," we discover, quite remarkably, that the text eschews *vayitzar* in favor of yet another mode of divine creation, *vayiven*: "And the Lord God *built* the rib that he had taken from Adam into a woman" (2:22). Genesis

Rabbah (18:1) reports the comments of R. Yose b. Zimra, who reads *vayiven* as a play on the Hebrew word for understanding, *havanah*. Since *vayiven* implies that greater understanding was given to woman than to man, R. Yose (not the R. Yose who embraced the fig tree) connects the advent of female sexuality with *reason* rather than with imagination; in so doing he reverses the more prevalent association—in both the rabbis and in Milton—of masculinity with the authority of biblical reasoning and femininity with the libertine romance of imagination. While we may wish to read this comment as further evidence of an antimisogynist strain within midrash, we must also attend to what the Bible and its rabbinic readers refuse to Eve in the use of *vayiven* instead of *vayitzar: yetzer*, desire (both proper and improper) and its concomitant, imagination. Just as Milton's poem plays out the tensions inherent in tying female sexuality to poetic creativity, so too the rabbis depict the redemptive aspect of sexuality only to delimit it by interrupting its associations with imagination.

These parallel textual-sexual histories in the rabbis and in Milton are, in and of themselves, noteworthy. What makes them of even greater interest is that they suggest a very different reading of the presence of Hebraic and rabbinic influences on the seventeenth-century English poet than is usually offered. Rather than seeing these influences as assertions of control, infusions of biblical authority, or embodiments of law (versus the Pauline spirit), we must view them as part of a more complex dynamic. The Hebraic (and potentially rabbinic) elements of the poem may partly serve to rein in the potentially corrupting influences of classical poetry, but they also function as a necessary complement to the redemptive sexuality itself contained within classical motifs and images. The reaffirmation of sexuality—both pre- and postlapsarian—is also a preservation of dialogical textuality. The dialectical possibilities inherent in sexuality, potentially both redemptive and corrupting, are also there in the plurivocal text. From a literary- and religious-historical perspective, these genealogies suggest that the rabbis' radical revision of postbiblical Judaism is analogous to Milton's own innovative refashioning of post-Reformation Christianity.

"MALE HE CREATED THEE"

WHEN WE FINALLY do arrive at Raphael's version of the creation of humanity, and then Adam's account of his own awakening in book 8, we have been witness to an important organization of gender and source text that serves as a meditation on the creative process generally. Raphael reports the divine pronouncement, following closely (with the notable aforementioned additions) the text of Genesis 1:26–30 (the Priestly account):

> Let us make now Man in our image, Man
> In our similitude, and let them rule
> Over the Fish, and Fowl of Sea and Air,
> Beast of the Field, and over all the Earth,
> And every creeping thing that creeps the ground.
> This said, he form'd thee, *Adam*, thee O Man
> Dust of the ground, and in thy nostrils breath'd
> The breath of Life; in his own Image hee
> Created thee, in the Image of God
> Express, and thou becam'st a living Soul.
> Male he created thee, but thy consort
> Female for race; then bless'd Mankind, and said,
> Be fruitful, multiply, and fill the Earth,
> Subdue it, and throughout Dominion hold
> Over Fish of the Sea, and Fowl of the Air,
> And every living thing that moves on the Earth. (519–34)

READINGS OF THIS rendition tend to emphasize the degree to which Raphael focuses on man's dominion, on his free will, reason, and ultimately his distance from God.[77] That this emphasis is grounded specifically in man's likeness to God and that it comes directly from the P text appear to contradict what has been called by many readers the more theocentric quality of Genesis 1 and of *Paradise Lost*, book 7. More remarkable still, Milton's interpretive undermining of man's dominion results from his incorporation of portions of the Yahwistic text (2:7), normally considered to be the more anthropocentric creation story: "This said, he form'd thee, *Adam*, thee O Man / Dust of the ground, and in thy nostrils breath'd / The breath of Life . . . and thou becamest a living Soul." Whereas in earlier moments of the creation Milton did not hesitate to augment the biblical narrative with his own hypotactic details of nature's fecundity, here, at this most crucial of creative moments, where man's authority threatens to jettison itself from the creating Authority and the poet's creative invention could potentially leave the biblical pretexts behind, Milton's interpretive *and* creative solution is to fold in a second biblical text that reminds man of his lowly origins and his debt to his maker. It is of the utmost significance that the source for this augmentation is the Bible, *and not a classical source,* since the mode of creativity that the poet endorses is specifically male. Milton grants to woman the essential role in procreation, but in such a way as to diminish its significance relative to other human forms of authorship. While the text states, "Male he created thee, but thy consort / Female for Race," the production of a multitudinous race is necessary primarily as a means to subordinate the rest of the created universe: "fill the Earth / Subdue it, and throughout Dominion hold." Raphael's augmentation of P, "Female for Race," enacts precisely the kind of interpretive supplement that constitutes the masculine form of creativity embodied in the text. In other words, Milton's incorporation of female procreativity in the form of discursive abundance and textual supplementation may initially threaten to overwhelm masculine creation-via-fiat, but it is eventually subsumed within the narrative in order to shore up further the authority of male dominion.

I have just said that if Raphael's augmentations of the creation of humanity have sources, they are necessarily to be found in the Bible. But this is not entirely the case, and the exception is worth noting. Before coming to the Priestly pronouncement in line 519, Raphael sets the stage with the following observation:

> There wanted yet the Master work, the end
> Of all yet done; a Creature who not prone
> And Brute as other Creatures, but endu'd
> With Sanctity of Reason, might erect
> His Stature, and upright with Front serene
> Govern the rest, self-knowing, and from thence
> Magnanimous to correspond with Heav'n,
> But grateful to acknowledge whence his good
> Descends, thither with heart and voice and eyes
> Directed in Devotion, to adore
> And worship God Supreme, who made him chief
> Of all his works . . . (505–16)

AS MANY ANNOTATORS have pointed out, this kind of prelude, which posits a difference between man and all other creations based on posture and destiny, was not uncommon in ancient, medieval, and early modern renditions of the creation of humanity. Milton's version, however, is especially close to that of Ovid, whose Narcissus story, as we have already seen, played an important role in shaping Eve's creation story:

Sanctius his animal mentisque capacius altae

deerat adhuc et quod dominari in cetera posset:

natus homo est, sive hunc divino semine fecit

ille opifex rerum, mundi melioris origo,

sive recens tellus seductaque nuper ab alto

aethere cognati retinebat semina caeli.

quam satus Iapeto, mixtam pluvialibus undis,

finxit in effigiem moderantum cuncta deorum,

pronaque cum spectent animalia cetera terram,

os homini sublime dedit caelumque videre

iussit et erectos ad sidera tollere vultus.

[A living creature of finer stuff than these, more capable of lofty thought, one who could have dominion over all the rest, was lacking yet. Then man was born: whether the god who made all else, designing a more perfect world, made man of his own divine substance, or whether the new earth, but lately drawn away from heavenly ether, retained still some elements of its kindred sky—that earth which the son of Iapetus mixed with fresh, running water, and moulded into the form of the all-controlling gods. And, though all other animals are prone, and fix their gaze upon the earth, he gave to man an up-lifted face and bade him stand erect and turn his eyes to heaven.][78]

HOW DOES THE PRESENCE of an Ovidian echo in Raphael's prelude to the creation of humanity reflect upon my earlier argument that the biblical creation sources represent, for Milton, masculine authority and male creativity? One possible answer would be that, since the Ovid reference comes just before the Genesis pronouncement, Milton has provided yet another instance of the masculine biblical voice supplanting the feminine classical one. But Raphael's Ovidian echo is *self*-correcting, as well. Ovid's characteristic deferral of agency in the creation through the use of the "sive . . . sive" disjunctive conditional—"*whether* the god who made all else . . . made man of his own divine substance, *or whether* the new earth . . . retained still some elements of its kindred sky"—never fully acknowledges the creating power. Raphael leaves no room for this kind of ambiguity in his version, calling man "a

Creature . . . to adore / And worship *God Supreme, who made him* chief / Of all his works." The Ovidian prelude also occurs within the opening description of the "golden age." We are told immediately following these lines,

> Golden was that first age, which, with no one to compel, without a law, of its own will, kept faith and did the right. There was no fear of punishment, no threatening words were to be read on brazen tablets . . . . The earth herself, without compulsion, untouched by hoe or plowshare, of herself gave all things needful. (1.89–92, 101–2)

RAPHAEL'S REVISION OF this classical idyllicism occurs within the subsequent paraphrase of Genesis 1, but it stands as *the* quintessential distinguishing feature of the Hebraic representation of the prelapsarian world:

> He brought thee into this delicious Grove,
> This Garden, planted with the Trees of God,
> Delectable both to behold and taste;
> And freely all thir pleasant fruit for food
> Gave thee, all sorts are here that all th'Earth yields . . . (537–41)

TO THIS POINT prelapsarian Eden sounds very much like Ovid's golden age.

> [B]ut of the Tree
> Which tasted works knowledge of Good and Evil,
> Thou may'st not; in the day thou eat'st, thou di'st;
> Death is the penalty impos'd, beware,
> And govern well thy appetite, lest Sin
> Surprise thee, and her black attendant Death. (542–47)

WHAT IS MOST BITTERSWEET about this moment of crowning creative achievement is that we are anything but surprised by the sin that already threatens it. The single prohibition makes all the difference in the world between Ovid's vision of the lawless golden age and the Bible's Eden with limits. Laws and limitations feel repressive to us because, as fallen readers, we can have no real conception of a limit that guards and orients our freedom without at the same time constraining it. It is this paradoxical sense of limit, however, that is what the J writer asks us to grant as a primordial and yet irretrievable state,

and which Milton adduces as the correction to the Ovidian "Aurea aetas
. . . sine lege."[79]

Furthermore, Raphael's use of this passage in Ovid alludes to Eve's narcissistic moment by revising it. Whereas Eve recalls "unexperienc't thought,"
here man is to be "endued / With sanctity of reason . . . self-knowing." If
Eve lay herself down at the lakeside, here man "might erect / His stature."
Eve looks into the lake, thinking it to be another sky; man "correspond[s]
with Heav'n . . . grateful to acknowledge whence his good descends." And
the most important correction, "thither with heart and voice and eyes / Directed in devotion," emends Eve's self-centered affections: "it return'd as soon
with answering looks / Of sympathy and love; there I had fixt / Mine eyes
till now." As I have already suggested, critics wishing to support the claim
that Milton fashioned a prelapsarian Eve already possessing the qualities that
would allow her to be seduced by Satan, as well as those who wish to demonstrate Milton's elevation of man by means of a denigration of woman, often
point to the counterpoint of Eve's and Adam's first moments of consciousness. But this counterpoint is preceded by Raphael's presentation, a book
earlier than Adam's. The juxtaposition of these passages from book 4 and
book 7, both of which stand as readings of Ovid, is informed by gender hierarchy—but this gender hierarchy grows out of Milton's structural homily
concerning the use of classical sources in his biblical epic. Theology and poetics serve as the basic organizing principles around which other political and
cultural terms cluster. The poem interprets Ovid's text by way of the biblical
text that supersedes it.

ADAM AT A CROSSROADS

While accommodation plays a significant, if unstated, role in the book 7 creation narrative, when we come to Adam's description of his first waking moments, this aspect of Miltonic poesis becomes an essential and explicit element. Geoffrey Hartman has discussed in detail the accommodative aspect
of Milton's use of the figure of the sun in Adam's creation and communication with Raphael.[80] In Adam's narration Milton offers a version of what he
considers to be the ideal mode of interpretation. This is true of both the
form in which the interpretation occurs and the end to which it brings the
interpreter. Although there can be no doubt that this model takes shape in a

prelapsarian world—both the events that Adam describes and the time of his description occur, of course, before the fall—Milton offers it as one transferable, or better, interpretable, to the postlapsarian world of his readers. Adam's retelling of events that have already been described, first in Genesis 1–2 and then in Raphael's hexameral paraphrase, serves as a two fold authorization of Milton's imaginative process. First and most obvious, Adam's narrative becomes a paradigm for the poet's: both mortals give their own revisions of a divine narrative. Second, Adam's revision attributes an essential role to the human actor—Adam himself—in the story. Just as a full rendition of the creation of humanity, male *and* female, would be incomplete without an emphasis on humanity's partnership with God in the creative endeavor, so too Milton's retelling must figure an active role for the human poet, whose report of these divinely produced events contains interpretive and creative augmentation.

This incorporation of human participation in the creative partnership can be found throughout rabbinic literature. In Genesis Rabbah contemplation of the act of creation gives rise to thought about human creation. The rabbis are quick to compare God's creative activities to their own imitations of them:

> R. Samuel bar Ami said, "From the beginning of the world's creation the Holy One Blessed be He sought a partner for Himself from among the earthly creatures. How ever you approach it, the manner of counting the days serves as proof of this. The verse should have either said '[day] one' '[day] two' '[day] three,' or 'first' 'second' 'third.' How is it that we have 'one' 'second' 'third'? When would the Holy One Blessed be He complete the sequence [by calling the day 'first' rather than 'one']? During the erection of the tabernacle, 'And he that made his offering on the first day . . .' (Num. 7:12) That is, on the first day of creation. For the Holy One Blessed be He said, 'It is as if I created the world on that day.'" (3:9)

TAKING AS HIS starting point a rather unremarkable inconsistency in the text's numbering of each day of creation—the cardinal "one" followed by the ordinal "second, third, fourth, etc."—R. Samuel bar Ami invents a connection between divine creation and human artifice. God sought mortal partnership in the originary act of creation, which was not fully completed until the erection of the *mishkan*, the tabernacle, in the wilderness. This portable house of worship, created by human craftsmanship, was thought by the rabbis to mirror God's creation and thereby complete it. Amid the wealth of detailed directions for the tabernacle's construction recounted twice in the Pentateuch—the first time, in Exodus 25–31, as prescriptive, and the second time, a virtually verbatim repetition in Exodus 36–40, as descriptive iteration—God explains the primary purpose of the tabernacle (*mishkan*): "And let them make me a sanctuary that I may dwell (*shakhanti*) among *them*" (Exodus 25:8, emphasis added).[81] The rabbis were fond of pointing out that the indirect object in the second part of the verse ("them") does not correspond to the direct object in the first part of the verse (the tabernacle). The Israelites were commanded to build a *tabernacle* (the etymology of which is the verb for "dwell"), but God promised to dwell among *them*, i.e., the people who had been instructed to build it. In other words, the verse insists by this deliberate shift in object that the tabernacle functions to bring God's presence into the midst of the people and not as a separate dwelling place. The rabbis perceived the tabernacle as facilitating divine condescension or accommodation. The *mishkan* was thought to bring God closer to humanity and, simultaneously, to elevate humanity to the realm of the divine. As an emblem of humanity's position vis-à-vis God's creation, the tabernacle served magnificently as the vehicle of human-divine communication. Though divinely inspired or occasioned, it had to be executed by human makers. The rabbis perceived the tabernacle as a human completion of divine creativity, the purpose of which was ultimately to facilitate the bridging of the terrestrial and celestial spheres.

Having been advised by Raphael to be lowly wise, Adam displays remarkable self-awareness in his introduction to his own birth narrative:

> But apt the Mind or Fancy is to rove
> Uncheckt, and of her roving is no end;
> Till warn'd, or by experience taught, she learn,
> That not to know at large of things remote
> From use, obscure and subtle, but to know
> That which before us lies in daily life,
> Is the prime Wisdom, what is more, is fume,
> Or emptiness, or fond impertinence,
> And renders us in things that most concern
> Unpractic'd, unprepar'd, and still to seek. (8.188–97)

IT IS DIFFICULT to imagine what experiences Adam might have had to this point in his brief life that would have enabled him to understand the tendency of the human mind to wander in mazes lost like the fallen angels. He has, to be sure, listened attentively to Raphael's narration of Satan's rebellion and the war in heaven. He has had to comfort Eve after her disconcerting, Satan-induced dream. And he has been gently rebuked by Raphael for pursuing too far matters like the private lives of angels or the apparent superfluity of the motions of the heavenly bodies. None of these propaedeutics, however, suggest that pursuit of "things remote from use" will necessarily "render us in things that most concern / Unpractic'd, unprepar'd, and still to seek." Adam is a good student, but the lessons he describes here ventriloquize the experiential wisdom of an aging blind poet who argued passionately in his younger days,

> Since therefore the knowledge and survay of vice is in this world so necessary to the constituting of human vertue, and the scanning of error to the confirmation of truth, how can we more safely, and with lesse danger scout into the regions of sin and falsity than by reading all manner of tractats, and hearing all manner of reason? (YP 2:516–17)

IT WILL BE objected that, unlike prelapsarian Adam, the writer of *Areopagitica* speaks to a fallen world, where good and evil "grow up together almost inseparably; and the knowledge of good is so involv'd and interwoven with the knowledge of evill . . . . This is that doom which *Adam* fell into of knowing good and evill, that is to say, of knowing good by evill" (YP 2:514). But I would like to suggest that Adam's statement here in book 8 marks something of a retreat from the position the poet defended so eloquently in his earlier career. Milton quite explicitly draws an analogy between Adam's pending narrative and this moment in his own composition of the poem. Adam concludes the statement I have quoted above, "Therefore from this high pitch let us descend / A lower flight, and speak of things at hand / Useful . . ." (198–200). It has not been all that long since we heard the poet beseech his Muse, "with like safety guided down / Return me to my Native Element / . . . Standing on Earth, not rapt above the Pole, / More safe I Sing with mortal voice" (7.15–16, 23–24). Adam's story of his first moments of consciousness has become an occasion for Milton to offer a representation of the proper form of mediated self-authorship, a form that is necessarily characterized by a "lower flight" or condescension—in other words, by accommodation.

What this parallel between the poet's self-consciousness and Adam's "descent" suggests is that the accommodative mode, which in the previous chapter I associated primarily with representations of divine truths and epistemological limits, asserts itself also as the proper mode for human communication (pre- and postlapsarian). That is to say, accommodation at this moment has become both the form and the content of Adam's narrative: on the one hand, the form of allegorical displacement is manifest in the connection drawn between the poet and Adam in their parallel downward turns and, on the other hand, the theme of descent serves as a trope for epistemological accommodation. Though Milton had long endorsed unfettered inquiry, and had advocated an uncloistered virtue, when it came time to compose this poem about the limits of knowledge and the perils of insisting on full self-authorship, a retreat from his earlier position became almost inevitable. The boundary between what Milton considered to be appropriate to prelapsarian investigation (which we can now only know indirectly, anyway) and postlapsarian inquiry is no longer as distinct as we might have earlier supposed. With the collapse of this division, however, comes the possibility of applying the insights of Adam's story to our own realms of readerly and writerly (interpretive and creative) experiences.[82]

Adam's waking upward gaze—"Straight toward Heav'n my wond'ring Eyes I turn'd, / And gaz'd a while the ample Sky" (257–58)—may indeed balance Eve's fascination with the pool of water at her feet. But the upward movement of Adam's first waking moments also contrasts with his aforementioned desire to "descend a lower flight." It will be recalled that accommodation serves two complementary yet contrasting goals. It brings the heavenly and the transcendent down to the level of human comprehension. This downward thrust, however, is meant ultimately to raise humanity up to the realm of the divine—what we may call the anagogic movement of accommodation. Adam's "quick instinctive motion" compels him anagogically upward.

This bidirectional manner of processing the world is immediately repeated and revised as Adam is brought to the garden that has been prepared for him. Receiving no answer from the physical universe to which he had addressed his first waking questions, "On a green shady Bank profuse of Flow'rs / Pensive I sat me down." The "soft oppression" that seizes Adam, producing the first of two important midday naps, emphasizes the descending motion. Not only does he "sit . . . down," but he calls his mood pensive, alluding to the etymological root, *pensare*, where thought weighs one down.

Almost immediately, as if to balance the downward turn of Adam's sleepy thoughts, the shape divine at Adam's head commands him to rise: "by the hand he took me rais'd, / And over Fields and Waters, as in Air / Smooth sliding without step, last led me up / A woody Mountain; whose high top was plain" (300–3). This God-induced somnambulism is, of course, Milton's version of the biblical statements in Genesis 2:8—"And the Lord God planted a garden eastward in Eden; and there he put the man whom he had formed"—and 2:15—"And the Lord God took the man, and put him into the garden of Eden to dress it and to keep it." The poet's augmentation of the biblical text not only makes more explicit the narrative's etiology, but it also characteristically projects the events of Adam's story onto an anagogic framework. That is, Adam is given to understand his ascent to Eden as a direct response to his initially unanswerable search for origin and end: "how came I thus, how here? . . . how may I know him, how adore, / From whom I have that thus I move and live." The journey to Eden, characterized by the downward and upward trajectories of accommodation, illustrates a mode of interpretation in which human participation is essential but insufficient by itself. As a first instance of this bidirectionality it stands somewhat incomplete. Adam is too passive. He asks the right questions but plays little part in formulating the answers.

The most dramatic instance of this human-divine partnership occurs in the ensuing description of Adam's request for a mate. It is in this episode that Adam discovers, by trial and error, the proper interpretive mode. Step one: observation. God brings all the animals "to receive / From thee thir Names" (343–44). In this process of observation Adam exercises his faculty of understanding, which in turn immediately corresponds to a power over language (step two): "I nam'd them, as they pass'd, and understood / Thir Nature, with such knowledge God endu'd / My sudden apprehension." Language at this moment wields the power to interpret, but it also stands as a tool for creation, both because it corresponds to the logos of divine (masculine) creativity and because it has been associated with man's possession and domination of the created world. Yet, since Adam's creativity must always remain subordinate to God's authority, this linguistic mastery soon reveals a lack. Adam first perceives this unnamable absence as an inability to name and to worship his creator: "O by what Name, for thou above all these, / Above mankind, or aught than mankind higher, / Surpassest far my naming, how may I / Adore thee, Author of this Universe" (357–60). Adam's naming capacity becomes precisely the criterion by which he is placed in the hierarchy ranging from the animals to God. He can name (and understand) the animals, so he stands above them; he cannot name (or understand) God, so he remains subordinate. Awestruck by his incapacity to name God (and therefore to understand the divine), Adam expresses this anxiety as a concern over worship. We would do well to separate these concerns, though. Mastery through interpretation—the other side of the creative coin—is what matters to Adam initially. But he senses that this would be to overstep his bounds considerably, especially with God's warning about the forbidden tree "resound[ing] yet dreadful in [his] ear." So he turns to another possibility, one that, we saw at the beginning of this chapter, is intimately connected with the creation narrative of Genesis: worship. The poesis of praise mitigates any threat to originary authority suggested by poetic creativity. Adam reverts to the same strategy used by Milton in Raphael's version of creation.

Almost as soon as he lights upon this approach, however, Adam discovers a different absence: "but with mee / I see not who partakes" (364–65). The transition from a need to praise to a need for companionship is as puzzling as it is immediate. The confusing litany of requests expressed in Adam's ten-line address to God (357–67) replicates, at least partially, the confusing, potentially arresting anxiety encountered and then elided here by the poet's use of Adam's prelapsarian voice. The compensation offered by poetic language as praise for the First Creator does not satisfy as the "large recompense" the younger poet found in his elegiac declaration of poetic independence.[83] Indeed, Wordsworth's echo of this phrase in "Tintern Abbey," "other gifts / Have followed, for such loss, I would believe, / *Abundant recompense*" (87–89, emphasis added), follows the solution offered by Milton in Adam's request for a mate. Wordsworth's abundant recompense consists in observing nature "not as in the hour / Of thoughtless youth, but hearing oftentimes / The still, sad music of humanity." Wordsworth's revision of *Lycidas* and *Paradise Lost* reveals that Adam's awareness of a lack (or loss) in his inability to name (know) God cannot be entirely offset by the human power of language to praise, *except* insofar as this praise occurs in the context of a social network. Adam's need for a human partner stems from his desire for fellowship "fit to participate / All rational delight" (390–91). Language, the gift of rationality bestowed upon humanity, serves its end of communication and creation only *between* people. I have been emphasizing the simultaneous upward and downward movements of accommodation. There is, of course, a term in rhetoric to describe this kind crisscross in directions: chiasmus. It is significant, then, that Adam's expression of his need for companionship is finally structured as a chiasmus: "In solitude / What happiness, who can enjoy alone, / Or all enjoying, what contentment find?" (364–66). The nature of this rhetorical crossing seems all the more peculiar—and thus significant primarily as a syntactical organization—when we recognize that happiness, enjoyment, and contentment, the terms of this chiasmus, are all virtual synonyms. By resorting to this purely formal structure Adam vividly demonstrates his new understanding of the dialectical nature of accommodation, upward and downward, divine and human.

Not only does Adam participate in the creation of Eve, but her presence will also serve to produce the social fabric so essential to a human language that at once interprets and creates, a social fabric that depends upon the ethical nature of such communication. The analogy between Eve and the poem—both of which are created through but not by their putative authors—unavoidably maintains Eve's subordination to Adam. Nevertheless, her "status as creature"[84] does not preclude a return of the feminine mode of creativity that we saw the poet trying to banish from his narrative of creation. Companionship, community, eros—these elements of human society can only exist with Eve's creation:

> . . . Man by number is to manifest
> His single imperfection, and beget
> Like of his like, his Image multipli'd,
> In unity defective, which requires
> Collateral love, and dearest amity. (422–26)

HUMAN PROCREATION CANNOT occur without woman, without the feminine aspect of creativity. Human creativity is inextricably tied to "collateral love," imagination and desire.

5

"So Shall the World Go On":
Martyrdom, Interpretation, and History

I F MIDRASH and *Paradise Lost* explore knowledge and being, they also interrogate the dynamics of experience and wrestle with the idea of history. The events of the past, both distant and more recent, posed a special challenge to the rabbis and Milton. With few exceptions, these events marked painful losses: the destruction of the Temple and the ensuing loss of political power within the Roman Empire on the one hand, the Restoration of the English monarchy and the disempowerment of more radical embodiments of Protestantism on the other. Yet if these texts purport to serve as theodicy—for the rabbis implicitly, for Milton explicitly—part of "this great argument" must offer some form of consolation by suggesting the possibility of redeeming the history of loss. One premise of this study's larger argument concerning the relationship between midrash and *Paradise Lost* has been the assertion of parallel historical circumstances out of which these texts arose. Both the rabbis and Milton were engaged in homologous struggles for ideological and theological survival in the wake of their respective experiences of defeat. We might therefore expect those portions of rabbinic writings and Milton's epic that most directly address the matter of history to bear the closest resemblance to one another, especially as they both struggle to make sense of what often looks to be the apparent disparity between God's word and human history.

In this chapter I shall examine references to the history of loss in midrash and *Paradise Lost*, arguing that these moments of mourning constitute distinctive phenomenologies of history. Certain elements of midrash do indeed bear structural and thematic affinities to portions of the final two books of Milton's poem. Imagining their own version of Michael's instructional encounter with Adam, the rabbis replace the "false surmise" of historical narration with a nonlinear folding together of the biblical past, the rabbinical present, and the hoped-for future of redemption. Similarly, Michael's visitation to the fallen couple posits a paradoxically cyclical teleology to the (future) history of humankind, the "Ages of endless date." "Adam's acceptance of the scene of exile," as one critic has put it, "constitutes the first stage of his moral ascent."[1] Historical phenomena (φαινεσθαι) are transformed into interpretive fantasies (φαινειν). In their respective meditations on the patterns and dynamics of history, the rabbis and Milton discover that linear historiography implies an eschatological teleology, which in turn depends on the typological assertion that the end gives *everything prior to it* its meaning, thereby rendering everything prior to it inherently meaningless. Cyclical time, however, preserves the specificity of history by endlessly deferring any presumed end of days. Rabbinic literature and *Paradise Lost* lament the death and loss they uncover in commemorating the past; yet they seek consolation in an elision of that past, producing a kind of antihistory with direct implications for the renewal of political agency.

Despite these overriding similarities, it is precisely in addressing the relationship between the past, present, and future that some of the most crucial differences between the rabbis and Milton arise. As I shall argue at the close of this chapter, the differing interpretive models offered by midrash and *Paradise Lost* not only demonstrate Milton's own assertion of Christianity's primary claim to the fulfillment and supersession of Judaism, they also highlight the poet's anxieties in recognizing the parallels between his own circumstances and those of post-Christian Jews.

A TALENT FOR SUFFERING

Such an untransmuted lump of futurity, coming in a position so momentous for the structural effect of the whole work, is inartistic.

And what makes it worse is that the actual writing in this passage is curiously bad.

C. S. LEWIS'S NOTORIOUS condemnation of the final two books of *Paradise Lost* have had a lasting effect on the subsequent critical career of this portion of the epic; nearly every writer since the 1942 publication of *A Preface to "Paradise Lost"* who has tried to deal with Michael's visitation to the newly fallen couple in books 11 and 12 has had to frame his or her comments in terms of either an agreement and expansion of Lewis's criticisms or a defense of Milton's poem.[2] What often goes unnoticed in discussions of Lewis's comments, however, is his own attempt at accounting for his disappointed sense of the decline in the final books. He goes on to speculate in biographical terms about Milton's apparent lapse:

> The truth is we know next to nothing about the causes governing the appearance and disappearance of a talent. Perhaps Milton was in ill health. Perhaps, being old, he yielded to a natural, though disastrous, impatience to get the work finished.[3]

ALTHOUGH MY ANALYSIS in this chapter will bracket the matter of aesthetic judgment raised by Lewis, I do think he is on the mark in regarding the final books of the epic as struggling under the burden of Milton's own contemporary circumstances in ways that the earlier portions of the poem managed to subsume more covertly into other concerns. What interests me especially in Lewis's speculation is his reference to "the appearance and disappearance of a talent." Deliberately or not, Lewis's comment resonates with one of Milton's best known sonnets (19), a poem that addresses many of the same issues of suffering and chosenness to which the poet turns again in books 11 and 12 of *Paradise Lost.*

When I consider how my light is spent
    Ere half my days, in this dark world and wide,
    And that one Talent which is death to hide,
    Lodg'd with me useless, though my Soul more bent
To serve therewith my Maker, and present
    My true account, lest he returning chide;
    "Doth God exact day-labour, light denied,"
    I fondly ask; But Patience, to prevent

That murmur, soon replies, "God doth not need
   Either man's work or his own gifts; who best
   Bear his mild yoke, they serve him best; his State
Is Kingly. Thousands at his bidding speed
   And post o'er Land and Ocean without rest:
   They also serve who only stand and wait."

I want to take seriously the possibility that the talent Lewis characterizes as having disappeared in books 11 and 12 of *Paradise Lost* is related to the "Talent which is death to hide" in the poet's meditation on his life's calling and achievement (or lack thereof). Milton's intense ambivalence concerning the nature of Christ's suffering is well-known. His fragmentary attempt at writing a poem about the Passion ends before it has really begun, as he labors to situate its expression of grief both within literary history and within a geographic landscape. His account of Christ's death on the cross in *Paradise Lost* garners a scant thirteen lines (12.401–14). The poem Milton devoted entirely to Jesus's earthly role ends even before Jesus is taken into custody and tried, as the hero "unobserv'd / Home to his Mother's house private return'd" (*Paradise Regained* 4.638–39). Perhaps one of the fullest and most personal investigations into the value of suffering Milton ever wrote, Sonnet 19 figures the matter of vocation—the same issue with which Jesus struggles in his temptations by Satan in *Paradise Regained*—specifically as a matter of talent. The voice of Patience assures the lyric "I" that burying one's talent, standing and waiting, can also effect salvation and earn one a right to enter into the kingdom of heaven. Anticipating the heroism of Abdiel and the series of individual faithful of whom Adam is given proleptic insight in *Paradise Lost*, Christ in *Paradise Regained*, and Samson in the dramatic poem that takes his name, Milton's sonnet insists that those who appear to be idle serve God, even if, as the third servant of Matthew's parable, they appear to be cast out in "outer darkness . . . weeping and gnashing [their] teeth" (25:30).[4] The shift in tone, style, perhaps even in artistic merit of books 11 and 12, of which Lewis is famously critical, is a direct result of the poet's meditation on history as a phenomenology of suffering. The value of this suffering remains uncertain, but, in the end, Milton seeks to combine the apparently contradictory human responses to history of standing and waiting, on the one hand, and the reaffirming of political agency, on the other. Milton's poetic talent may not so much have disappeared in books 11 and 12 as been deliberately buried.[5]

"THIS MUST NOT YET BE SO"

IT WOULD INDEED be surprising to find little or no change in Milton's thinking about history and political agency from his earliest writings prior to the Civil War to his Restoration poetry. The mere change in form—from an early career as a lyric poet and political/religious pamphleteer to a late explosion in epic poetry—deserves to be read as indicative of a shift in attitude. Even in light of some of the more recent attempts at restoring a politicized late Milton, I think the nature of this shift deserves further attention. When Adam hears Michael's final prophecy concerning the "Ages of endless date," he marvels "how soon [the archangel's] prediction" (12.553) has "Measur'd this transient World, the Race of time, / Till time stand fixt" (554–55). The "soon" here most literally refers to the rapidity with which Michael has narrated the entire course of world history, from Cain and Abel to the triumphant return of Christ on the day of the last judgment. Yet it must also surely suggest that Michael's prediction—literally his "speech before" the course of history—prevents or foreshortens that course of history. To put this matter in terms of Milton's own poetic career, Adam seems to be making the same assumption that the poetic voice of the younger Milton's "On the Morning of Christ's Nativity" makes. In that very early poem the singer imagines the "holy Song" produced by the birth of Christ to wield the power to interrupt history:

> Time will run back, and fetch the age of gold,
> And speckl'd vanity
> Will sicken soon and die,
>   And leprous sin will melt from earthly mold,
> And Hell itself will pass away,
> And leave her dolorous mansions to the peering day.
>
> Yea, Truth and Justice, then
> Will down return to men,
>   The'enamel'd *Arras* of the Rainbow wearing,
> And Mercy set between,
> Thron'd in Celestial sheen,
>   With radiant feet the tissued clouds down steering,
> And Heav'n as at some festival,
> Will open wide the Gates of her high Palace Hall. (135–48)

REDEMPTION PROMISES TO BE complete at that very instant; the "prevent[ion]" (24) of the "Star-led Wizards" (23) would indeed be achieved by this far from "humble ode" (24). Before this false surmise can continue any further, however, the poetic voice is interrupted by "wisest Fate," who "says no, / This must not yet be so" (149–50). The infant who now sleeps quietly must grow to adulthood so that he can achieve salvation in his suffering and crucifixion. History, specifically the history of loss and martyrdom, serves a necessary function.

If we turn back to Adam's assessment of Michael's prediction, we discover that he has internalized something of that corrective voice that had to be personified as Fate in the earlier poem. On the other side of time standing "fixt," Adam perceives only "abyss, / Eternity, whose end no eye can reach" (12.555–56). His concluding lesson reveals a thorough understanding of the problematics of history and the political, as well as religious, value of martyrdom:

> Henceforth I learn, that to obey is best,
> And love with fear the only God, to walk
> As in his presence, ever to observe
> His providence, and on him sole depend,
> Merciful over all his works, with good
> Still overcoming evil, and by small
> Accomplishing great things, by things deem'd weak
> Subverting worldly strong, and worldly wise
> By simply meek; that suffering for Truth's sake
> Is fortitude to highest victory,
> And to the faithful Death the Gate of Life. (12.561–71)

WHAT IN MILTON'S own historical experience could have provided the basis for such a view? For a thoroughly disempowered Milton, writing from a self-imposed exile, "suffering for Truth's sake" could easily be read as an abdication of historical, worldly, political agency. Indeed, even recent critics who wish to resist the notion of a late Miltonic quietism have noted that Adam's lesson seems to constitute a withdrawal from collective political action and a turning away from the public spirit of Milton's controversialist prose tracts. Adam's words posit a curious set of ostensible antitheses, however, in their chiastic bracketing of "worldly strong" and "worldly wise" with "things deem'd weak" and "simply meek." The lines offer a hopeful containment of worldly strength and wisdom so that the subversive act of "suffering for Truth's sake" becomes "fortitude to highest victory." Not so much an antithesis, these lines sublate worldly power to effect a synthesis.

But Adam here is concerned less with theory—he and Michael will soon descend from the top of Speculation—than with praxis. Michael, after all, supplements this conclusion with the famous lines, "only add / Deeds to thy knowledge, answerable, add Faith, / Add Virtue, Patience, Temperance, add Love, / By name to come call'd Charity, the soul / Of all the rest" (581–85). What would it mean to put into practice the history lesson of books 11 and 12? Jason Rosenblatt has argued, "Milton's Adam falls from nature, history, and Torah as understood by the Hebrew Bible into the Gospel's abrogation of the world, of temporality, and of the law as understood by typology."[6] Despite Rosenblatt's convincing argument, it seems to me that an analysis of books 11 and 12 still stands to gain from a comparison to the "Hebraic" view of history as revealed in some of the rabbis' observations on the Bible.

RABBINIC HISTORY

THE PRECISE CONTINUITIES and discontinuities between biblical and rabbinic perspectives on history—insofar as it is at all possible to generalize about either of the heterogeneous bodies of texts that embody these perspectives—could fill more than one volume and are largely beyond the scope of this study. Nevertheless, it is necessary briefly to consider the relationship between biblical and rabbinic views on history, since it is only within the context of this relationship that we may begin to appreciate the dynamics of the rabbinic response to contemporary political, cultural, and social circumstances.

Beginning "In the beginning," marching irresistibly forward in time, the Hebrew Bible depicts existence as both particular and historical. Though they may participate in mythic, paradigmatic structures, the biblical accounts of the Patriarchs, of Exodus, of the conquest of Canaan, the fitful rise of the Israelite monarchy, the division of the Kingdoms, of exile and destruction, resist any transcendent ahistorical impulse. As Yosef Hayim Yerushalmi has noted in his classic study of Jewish historiography,

With the departure of Adam and Eve from Eden, history begins, historical time becomes real, and the way back is closed forever. . . . Thrust reluctantly into history, man in Hebrew thought comes to affirm his historical existence despite the suffering it entails, and gradually, ploddingly, he discovers that God reveals himself in the course of it. Rituals and festivals in ancient Israel are themselves no longer primarily repetitions of mythic archetypes meant to annihilate historical time. Where they evoke the past, it is not the primeval but the historical past, in which the great and critical moments of Israel's history were fulfilled.[7]

FOR EXAMPLE, while the festival of Passover may have its origins in a primordial springtime harvest ritual—one of its biblical names is *chag ha'aviv*, the festival of spring—its value in biblical terms stems from its commemoration of the Exodus. This is not to say that the Bible functions primarily as a history book, providing exhaustively detailed accounts of events of the distant past. Indeed, as Erich Auerbach famously observed, biblical accounts are "fraught with background," providing only the most minimal details.[8] The historical aspect of the Hebrew Bible depends on its location of meaning in the past, i.e., God's role in history and the special relationship between God and the Israelites.

The Hebrew Bible also retains a historical aspect precisely in the minimalism of the details discussed by Auerbach; it is within the lacunae of the biblical text that the rabbis project their own historical situations. The rabbis were expert at attending to the biblical phenomenology of history, perceiving within the scriptural accounts diverse manifestations of God's once and future hand in the welfare of his chosen nation. Genesis Rabbah is filled with statements arguing explicitly or implicitly that the world was created to afford the Jews the opportunity to uphold and observe the Torah.

> R. Tanhuma in the name of R. Joshua b. Levi said, "In the future the Holy One Blessed be He will give to the nations of the world a cup of bitterness to drink drawn from the source of judgment [*hadin*]. This is the purpose of "And a river went out of Eden to water the garden" (Gen. 2:10). The four river heads refer to the four kingdoms: "The name of the first is Pishon," this is Babylonia because "and their horsemen shall spread [*upashu*] themselves" (Hab. 1:8). . . . "And the name of the second river is Gihon," this is Media, because Haman's eyes were inflamed like a serpent's, [and the serpent was condemned] "upon thy belly [*gichonkha*] thou shalt go, and dust thou shalt eat all the days of thy life" (Gen. 3:14). . . . "And the name of the third river is Tigris [*chideqel*]," this is Greece, because it was sharp and quick [*chadah v'qalah*]

with its proclamations [against Israel]. . . . "And the fourth river is the Euphrates [*p'rath*]," this is Edom [Rome], because it corrupted [*hephirah*] and harrassed God's world; because it became fruitful [*parath*] and great from the blessing of the old man [Jacob]; because "I am going to destroy [*l'hapher*] it in the end"; because of its demise, "I have trodden the winepress [*poreh*] alone" (Isa. 63:3). (17:4)

THE RABBIS SEEM genuinely to relish this word game, finding all sorts of hints about the four oppressive regimes. The midrash saves its greatest display of interpretive ingenuity for Edom, a.k.a. Rome, the current regime. Characteristic of rabbinic interpretations (in Genesis, especially), the beginning is read as anticipating—containing—historical developments. In the middle of their protracted investigation of the four rivers in Eden, however, R. Huna and others interject what seems to be a contradiction of the historical bent of this political polemic:

> R. Huna in the name of R. Aha: All [oppressive] kingdoms are called Assyria [*ashur*], because they become rich [*mith'ashroth*] from Israel. R. Yose b. R. Judah said, "All kingdoms are called Nineveh, because they ornament themselves [*mith'na'oth*] at Israel's expense." R. Yose b. R. Halapta said, "All kingdoms are called Egypt [*mitzrayim*], because they oppress [*m'tzaroth*] Israel."

THE MIDRASH POSITS a radically ahistorical continuity between oppressive regimes. Yerushalmi argues that this disintegration of time is what distinguishes the rabbinic approach to history from an earlier biblical attitude. "Unlike the biblical writers," he writes, "the Rabbis seem to play with Time as though an accordion, expanding and collapsing it at will. Where historical specificity is a hallmark of the biblical narratives, here that acute biblical sense of time and place often gives way to rampant and seemingly unselfconscious anachronism."[9] That the rabbis play fast and loose with time, however, does not necessarily mean that the rabbis were uninterested in history. We must be cautious about any formulation of rabbinic writing that implies its total lack of concern with the meaning and nature of contemporary events, or even that it avoids reflecting on the proper mode of action—religious, but also political—in response to those contemporary events. Anachronism and immediate historical application are two sides of the same coin.[10]

The favorite midrashic method of folding in intertexts from Prophets and Writings grows out of an ongoing project of contemporization, of perceiving the past in terms of the present. Since the prophets served as prototypes for mediation through interpretation, positioned as they were between divine revelation and human understanding, the rabbis considered the prophetic mediation of the creation account to function as an important justification of their own roles as interpreters. The following interpretive chiasmus serves as a rich example of the scriptural bricolage produced by rabbinic intercalation of the writing of the prophets into the creation account:

> R. Berakhiah, R. Jacob b. R. Avina in the name of R. Abbah bar Kahana: The account of creation comes to teach us about the giving of the Torah and, in turn, achieves greater clarity, "As when the melting [*hamasim*] fire burneth" (Isa. 64:1), that is, they divided [*heymisu*]. When did the fire divide between the upper and lower realms? Was it not during the giving of the Torah? This was also the case when the world was created [i.e., the firmament was separated out for the lower waters by fire]. (4:2)

THE PRESENCE OF fire from heavens is explicit only in Exodus's story of the giving of the Torah: "And mount Sinai was altogether on a smoke, because the Lord descended upon it in fire" (Exodus 19:18). The division of the upper and lower waters appears explicitly only in the story of creation: "And God made the firmament, and divided the waters which were under the firmament from the waters which were above the firmament" (Genesis 1:7). Isaiah describes God's descent at Sinai as a rent in the heavens and then compares it to the division in the creation story when the waters were split. From images in the story of the giving of the Torah, the rabbis reason, we know that the splitting of waters was achieved by fire. Hence, the unity of Scripture, especially between two central historical moments—the creation and the giving of the Torah—is achieved through a *third* intertext from Isaiah. The prophet, as prototype for the midrashist, facilitates this reading.

By simultaneously reaffirming the completely intertextual quality of Scripture and establishing the role of the rabbinic interpreter in the perception of this intertextuality, the midrashic hermeneutic confirms its historicity even as it "play[s] with Time as though with an accordion." The second verse of Genesis occasions the following teleological homily, an account of biblical history that also projects forward into the lived experience of the rabbis:

> "And the earth was formless, etc." R. Yudah b. R. Simon interpreted the

Scripture with reference to coming generations: "And the earth was form-less," this refers to Adam, who was reduced to naught and nothing [by eating from the Tree of Knowledge]. ". . . and empty," this refers to Cain, who sought to return the world to formlessness and nothing [by killing Abel]. ". . . and darkness," this refers to the generation of Enoch, "and their deeds were in the dark" (Isa. 29:15). ". . . was on the face of the deep," this is the generation of the flood, "the same day were all the fountains of the great deep broken up" (Gen. 7:11). "And the spirit [*ru'ach*] of God hovered over the face of the water," "And God made a wind [*ru'ach*] pass over the earth" (Gen. 8:1). The Holy One Blessed be He said, "How long will the world endure in darkness. Let light come," "And the Lord said let there be light," this refers to Abraham, as it says, "Who raised up the righteous man from the east" (Isa. 41:2) [that is, from the same direction that the light comes]. "And the lord called the light day," this refers to Jacob, "And the darkness He called night," this refers to Esau. "And there was an evening," this is Esau, "And there was a morning," this is Jacob, "one day" which the Holy One Blessed be He gave to them, What is that day? Yom Kippur [that is, a day on which they could both atone]. (2:3)

R. YUDAH REFORMULATES each phrase of the first five verses as a prolepsis of the ensuing biblical narrative of Genesis. The opening verses of the book have now become a statement of theme, the development of which has become the task of the rest of Genesis. What is more, in light of the common midrashic association of Esau with Rome, this proleptic reading looks forward not only to the ensuing narration of fraternal conflict in Genesis but also to the contemporary divisions between Israel and an increasingly Christianized Rome. Searching for a way to understand the astonishing success of their prodigal son, Christianity, the rabbis perceived historical developments through the paradigm of family. As Jacob Neusner has observed, "Sages found a place for Rome in Israel's history only by assigning to Rome a place in the family."[11] Rome became Israel's twin brother and hence, in the model of all fraternal relationships depicted in Genesis, its primary nemesis. R. Simeon b. Laqish makes this associative chain more explicit in the sequel of the midrash cited above, reading the verses as a rendition of the succession of kingdoms under which Israel was to—and continues to—suffer:

"And the earth was formless," this refers to Babylonia, "I beheld the earth, and, lo, it was without form" (Jer. 4:23). "And empty [*vavohu*]," this refers to

Media [Persia], "and they hastened [*vayivhalu*] to bring Haman" (Est. 6:14). "And darkness," this refers to Greece, which darkened the eyes of Israel with its statutes, commanding Israel, "Write on the horn of an ox [a form of public proclamation] that you have no part in the God of Israel." "On the face of the deep," this refers to this evil kingdom [Rome], just as this deep is beyond investigation, so too the evil kingdom is beyond investigation. "And the spirit of God hovers," this refers to the spirit of the Messiah, as it says, "And the spirit of the Lord shall rest upon him" (Isa. 11:2). (2:4)

THE CREATION NARRATIVE thus contains the biblical past, the midrashic present, and the messianic future. The relevance of creation to the (pre)history of Israel has not only been clarified, it has been made into an underlying theme of the hexameral narrative in its entirety. The rabbis nowhere deny the historicity of the creation account. They do assert, however, that the divine author's creation is ongoing, not fully complete until the end of days. Perceived initially as God's victory over the destructiveness that inheres in formlessness, emptiness, darkness, and deep obscurity, the acts described in creation signify the coming victory of God's order, manifested in his people, over the kingdoms of chaos and destruction. The rabbis have recaptured what is considered to have been the operative spirit behind those prebiblical creation stories that describe the battle between the forces of chaos and order. Just as these creation epics (like the Enuma Elish) functioned ideologically to support political orders as they vied for control with competing powers, so too the rabbis project the biblical hexameron onto a political template. The theodical range of this argument is staggering, and its political ambitions are impressive; especially remarkable, though, are the textual strategies deployed in its execution. The rabbis open the text onto their world, using the words of the Scripture as the thin end of the wedge.

A similar dynamic is at work as *Paradise Lost* comes to a close. Books 11 and 12 of Milton's epic thematize interpretation more explicitly than the rest of the poem; in so doing, however, they also thematize creation, since the two are necessarily related. In his account of the creation, Raphael highlights the interpretive elements of creation; in his account of history, Michael underscores the creative elements of interpretation. The end of vision in book 11 corresponds to Adam's death, but it also corresponds to Milton's blindness. It must be read as a deeply personal moment. Milton loses his sight "Betwixt the world destroy'd and world restor'd" (12.3). He can only see this restoration (as opposed to the Restoration) through narration, a narration that thematizes mediation and interpretation.

Book 12's representation of Moses, Israel, and law reveals an aspect of Miltonic typology that distinguishes it from a more standard Calvinist approach. As I have argued earlier, despite its supersessionary account of history and interpretation, for Milton as well as for others, typology never totally eliminates an inassimilable historical residuum, one that is inextricably bound up with the figure (and the body) of the Jew. As a critical aspect of the matter of typology, Michael's account of the Sinai theophany provides further insight into the fraught question (especially post-Restoration) of England's status as the new Israel.

> God from the Mount of *Sinai*, whose gray top
> Shall tremble, he descending, will himself
> In Thunder, Lightning, and loud Trumpet's sound,
> Ordain them Laws; part, such as appertain
> To civil Justice, part religious Rites
> Of sacrifice; informing them, by types
> And shadows, of that destin'd Seed to bruise
> The Serpent, by what means he shall achieve
> Mankind's deliverance. But the voice of God
> To mortal ear is dreadful: They beseech
> That *Moses* might report to them his will,
> And terror cease; he grants what they besought,
> Instructed that to God is no access
> Without Mediator, whose high Office now
> *Moses* in figure bears; to introduce
> One greater, of whose day he shall foretell,
> And all the Prophets in thir age the times
> Of great *Messiah* shall sing. Thus, Laws and Rites
> Establisht, such delight hath God in Men
> Obedient to his will, that he voutsafes
> Among them to set up his Tabernacle,
> The holy One with mortal Men to dwell. (12.227–48)

MICHAEL'S RENDITION SEEMS especially to struggle with the problem of mediation. On the one hand, it has to present Moses as a necessary intermediary, citing the Israelites' terror at hearing God's voice directly (Exodus 20:18–21), so as to foreshadow the intermediary role of Christ, whose arrival Moses himself is said to have foretold. Thus, Moses's mediation serves a rhetorical function, too; it may be said to enact a typological mediation, which is in turn fulfilled in the mediation of Christ: "to God is no access / Without Mediator, who high Office now / *Moses* in figure bears." In this respect, though, mediation never fully disappears; rather, it only finds improved expression (however immeasurably) in the advent of Christ: "to introduce / One greater, of whose day he shall foretell." On the other hand, as a result of this mediation and the "Laws and Rites / Establisht," themselves formulated by Michael as shadowy Types, God will dwell among mortal men, apparently without the need of an intermediary. Milton captures some of the ambivalence felt within the Exodus narrative of the theophany itself. Yahweh reveals himself, his glory, to the newly liberated Israelites, while at the same time insisting on a literal boundary to be established between himself and the people (Exodus 19:12). To say that Moses served as intermediary between God and the people at the behest of the Israelites is to report only half the story. The other half, the more "uncanny" in Harold Bloom's view, is the repeated warnings to Moses that the people not get too close to God on the mountain top (Exodus 19:12–13 and again at verses 21–22 and 24). Milton's description of Christ's mediating role having been figured by Moses and foretold by "all the Prophets in thir age" transpires within a larger context that already depends on several degrees of mediation: Michael narrates the events to Adam and Milton reports this angelic mediation in his epic poem. For the rabbis and for Milton scriptural, as well as midrashic or poetic, instances of mediation occasion and are occasioned by the need to acknowledge historical change.[12]

"THE SPIRIT OF THE ANOINTED"

R. SIMEON B. LAQISH'S reference to the spirit of the Messiah (*rucho shel moshiach*) at the end of his homily deserves further examination. The eschatological impulse of the midrash is undeniable. It seeks deliverance from the oppressive Roman regime through messianic intervention. Yet the role of the Messiah was far from clearly defined during the rabbinic period; indeed, attitudes toward the Messiah underwent enormous change during the centuries that followed the destruction of the Temple. R. Simeon b. Laqish's Messiah need not be the spiritual deliverer he became in later Jewish writing, especially in the wake of Christianity's successful rise. For much of the first century following the destruction, Jewish messianic expectations focused on a military and political leader, a newly anointed (the literal meaning of Messiah) king to liberate Israel from Roman oppression. This attitude toward the Messiah was widely held among the early rabbis. Did the redactors of R. Simeon b. Laqish's interpretation share this view? We do not have to look far for an answer. The midrash concludes:

> On what merit will he [the Messiah] come? ". . . moved upon the face of the waters" (Gen. 1:2), [that is,] the merit of repentance, which has been compared to water, "pour out thine heart like water" (Lam. 2:19).

THIS MESSIAH, imbued with the spirit of God, will only come in response to Israel's atonement of its sins. Far from a military leader or capable politician, the Messiah to whom the midrash looks forward bears a suggestive relationship to the Christian Messiah, Jesus of Nazareth. Both Christianity's Messiah and the Messiah described in this rabbinic text are associated with atonement. The difference, however, is that Pauline theology stresses the atonement made available *only* through the self-sacrifice of the Christ, whereas the rabbis in this midrash suggest that humanity's atonement must *precede* the advent of the Messiah: human agency plays an irreplaceable role in rabbinic salvation history. Rabbinic literature that can, with reasonable certainty, be attributed to the Tannaitic period (up until 200 *c.e.*) has virtually nothing to say about the Messiah as transcendent redeemer, harbinger of the eschaton. Texts of the period immediately following, however, present a messianic eschatology that both acknowledges the necessity of history and formulates an antihistorical response. A crucial, albeit unspoken, factor in this evolution of rabbinic messianism is the advent and growing success of Christianity. What are the dynamics of this transformation? Why did it occur and what were the implications for a rabbinic phenomenology of history?

If Christianity posited the cross as the source of redemption, rabbinic Judaism, according to Jacob Neusner, offered the Torah, first in its written and oral formulations (i.e., rabbinic writings), second as the symbol of Israel's salvation, and third "in the person of the Messiah who, of course, would be a rabbi. The Torah in all three modes confronted the cross with its doctrine of the triumphant Christ, Messiah and King, ruler now of heaven and earth."[13] Not only were the terms of their respective messianic ideologies parallel, reasons Neusner, but the interpretive methods by which rabbinic Judaism and Christianity arrived at these beliefs are analogous.

> The Judaic sages worked out a view of history consisting in a rereading of the Book of Genesis in light of the entire history of Israel, read under the aspect of eternity. The Book of Genesis then provided a complete, profoundly typological interpretation of everything that had happened as well as a reliable picture of what, following the rules of history laid down in Genesis, was going to happen in the future. . . . Just as the Christians read stories of the (to them) Old Testament as types of the life of Christ, so the sages understood the tales of Genesis in a similarly typological manner. For neither party can history have retained that singular, one-dimensional, linear quality that it had had in Scripture itself.[14]

CHARACTERIZING RABBINIC JUDAISM'S messianic eschatology as "essentially ahistorical," Neusner writes, "if people wanted to reach the end of time they had to rise above time, that is, history, and stand off at the side of great moments of political and military character."[15] From a slightly different perspective, Yerushalmi has drawn the same conclusion in his survey of rabbinic literature, noting that "the Rabbis neither wrote postbiblical history nor made any special effort to preserve what they may have known of the course of historical events in the ages immediately preceding them or in their own time."[16]

Reading their own contemporary circumstances into the biblical narrative, the rabbis certainly regarded history as having rhythms and cycles to it. Indeed, as the passages I have cited above from Genesis Rabbah demonstrate, the rabbis ingeniously interpreted even the most superficially innocuous details through a prophetic lens. Yet this approach to reading the Scriptures is a far cry from Christian typology. As Neusner's frequent collaborator, Bruce Chilton, carefully argues, the Synoptic Gospels, and even Paul's letters, constructed an analogical relationship between the Hebrew Bible and the details of Christ's life that may have resembled the analogies drawn by the rabbis. This mode of analogy, however, ceased to be operative in the anonymous letter to the Hebrews,[17] whose author

> understands Israel, literally, as a thing of the past, the husk of the first, now antiquated covenant. . . . The Christian Judaism of Hebrews is . . . self-consciously a system of Christianity, because all that is Judaic is held to have

been provisional until the coming of the Son, after which point it is no longer meaningful.[18]

CHRISTIAN TYPOLOGY, following the Letter to the Hebrews (and especially as it became further elaborated in Reformation writings), constitutes an allegorical mode of reading that "effectively treats history as God's fictional representation of the something else that lies outside of history."[19] In other words, typology evacuates history of any internal significance; this is true both of contemporary historical events and the presumptive histories detailed in the Hebrew Scriptures. The same cannot be said of rabbinic Judaism's hermeneutics of history.

The oscillation between the particularities of a specific historical period and the generalities of an apparently continuous history of oppression find their counterpart, for the rabbis, in the succession of biblical characters who, when faced with adversity, each looked to an act of divine intervention for salvation. The relationship between these moments that exemplify God's personal relationship with individuals and the history of God's social commitment to the political entity, Israel, becomes more meaningful within the framework of the narrative of creation. The following homily begins with a seemingly unrelated intertext from the episode of the crossing of the Red Sea in Exodus but quickly finds its way through the entirety of biblical history, back to the six days of creation:

> R. Jonathan said, "The Holy One Blessed be He made an agreement with the Sea that it would split before Israel, as it is written, 'and the sea returned to its strength [l'eythano] when the morning appeared' (Ex. 14:27), [that is,] according to his agreement [l'tha'anoh]." R. Jeremiah b. Elazar said, "Not only with the Sea did God make an agreement, but with all those things created during the six days of creation. As it says, 'I, even my hands, have stretched out the heavens, and all their host have I commanded' (Isa. 45:12). I commanded the Sea to split, and the heavens to be silent before Moses, 'Give ear, O ye heavens' (Deut. 32:1), I commanded the sun and moon to stand before Joshua, I commanded the ravens to sustain Elijah, I commanded the fire not to harm Hananiah, Mishael, and Azariah, I commanded the lions not to harm Daniel, the heavens to open before Ezekiel, the fish to spit out Jonah." (5:5)

AS A SYSTEMATIC effort to correlate the story of creation with the history of Israel, the underlying premise of these remarks is that there was, is, and always shall be a relationship between the natural world and the historical experiences of Israel. The scriptural events listed here all share one major theme in common: each one relates to a moment in which Israel (or some portion of it) was saved through divine intervention. In other words, Israel was—*and will be*—saved by God's activity in history, just as the world was brought into existence through God's act of creating the physical universe.

Readers of Milton will no doubt recognize a parallel approach to the history of the One Just Man in books 11 and 12 of the epic. Having observed these structural and homiletical similarities, we should nevertheless note that Michael's narrative in book 12 contains Milton's most explicit pronouncement on the apparently typological relationship between the Law of the Old Covenant and the Gospel of the New.[20] Having heard Michael describe the Mosaic covenant, Adam asks his angelic guide about the necessity of the covenant's legal structures:

> This yet I apprehend not, why to those
> Among whom God will deign to dwell on Earth
> So many and so various Laws are giv'n;
> So many Laws argue so many sins
> Among them; how can God with such reside?
> To whom thus *Michael*. Doubt not but that sin
> Will reign among them, as of thee begot;
> And therefore was Law given them to evince
> Thir natural pravity, by stirring up
> Sin against Law to fight; that when they see
> Law can discover sin, but not remove,
> Save by those shadowy expiations weak,
> The blood of Bulls and Goats, they may conclude
> Some blood more precious must be paid for Man,
> Just for unjust, that in such righteousness
> To them by Faith imputed, they may find
> Justification towards God, and peace
> Of Conscience, which the Law by Ceremonies
> Cannot appease, nor Man the moral part
> Perform, and not performing cannot live.

THE LAW DOES NOT produce sin, as some readers of Paul, especially among many antinomian reformers contemporary to Milton, have argued. Neither is the law equal to sin or cut from the same cloth. Rather, the law functions to reveal sin, sin that cannot be removed by the law but whose remedy begins with its exposure by the law. As I have argued in chapter 2, from his very earliest writings against the prelacy Milton regarded the Church as having resulted from a process of evolution from the Mosaic covenant; he did not assert, as many of his Calvinist contemporaries did, that the Old Testament was always already Christianized. Though he may have changed his views in many respects from the 1641 publication of *Of Reformation*, it appears from this passage in *Paradise Lost* that here is one aspect of Milton's thinking that remained much the same. Yet, even if Michael constructs the Law as a necessary stage in the salvation of humanity, his account does quickly replace linear progress with typological fulfillment.

> So Law appears imperfet, and but giv'n
> With purpose to resign them in full time
> Up to a better Cov'nant, disciplin'd
> From shadowy Types to Truth, from Flesh to Spirit,
> From imposition of strict Laws, to free
> Acceptance of large Grace, from servile fear
> To filial, works of Law to works of Faith.
> And therefore, shall not *Moses*, though of God
> Highly belov'd, being but the minister
> Of Law, his people into *Canaan* lead;
> But *Joshua*, whom the Gentiles *Jesus* call,
> His Name and Office bearing, who shall quell
> The adversary Serpent, and bring back
> Through the world's wilderness long wander'd man
> Safe to eternal Paradise of rest. (12.280–314)

RATHER THAN MAINTAINING a strictly linear account of the biblical progression from Moses to Joshua, Michael's account overleaps much of biblical history. Joshua not only anticipates Jesus typologically; Milton's presentation here effectively elides Joshua's own historical importance in favor of the exclusively salvific power of Jesus's role, which Joshua merely adumbrates.[21] If, as Grossman asserts, "Typology emphasizes the historical development of the Christian revelation,"[22] it seems to so as repeatedly to shift Adam's attention from "historical development" onto "Christian revelation." While both the rabbis and Milton use the very beginning of the Genesis narrative to anticipate the progress of history, they construct the relationship between past, present, and future in notably different ways. For the rabbis, the story of creation contains hints of future moments of redemption, each of which stands independently as an example of God's hand in the salvation of the faithful. Yet this prolepsis remains fully open-ended, without any delimiting or teleological reference to the final redemption. For Milton, reading through a far more typological lens, Michael's litany of lonely men of faith obtains its full significance only in the blinding light of Christ's Incarnation, Passion, and Resurrection.

RABBINIC SCENE OF INSTRUCTION

THE RABBIS THEMSELVES imagined a human-divine exchange not unlike the two-book scene of instruction described by Milton. Significantly, however, the rabbinic version occurs as part of the Sinai theophany rather than as consolation for the Fall. BT Menachot reports the following story:

> When Moses ascended on high [to receive the Torah] he found the Holy One, blessed be He, seated, attaching coronets to the letters [of the Torah]. Said Moses, "Master of the Universe, Who holds your hand [forcing you to add these crowns]?" He answered, "There is a man who will arise at the end of many generations, Akiba b. Joseph by name, who will expound upon each tittle many, many laws." "Lord of the Universe," said Moses, "show him to me." He replied, "Turn around." Moses went to sit down behind eight rows [, listened to Akiba's discourses upon the law] and was unable to understand what he was saying. His resolve weakened. When they came to a certain matter, the disciples said, "Rabbi, whence do you know this?" He replied "It is a law given unto Moses at Sinai." [Moses] was comforted [by this]. Moses returned to the Holy One, blessed be He, and said, "Lord of the Universe, You have a man like this one and yet you give the Torah through me?" He replied, "Silence! such is my will." Then Moses said, "Lord of the Universe, You have shown me his Torah, now show me his reward." He said, "Turn around." Moses turned round and saw them weighing out [Akiba's] flesh at the market-stalls. "Lord of the Universe," cried Moses, "This is the Torah, and this is its reward?" He replied, "Silence! such is my will."[23]

LIKE MILTON'S LENGTHY dialogue between Michael and Adam in books II and

12, this rabbinic legend imagines a scene of instruction in which the divine interlocutor is called upon to correct and interpret a vision that may be misunderstood by the human witness. Furthermore, the Menachot legend describes a scene of instruction in which the human figure observes yet another scene of instruction. Rather than gaining insight or wisdom from the witnessing of this later pedagogical vignette, Moses must directly confront his ignorance, his failure to comprehend. Indeed, Moses is forced to acknowledge his own belatedness, a belatedness made all the more remarkable by virtue of what Akiba's response to his student's query suggests. If, as Leopold Damrosch has argued, Adam experiences a parody of God's foreknowledge in the epic's last books, what he calls "the pastness of the future,"[24] in this rabbinic legend Moses seems to be suffering from a belatedness with respect to *himself* and his own task as lawgiver to the Israelites.

In the first portion of the aggadah Moses confronts the astonishing ingenuity of a scholar manipulating and reforming the biblical texts in ways that he could never have anticipated. Moses's initial response of consternation and discouragement is difficult to read. It may be the typical reaction of a frustrated student struggling vainly to keep up with the lesson. But it also embodies the perpetual rabbinic anxiety concerning the validity of newer interpretations. Moses gives voice to that same nagging doubt every literary critic lives with (even if the "intentional fallacy" has been recognized as such) as he or she offers a reading whose connection to the "text itself" (let alone any notion of authorial intention) seems strained. As remarkable as it is to find the rabbis voicing this anxiety, more remarkable still is the answer they give to it. When asked about the source of one of his interpretations, Akiba does not simply attribute it to God by asserting that, while the Torah doesn't say so explicitly, the interpretation is suggested by God's words in the Torah. This view of the divine transmission of the Dual Torah was a crucial means of rabbinic self-justification. The Palestinian midrash, Leviticus Rabbah, provides a succinctly direct statement of this view:

"And the Lord delivered unto me two tables of stone written with the finger of God; and on them was written according to all the words (*k'khol had'varim*) . . ." (Deut. 9:10). R. Joshua b. Levi explained: "It says, 'on them . . . according to all the words (*k'khol had'varim*),' and it is also written, 'All the commandments (*kol hamitzvah*) which I command thee' (Deut 8:1). Instead of the expression *kol* the expression *k'khol* is used, instead of *d'varim*, *had'varim* is used, instead of *mitzvah*, *hamitzvah* is used, implying that Scripture, Mishnah, laws,

Talmud, *Toseftoth,* Aggadoth, and even what a faithful disciple would in the future say in the presence of his master, were all communicated to Moses on Sinai; for it says, 'Is there any thing whereof it is said, See, this is new?' (Eccl. 1:10). And the other part of the verse provides the reply to this: 'It hath been already.' "[25]

AKIBA'S REPLY TO his student's query does not make the same claim as R. Joshua b. Levi, a first-generation Palestinian amorah. Instead, Akiba locates the source of his innovative reading precisely in the *transmission* of the law from God to Moses. Hearing Akiba attribute his interpretation to that transmission seems to have sufficed for Moses: *nityashvah da'ato,* "he was comforted" [lit. "his mind eased itself"]. With canny self-awareness, Rav acknowledges the *dis*continuity between the biblical text and rabbinic interpretations at the same time that he bridges that gap with a concise statement of the ideology of the Dual Torah, i.e., that both the Written Torah and the Oral Torah were given at Sinai and that the Oral Torah is intimately tied to the written word. Moses does not appear to be appeased by being reminded (or foretold) of the lessons he will learn outside of the written law. He gains comfort instead from Akiba's gesture of attribution itself. This first part of Rav's legend identifies the remarkable originary powers of the rabbis (exemplified by the paradigmatic figure of Akiba), enlisting the authority of tradition to support their new interpretations essentially by fiat. This power of fiat comes through especially strongly in God's reply to Moses's modest self-abnegation: "Silence! such is my will." For once, human interrogation of the divine is unacceptable. How remarkable that the possibility of questioning God is foreclosed precisely at the moment when the validity of the interpretive powers of humanity is established.

If the first half of this imaginative tale functions largely as an apotheosis of Akiba, the second half of the legend opposes the vastly creative skill of the interpreter with his catastrophically wrong-headed political acumen. When the tale describes Moses looking on as Akiba's flesh is weighed out in the market stalls, it directly recalls the story of the rabbi's execution at the hands of the Roman Empire:

The hour at which R. Akiba was taken to be executed was also the hour for the recital of the Shema.[26] As they were combing his flesh with combs of iron he was accepting upon himself the yoke of the Kingdom of Heaven. His students said to him, "Rabbi, [you insist on committing yourself to heaven] even at this moment?" He replied, "All my life I was troubled by the verse, '[you shall love the Lord] with all your soul' [Num. 6:5], [which I understood to mean,] 'even if the Lord took your soul.' I wondered when I would be given the opportunity to fulfill [this commandment]. Now that I have the opportunity, shall I not fulfill it?"[27]

ONE OF SEVERAL legends recounting the violent deaths of rabbinic leaders at the hands of the Roman Empire, this narrative has since become part of a much more extensive liturgical martyrology recited to this day in traditional Yom Kippur services, known as the Eleh Ezkerah, "These I will remember." As Solomon Zeitlin has argued, while accounts of the execution of individual rabbis may have some relation to the events as they actually transpired, the collation of these accounts into stories of the "Ten Martyrs to the Kingdom" in various locations is a much later occurrence. This must be so, first, because each version of the martyrology uses a different list of ten rabbis and, second, because the ten rabbis included in any of the extant versions were not all contemporaries. Furthermore, Zeitlin points out that these martyrologies all rely on the premise of a transgenerational guilt that must be redeemed by the ten rabbis. "The theological conception of the redemption of the Original Sin," writes Zeitlin, "that a sinless man, a righteous man, can redeem with his blood a sin committed in antiquity, was in vogue among the Jewish Apocalypticists, but was strongly opposed by the Rabbis."[28] Indeed, in its talmudic context, the story of R. Akiba's execution notably avoids any assignment of guilt or redemption. Akiba is executed, according to an earlier part of the same account, because when "the wicked Government decreed that Israel should not involve itself in the Torah," Akiba nevertheless encouraged large gatherings at which the Torah was publicly studied. No mention is made of the sin of Joseph's brothers, which, in the later martyrologies, would become the transgenerational guilt that the ten rabbis were killed to expiate. The similarities to a developing Christology of sacrifice and redemption would have been too great. Neither does this account record any connection between Akiba's arrest and execution and his active support of Bar Kokhba's revolt. The story describes the gruesome mode of Akiba's death merely incidentally, in a subordinate adverbial clause. Yet it is flesh combed from Akiba's body that Moses is imagined to have seen during his instructional visit with God on Sinai.

The legends concerning the martyrdom of R. Akiba and his companions in 135 *c.e.* constitute a rich field of inquiry because they display a number of tensions concerning the development and promulgation of a rabbinic theory of history and political action. I cite this compelling story of Moses visiting R. Akiba's *bet midrash* (house of study) because it allows us to see these tensions and anxieties and because it suggests a crucial parallel with Milton's own anxious reassessment of history and political action as it appears in books 11 and 12 of *Paradise Lost*. Rav's legend of Moses in Akiba's bet midrash pits political and military defiance against interpretive and intellectual resistance, showing the perils of both approaches but ultimately favoring the latter over the former.

Rav presents Akiba at both the height of his interpretive powers and at the utter depths of his political failures. As Akiba's body is literally fragmented, his flesh torn from his limbs, we witness the reversal of Ezekiel's compellingly hopeful vision of the dry bones.

> And as I prophesied, there was a noise, and behold a shaking, and the bones came together, bone to his bone. And when I beheld, lo, the sinews and the flesh came up upon them, and the skin covered them above; but there was no breath in them. Then said he unto me, Prophesy unto the wind, prophesy, son of man, and say to the wind, Thus saith the Lord God; Come from the four winds, O breath, and breathe upon these slain, that they may live. So I prophesied as he commanded me, and the breath came into them, and they lived, and stood up upon their feet, an exceeding army. (Ez. 37:7–10)

EZEKIEL'S VISION OFFERED comfort to a fragmented and disheartened people: "these bones are the whole house of Israel . . . Thus saith the Lord God; Behold, O my people, I will open your graves, and cause you to come up out of your graves, and bring you into the land of Israel" (11–13). While the present situation looked bleak, Ezekiel's prophecy promised the return of Israel's glory, both spiritual and political. Indeed, in the larger chapter of the vision of the dry bones, the prophet devotes much of his attention to the geopolitical future of the Israelites, predicting a reunification of the kingdoms of Israel and Judah under the sovereignty of a renewed Davidic dynasty. In light of this powerful hope for political as well as spiritual redemption, Akiba's body takes on a synecdochic value. If Ezekiel predicted the resumption of political power, then Akiba's execution vividly figures the final blow to any hopes for Jewish political autonomy and self-determination. Rent asunder by the Roman Empire, its heart (the Temple in Jerusalem) cut out from its midst, the body of Israel looks very much as though it will not survive. And the rabbis rightly ask, "This is the Torah, and this is its reward?"

God's reply is even more remarkable: "Silence! Such is my will."[29] Does this tale teach us the necessity of history, or of a retreat from history?

R. AKIBA AND BAR KOKHBA

TO UNDERSTAND THE complicated historico-political tensions of these rabbinic accounts of Akiba's magnificent strengths and fatal weaknesses, we must first gain a fuller understanding of the Bar Kokhba revolt and its rabbinic legacy. The destruction of the Temple in 70 *c.e.*, as part of a larger military defeat of Jewish self-rule, prompted many community leaders to reconsider the value of active political engagement with the sovereign power of Rome. The Pharisees, advocates of an ascetic, meditative, and scholarly religious sensibility, enjoyed a de facto victory over their primary sectarian opponents, the Sadducees, for whom the Temple and its attendant cult functioned as a raison d'être. The Sadducees had not only served in religious and clerical capacities. They had also occupied prominent civic and political positions, serving as the governors (and sometimes royalty) of the Palestinian Jewish community. Indeed, members of priestly families affiliated with the Sadducees claimed royal heritage, merging Davidic and Levitical dynasties so as to legitimize their positions of political power. During the brief periods of greater political independence from Rome, the Sadducees, because of their control of the Temple, functioned as rulers of the Jewish community. Even during the puppet regime of Herod members of the Sadducean sect tended to ally themselves with the royal house more so than the Pharisees. With the elimination of the Temple cult, the distribution of power within the Jewish community, such as it was, changed dramatically. What was soon to become recognizable as rabbinic Judaism, with its concern for the minutia of ritual purity, religious practice, and the scholarly expertise necessary to enact them, owes its origins to the period immediately following the destruction of the Temple.

Changes from an outward-looking, politically engaged community to an inward-looking one did not occur overnight.[30] For much of the century that followed the destruction of the Temple, there occurred a number of abortive military attempts at reasserting Jewish political autonomy and reestablishing the Kingdom of Israel, led by groups like the Zealots and the *Sicarii*, the "daggermen" or "assassins." The best known of these attempts occurred between 132 and 135 *c.e.* under the leadership of Bar Kokhba. Reports of this revolt against Rome vary, but by all accounts it was an unmitigated disaster for the Palestinian Jewish community: Lamentations Rabbah (2:4), the midrash on the book of Lamentations, reports that the Emperor Hadrian slew "eighty thousand myriads of human beings" [*sic!*] at Bethar, the seat of Bar Kokhba's revolt; according to Dio Cassius, "580,000 men were slain in the various raids and battle, and the number of those that perished by famine, disease, and fire was past finding out."[31]

This massive loss of life was further aggravated by the death of a number of important scholarly leaders, many of whom had thrown their lot in with Bar Kokhba, believing him to be a messianic figure appointed by God to deliver Israel from bondage. The most prominent supporter of Bar Kokhba was R. Akiba b. Joseph. According to various accounts—and these accounts are dispersed throughout rabbinic literature, from different periods and locations—Akiba and his fellow rabbis were executed by Roman authorities during the period of the rebellion. Significantly, none of the *rabbinic* accounts report that the cause for execution was political sedition or participation in a military revolt; where charges are reported, they suggest Jewish disobedience of Roman injunctions against the teaching of the Torah (the very activity in which Akiba is engaged when Moses visits his bet midrash), ordination of new rabbis, or the observance of various ritual laws like circumcision. Whatever the real charges might have been, the rabbinic texts make a point of shifting the focus away from political rebellion to religious fulfillment and self-realization.

We find extensive mention of the Bar Kokhba revolt in rabbinic literature—in and of itself, an indication of the exceptional quality of this historical event, since rabbinic writing is usually quite laconic concerning contemporary historical occurrences—partly because the final editing of the earliest rabbinic text, the Mishnah, took place not very long after the war.[32] Isaac and Oppenheimer argue that Jewish unity fostered by the Patriarchate and Sanhedrin immediately following the destruction of the Temple was temporarily so powerful that during its occurrence there was no Jewish party of any note opposed to the revolt.[33] Yet in virtually all extant accounts of the Bar Kokhba rebellion we find a profound ambivalence concerning the legacy of this military action and, even more notably, in the representation of Bar Kokhba himself. While many of the rabbinic legends reveal an admiration for Bar Kokhba's physical and military prowess—he is portrayed with superhuman strength—they emphasize, even more so, his shortcomings, e.g., his lack of humility, his brutality, and his short temper. Indeed, one legend recounts Bar Kokhba's dispute with R. El'azar of Modi'im, a supporter of the revolt and a resident of Bethar, Bar Kokhba's military command post. R. El'azar demonstrated his support of the rebellion by sitting in sackcloth, fasting and praying continuously for the well-being of Bethar. This rankled Bar Kokhba because, as a fighting man confident in his own strength, he put no faith in divine assistance. His suspicions regarding R. El'azar's loyalty were raised and, in a fit of rage, Bar Kokhba kicked the rabbi so powerfully that he killed him. The midrash on Lamentations reports that it was immediately following this act of internal violence that the Roman army succeeded in conquering Bethar and killing Bar Kokhba. As Yael Zerubavel observes, this legend and others "show more appreciation of the rabbi than the leader of the revolt, suggesting that Rabbi El'azar of Modi'im . . . contributed more to the revolt's potential success than Bar Kokhba."[34] Further, it seems to contain a very important rabbinic lesson on the self-reproducing nature of violence.

Richard Marks has suggested that the rabbinic legends about Bar Kokhba invoke the biblical *gibborim*—heroes like Ehud, Jephthah, and, especially, Samson—complex individuals, characterized by virtues and vices. The legends of Bar Kokhba "understand his failure as a consequence of sins characteristic of *gibborim*."[35] Examining the Bar Kokhba legends in relation to other rabbinic accounts of gibborim, Marks speculates that the rabbis may have drawn some of the narrative elements for their tales from Greek and Roman legends of heroes like Hercules. What is more, the structure of the legend of Bar Kokhba and R. El'azar of Modi'im bears a resemblance to that of Aristotle's codification of Greek tragedy.[36] In addition to having its own hero in possession of only limited information, marred by a hamartia, the tale describes an anagnorisis and peripateia, as Hadrian's forces overrun the defeated rebels of Bethar:

Bar Koziba was slain and his head taken to Hadrian. "Who killed him?" asked Hadrian. A Cuthean said to him, "I killed him." "Bring his body to me," he ordered. He went and found a snake encircling its neck; so [when Hadrian was told of this he] exclaimed, "If God had not slain him who could have overcome him?"[37]

WE HAVE HERE another instance of the presence of Hellenic influences in Hebraic sources, all the more noteworthy for its occurrence in an extended account of the (military) defeat of Jewish forces by Hellenic forces. What is more, the image of the serpent encircling the severed head of Bar Kokhba resonates powerfully across Hebraic and Hellenic cultures. It is no wonder that Hadrian quickly draws his own conclusion upon receiving the Cuthean's report. Nor is it any wonder that the rabbinic composers of this legend seem to have given their tacit approval to Hadrian's interpretation. Hadrian might have been thinking of Laocoön, the Trojan priest whose disobedience of Apollo lead to the destruction of Troy and who met his own death in the crushing embrace of two serpents;[38] the rabbis might have thought of the serpent whose temptation of Eve brought about the loss of Eden and human mortality. In either case, the serpent signifies the repercussions of human audacity and competition with God.

The serpent encircles Bar Kokhba's once glorified head as if to say that this man may have had truly remarkable abilities, and ambitions to match them, but as a human being he was necessarily doomed to failure without God's help. Just as the midrashic embrace of the fig tree marks that rabbinic text as one fraught with the tensions of competing Hebraic and Hellenic ontologies, so too this image of the serpent around Bar Kokhba's neck reveals an intense political ambivalence concerning the nature of interactions between Hebraism/Judaism and Hellenism/paganism. The larger story in which this image appears describes the abject defeat of Jewish forces at the hands of the Roman army, an event that is commemorated to this day as having occurred on the ninth day of the month of Ab (also the day given for the destruction of both Temples). Yet this defeat is recognized, i.e., the legend's anagnorisis occurs, *at the moment the Roman emperor interprets the symbology of the serpent.* And the rabbis give prominence to this infiltration of Hellenic images and interpretation by allowing Hadrian to have the last words, words that simultaneously condemn Bar Kokhba for his hubris[39] and acknowledge the supremacy of the God of Israel: "If God had not slain him who could have overcome him?"

If parallels do exist between Virgil's account of the fall of Troy and this rabbinic legend of Bar Kokhba's demise—both recount the breach of seemingly impregnable walls, linking the defeat that ensues with the offenses given by the cities' human defenders (Laocoön and Bar Kokhba) to the same cities' divine defenders (Apollo and the God of Israel)—it is crucial to recognize one essential difference. Though Aeneas describes the fall of Troy to

his Cartheginian audience with the necessary bitterness of a defeated war-
rior, that defeat functions as a prelude to the founding of the Roman Empire
by a series of successful military campaigns and political alliances. Virgil's
epic begins with its hero drowning helplessly at sea—*Aeneae solvuntur frigore
membra* (1.92)—but ends with that same hero convincingly defeating his foe,
Turnus: *Ast illi* (i.e., Turnus) *solvuntur frigore membra* (12.951). The direct echo reveals how the *Aeneid* charts the transformation of its hero's passive state to an
aggressive hypermasculine virility; having earlier been defeated, he is now
pure action and agency.

Unlike Virgil's epic, however, the rabbinic account of the defeat of Bar
Kokhba's forces explores the catastrophic losses so as to elaborate a version
of political agency *against which* the rabbis define themselves. The rabbinic victory that follows this defeat is precisely not of the same order; rabbinic Judaism of the Diaspora managed to ensure its survival precisely by not following the path of military aggression exemplified by the Bar Kokhba
rebellion. In order to assert this new mode of existence within the forces of
history, the rabbis had to elaborate a version of Israel's chosenness that did
not depend for its validity on political and military success. Indeed, the rabbis sought ways of validating their sense of divine election through a new
theory of suffering.[40]

The equivocal characterization of the military nature of Bar Kokhba's rebellion and the specifically political ambitions of a figure like R. Akiba is
matched by a highly ambivalent textual account of R. Akiba's support of Bar
Kokhba. Bar Kokhba's given name was Bar Koziva. He took (or was awarded)
the name Bar Kokhba, "son of the Star," as an indication of his messianic
claims. The midrash on Lamentations provides a lengthy diatribe on the
legacy of the revolt, which includes the following observations on its leader's
name:

> R. Jochanan said: Rabbi used to expound the verse, "There shall step forth a
> star [*kokhav*] out of Jacob" [Num. 24:17], as follows: do not read it as *kokhav*
> but as *kozav* (lie). When R. Akiba beheld Bar Koziva he exclaimed, "This is
> the Messianic King!" R. Yochanan b. Tortha replied, "Akiba, grass will grow
> in your cheeks before he [i.e., the Messiah] will come!"[41]

MARKS SUGGESTS THAT well before Akiba's time the verse cited from Numbers, "There shall step forth a star [kokhav] out of Jacob," had acquired a set
of meanings linking it specifically to the Jewish messianic and apocalyptic tra-

dition. In a portion of Akiba's own reading of the verse now excised from the text, Marks speculates that Akiba must have linked the star (kokhav) to Bar Koziva (the rebel leader's real name), thereby participating in the renaming of Bar Koziva as Bar Kokhba. Marks concludes that R. Akiba's (now elided) quotation of Numbers 24:17 means that he regarded Bar Koziva as a "national warrior-king arisen to conquer and destroy Rome."[42] We know from other passages in rabbinic literature that Akiba espoused a messianic view that was explicitly national, historical, and of this world.[43]

Reversing the process whereby Bar Koziva acquired the name promising deliverance, Bar Kokhba, Rabbi *rewrites the biblical verse*, suggesting that instead of promising salvation the prophecy in Numbers predicts the Bar Kokhba fiasco by alluding to the false promises made by its leader. Rabbi's condemnation of Bar Kokhba serves as a necessary prologue to the introduction of Akiba's mistaken hope. Akiba, who is otherwise celebrated throughout rabbinic literature as a visionary figure, bestowed with the gifts of intellectual acuity, spiritual insight, and charismatic leadership second to none, is shown here as the tragic victim of Bar Kokhba's deception. And if that is not enough, R. Yochanan b. Tortha (an extremely minor figure in rabbinic literature, whose only claim to fame is this statement contra the much greater Akiba) is given the last word—Akiba's expectations are bitterly disappointed and, with the benefit of hindsight, the audience to whom this midrash was addressed would have recognized how true R. Yochanan b. Tortha's warning was.[44]

We may observe a dynamic engagement with suffering and its sources in the account of Akiba's martyrdom itself. As the iron combs tear at his flesh, he completes his final recitation of the Shema. The story in Berakhot continues:

[Akiba] lengthened the word *echad* ["one," the final word of the first verse] until his soul left his body. A heavenly voice went forth and proclaimed, "Happy are you, R. Akiba, for your soul departed [as you said the word] *echad*."

The ministering angels said to the Holy One Blessed be He, "This is the Torah, and this is its reward? [He deserved to be] 'of those who died by Thy hand, Lord'" [Ps. 17:14]. He replied, "'Their portion is in life'" [ibid.]. A heavenly voice went forth and said, "Happy are you, R. Akiba, for you have been invited to life in the world to come."

AKIBA DIES WITH the defiant assertion of God's unity and singularity on his lips, resisting the potential conclusion one might draw from his execution of Roman/pagan supremacy.[45] Bearing witness to his unwavering devotion to God and his legacy of study, angels give voice to the same objection uttered by Moses in the legend recounted in Menachot: "This is the Torah, and this is its reward?" Akiba's execution seems to contradict the rabbinic reading of Isaiah 53, and the rabbis address this potential contradiction by giving it voice through Moses (in Menachot) and angels (in Berakhot)!

The exchange between the ministering angels and God that ensues leaves wonderfully ambiguous the real agent of Akiba's death. The initial objection posed by the angels—in the form of a verse from Psalms—suggests that they perceive Akiba's death to be at the hands of the Romans. Yet God's reply—the conclusion of the same verse—implies an acceptance of responsibility. This acceptance functions as the necessary prerequisite for Akiba's invitation to the world to come. Yet the invitation raises further questions, as it shifts the legend's focus from a pragmatically historical one—the outcome of Akiba's conflict with Roman authorities—to an eschatologically reassuring one. No modern scholar of the rabbinic period that I can find supports the argument suggested in the rabbinic sources themselves, i.e., that R. Akiba was executed because he had disobeyed the Roman prohibition against the study of Torah. The prevailing opinion is that Akiba was charged as a rebel and executed for sedition. By making the study of Torah the act of defiance—rather than an involvement in an illegal or seditious political/military movement—the rabbis transform their characteristic self-defining activity, study, into a highly politicized undertaking. This, whether it was viewed as such by the Romans or not. By giving Akiba his reward in the apocalyptic world to come, however, this politicization has a very different dynamic than that of the Roman world of power politics.

In addition to constructing Akiba's defiance as a hermeneutic activity, the rabbis formulated a specific ideology of suffering at the hands of God. Citing Isaiah's suffering servant, BT Berakhot 5a reports the following account of divinely inflicted suffering by Raba, in the name of R. Sahorah, in the name of R. Huna,

> Anyone in whom the Holy One, blessed be He, is pleased [*chafetz*], He crushes him with painful sufferings as it says, "And the Lord was pleased [*chafetz*] with [him, hence] he crushed him by disease" [Isa. 53:10]. You might think that this is so even if he did not accept them out of love. Thus it says, "To

see if his soul would offer itself in restitution [*asham*]" [ibid.]. Just as the trespass-offering [*asham*] must be brought by consent, so the sufferings must be endured with consent. And if he does accept them, what is his reward? "He will see his seed, prolong his days" [ibid.] And more than that, his learning [*talmudo*] will endure by his hand. As it says, "The purpose [*chefetz*] of the Lord will prosper in his hand" [ibid.].

R. HUNA'S HOMILY draws its impact from a number of interpretive strategies typical of such talmudic and midrashic homilies, especially wordplay. There are at least three different wordplays in this passage. The first has its origins in the biblical text itself. Noting that "pleased" and "purpose" are derived from the same root, *ch*, *f*, *tz*, the rabbinic interpreter argues that God reveals his pleasure in a believer by fulfilling his purpose through him—even (or especially) if that fulfillment must come about through suffering. The second and third wordplays function to prioritize the emergent rabbinic worldview, particularly as it supersedes a perspective dependent on the Temple and the sacrificial cult. The Hebrew word *asham* refers to a specific kind of sin offering described in the Pentateuch (see, e.g., Leviticus 5) and as such pertains to the ritual forms that had ceased to be operative following the destruction of the Temple. Without entirely negating the value of this antiquated mode of restitution, R. Huna seems to be suggesting that it has been replaced by a more generalized form of suffering that would have been familiar to his contemporary audience. Where the specialized ritual forms of the Temple had once been the only way to achieve atonement, now this atonement is available to anyone undergoing divinely inflicted torment. But R. Huna argues even further, that the legacy of this patient sufferer is assured specifically as *talmudo*, "his learning," the word that would become the generic term for rabbinic study. Thus, in place of a prophetic utterance speaking to a people dependant on the Temple, Isaiah's song of the suffering servant comes to refer directly to rabbinic Judaism's firm valuation of textual study over everything else.

Daniel Boyarin has recently argued that much of rabbinic literature from the second through sixth centuries *c.e.* is engaged in the formulation of a diasporic mode of resistance directly in response to modes of power embodied by Rome. Rabbinic masculinity transforms itself into the direct antithesis of Roman *virtus* by valorizing "the grotesque, dismembered, dephallicized male body, [defining] resistance not as the assumption of power and dominance but as resistance *to* the assumption of dominance."[46] Especially in their accounts of rabbinic martyrs, the writings of the rabbis celebrate a kind of cultural masochism in which the male body is open, permeable, susceptible to pleasure and pain (often simultaneously), and therefore (in Roman/pagan eyes) feminine.[47] Boyarin's argument concerning rabbinic masculinity and its characteristic modes of political resistance to Roman masculinity allows us to draw some further conclusions concerning the rabbinic phenomenology of suffering. First, as Boyarin himself suggests, *"already existing* pain is transformed into pleasure through interpreting and experiencing it as submission to an idealized figure. Thus if 'anyone whom God desires, He will cause them physical sufferings' [BT Berakhot 5a], then it follows that anyone to whom God causes physical sufferings, He desires."[48] Furthermore, the rabbis assert their own version of suffering by staking a claim to Isaiah's suffering servant and proclaiming that the prophet refers to all Jews who have suffered, rather than to a single man (in whose name many Jews eventually would suffer).

Of course, the prophetic precedent for this correlation of suffering with election meant that it wielded special significance for early Christian thought as well as for Hebraic/Jewish self-fashioning. The rabbis' reading of Isaiah 53 seems to me to share more in common with Christianity's understanding of that text than has often been acknowledged, in its assertion of a common legacy of suffering. In both cases Isaiah 53 (and its prophecy of faithful suffering) comes to anticipate the contemporary suffering of the respective biblical interpreters as much as it establishes any divine or semidivine paradigm. Yet, where Christianity asserts the suffering of Christ as a typological model that fulfills the text of the Hebrew Bible in order to supersede it, rabbinic Judaism posits the suffering of all those with whom God is pleased as guarantee of a textual and hermeneutic durability. Study and interpretation become the new terrain on which survival and human agency are negotiated. The suffering is given meaning by references to other versions of suffering; history supplants typology.[49]

"SUFFERING FOR TRUTH'S SAKE"

MATTHEW'S GOSPEL CONCLUDES the account of Jesus having healed Peter's mother-in-law, "that it might be fulfilled which was spoken by Isaiah the prophet, saying, Himself took our infirmities, and bare our sicknesses" (Matthew 8:17). Mark and Luke cite Isaiah 53:12, "and he was numbered with the transgressors," in their respective Passion narratives (Mark 15:28, Luke 22:37). As prophetic utterance Isaiah's powerful vision predicts the life and death of Jesus and helps to formulate the salvific mode through which his death comes to be read as victorious rather than ignominious.

Paul's letters also invoke the image of the suffering servant (explicitly and implicitly) as part of an analogy between the suffering of Christ and the suffering of his followers. Though this parallel would be developed far more elaborately in later Christian writings, Paul portrays the suffering endured by his addressees as a temporary inconvenience and not, as the Hebrew prophetic tradition might suggest, as an indirect demonstration of intimacy with God. In Romans 8:35–39, Paul asks,

> Who shall separate us from the love of Christ? shall tribulation, or distress, or persecution, or famine, or nakedness, or peril, or sword? As it is written, For thy sake we are killed all the day long; we are accounted as sheep for the slaughter. Nay, in all these things we are more than conquerors through him that loved us. For I am persuaded, that neither death, nor life, nor angels, nor principalities, nor powers, nor things present, nor things to come, Nor height, nor depth, nor any other creature, shall be able to separate us from the love of God, which is in Christ Jesus our Lord.

OF SPECIAL INTEREST in this letter is its probable audience: a growing Jewish-Christian community in the imperial capital. We might well expect that Paul would work especially hard in this letter to distinguish his views from those circulating in the general Jewish community. While these distinctions are more readily apparent in Paul's discussion of justification through faith, even in this passage concerning suffering we may perceive a tacit attack on the Jewish approach to living in a hostile environment. Paul is believed to have written his letter to the Romans in 55 or 56 *c.e.*,[50] fifteen years before the destruction of the Temple, during a period when many Jews, especially in Palestine, expressed their defiance of Rome in overt military resistance. There were, no doubt, those Jews who advocated a more passive response to Roman oppression, but a thoroughgoing theory of the dignity inherent in suffering in God's name was still several centuries in the future. The tone in Paul's letter is clearly defiant, but it makes no claims for the positive power of suffering, either. Indeed, in 2 Corinthians 6:2–10 Paul resorts again to the rhetorical digest of factors, this time to suggest the power of Christian salvation over the evils of this world:

Behold, now is the accepted time; behold, now is the day of salvation. Giving no offence in any thing, that the ministry be not blamed: But in all things approving ourselves as the ministers of God, in much patience, in afflictions, in necessities, in distresses; In stripes, in imprisonments, in tumults, in labors, in watchings, in fastings; By pureness, by knowledge, by longsuffering, by kindness, by the Holy Ghost, by love unfeigned; By the word of truth, by the power of God, by the armor of righteousness on the right hand and on the left; By honor and dishonor, by evil report and good report: as deceivers, and yet true; As unknown, and yet well known; as dying, and, behold, we live; as chastened, and not killed; As sorrowful, yet always rejoicing; as poor, yet making many rich; as having nothing, and yet possessing all things.

FOR PAUL, SUFFERING is relevant less because it affords the believer the opportunity to earn his salvation or display his merit than because it poses the challenge of endurance, perseverance, and transcendence.

But the suffering servant, and Christ's embodiment of that prophecy, have a further function in other early Christian writings, becoming typological models for believers in Christ as *they* endure the physical pain, humiliation, rejection, and systematic oppression that characterized the lives of many early Christians. 1 Peter, an early pastoral epistle addressed to "strangers scattered throughout Pontus, Galatia, Cappadocia, Asia, and Bithynia" (1 Peter 1:1), i.e., Christian communities of the diaspora, far from Palestinian or Roman centers, concerns itself largely with the nature and meaning of suffering endured and to be endured by these communities.[51] Though it repeatedly invokes Isaiah's suffering servant as its intersecting text (especially the direct citations of Isaiah at 2:22–25), the epistle presents an ambiguous account of the nature of Christian suffering. On the one hand, the letter suggests that those who suffer as did Christ, i.e., blamelessly, can expect redemption: "because Christ also suffered for us, leaving us an example, that ye should follow his steps" (2:21). In other words, redemption is earned by modeling one's behavior after Christ, who showed the way to salvation by suffering patiently as God's faithful servant. On the other hand, 1 Peter implies that a Christian's blameless suffering obtains value only insofar as it partakes of Christ's suffering: "But rejoice, inasmuch as ye are partakers of Christ's sufferings" (4:13). Suffering derives its meaning not solely from its mimetic properties but from its subordinate aspect.

Alan Segal has noted that the New Testament never specifically invokes

Isaiah 53 "to prove the vicarious atonement of the messiah."[52] That is, while the notion of redemptive suffering, wherein one figure undergoes punishment so as to absolve those who are guilty, was a concept familiar to members of the Jewish community living during the time of the Temple and its sacrificial cult, the application of Isaiah 53 directly to the Messiah was a Christian innovation. Segal continues, "In I Peter, Isaiah 53 is used to explain the death of the martyrs as an emulation of the Christ, but even here vicarious atonement is not proven by scriptural passage."[53] The split, in Segal's reading, between the necessity of imitatio Christi in suffering, on the one hand, and vicarious atonement through Christ's passion, on the other, is indicative of what I have referred to above as the ambiguous presence of Isaiah 53 in early Christian writing. It is not until the third and fourth centuries *c.e.*—coincident with the political rise of Christianity—that a coherent theology of vicarious atonement emerges, one that deemphasizes the suffering of the believer as a necessary aspect of redemption, one that fulfills the model established by Christ.

An early Greek Christian document, *Constitutions of the Holy Apostles*, probably dating from the first half of the second century *c.e.*, asserts that followers of Christ ought to imitate him in suffering:

> If therefore He for our sakes renounced His repose, was not ashamed of the cross, and did not esteem death inglorious, why do not we imitate His sufferings, and renounce on His account even our own life, with that patience which He gives us? For He did all for our sakes, but we do it for our own sakes: for He does not stand in need of us, but we stand in need of His mercy. He only requires the sincerity and readiness of our faith.[54]

THIS EARLY ARTICULATION of the concept of imitatio Christi posits human suffering as a constitutive element of future redemption. The believer renounces his own life, suffering patiently, as a necessary means of demonstrating "the sincerity and readiness" of his or her faith. Without Christ's passion, redemption would be unavailable; yet without the believer's imitative passion, redemption would be equally impossible.

By the end of the second century *c.e.* and the beginning of the third, one of the most important founders of the Latin Church, Tertullian, would expound a much more detailed theory of human suffering. Addressing himself to fellow Christians languishing in prison as they prepared for their certain martyrdom at the hands of Roman gladiators, Tertullian assured them,

We, with the crown eternal in our eye, look upon the prison as our training-ground, that at the goal of final judgment we may be brought forth well disciplined by many a trial; since virtue is built up by hardships, as by voluptuous indulgence it is overthrown.[55]

Tertullian's words of encouragement compare the passing qualities of earthly pain to the triumphant redemption that awaits the spirit. Central to his diminishment of corporeal suffering is the Pauline division of body and soul. The soul triumphs precisely in its renunciation of the body, of the world, of action (personal and political) in the historical present: "It is of no consequence where you are in the world—you who are not of it."[56]

About five years later Tertullian composed a more sustained meditation on these matters entitled *Of Patience*. Enumerating the extensive instances of Christ's patience, Tertullian argues that though we may not hope to achieve the perfect patience of God we must nevertheless strive to learn from this quality, just as "we see all servants of probity and right feeling shaping their conduct suitably to the disposition of their lord."[57] But this patience is a complex matter, self-perpetuating for those who are already believers and difficult to obtain for those who do not believe: "It is patience which is both subsequent and antecedent to faith."[58] In Tertullian's view patience is an essential quality to distinguish the old law from the new: "So faith, illumined by patience, when it was becoming propagated among the nations through 'Abraham's seed, which is Christ' [Galatians 3:16], and was superinducing grace over the law, made patience her preeminent coadjutrix for amplifying and fulfilling the law, because that alone had been lacking unto the doctrine of righteousness."[59] In Tertullian we first discover that what Milton would call "suffering for truth's sake," that is, a believer's Christlike patience, directly supplants the Old Covenant's reliance on law as the means to salvation. Suffering and patience are the human counterparts to the divine grace that constitutes the New Covenant.

Writing at a far more secure moment in the rise of Christianity (ca. 391 *c.e.*), a period in which early Christian martyrs were admired as recent reminders of past suffering rather than as contemporary exempla, Ambrose formulates a view more in keeping with the growing confidence of the Church: "It is not a blessed thing to be in the midst of suffering; but it is blessed to be victorious over it, and not to be cowed by the power of temporal pain."[60] In this view pain and suffering do not possess a value (salvific or otherwise) in and of themselves. Rather, they present obstacles to be transcended by the faithful. No longer are believers asked to endure patiently as *a necessary means* to achieve redemption. Ambrose now calls on the Christian community to overcome temporal pain, "not to be cowed" by it. Redemption comes by other means. What is more, this dismissal of suffering appears within a larger account of the "blessed life . . . in this body," that is, living in this historical moment. As the Church grows in worldly influence and power, so it must reformulate a theory of suffering that makes room for a faithful and meaningful life in the *absence* of extreme pain and oppression. Imitating Christ's passion in the first three centuries was almost a matter of course—unlike their Jewish counterparts, many early Christians could expect an ignominious death not unlike their messiah. As those at whose hands these early believers were persecuted came more and more under Christian influence, however, the faithful could no longer anticipate (or need no longer dread) a difficult life and/or a painful death. Imitatio Christi, if it was to retain any meaningful theological value, required a new explanation. The notion of imitatio Christi through suffering would not disappear altogether, however, and during the period of the Reformation and later, in Milton's time, it would inspire renewed interest.

During the eleven centuries of Christian religious and political domination centralized in the Roman Church, we find relatively little emphasis within Christian theology placed on the value of defiant suffering, especially as a means of forging a collective identity. Suffering—in forms like the monastic mortification of the flesh—becomes almost exclusively an individualized matter; it could not serve in any more overtly political fashion simply because the distribution of worldly power mitigated against its efficacy for such matters. This approach to suffering would not disappear entirely from Christian thought, but it is to be found much more deeply entrenched in Jewish writings—both interpretive and liturgical—of the same period. It took the fierce confessional divisions of the Reformation, along with the often violent struggles between adherents of Rome and the growing body of followers of Luther, and especially Calvin, to precipitate a renewed interest in the Christian phenomenology of suffering.

As several of his biographers have observed, much of Calvin's thinking about the value of suffering, especially as a barometer for the determination of election, took shape in the aftermath of his flights from Paris in 1535 and Geneva in 1538. Attacks on Protestants were occurring with increased frequency and intensity; there can be little doubt that this context of collective persecution contributed to Calvin's conceptualization of election as limited, a status shared by a chosen few. Here again, after over a millennium of Christian supremacy, was a way of formulating a collective oppositional identity via the phenomenology of suffering. Yet suffering for Calvin did not have the same value it had for some of the earliest Church fathers. Calvinist theology—which would come to dominate the Puritan reforms of the English Interregnum—saw Christ's crucifixion as a necessary price to be paid in order to redeem man's inherent corruption. Man only deserves salvation because Christ willingly gave his life; *man's* actions in and of themselves are essentially meaningless. In his *Institutes of the Christian Religion* Calvin writes at length concerning the meaning and value of suffering. The eighth chapter of book 3 concerns itself with "Bearing the Cross, a Part of Self-Denial," asking, "Why should we exempt ourselves, therefore, from the condition to which Christ our Head had to submit, especially since he submitted to it for our sake to show us an example of patience in himself?"[61] Calvin goes on to assert, however, that this imitative self-denial is without value except as part of a preceding faith in Christ. Throughout this chapter, and the *Institutes* more generally, Calvin resolutely denies anything that might suggest the possibility of humanity's self-justification. This being so, any suffering a believer endures is a manifestation of faithful justification that precedes it; in and of itself it has no salvific force. Pursuing this notion further, Calvin writes that God afflicts his people

> to test their patience and to instruct them to obedience. *Not that they can manifest any other obedience to him save what he has given them.* But it so pleases him by unmistakable proofs to make manifest and clear the graces which he has conferred upon the saints, that these may not lie idle, hidden within. . . . Obviously, if everything went according to their own liking, they would not know what it is to follow God.[62]

What may look like the rewarding of meritorious suffering is really the fulfillment of a predestined salvation that had manifested itself in the elect believer's willingness to suffer persecution.[63] A faithful Christian who imitates Christ by patiently suffering reveals the increasingly intimate union all the elect enjoy with Christ.

RESTORATION OF/AND POLITICAL AGENCY

IF MILTON WERE to have adopted this more orthodox Calvinist view of predestined salvation, then his typological account of individual moments of "suffering for truth's sake" in books 11 and 12 would indeed treat these moments as "God's fictional representation of the something else that lies outside of history."[64] As such, Jason Rosenblatt's assertion that the final books of *Paradise Lost* mark a retreat from the Hebraism of the prelapsarian books would find further validation.[65] Books 11 and 12 may indeed draw on the far more explicit typology of the Letter to the Hebrews than other portions of the epic. I want to suggest, however, that, largely as a result of Milton's doctrinal heterodoxies, especially his Arminianism,[66] there remains a historical surplus, one that I have connected earlier with Hebraism/Judaism. While this Hebraic/Judaic presence—or what I have described as the striking similarities between midrash and *Paradise Lost*—is muted in these final books, it is nevertheless a feature that deserves further attention.

Reviving a view we first saw associated with Tertullian in the very earliest stages of the Church, Milton sees Christ's patient suffering as a crucial model for human action (or, as is often the case, inaction) *and* as a necessary element of salvation. Imitatio Christi becomes an essential aspect of one's ability to *earn* salvation. In his most extensive meditations on these matters in the *De Doctrina Christiana*, Milton wrestles with the Arminian question of how salvation is to be achieved through a combination of divine mercy and human faith freely given. While he does not shy away from the strict language of redemption as necessary, Milton insists that humanity must show its willingness to accept salvation.[67] Writing of the virtues "which relate to our duty . . . toward God," Milton includes Patience, "a virtue which shows itself when . . . we bear any evils that we have to bear calmly, as things which our supreme Father has sent for our good."[68] It is not a foregone conclusion—as it is for Calvin—that the elect will endure these evils patiently and not fall away. As Milton writes earlier, in one of the most explicitly Arminian chapters of the *De Doctrina Christiana*,

> God . . . promises to put reverence for him into [believers'] minds, so that they may not depart from him. In other words, he promises to fulfil his own responsibility and give them enough grace to prevent their departure. He also makes a covenant, however, and the conditions of the covenant have to be fulfilled not by one party alone but by both.[69]

AS AN ACCOUNT of suffering Milton's argument distinguishes itself from more standard Calvinist readings insofar as it restores human agency. Even when larger or more public political activities are no longer possible, human engagement with the world as it is experienced materially and historically is essential. Similarly, despite its superficially Calvinist flavor, Milton's suggestion at the beginning of book 11 of *Paradise Lost* that Adam and Eve found the ability to pray only because "Prevenient Grace descending had remov'd / The stony from thir hearts" (3–4), must be read in the context of the final lines of the preceding book, where, following the imitationes Christi of Eve and Adam,[70]

> they forthwith to the place
> Repairing where he judg'd them prostrate fell
> Before him reverent, and both confess'd
> Humbly thir faults, and pardon begg'd, with tears
> Watering the ground, and with thir sighs the Air
> Frequenting, sent from hearts contrite, in sign
> Of sorrow unfeign'd, and humiliation meek. (10.1098–1104)

ADAM AND EVE demonstrate a willingness to fulfill their part of the covenant, which in turn leads God to facilitate the slow process of redemption.

Given the dynamics of Milton's theodicy, with its dependence on parallel assertions of responsibility by God and humanity, nothing short of this reciprocal repentance at the close of book 10 would have been acceptable. Yet the assertion of human agency in the realm of salvation is not identical to the insistence on the efficacy and necessity of human involvement in the material and political world. We might easily imagine Milton adopting a fully eschatological view of history that would regard any human attempts at effecting change as at best futile, at worst sacrilegious. As his final prose tracts suggest, and as his great Restoration poems reveal, Milton does not choose the path of least resistance. "The experience of defeat," to cite Christopher Hill's study of the Restoration, left Milton wiser but no less interested in the world and his role in it.[71]

Whatever lingering hopes Milton might have had for the institution of a republican government just prior to the Restoration were given voice in his second edition of *The Readie and Easie Way to Establish a Free Commonwealth* (April 1660). Milton's tract vigorously advocates the institution of a "Grand Councel . . . firmly constituted to perpetuitie" (YP 7:444) to replace the now disbanded Rump Parliament. Supplementing the arguments from England's own recent and more distant past with evidence from classical antiquity and biblical history, Milton turns most frequently to the example of the Israelites in the desert, for both positive and negative instruction. As was the case in Milton's antiprelatical tracts (see chapter 2), the Jewish and pagan Ancients first appear in the same breath: "Therefor among the *Jews,* the supreme councel of seaventie, call'd the *Sanhedrim,* founded by *Moses,* in *Athens,* that of *Areopagus,* in *Sparta,* that of the Ancients, in *Rome,* the Senat, consisted of members chosen for term of life" (YP 7:436). Yet this affirmative synthesis of the wisdom of England's Hebraic and classical antecedents is quickly tempered by Milton's admonitory reference to "the gentilizing *Israelites*" who "clamoured for a king" in 1 Samuel 8 to set them—so they felt—on equal footing with their neighboring nations (449–50). Should Milton's English contemporaries "return precipitantly" to a monarchy whence God had just delivered them, then they would follow in the pattern of their Jewish antecedents precisely by adopting this gentile/heathen mode of government. As we have seen elsewhere in Milton's writings, both early and late, the coupling of Judaism and paganism cuts both ways. On the one hand, they offer mutually supporting examples, where the wisdom of the Hebrew and classical ancients function as aspects of England's heritage deserving of revival and preservation. On the other hand, they pose the danger of a mutual contamination so profound that it seems to justify the disowning of England's previously acknowledged cultural, political, and religious lineage.

This complex folding together of Jewish and pagan precedents to England's current predicament recurs at the close of the tract, where Milton cites another biblical topos long favored by disputants in the debates over monarchy. With a bitterness and scorn especially characteristic of Milton's final forays in prose, he writes that if, after England has tasted of the liberty of the Commonwealth,

> the same reason shall pass for current to put our necks again under kingship, as was made use of by the *Jews* to returne back to *Egypt* and to the worship of thir idol queen, because they falsly imagind that they then livd in more plentie and prosperitie, our condition is not sound but rotten, both in religion and all civil prudence. (YP 7:462)

AS IN THE EXAMPLE from 1 Samuel, the Jews who are adduced as an example not to follow, i.e., those who sought to return to Egypt, are depicted as idolatrous and heathen. By implicit contrast, then, were Milton's fellow Englishmen to choose to resist the restoration of the monarchy by adopting his plan for a free Commonwealth, England would reveal itself as the faithful Israel, uncorrupted by pagan influence. By appealing to whom he identifies as "sensible and ingenuous men" (YP 7:463), the tract's fit audience though few, Milton's embrace of "reviving liberty" functions to resist "the deluge of this epidemic madness" leading inexorably back to the idol queen of Egyptian monarchy, a movement that, from the perspective of the "abus'd multitude" appears to be a far readier and easier way than the path Milton advocates. Against a mounting body of evidence to the contrary, this last desperate plea in prose avers the difference between a pagan impulse toward the abdication of political agency and the true Israelite assertion of political self-determination, the eponymous "ready and easy way."

By the time he comes to write his epic poem, biblical example, pagan precedent, and political agency have been transformed. The shift from vision to narration between books 11 and 12 occurs to encourage Adam to become a good reader and, thus, a historical agent. Pictures are of limited use to a propaedeutics that prepares Adam for a world in which he will not have direct unmediated contact with God's will. In this respect, book 12's modal change from vision to narrative is analogous to the rabbinic replacement of the visionary mode of prophecy with the hermeneutic mode of midrash. Before textual strategies can adequately develop, *prophecy has to fail.* Adam's inability to read the scenes correctly embodies the failure of prophecy, a failure that must be experienced before an interpretive mode can develop. Milton, the passionate iconoclast, first banishes the images, shatters the idols, before he expounds on the words. What is more, the narrative mode of book 12 balances our attention between the episode under narration and the act of narration itself so as to render a purely typological reading of the account incomplete. The visionary mode of book 11 elides the function and historical context of interpretation in ways that Michael's telling of events do not. The result in book 12 is a network of associations between the specific biblical history of Michael's narrative, the gradual education of Adam, the life and death of Christ, and, unspoken but always present, the historical circumstances of a politically and religiously disappointed John Milton. In a passage that revises Milton's late political tract, Michael describes the Israelites' journey through the desert following the splitting of the Red Sea:

> the Race elect
> Safe toward *Canaan* from the shore advance
> Through the wild Desert, not the readiest way,
> Lest ent'ring on the *Canaanite* alarm'd

War terrify them inexpert, and fear
Return them back to *Egypt*, choosing rather
Inglorious life with servitude; for life
To noble and ignoble is more sweet
Untrain'd in Arms, where rashness leads not on.
This also shall they gain by thir delay
In the wide Wilderness, there they shall found
Thir government, and thir great Senate choose
Through the twelve Tribes, to rule by laws ordain'd. (12:214–26)

THE GOSPEL ACCOUNTS of Jesus's isolation in the wilderness for forty days, where he was tempted by the devil, read the wandering of the Israelites for forty years as their prototype. Yet typology is only one lens through which to read these wanderings. First, Adam's own immediate future is anticipated by (or, if one wishes to reassert chronology, reflected in) the uncertain yet divinely guided wanderings of the Israelites. The poignant and beautiful final lines of the poem describe Adam and Eve departing from Eden with the world all before them, "where to choose / Thir place of rest, and Providence thir guide: / They hand in hand with wand'ring steps and slow, / Through *Eden* took thir solitary way." Second, echoing the title of Milton's final, desperate, and ultimately futile plea to resist the restoration of the monarchy, the Israelites "advance / Through the wild Desert, *not the readiest way*, / . . . choosing rather / Inglorious life with servitude" [emphasis added]. The particularities of the biblical wanderings are preserved; yet the historical details of Milton's own political struggles resonate through this passage. Indeed, the passage not only recollects (and resists) Milton's final public engagement in matters of government through a reference to its title, it also revises how *The Readie and Easie Way* invoked the Mosaic past as precedent for alternatives to monarchy.[72]

Michael's epic revision of the "ready and easy way" also differs from the earlier prose tract in how it addresses the differences between Hebrew and pagan political agency. The prose tract had condemned those Israelites who clamored for a return to Egypt to worship "thir idol queen"; yet it made no mention of the dangers of entering "on the *Canaanite* alarm'd / [Lest] War terrify them inexpert." The poem, however, suggests that had the Israelites chosen to advance immediately into Canaan they would have been required to embrace a pagan militarized mode of historical action, for which they were not at all prepared, and from which they would have fled, back into the pagan world of Egypt. "Not the readiest way" in the poem comes to mean an Hebraic form of political organization positioned in the "wide Wilderness" between the paganism of Egyptian servitude and the paganism of Canaanite militarism. The most significant by-products of this delay are "Laws; part such as appertain / To civil Justice, part religious Rites" (230–31). While it is true that these Laws function explicitly as "types / And shadows, of that destin'd Seed to bruise / The Serpent, by what means he shall achieve / Mankind's deliverance" (232–35), what they typify is a resistance to an aggressive political agency, a self-discipline to which Milton returns in far greater detail in *Paradise Regained*. That is, though Milton does not dissent from the central Christian tenet that the Gospel supersedes the law, the law nevertheless manifests the ideal mode of being in the world, in history, that Christ's own life fulfills and exemplifies. The Hebraic choice to follow "not the readiest way" is the choice a Restoration Milton himself seeks to follow, neither fully abdicating his political and historical responsibilities nor asserting an aggressive pagan agency.[73]

While he was still an advocate of this more aggressive political activity as a defender of the execution of Charles I, Milton characterized some of his opponents as "Zelots," using the term pejoratively to equate erstwhile antagonists of the religious and civil hierarchies with those Jews who were implicated in the betrayal of the Temple priests during the period of the destruction of the Second Temple.[74] For the author of *Eikonoklastes* in late 1649, both groups were guilty of a catastrophic lack of courage in their convictions. Their unwillingness to carry out the full implications of their respective political stances made them not only ineffective but counterproductive. Only three years later, Menasseh ben Israel gave voice to an alternative mode of political opposition, drawing on a similar episode in Jewish history toward very different ends. In his most extended plea for the readmission of the Jews to England, Menasseh offered a prophetic view of history that grew out of his own reading of rabbinic texts:

> If the Lord fulfilled his word in calamities, he will fulfill it also in felicities. Therefore *Rabbi Aquibah* laughed, when hee saw a Fox run out of the Temple being destroyed, though his companions wept; he saying, Now is fulfilled that prophecy of *Jeremiah*, *Lamentations* 5:18. *And the foxes shall run therein*; and he hadded, and those blessings also shall follow, which the Lord hath promised. We see all the curses of God come to passe, which are mentioned in *Leviticus* and *Deuteronomy*; as well as those, which concerne our being scattered to the

ends of the earth (which is *Portugall*) and those concerning the calamities of
the Inquisition; and those of our banishments . . . from whence it appears,
that all the happy prophesies shall be fulfilled. And as we have perished, so
also shall *Bozra* (that is, *Rome*), perish. See Isaiah 34:6.[75]

THE R. AKIBA whom Menasseh cites gives voice only tacitly to the kind of
worldly messianic hopes for which he was executed by Rome. This famous
rabbinic legend functions to restrain Akiba's messianism. It does not serve as
a call to arms, to join the Bar Kokhba rebellion, which, as I have argued earlier, is likely to have been its original context. And it is precisely because of the
absence of any aggressive politico-military ambitions that the story serves
Menasseh's purposes so well. The legend allows Menasseh to predict the fall
of Rome, that is, England's Catholic enemies, showing their defeat as inseparable from other biblical prophecies that include the scattering of the Jews,
presumably to England as well as Portugal. Even in Milton's England, R. Akiba figures prominently in the articulation of a history and politics that is crit-
ically engaged with the conventional aggressive models of army and empire.[76]

It would take the Restoration of Charles II for Milton to embrace the
nuances of Menasseh's assertion. Michael Fixler has read *Paradise Regained*
against the background of the earliest debates between Jews and Christians
over the role of the Messiah. Citing the "universal temporal theocracy" anticipated in the Hebrew prophets as evidence of the Jewish perception of the
Messiah as having a directly political role to play, Fixler argues that Milton
was fully aware of the fact that Christ's kingship took shape as a response to
the mistakenly temporal messianic hopes of the Jews in the first and second
centuries of the Common Era. This awareness combined with Milton's
knowledge of two contemporary events, the Whitehall conference on the
question of Jewish readmission and the spectacular rise of Sabbatai Zvi, the
self-proclaimed Jewish messiah, "make it even more likely that with a vivid
apprehension of the perennial opposition between the two concepts [of
messianism] Milton would have been predisposed to contrast them dramatically as spiritual reality and dramatic delusion."[77]

I think Fixler has identified a crucial aspect of Milton's formulation of
Satan's temptations of Christ in the wilderness, an aspect that is already suggested in the final books of *Paradise Lost*. Certainly, Milton was familiar
enough with the history of the destruction of the Second Temple and its aftermath from his readings in Josephus to be able to draw the contrast be-

tween a Jewish messianism centered on the recovery of worldly power and a Christology that focused on the spiritual character of the Messiah. As my discussion of the Bar Kokhba rebellion has shown, however, Jewish conceptions of the Messiah underwent an evolution parallel and in response to early Christianity. *Paradise Lost* recapitulates the evolution of a messianism that rejects the aggressive military reassertion of political power. This is an evolution characteristic not only of Christianity but also of rabbinic Judaism. Milton nevertheless identifies the wrong kind of messianism with Judaism, in both *Paradise Lost* and *Paradise Regained*, associating the worldly struggle for power with the law. He does so, I suggest, because the similarities between his own Restoration messianism and that of rabbinic Judaism of the Diaspora are so threatening to his own self-construction.

Yet, despite his efforts in these final books to distance himself from a Hebraic phenomenology, Milton's account of history nevertheless brings him closer to rabbinic models than he would willingly admit. Although he repeatedly deploys the language of type, the poem nevertheless resists a totalizing typology characteristic of Christian biblical hermeneutics. Typology evacuates history—both the presumptive histories detailed in the Hebrew Scriptures and contemporary events—of any internal significance. Whereas a fully typological account of history finally cancels out lived history in all its particularities—historical experiences carry no significance outside their relations to, and shadowy figurations of, Christ's life, death, resurrection, and the salvation of the kingdom of Heaven—Milton's pseudotypology amounts to a revalidation of history, consistent with his Arminian retrieval of the significance of human agency, no matter how small or "simply meek" it might seem.[78] In this respect *Paradise Lost* offers an uncanny embodiment of what the radical theologian Rosemary Reuther formulates in her remarkable book *Faith and Fratricide*. Reuther writes that, in order to free itself of what is otherwise an unavoidable antisemitism, Christianity must begin to think of itself as a diaspora religion.

> The assertion that the Jews are reprobate because they did not accept Christ as having already come is really a projection upon Judaism of that unredeemed side of itself that Christianity must constantly deny in order to assert that Christ has already come and founded "the Church." The Jews represent that which Christianity must express in itself, namely the recognition of history and Christian existence as unredeemed.[79]

ESPECIALLY IN THE wake of the Restoration, Milton would have recognized history and Christian existence in precisely this way. Yet he was unable to embrace the full implications of this recognition, elaborated by Ruether three hundred years later. Milton's inability—or unwillingness—to identify himself as a "diaspora Christian" accounts, in my view, for the apparent retreat from Hebraism in the final books of *Paradise Lost* (and, for that matter, all of *Paradise Regained*).

INTERPRETIVE THEURGY AS POLITICAL RESISTANCE

IN THEIR INNER core and essence, both midrash and *Paradise Lost* serve as consolations, responses to tragic circumstances, mirrored textually in moments that defy direct signification. In his beautifully consolatory essay, Henry Slonimsky has described the midrashic condition in the following terms:

> That the Torah will be made real in the end, and that all men will accept it in the end, that there is a far-off goal towards which all history converges, and that time and event are no mere welter or chaos but a meaningful process, and that the protagonist in that progress is a tragic-heroic figure, wounded and smitten but undismayed: that is the theology and the philosophy of history implicit in the Midrash.[80]

THE PRIMARY MODE of belief in midrash takes shape as a search for meaning, a faith in the availability of sense and the providence of interpretation. When Adam and Eve leave Eden in the final lines of Milton's poem, they do so with the same bittersweet hope described by Slonimsky: "Some natural tears they dropped, but wiped them soon; / The world was all before them, where to choose / Their place of rest, and providence their guide" (12.645–47). The exile with which *Paradise Lost* ends has been the determining condition of its composition from the very start, "Of man's first disobedience"—not merely the Fall of humanity but also Milton's fall from political favor during the Restoration. It is the same determining factor that conditions the midrashic hermeneutic.

The active, embattled engagement with the text describes the condition of exile. All interpretation, but especially the midrashic hermeneutic, posits as its final goal the unattainable return to a prelapsarian state, analogous to the pure or originary meaning of the text. As Paul Ricoeur has shown, the meaning of the state of innocence described in Genesis 2 can be understood only as an imaginary antithesis, an inaccessible antiontology that gives definition to our always already fallen existence: "The *imago Dei*—there we have both our being-created and our innocence; for the 'goodness' of creation is no other than its status as creature."[81] For Milton and the rabbis this imago Dei is best fulfilled by an ongoing reinvention of the text, a re-creation that mirrors the originary creation. Such a project can only transpire as part of the corporate and personal identities formulated by the condition of exile. The narrative of Genesis 1–3 begins in creative triumph—"Let there be light"—and ends in human alienation, exile from Eden. But it is this exile that contains within it the opportunity for redemption, the seeds of consolation, the possibility of interpretation. Genesis Rabbah concludes its consideration of the story of man's first disobedience with the following meticulous analogy between the details of the Fall narrative and the contemporary political history of transgression, destruction, and exile:

> "And the Lord called unto Adam, and said unto him, 'Where art thou [*ayekah*]?'" (Gen. 3:9): "How did this happen to you [*ekh havah lekha*]? Yesterday [you abided] by my will, now [you abide] by the will of the serpent; yesterday [you ranged] from one end of the world to the other, now [you hide] among the trees of the garden.

> R. Abahu in the name of R. Yose b. R. Haninah: It is written, "But they like men [*adam*] have transgressed the covenant, etc." (Hos. 6:7). Like men, like Adam: I placed Adam in the Garden of Eden, commanded him, he transgressed my commandment, I judged him, exiled him, and mourned over him saying, "How [*eykhah*]?" I placed Adam in the Garden of Eden, as it is written, And the Lord took the man, and put him into the Garden of Eden" (Gen. 2:15); I commanded him, as it is written, "And the Lord commanded" (Gen. 2:16); he transgressed my commandment, as it is written, "Hast thou eaten of the tree, whereof I commanded thee?" (Gen. 3:11); I judged him, as it is written, "therefore the Lord sent him forth from the garden of Eden" (Gen. 3:23); I exiled him, as it is written, "So he drove out the man" (Gen. 3:24), and I mourned over him saying, "How [*eykhah*]?" as it is written, "and said unto him, 'Where art thou [*ayekah*]?" which is written like How [*eykhah*].

> Similarly, I placed his children in the Land of Israel, I commanded them, they transgressed my commandments, I judged them, I exiled them, and I

mourned over them, saying, "How [*eykhah*]?" I placed his children in the Land of Israel, as it is written, "And I brought you into a plentiful country" (Jer. 2:7); I commanded them, as it is written, "And thou shalt command the children of Israel" (Ex. 27:20); they transgressed my commandments, as it is written, "all Israel have transgressed thy law" (Dan. 9:11); I judged them, as it is written, "cast them out of my sight and let them go forth" (Jer. 15:1); I exiled them, as it is written, "I will drive them out of my house" (Hos. 9:15); and I mourned over them, saying, "How [*eykhah*]?" as it is written, "How doth the city sit solitary" (Lam. 1:1). (19:9)

FOR REASONS THAT I have discussed in chapter 2, the Temple in Jerusalem does not function as centrally for Milton as it does for the rabbis, who cite Lamentations, that bitter threnody on the destruction of the Temple, as corollary to God's lament over humanity's disobedience and consequent exile from Eden. The absence of any reference to the Second Temple's destruction and its aftermath is most notable in book 12, where, once Christ's life is described, the only Temple that has any significance is the "living Temples, built by Faith to stand" (527). Milton nevertheless refers to the destruction of the First Temple and the exile that ensued (the same temple over which Lamentations weeps) so as to correlate these events with the loss of paradise.[82] The exile from Eden functions for the rabbis and for Milton as the key to all mythologies, the sine qua non of all subsequent acts of creation and interpretation, both divine and human.

Each historical event described in books 11 and 12 offsets triumph with downfall. The failures seem so definitive that Michael's history threatens to undermine its initial purpose of sending the first couple forth "though sorrowing, yet in peace." Indeed, the repeated snatching of defeat from the jaws of victory becomes so predictable that Michael finally gives up on detail and summarizes, "so shall the world go on, / To good malignant, to bad men benign" (12.537–38). What prevents this pattern from overwhelming history entirely, from evacuating it of its details in anticipation of Christ's final victory, is the written word, textual legacies, or, as the rabbis would call it, *talmud*. Time and again, before an interim victory is abrogated by the infiltration of evil, Michael pauses to recall the written accounts. The first apostles, for example, perform their ministry, "and race well run / Thir doctrine and thir story written left, / They die" (505–7). The corruption that follows is even described in textual terms, as the "grievous Wolves" who succeed these teachers "all the sacred mysteries of Heav'n / To thir own vile advantage shall turn / . . . With superstitions and traditions taint, / Left only in those written Records pure, / Though not but by the Spirit understood" (508–14).

If this is the way the world shall go on what, finally, is the correct response? What value does history have? The answer suggested by these final books of *Paradise Lost* seems to me to be a cautious assertion of the power of the written word. Not so much a blind, politically disempowered writer's pathetic rejection of worldly history, it is rather a reassertion of the political and religious importance of writing, both its transmission and its reception. The representation of history—its poetics—is only one side of Milton's story in books 11 and 12. The other, equally crucial element, is the interpretation of history, that is, its politics.

Epilogue: Toward Interpreting
the Hebraism of Samson Agonistes

I N CHAPTER 5 I suggested a parallel between Milton's imagined forecast
of future times in the final books of *Paradise Lost* and the rabbinic fantasy of Moses's visit to the bet midrash of R. Akiba. Both mountaintop scenes
render complex perspectives on history, politics, belief, and human agency.
These two scenes of instruction offer useful insights into one another, but
Milton's portrayal of Michael's postlapsarian instructions to Adam has for
its precursor a more explicit biblical account of divinely granted vistas,
Moses's Pisgah sight, just before his death, in Deuteronomy 34.[1] Anticipating
Milton's own reworking of this culminating biblical episode, rabbinic interpreters have read the scene as one that offers Moses a glimpse not only of Israel's geopolitical future (the substance of the chapter in Deuteronomy) but
also of its religious and judicial future. In one of two extant versions of the
midrashic collection on the book of Exodus, the Mekhilta, the rabbis assert
the following claim:

> From where do we know that all the requests Moses made to the Holy One
> were granted? He asked to see the land of Israel and God granted it, as it
> says, "and the Lord showed him all the land of Gilead, unto Dan" (Deut.

34:1). He asked to see the Holy Temple and God granted it, as it says, "Gilead," and Gilead is none other than the Temple, as it says, "Thou art Gilead unto me, and the head of Lebanon" (Jer. 22:6). From where do we know that God showed [Moses] Samson the son of Manoa? As it says, "unto Dan" and later it says, "And there was a certain man of Zora, of the family of the Danites, whose name was Manoa" (Judg. 13:2).[2]

AS OPENING AND closing brackets to Moses's vision, the rabbis offer the Temple and Samson, the pinnacle of Israel's cultic experience, on one side, and one of the most dubious episodes in premonarchic Israelite history, on the other. Between these two limits the midrash suggests, Moses was given prophetic access to the entire sweep of Israelite history, its peaks and valleys, triumphs and tribulations.

While the final two books of *Paradise Lost* may have offered Milton the opportunity to compose his own version of this prospective sweep through the history of the faithful, Michael's visitation to Adam was not the poet's final word on the matter. In 1671, sandwiched between the publication of the first (1667) and second (1674) editions of *Paradise Lost*, Milton published *Paradise Regained. A Poem in Four Books. To Which Is Added Samson Agonistes.* In his pairing of the four-book epic and dramatic poem, Milton revisited many of the issues he had addressed in the longer poem—the messianic role of Jesus, the Arminian retrieval of human agency, the relevance of history, the value of political and military defiance against interpretive and intellectual resistance.[3] He did so via almost the same two bracketing terms invoked by the rabbis in their account of Moses's Pisgah vision. On the one side stands (though it is about to fall) the Temple in Jerusalem, since to an early modern Christian audience *Paradise Regained*'s concern with the events preceding Jesus's crucifixion would have necessarily evoked the imminent destruction of the Temple; these two events were inextricably intertwined. On the other side stands (though he, too, is about to fall) Samson.[4]

MILTON'S HEBRAIC SAMSON IN THE CRITICAL TRADITION

LIKE *Paradise Lost* (and *Paradise Regained*, for that matter), *Samson Agonistes* offers itself as an ostensible synthesis of so-called Hebraic and so-called Hellenic features. Described by its author in the preface as a play modeled after Greek tragedy, the drama depicts a story whose source is specifically to be located in the Hebrew Bible. Criticism of *Samson*, at least of the last century, has sought to situate the text in relation to its Hebraic and Hellenic antecedents. What may have begun with Sir Richard Jebb's assertion, that the drama uses Dagon's struggle with the God of Israel to figure the conflict between Hellenism and Hebraism, has been revisted time and again by critics wishing to argue for either the primacy of Hebraic precedent or the predominance of classical influence.[5] William Riley Parker has argued for Milton's extensive debts to Greek tragedy; Michael Krouse has countered that Milton's Samson is a type of Christ, thereby verifying the dominance of the Hebraic tradition in its Protestant Christian fulfillment.[6] In his study of "the Hebraic Factor" in seventeenth-century English literature, Harold Fisch has described the matter teleologically, in terms of Milton's poetic development:

> The traditional epic form, the heavy style of orotundity in *Paradise Lost*, is comparable to the grand style in prose which we discerned in Hooker; the style of *Paradise Regained* reminds us of the Puritan and Baconian revolt against this—the new realism; whilst the style of *Samson Agonistes* represents Milton's ultimate synthesis. It is the most completely realized of Milton's poems and also . . . the most genuinely Hebraic.[7]

WEARING HIS PERSONAL predelictions on his sleeve, Fisch equates maturity with synthesis, fulfillment with Hebraism. Against what he considers the static heroes of Aeschylus and Sophocles, Fisch posits Milton's Samson, "a dynamic Old Testament hero," one who distinguishes himself not only from the passive sufferings of Oedipus at Colonus but also from the "evangelical piety" of seventeenth-century Calvinists.[8] Subsequent advocates of the "Hebraic factor" in Milton's dramatic poem have identified other features that tip the scales away from classical influence. Samuel Stollman has argued that while Milton's Samson differs strikingly from the rabbis' Samson, he does exemplify particularly Hebraic ideals, which, in Stollman's view, are effectively "Christian or that constellation of concepts and values of the Old Testament which Milton found entirely compatible with his Christian doctrine."[9] Marta Shapiro and Miriam Muskin have asserted the Hebraic aspects of Samson's heroism, faithfulness, and triumph in adversity.[10]

As I hope I have made clear by this point, I regard such attempts at distilling out from Milton's writings specifically Hebraic, Hellenic, or Christian aspects and influences with a good deal of suspicion. If the complex interweavings of these cultural, religious, and philosophical forces in *Paradise Lost*

make it difficult to determine what precisely is Hebraic or Hellenic about
any one aspect of the poem, the same is equally true of *Samson Agonistes*, a text
whose theme is so ostensibly Hebraic and whose form is so deliberately classical. Even more pertinent to the argument of this book, *Samson* directly thematizes the challenge of maintaining a religiously, ethnically, and culturally
specific identity in the face of considerable influences and pressures. In expressing its pride in Samson's felling of "a thousand foreskins" (144) the
Chorus anchors identity metonymically in the body. As I have argued above
in chapter 2, circumcision's corporeality shifts in Milton's use of the term,
serving to signify, on the one hand, the continuity between Israel of the Old
Covenant and England of the New Covenant through a metonymic relationship and, on the other hand, the break between the old and the new through
a metaphoric substitution. The fact and the figure of circumcision do indeed
serve the function of distinguishing Samson and the Israelites from Harapha
and the Philistines: "So had the glory and Prowess been recover'd / To *Palestine*, won by a *Philistine* / From the unforeskinn'd race, of whom thou bear'st
/ The highest name for valiant Acts" (1098–1101). Yet this is Harapha speaking, a character for whom the stakes of maintaining national distinctions are
quite different than for Milton.[11] As Harapha taunts Samson, "Is not thy
Nation subject to our Lords?" (1182), Samson's controversial decisions to
marry the woman of Timnah and Dalila—and Milton's modification of the
biblical account by asserting that Samson did marry Dalila—surely place the
matters of homogeneity and heterogeneity in the foreground. The Chorus
wonders, "Why thou shouldst wed *Philistian* women rather / Than of thine
own Tribe fairer, or as fair. / At least of thy own Nation, and as noble"
(216–18). Samson's reply, that his first marriage was divinely motivated and
that his marriage to Dalila, "I thought . . . lawful from my former act"
(231), only serves to exaggerate the problem. There seem to be occasions
when such cultural and ethnic cross-pollinations have a salvific potential:
"that by occasion hence / I might begin *Israel's* Deliverance" (224–25); there
are others, dangerously indistinguishable from the former, that function only
as a trap and prelude to self-destruction. Any desire for clear categories and
distinctions breaks down in the face of these interminglings and hybridiza-
tions.

Yet once more, Milton's use of Samson's marriage choices in the service
of a meditation on the problematics of religious and cultural purity was anticipated by rabbinic commentary on the Samson account in Judges. The
Palestinian Talmud reports the following observations:

It is written, "They came to the vineyards of Timnah" (Judg. 14:5). R. Samuel b. R. Isaac said, "This teaches us that his father and mother showed him that the vineyards of Timnah were planted with improperly mixed seeds [*kilayim*, prohibited in Deut. 22: 9] and said, 'Son, just as their vineyards are sewn with mixed seeds, so too their daughters are sewn with mixed seeds': 'His father and mother did not know that this was from the Lord, for he was seeking a cause of action against the Philistines'" (Judg. 14:4). R. Eliezer said, "It is written in seven places, 'do not marry with them.'" R. Abin [said], "In order to prohibit [marriage] with the seven nations [the Philistines were not among the seven, and thus implicitly permitted]. And here you say he was forbidden?" R. Isaac said, "To the scorners he was scornful" (Prov. 3:34) [i.e., because he associated himself with the wicked, he was punished].[12]

THIS COLLOQUY APPEARS to offer a series of arguments against Samson's exogamous relationships, only to undermine each of them. Samson's parents' objection to their son's marriage—that it threatens to contaminate his Hebraic purity just as the prohibition against mixed seeds is part of the biblical holiness code—loses its persuasiveness in light of their apparent ignorance of Samson's divine mission. Sometimes, R. Samuel the son of R. Isaac argues, heterogeneity has its redemptive uses. Even the biblical command against cross-cultural pollination with the seven nations offers no real argument against Samson's marriage choice. The rabbis seem to be suggesting that it is improper to expand this biblical prohibition into a generalized pronouncement on the illicit nature of encounters between Israelites and their surrounding cultures. Samson's error was not the abstract choice of a non-Israelite for a wife; it was his failure to recognize the morally deficient qualities of his particular choice. Milton's Samson offers the same analysis of his fault: "I thought it lawful from my former act, / And the same end" (231–32). Both the rabbinic and the Miltonic Samson make the mistake of categorical abstraction in the face of historical particularities and contingencies.

Furthermore, rabbinic observations constitute only one stream of Judaic traditions regarding Samson, making the isolation of Hebraic, Hellenistic, and Christian influences even more intricate. There is an extensive tradition within *Judaism* of the first century *b.c.e.* through the second century *c.e.* of Hellenizing the Samson narrative. Pseudo-Philo, in his *Biblical Antiquities*, devotes a good deal of energy to exaggerating Samson's physical prowess by embelleshing many of his exploits. In so doing, he stresses Samson's strengths but also identifies his weaknesses, most directly by comparing him unfavorably to the morally superior Joseph. More important for our purposes, Josephus, in his *Jewish Antiquities*, renders Samson as a prototypically Aristotelean "great-souled man," whose similarities to Hercules are unmistakable. As Louis Feldman has argued, Josephus's Samson constitutes a parallel, rather than subordinate, tradition to the rabbinic accounts of the biblical judge.[13] According to Feldman, by singling out four admirable qualities in Samson's character—valor, strength, high spirit, and wrath—Josephus constructed a Samson consistent with his larger apologetic project of defending the Jews against the charges of weakness being leveled by their Greek and Roman antagonists.

As early as Henry Todd's annotations on *Samson Agonistes*, Milton's account has been thought to draw upon the writings of Josephus.[14] When this Greek-writing Jew is cited, however, he is typically aligned with the classical influences said to be at work on Milton. Josephus, like the rabbis and Milton, read the Bible through multifaceted perspectives, heavily influenced by Platonic and Aristotelean philosophy but equally indebted to a plurivocal semitic tradition of legends and hermeneutics. Given Milton's certain familiarity with Josephus, not to mention the extensive influence Josephus's writings exercised on the Church fathers and developing Christian interpretations of the Bible, we would be hard-pressed to make any definitive claims about the specifically "Hebraic" or "classical" qualities the poet drew upon in his reading, mediated or otherwise, of Jewish sources. In his preface to the closet drama, Milton speaks of the classical models of tragedy, citing Aristotle's view that tragedy's power stems from its ability to raise "pity and fear, or terror, to purge the mind of those such like passions, that is to temper and reduce them to just measure with a kind of delight, stirr'd up by reading or seeing those passions well imitated." While this view of tragic catharsis may indeed have come most directly to Milton from his readings of "*Aeschylus, Sophocles*, and *Euripides*, the three Tragic Poets unequall'd yet by any," he may have also encountered a Samson already filled with οργη (fury), frustrated by the υβρις of the Philistines, and destroyed by a fate-driven περιπετεια in his readings of Josephus and those Christian writers influenced by the Josephan tradition.[15]

It is in what most regard as Milton's final poetic achievement that we may further recognize how inextricably intertwined are the discourses of Hebraism, Hellenism, and Christianity. The Samson of both Milton and the rabbis embodies a range of contradictory impulses, from faithfulness to heretical obstinance, from productive to destructive sexuality, from violence to passivity. By way of summarizing my arguments in the preceding chapters, I want to recapitulate some of my assertions concerning the interactions and parallels between Miltonic and rabbinic epistemologies, ontologies, and phenomenologies in the context of a brief discussion—more prospective than exhaustive—of Milton's dramatic poem.

EPISTEMOLOGY AND THEODICY: GOD'S WAYS AND SAMSON'S

Samson Agonistes gestures toward a similar theodical project to that of Milton's twelve-book epic, both in its thematic associations and in its language. The Chorus's reply to Samson early in the play, "Just are the ways of God, / And justifiable to men" (293–94), clearly echoes the epic's great argument to "justify the ways of God to men." In this dramatic context, however, the claim rings more hollow, failing in its primary purpose, which is to console Samson for his pain and sorrow. Indeed, any attempt at locating theological and epistemological refinement in this, Milton's last work of poetry, encounters a number of complicating features, not the least of which is the replacement of the voice of the epic narrator—however distinct it may be from Milton's own persona—with the polyphony of the play's dramatis personae. If the epic narrator is less than fully reliable, how much more unreliable are the diverse voices of Samson, Manoa, and the Chorus? The invocation to book 3 of *Paradise Lost* simultaneously acknowledges the challenge posed by the poem's great argument—"May I express thee unblam'd?" (3)—and claims to rise to this challenge—"I may see and tell / Of things invisible to mortal sight" (54–55). Samson draws a parallel connection between the search for God's justice and the dynamics of blindness and insight. His opening lament begins with what looks like an embrace of Raphael's charge to be "lowly wise," as he willingly accepts the limitations of his epistemological horizon: "I must not quarrel with the will / Of highest dispensation, which herein / Haply had ends above my reach to know" (60–62). Immediately following this acceptance, however, Samson launches into an extended lament on his blindness, one that reverses the trajectory toward inner vision charted by the invocation to book 3. The comparative economy of that earlier meditation on loss of physical sight, which hopefully looks to the compensatory gain of prophetic poetry—"So

much the rather thou Celestial Light / Shine inward" (51–52)—becomes in
the later drama an economy that finds Samson's current status wanting: "but
O yet more miserable! / Myself my Sepulcher" (101–2).[16]

Furthermore, as I have argued in chapter 3, the theodical project of *Paradise Lost* depends upon the poetically rich, but theologically risky, tactic of
humanizing God, embracing and exploring those anthropomorphic and anthropopathic characteristics regarded by other writers and theologians as the
markers of humanity's inability fully to comprehend divinity. In *Samson Agonistes* the reciprocity of this mimesis, the simultaneous location of God's behavior in human pathos and humanity's salvation in its imitatio Dei, obtains
even more complex expression. The Chorus's assertion of the justice of
God's ways early in the play is repeated by Samson just prior to his departure
for the feast of Dagon, with a key difference. Distinguishing himself from
those who are powerless to resist the commands of their mortal masters,
Samson attributes his willingness to attend the feast to "Some rousing motions" (1382), concluding, "And for a life who will not change his purpose? /
(So mutable are all the ways of men)" (1406–7). If God's ways are just, man's
ways are mutable; yet because God's ways can only be known through the
ways of men, justice and mutability stand not in opposition to each other
but rather as mutually constitutive. The mutability of God's ways is precisely what makes them both just and difficult, if not impossible, to construe.
Even the Chorus's infuriatingly facile summation of Samson's story, a passage that contributes to much of the ongoing debate over the presence or absence of salvific resolution in the drama, acknowledges the convergence of
divine justice and mutability:

> All is best, though we oft doubt,
> What th' unsearchable dispose
> Of highest wisdom brings about,
> And ever best found in the close.
> Oft he seems to hide his face,
> But unexpectedly returns. (1745–50)

THE CHORIC ASSERTION that "All is best" stands in stark contrast to the
events that have just transpired and demand a highly revisionary account of
history, one that either elides the ever shifting fortunes of individual and collective human existence or renders these ceaseless changes as inherent to the
providential justice of God's ways.

Turning to the rabbis, we find a similar acknowledgment of historical contingency as functional evidence of a system of justice. And yet, as in *Samson Agonistes*, it is hard to read this kind of justice as a source of comfort or as a means to clarifying the epistemological challenge of interpreting God and history. The rabbis locate a dynamic lex talionis in the story of Samson, both as it applies to the individual man and as it applies to the Philistines:

> So too do you find in the case of Samson, that he was punished by the very thing for which he was proud, as it says, "And Samson said unto his father, Get her for me, for she pleaseth me well [Heb. *y'shara b'eynai*, she is pleasing to my eyes"] (Judg. 14:3). What is written afterward? "But the Philistines took him and put out his eyes and brought him down to Gaza" (ibid. 16:21). R. Judah says, "Just as the beginning of his corruption occurred in Gaza, so too his punishment occurred nowhere else but in Gaza."[17]

IN THIS RABBINIC account God measures out Samson's punishment with the elegance of a Dantean contrapasso, coordinated physiologically and geographically. But Samson is not merely the bodily site on which God's justice is made manifest. He also serves as the human agent enacting a parallel lex talionis on the Philistines. As the rabbis present it in the following talmudic investigation, however, the human execution of talionic justice loses its simplicity, its elegance, and especially its satisfying justification. The Babylonian Talmud (Tractate Sotah 10a) comments on Samson's use of the three hundred foxes in Judges 15:4 as the mechanism for destroying the fields of the Philistines. Superficially, at least, Samson's destruction of his enemies' crops responds directly to an injustice he feels he has experienced. At verse 3 he asserts his blamelessness and the rabbis seem, initially, to support this claim of just desert: "Why especially foxes? R. Aibu b. Nagari said in the name of R. Hiya b. Abba, 'Samson said, "Let it be [an animal] that turns backward and metes out a punishment on the Philistines who went back on their oath.'" The medieval exegete, Rashi, explains that the rabbis believed the fox turns backward when it is hunted rather than trying to escape by running further away. This characteristic makes it the ideal vehicle for attacking the Philistines, who were thought to have gone back on a nonaggression treaty reported in Genesis 21:23 and 26:28–31 between Abimelech, the legendary ancestor of the Philistines, and Abraham and Isaac, the ancestors of the Israelites.

But this penal economy—really, an economy built upon ideas of vengeance—is only superficially embodied in the fox's proverbial tendency to backtrack when it flees an enemy. Clearly, the fox does not double back to *attack* its enemy but rather to evade it by trickery. The rabbinic interpretation of Samson's deployment of the foxes may thus be said to pay lip service to a talionic justice attributable to both God and humanity, but not far beneath the surface of this homily is an impulse toward a kind of tricksterism that depends on nonvengeful mutability and contingency. Samson's revenge, precisely because it answers the treachery of the Philistines in kind, becomes less distinguishable from the world of pagan violence, whether it is legitimized or not. In the larger context of the biblical Samson account, the story of the foxes is only one installment in a cycle of retaliatory violence in which Samson indulges as avidly as (if not more so than) the Philistines. The foxes, on the other hand, offer the trickster alternative that, as Boyarin and others have recently shown, was especially appealing to the world of the rabbis.[18] Samson, the seemingly Hebraic hero, becomes yet another non-Hebraic bully, the emulation of whom raises more difficulties than it solves, if only because it continues the endless cycle of vengeance.[19]

As I have shown, in the *De Doctrina Christiana* and in *Paradise Lost* Milton posits an accommodative mode for representing divine truths that is epistemological in nature, insisting that the representation of God in terms of human forms and emotions marks the limits of human understanding. Accommodation thus becomes a representational and poetic advantage to be exploited rather than a limitation to be transcended. The justification and salvation through human-divine imitation, such a central aspect of the theodicy of *Paradise Lost*, comes under further scrutiny in Milton's late drama. There continues to be a debate among scholars as to whether Milton's Samson serves as a type of Christ, following Samson's inclusion among the list of the faithful in Hebrews 11:32. As the conclusion of that portion of the Letter to the Hebrews makes clear, and as I have argued in chapter 2, such a typological account evacuates Samson of any historical value: "And these all, having obtained a good report through faith, received not the promise: God having provided some better thing for us, that they without us should not be made perfect" (39–40). In these terms Samson may foreshadow Christ, but Christ's behavior gains no further definition in reference to Samson.

It seems to me, however, that the drama tempts us to follow such a typological reading only to undermine it. Manoa recounts to the Chorus his attempts at freeing Samson through appeals to the lords of the Philistines specifically by trying to redeem his son with money. Refused initially by both the proud and the greedy, he finally identifies a third group,

> More generous far and civil, who confess'd
> They had anough reveng'd, having reduc't
> Thir foe to misery beneath thir fears,
> The rest was magnanimity to remit,
> If some convenient ransom were propos'd. (1467–71)

INDICATING A WILLINGNESS to empty himself of his belongings for the sake of redeeming his son, Manoa appears very much like Christ, whose own *kenosis* begins the process of human redemption. The parallels between Manoa and Christ are both striking and inexact. As a father who is ready to forgo "all my Patrimony" (1482) for the sake of his son, Manoa seems to serve as both the Father and the Son. Indeed, the Chorus acknowledges this odd reversal at lines 1485–89, "Thou for thy Son art bent to lay out all." Even as he offers himself as a redeemer, however, his own son performs a different kind of imitatio Christi, one that tears the fabric of Manoa's account. Interrupting his own story, Manoa remarks, "What noise or shout was that? It tore the Skie" (1472). The tearing of the sky must remind us of the tearing of the veil in the Temple at the moment of Christ's death, recounted in the Synoptic Gospels (Mark 15:38, Matthew 27:51, Luke 23:45). There, the rending signifies the elimination upon Christ's death of the ritual boundary between God's sanctity and the people, as described in Exodus 27:33. Here, this rip in the firmament invites different interpretations, as is made evident by the most immediate misreading offered by the Chorus. Through this verbal echo of the gospel Passion accounts, Milton dangles before us the temptation to read Samson's self-sacrifice as a type of Christ's death, but such a typological interpretation founders on the vast differences. Once the source of that "noise or shout" is discovered as Samson's slaughter of the Philistines through his own self-immolation, the meaning of the act does not gain any further clarity. It is true that the Chorus insists upon a salvific reading, but the "copious legend, or sweet lyric song" (1737) with which Manoa hopes to commemorate his son's life reinstalls the events into the ambiguous frame of classical conventions, the same conventions apparently dismissed by Milton in the invocation to book 9 of *Paradise Lost* as "long and tedious" (30). Most important of all, the core of Christian theology regards Christ's death as a *conquest* of fallen mortality; Michael assures Adam that Christ's voluntary death, "this God-like act / Annuls thy doom, *the death thou shouldst have di'd*" (*PL* 12.427–28, emphasis added). Samson's death not only does not adumbrate this overcoming of death, it immerses itself neck-deep in the blood of human mortality. How can we locate redemption in the dead bodies of the Philistines? Insofar as Samson's act bears a structural resemblance to Christ's self-sacrifice, while at the same time not eliminating the veil that divides God from the people, any potential typological relationship between Samson and Christ can hardly be said to offer a reassuring theodicy.

For obvious theological reasons the rabbis would not want to read Samson in relation to Christ. They do, however, use the story of Samson to meditate on the nature of (human!) sacrifice and its ability to effect redemption or absolution. Recounting Samson's discovery of the honey bees in the carcass of the lion he had killed earlier, the rabbis imagine Samson's surprised reaction: "'A lion feasts on other animals, yet now it has produced food!' It is similar to Aaron and his sons, who eat of all the sacrificial offerings and then become an offering themselves: 'This is the offering of Aaron and his sons' (Lev. 6:13) [20 in the Protestant Bible]."[20] Referring to Aaron's sons, Nadav and Abihu, who were killed by God in Leviticus 10, the rabbis figure this striking moment of divine wrath as a kind of sacrifice. In a punishment that bears all the trappings of divine justice, God devoured Aaron's sons with fire for the transgression of bringing an illicit "strange fire" (*esh zarah* in Hebrew) as an offering. The rabbis extend the talionic nature of this story by construing the death of Nadav and Abihu as itself an offering, one that mirrors the priestly privilege of eating from the (licit) offerings described immediately following, in Leviticus 10:12–20. A disturbing economy of sacrifice and redemption emerges from this reading, one that posits the eye-for-an-eye vengeance enacted on Aaron's sons as a necessary sacrifice, equivalent to the animal sacrifices that made up the Tabernacle rituals. That the rabbis attach this rendering of the Nadav and Abihu story to Samson's musings on the lion and the bees is of further note, since the riddle Samson generates from his surprising realization is one of the precipitating factors in the cycles of vengeance in Judges 14–15: the Philistines threaten the woman of Timnah in order to learn the answer and Samson murders thirty men in Ashkelon and abandons his wife when the Philistines are able to solve the riddle. This rabbinic observation also offers a third level of comparison, one that further interrogates the value of sacrifice, human and otherwise. Samson, like the lion he has slain, distinguishes himself by the violence he commits, whether it is justified or not. He resembles the lion in his death, as well, in the context of the rabbinic interpolation of the Nadav and Abihu story. The lion's carcass fosters the nourishment of the honey. Nadav and Abihu become the offerings they were once privileged to consume. Samson, in his death, offers the possibility of redemption. Yet in all these cases the potential for salvation is inscribed with talionic urgency on dead bodies.

ONTOLOGY AND SEXUALITY: SAMSON'S BODY

INASMUCH AS SAMSON'S physical strength plays such a central role in his biblical characterization and insofar as his downfall is precipitated by an erotic relationship with a Philistine woman, it should come as no surprise that Samson's body constitutes a critical site for interpretation and elaboration for both the rabbis and Milton. For the rabbis Samson's sexuality functions as the means of both corruption and (potential) salvation. Invoking the dynamics of talionic justice so essential to the rabbinic reading of the Judges narrative, the rabbis observe an adverbial inconsistency between the Samson account and the story of Judah and Tamar:

> Rav said, "Since the beginning of his corruption was in Gaza, so too he was punished in Gaza" [cf. Tosefta Sotah 3.4]. But isn't it written, "Samson went down to Timnath" (Judg. 14:1)? R. Samuel b. Nahman replied, "[Samson went down to Timnah] for the sake of marriage [and not for an illicit erotic liaison]."

> One verse reads, "Samson went down to Timnah," and another verse reads, "Behold your father-in-law is going up to Timnah" (Gen. 38:13). Rav said, "There are two Timnahs, one associated with Judah and the other associated with Samson." R. Simon said, "There is only one Timnah; why does Scripture refer to it with both the language of ascent and the language of descent? In the case of Judah, because his journey was for the sake of heaven, the text refers to an ascent. In the case of Samson, because his journey was not for the sake of heaven, the text refers to a descent.[21]

IN THE CHARACTERISTICALLY plurivocal fashion of all rabbinic texts, this discussion of Samson's "descent" to Timnah points in the direction of two conflicting readings. Although R. Samuel b. Nathan works to clear Samson of any specifically sexual wrongdoings in his liaison with the woman from

Timnah, R. Simon's reading of Judah's story against Samson's necessarily condemns the latter for its improper expression of erotic desire. As is often the case in midrash aggadah, no effort at reconciling the two follows. Indeed, the very absence of such a reconciliation suggests a rabbinic perspective on sexuality as an ambivalent force, consistent with the unmodified yetzer I discuss in chapter 4. Samson's desire in absolute terms was neither good nor bad; as the story of Judah seems to suggest, erotic desire can have salutary effects. Rather, the particular details of that desire determine its moral and salvific valence. We have already seen a version of this reconfiguration of desire in the younger Milton's own use of the Judah and Tamar story in *Animadversions* (YP 1:688–89). There Milton presented the story for condemnation rather than approbation, as it figured the prelatical indulgence in ritual seductiveness for the sake of Christianizing pagans.[22] In that case, as in this rabbinic example, the biblical accounts are mined for their rich ambiguity to illustrate a parallel rich ambiguity in the dynamics of sexuality.

The rabbinic interest in the erotics of Samson's story continues, however, by relating it specifically to—or rather, distinguishing it from—his other bodily traits. In a statement from the Palestinian Talmud that is almost comical in its salaciousness, R. Huna in the name of R. Yosse carefully assures us that although God blessed Samson with unusual physical strength, "His sexual performance was like that of any man."[23] Unable to imagine how any mortal woman would have been able to bear the sexual appetite and performance of a superman like Samson, R. Yosse offers the only feasible solution: in this respect, at least, Samson was no different than any other man. The Babylonian Talmud's counterpart to this discussion argues precisely the opposite:

> "And the child grew and the Lord blessed him" [Judg. 13:24], In what did he bless him? R. Judah said in the name of Rav, "He blessed him with strength. His strength was like any other man, but his virility was as an overflowing stream."[24]

AGAINST R. YOSSE'S ASSERTION of the quotidian nature of Samson's sexual powers, Rav insists that God's blessing was specifically sexual in nature, suggesting that Samson's extraordinary sexual appetite drew him to the Philistine women, which in turn led him to begin the process of freeing the Israelites from Philistine power.[25] How might we account for such diametrically opposed readings? The differing historical circumstances in which the two talmudim were redacted may offer us one possible path. Faced with the daily threat of religious and cultural annihilation by a political power claiming to be the new or true Israel, the Palestinian rabbis responsible for editing the Talmud would have wanted to steer clear of suggestions of the salvific potential of sexual intercourse with the non-Jewish (read: Christian) world. The editors of the Babylonian Talmud, though certainly not enjoying any real political power, were not confronted as immediately with the challenges of a Christian Roman empire with whom any intermingling—sexual or otherwise—would have been regarded as extremely dangerous. To suggest that Samson's erotic desire for the woman of Timnah or for Dalila was a path toward redemption would not have raised the same concerns it would have raised for the rabbis of the Palestinian Talmud. For these Babylonian rabbis Samson's sexuality was extraordinary, both for good and for ill. The commentary there continues,

> "And he ground in the prison-house" (Judg 16:21). R. Yochanan said, "Grinding always refers to [sexual] transgression, as it says, 'Let my wife grind after another' (Job 31:10). This comes to teach us that every Philistine would bring his wife to [Samson] in the prison-house so that she might be impregnated by him [and bear a son of Samson's strength]."

THE IMAGE OF Samson helping to populate the Philistine nation with numerous infant supermen, as amusing as it is, depends upon an implicit condemnation of Samson's sexual prowess as a contributing factor to the once and future oppression of the Israelites by a physically strengthened pagan world. Once, because it allowed Dalila to learn the secret of his strength: earlier in this same discussion the rabbis had commented on Judges 16:16, "And it came to pass that she pressed him daily with her words and urged him." What, they ask, does "urged him" mean? R. Isaac from the school of R. Ami said, "Just at the moment of sexual climax, [Dalila] would pull herself out from under him." That is, the frustration of his sexual desire produces his physical impotence. Future, because these superhuman offspring were to serve as the mechanism for the Philistines' ongoing enslavement of Israel.

Alas, Milton does not speculate on the interesting question of Samson's alternatively ordinary or extraordinary sexual powers. He does, nevertheless, offer his readers a Samson who is only too familiar with the similarities and disjunctions between physical strength and sexual appetite, one for whom "urging" presents a serious hermeneutical challenge. In his earliest speech Samson muses over his apparent seduction by Dalila:

Whom have I to complain of but myself?
Who this high gift of strength committed to me,
In what part lodg'd, how easily bereft me,
Under the Seal of silence could not keep,
But weakly to a woman must reveal it,
O'ercome with importunity and tears.
O impotence of mind, in body strong!
But what is strength without a double share
Of wisdom? Vast, unwieldy, burdensom,
Proudly secure, yet liable to fall
By weakest subtleties, not made to rule,
But to subserve where wisdom bears command. (46–57)

WHEREAS SOME RABBIS distinguish between Samson's physical strength and his sexual virility by making the latter ordinary (that is, entirely functional, but not unusual), Milton's Samson takes the further step of contrasting his "body strong" with his "impotence of mind." The paradox, in Samson's mind, is not in the incommensurability of his physical and sexual abilities; rather, it is in the impotence that seems to arise precisely from his pursuit of an erotic desire. Now while this dynamic owes something to the early modern association of excessive sexuality (male or female) with what Samson later calls "foul effeminacy" (410), it has at least as much to do with the deeply ambivalent nature of desire in the drama. In speaking of his first marriage to the woman of Timnah, Samson insists, "what I motion'd was of God; I knew / From intimate impulse, and therefore urg'd / The Marriage on" (222–24). The language does not distinguish between a specifically sexual intimate impulse and a divinely motivated urge, inextricably (and ambiguously) linking the two. By the time Samson claims to feel a "rousing motion" to attend the festival of the Philistines, arousal conveys erotic and divine potentials, each of which bear on Samson's masculine fulfillment of his calling through a display of physical strength.

Dalila's function as pagan enticement is surely an aspect of any meditation on the role of sexuality in either Milton or the rabbis. In Milton's drama this issue arises, among other places, as part of Samson's extended tirade against his wife: "To please thy gods thou didst it; gods unable / To acquit themselves and prosecute their foes / But by ungodly deeds, the contradiction / Of thir own deity, Gods cannot be" (896–99). As we have seen, Milton often associates the dangers of unproductive erotic desire with the empty seductions of the pagan world, even if he is never able to excise either from his writings. In rabbinic writing Samson's story also serves as a nexus of sexuality and paganism while at the same time coordinating a third, equally problematic cultural force, Christianity. In commenting on Numbers 15:39, "and that ye seek not after your own heart and your own eyes, after which ye use to go a whoring," the rabbis align each of these biblical warnings with external cultural temptations:

> As we learn in a mishnah, "After your heart" refers to Christianity [*minuth*], as it is written, "The fool says in his heart, there is no God" (Ps. 14:1). "After your eyes" refers to the desire for sexual transgression, as it says, "And Samson said to his father, 'Take her for me, for she is pleasing to me eye'"(Judg. 14:3). "You go astray" refers to the desire for idolatry, as it is written, "And they strayed after baalim" (Judg. 8:33).[26]

THE RABBIS POSITION Samson's erotic desire between the seductions of Christianity and idolatry, suggesting a common bond between all three. Most remarkably, by equating *minuth* with a denial of God, the rabbis misread Christianity's formulation of its own self-proclaimed biblical heritage. While other (and especially later) Jewish traditions construct Christianity as a form of idolatry (most notably, Maimonides), this text seems to want to distinguish between these two heresies even as it relates them. That Samson's improper sexuality functions to hold Christianity and idolatry apart places special emphasis on the mediating role of eros in rabbinic meditations on Hebraism, Hellenism, and Christianity.[27]

PHENOMENOLOGY AND HISTORY: SAMSON AS SAVIOR

AS I HAVE ARGUED in chapter 5, the messianic and eschatalogical emphases of Christianity posed special challenges to the rabbis of the third through sixth centuries of the Common Era. Rabbinic Judaism's strikingly ambiguous, heterogeneous accounts of God's future anointed one (*melekh hamashiach*) and its related anticipations of the world to come (*olam habah*) were formulated in relation to an emergent christology, an essential claim of which was the supersession of Old Testament Judaism. Ongoing encounters with a Christian community claiming to be the true Israel resulted in a rabbinic messianism, at times diverging sharply from Christianity, at other times sounding very much like the followers of Jesus and Paul. This tension in rabbinic thought produced a number of meditations on disappointed or mistaken messianic hopes, the most dramatic of which are the extended accounts of Bar Kokhba and R. Akiba, which I have discussed in the preceding chapter. In a passage that uncannily anticipates many of the contemporary critical controversies regarding the Miltonic Samson's status as a type of Christ, the rabbis offer an imaginative description of Jacob's confusion over the meaning of the biblical Samson narrative: "When Jacob our father foresaw [Samson] he believed him to be the Anointed King (*hamelekh hamashiach*), but when he foresaw him dead he said, 'Even he has died, "I have waited for thy salvation, O Lord"' (Gen. 49:18)."[28] While the midrash makes no explicit mention of Christianity, I am convinced that it has been offered as a polemic against the misguided messianism of the followers of Jesus. The death of a mighty leader at one point believed to be the melekh hamashiach provokes Jacob's unflinching conclusion that the messiah has yet to come, directly in opposition to the christological assertion that Jesus's death served as *the* sign of his messianic status. Jesus is no more the Christ than Samson was. The Samson story's dubious account of cyclical violence and revenge serves as its primary value, offering the rabbis the possibility of aligning (however obliquely) those qualities with the Christian story of salvation via Jesus's crucifixion. The parallel version of this midrash in the Albeck edition of Genesis Rabbah omits Jacob's mistaken hopes for a messianic Samson, moving immediately to an alternative account of who the *Jewish* messiah will be:

> When Jacob foresaw [Samson], he said, "I await your salvation, Lord," that is, he will not bring the redemption, but rather [it will come] from Gad, as it says, "Gad, a troop shall troop overcome him, but he shall overcome at the last (*aqev*)" (Gen. 49:19), that is, he who comes at the end (*eqev*): "Behold, I will send you Elijah the prophet" (Mal. 3:23) [4:5 in the Protestant Bible], who is from the tribe of Gad. Thus the verse reads, "but he shall overcome (*yagud*) at the last."[29]

THIS JACOB ISN'T FOOLED at all, in part because he is a better reader of the prophetic writings than the evangelists. Mark (1:2) and Luke (1:76) both cite Malachi 3:1 in their accounts of John the Baptist (the gospel's Elijah figure), but neither of them includes Elijah's origins in the tribe of Gad.[30] In this rabbinic reading the Samson story thus becomes an occasion for insight into who the messiah is—and, especially, who he is *not*. Charting a middle path between the aggressive military and political agency of Samson's story on the one hand and the passive withdrawal from history that attends early Christianity's eschatology, the rabbis offer the importance of interpretive politics—a reading of both biblical texts and historical events—as the proper form of human action in the world.

In the preface to his dramatic poem, defending the classical tragic form as appropriate to the biblical matter of Samson's story, Milton identifies an early precedent for Christian tragedy: "*Gregory Nazianzen* a Father of the Church, thought it not unbeseeming the sanctity of his person to write a Tragedy, which he entitl'd *Christ Suffering.*" Given Milton's notorious discomfort with the Passion—his inability to complete his early passion poem, his superficial references to it in *Paradise Lost*, and especially, his displacement of the crucifixion story onto the wilderness story in *Paradise Regained*—it is striking that the poet would have chosen *Christus Patiens* as evidence of the propriety of tragedy for biblical themes. Such a reference functions partially to do the work Milton found himself personally unable to do: he need not write a tragedy about Christ's passion since it is something already attempted in prose or rhyme. Indeed, Milton frames his reference so as to shift the attention from the sanctity of the subject matter to the "sanctity of [the] person," that is, the poet doing the writing. In yet another deferral of the passion, Milton seems to be more concerned with the integrity of his own poetic vocation—his agency as a reader and writer—than with the integrity of the theme of salvation through suffering. What is more, *Christus Patiens* itself swerves from any kind of phenomenological account of the crucifixion to contemplate in far greater depth the effect of Christ's passion on the human community, most vividly Jesus's mother. Though the occasion for the tragedy may be Christ's suffering, the drama devotes most of its attention and energy to Mary's suffering; Christ hardly seems to suffer at all! At the moment of Christ's death, Mary cries, "seeing your crucified corpse, / I lament for myself more than for you, for your absence, / For you killed me more than you were destroyed" (894–96).[31]

Critics of *Samson Agonistes* have tended to equate its so-called Hebraism with a parochial nationalism, a particularism that stands in the way of Samson finally achieving his transcendent, extrahistorical (perhaps even Christlike) redemption.[32] That is, when Samson insists on the particularities of history and law, he is being Hebraic, carnal, political, and therefore unredeemed. At the end, when he finally transcends this—or when, in the view of those who posit an unregenerate Samson, he fails to transcend the contingencies of history—readers are given a lesson in true redemption, i.e., what it is and/or what it is not. In keeping with my quarrel with these polarizing tendencies, I think that Milton's citation of *Christus Patiens* serves to underscore the same ambivalence regarding the particularities of history and human agency I identified in my discussion of the final books of *Paradise Lost.* Milton's resistance to a diasporic Christian identity resembling the rabbinic refashioning of Judaism, as I have argued in chapter 5, accounts for the (partial) retreat from a Hebraic attention to historical contingency at the end of the twelve-book epic. The homologous responses to history as a phenomenology of suffering in both rabbinic literature and Milton's writings, however, bespeak a shared interpretive politics of survival. As Milton's memorable phrase in book 12 indicates, historical agency depends on "suffering for Truth's sake," not dying for it.

In both rabbinic literature and Milton's drama, Samson comes to embody an intense ambivalence concerning the distinctiveness—the chosenness—of ethnic or national identity. In Samson's debate with Harapha Milton presents conflicting understandings of Samson's alternatively private and public personae. Harapha accuses Samson of having been a "League-breaker" (1184), simultaneously justifying Samson's incarceration and the Philistines' refraining from "violence or spoil" to Samson's countrymen. Samson replies that his fellow Hebrews misread his behavior as that of an individual rather than as a representative of the Nation:

> When I perceiv'd all set on enmity,
> As on my enemies, where ever chanc'd,
> I us'd hostility, and took thir spoil
> To pay my underminers in thir coin.
> My Nation was subjected to your Lords.
> It was the force of Conquest; force with force
> Is well ejected when the Conquer'd can.
> But I a private person, whom my Country
> As a league-breaker gave up bound, presum'd
> Single Rebellion and did Hostile Acts.
> I was no private but a person rais'd
> With strength sufficient and command from Heav'n
> To free my Country; if their servile minds
> Me their Deliverer sent would not receive,
> But to thir Masters gave me up for nought,

Th' unworthier they; whence to this day they serve. (1201–16)

FILLED WITH A POWERFUL disdain for his own nation, far more, it would seem, than for his enemies, Samson tries hard to justify his own actions. The poet's own biographical circumstances offer themselves as a tempting interpretive key to this moment. Resentful and unappreciated, Milton resisted identifying himself with Restoration England; his sympathies had disappeared for those countrymen who, in his view, had failed to lay claim to the political and religious salvation with which the Interregnum began. "Patria est," Milton wrote to Peter Heimbach, "ubicunque est bene." Rather than trying to assert the validity of this application of Milton's own life to the circumstances surrounding Samson, I want to call attention to how Samson's statement combines the talionic justice so often associated, for better or for worse, with a pre-Christian Hebraism—"force with force / Is well ejected when the Conquer'd can"—with Samson's apparent disavowal of any protopatriotic allegiance to the Hebrew nation: "Th' unworthier they; whence to this day they serve." Samson seems to undermine his function as a hero of the Hebrews even as he lays claim to the very qualities that have made him Hebraic in the subsequent critical tradition.

In the midrashic commentary on Jacob's blessings to his sons at the end of the book of Genesis, the rabbis present alternative evaluations of Samson's distinctiveness in light of his physical strength. Quoting a truncated passage from Genesis 49:16, "Dan shall judge his nation as one (*k'echad*)," the midrash offers two readings of "as one":

> as the unique (*ki'm'yuchad*) among the tribes, i.e., Judah. Another interpretation of "as one": like the singular one (*k'yichudo*) in the world [i.e., God], who requires no help in war, as it is written, "I have trodden the winepress alone" (Isa. 63:3). In this way, Samson, who comes from the tribe of Dan, required no assistance from anyone, not even a sword, but rather only the jawbone of an ass.[33]

THE RABBINIC TRUNCATION of the biblical verse—by omitting "of the tribes of Israel"—enacts at a syntactic level what the comments seek to clarify at an interpretive level. They underscore the isolation of Dan and, by extension, Samson. The first interpretation, however, depends on something of a paradox. If "as one" is to mean "unique," and that uniqueness is to suggest the equation of Dan with Judah, then the very equivalence seems to contradict the uniqueness that had constituted their conjunction. Dan's distinctiveness is recognizable, according to this reading, when it is no longer distinctive. The second interpretation presents a parallel tension, since the passage cited from Isaiah speaks in the voice of God. That Samson's acts of independent physical strength resemble God's singularity returns us to the complex matter of simultaneously locating God's behavior in human action and humanity's agency in an imitatio Dei. What is more, it begs the further question: is Samson's physical prowess, which is here taken as an indication of his independence, therefore *not* a sign of divine assistance?

Manoa's famously solipsistic coda, "Samson has quit himself / Like Samson" (1709–10) stands in tension with his assurance, several lines later, that "all this / With God not parted from him" (1718–19). It is a tension that parallels the rabbinic ambivalence concerning Samson's resemblance to and distinction from God. While his father may wish to regard Samson's heroic achievements as a sign of God's irrevocable favor, the reader is left to wonder whether the "calm of mind, all passion spent" at the end of the drama applies to Samson alone or whether it has value for the chorus of survivors whose passions Milton has deferred one last time.

Notes

Introduction: Hebraism and Literary History

1. Arnold, *Culture and Anarchy*, p. 466.
2. For a useful account of the intellectual context of Arnold's paradigm, particularly its debt to the German Enlightenment, see Gossman, "Philhellinism and Anti-semitism." Gossman specifically connects Arnold's essay with the dialectical models of Hegel and Heine.
3. Arnold, *Culture and Anarchy*, p. 472.
4. Among the most noteworthy of these studies are Saurat, *Milton*; Fletcher, *Milton's Semitic Studies*; Fletcher, *Milton's Rabbinical Readings*; Baldwin, "Some Extra-Biblical Semitic Influences; Conklin, *Biblical Criticism*; Adams, *Ikon*; Werblowsky, "Milton and the *Conjectura Cabbalistica*"; Fisch, "Hebraic Styles and Motifs"; Stollman, "Milton's Rabbinical Readings"; Mendelsohn, "Milton and the Rabbis"; Fresch, "The Hebraic Influence."
5. Rosenblatt, *Torah and Law*. Rosenblatt's essential study includes an astute discussion of the relationship between modern trends in the discussion of Milton's Hebraism and larger religious, political, and ideological issues in Milton studies. See especially pp. 3–11 and pp. 82–85.

6. Werman, *Milton and Midrash.*

7. Ibid., p. 169.

8. W. B. Hunter, in his "The Provenance of the *Christian Doctrine*," was the first to raise doubts. In the next two volumes of *Studies in English Literature* Hunter's challenges were in turn challenged by Barbara K. Lewalski, John T. Shawcross, Maurice Kelley, and Christopher Hill. In 1997 a committee comprised of Gordon Campbell, Thomas N. Corns, John K. Hale, David I. Holmes, and Fiona J. Tweedie assembled a report entitled "The Provenance of *De Doctrina Christiana*."

9. Hunter, "The Provenance of the *Christian Doctrine*," 132. As Barbara Lewalski has astutely replied, "The biblical images, metaphors, and allusions suffusing both *Paradise Lost* and *Paradise Regained* . . . allowed readers early and late to invest such terms with traditional meanings of their own understandings, eliding what might contradict them." See her response in "Forum," 152.

10. For an insightful analysis of the controversy, see Stephen B. Dobranski and John P. Rumrich, "Introduction: Heretical Milton," Dobranski and Rumrich, *Milton and Heresy*, 6–12. While it is not my intention to enter into this controversy in an extended fashion, I do want to make clear that in light of what I take to be essential aspects of Milton's theological, philosophical, and political outlook (especially his Armnianism and his monism), I see no reason to doubt Milton's authorship of the theological treatise. Indeed, although I did not write them to serve such an end, in the chapters that follow there may be found additional arguments in support of Milton's authorship.

11. See the beginning of chapter 1 for some working definitions of various terms used to describe rabbinic literature.

1. Diaspora and Restoration

1. My account of rabbinic literature in the following pages draws upon many recent studies, especially Boyarin, *Intertextuality and the Reading of Midrash;* Frankel, *Darkhei ha-Aggadah veha-Midrash;* Goldin, *Studies in Midrash;* Heinemann, *Darkhei ha-Aggadah;* and Stern, *Parables in Midrash.*

2. I mean this in a figurative sense, although the publication history of many midrashim consists in their physical placement on the page around the text of the Bible.

3. Halivni, "From Midrash to Mishnah."

4. Bialik, *Law and Legend.* See also the annotations and commentary to his collection

of aggadic tales, *Sefer Ha-Aggadah*. To be fair to Bialik, it should also be recalled that much of the subsequent essay is devoted to saving the category of halakhah from this dubious characterization.

5. Classical rabbinic literature is normally divided into two chronologically specific periods: the period of the tannaim, dating from the middle of the first century *c.e.* to the beginning of the third century, followed by the period of the amoraim, which ended at the beginning of the sixth century. There is a third period, associated with the saboraim, who are considered the editors of the Babylonian Talmud, but this period produced very little of its own writings.

6. Judah Goldin, "The Freedom and Restraint of Haggadah," Hartman and Budick, *Midrash and Literature*, 69.

7. The Tosefta ("addition, supplement" in Aramaic) corresponds in structure to the Mishnah and serves as a supplement to that collection, which was codified as authoritative by Rabbi Yehudah Ha-Nasi at the end of the second or beginning of the third century *c.e.*

8. Aramaic for "book," the Sifra is a halakhic midrash on the book of Leviticus and was probably redacted in the second half of the third century *c.e.*

9. The dating of this relatively obscure midrash is disputed, although its core probably goes back to the Tannaitic period (second or third century *c.e.*).

10. See Joseph Heinemann's essay in Hartman and Budick's *Midrash and Literature*, "The Nature of the Aggadah," and especially Strack and Stemberger's essential guidebook, *Introduction to the Talmud and Midrash*, for further elaborations on these different aggadic forms.

11. Shinan and Zakovitch, "Midrash on Scripture," 263.

12. Bloom, *The Book of J*; Brisman, *The Voice of Jacob*; and Pardes, *Countertraditions* stand out as some of the more noteworthy examples of this kind of literary reading.

13. See, for example, Neusner, "Genesis and Judaism."

14. Heinemann, *Darkhei Ha-Aggadah*.

15. The periods surrounding the destruction of the Second Temple in 70 *c.e.* and the Bar Kokhba rebellion in 132 *c.e.* are important exceptions, to which I shall return in greater detail in my final chapter.

16. Rosemary Radford Reuther observes, "It was Christian Rome that gradually repealed this protected status of the Jews and began to create the legal instruments of the ghetto." See her *Faith and Fratricide*, p. 28. Also see Jacob Neusner, "Stable Symbols in a Shifting Society: The Delusion of the Monolithic Gentile in Documents of Late Fourth-Century Judaism," Neusner and Frerichs, *"To See Ourselves as Others See Us."*

17. See Augustine, *The City of God*, 20.7–10.

18. On these parallel histories, see Reuther, *Faith and Fratricide*, p. 28, and "Judaism and Christianity"; and Boyarin, *A Radical Jew*.

19. A good deal has been written on this question, including Ruether, *Faith and Fratricide*; Neusner, *Judaism and Christianity*; Boyarin, *Carnal Israel*; and Boyarin, *Unheroic Conduct*, especially part 1.

20. Ruether's observations concerning Pharisaic Judaism's surpassing "universalism" betray her Roman Catholic emphasis and thus inadvertently allude precisely to the nature of the split between reformers and adherents to the pope in the early modern period: "Pharisaism also emancipated the Jew from the need for priestly mediatorship and for historical vindication, whereas the Church continued to be tied to the latter through its messianic heritage, and redeveloped the former in a revived priesthood and vicarious sacrificial system. The Pharisaic Jew, by contrast, carried his temple with him wherever he went. He needed no priest, for he was his own high priest, making acceptable offerings to God through prayer, penitence, and deeds of loving-kindness. Each man made his own decision to incorporate himself into the way of salvation. Rabbinic learning was a pathway open to all men." *Faith and Fratricide*, p. 57. Milton would likely have been quite content to describe his own view of Christian salvation in the words Ruether uses for rabbinic Judaism.

21. Worth bearing in mind is Tessa Rajak's observation on this matter: "It is probably right to see the development of rabbinic Judaism, and perhaps also its beginnings, as in some ways a response to the Christian challenge, a sharpening of self-definition . . . yet it is highly significant that no such purpose is made explicit." See "The Jewish Community and Its Boundaries," Lieu, North, and Rajak, *The Jews Among Pagans and Christians*, p. 12.

22. The term *minim*, "heretics," is almost always the rabbinic code word for followers of Jesus and Paul.

23. My debt to Geoffrey Hartman's mode of literary criticism should be apparent in these two terms, as they echo Hartman's *Saving the Text* and his essay "The Struggle for the Text," Hartman and Budick, *Midrash and Literature*, pp. 3–18.

24. Lightfoot, *In Evangelium*, A3^v-A4^r. This volume contains the first installments of a work that was published serially between 1658 and 1674.

25. Peter van Rooden, "Conceptions of Judaism as a Religion in the Seventeenth-Century Dutch Republic," Wood, *Christianity and Judaism*, p. 302.

26. van Rooden, "Conceptions of Judaism," p. 308.

27. See, for instance, David S. Katz, "The Phenomenon of Philo-Semitism," Wood, *Christianity and Judaism*, pp. 327–61.

28. Shapiro, *Shakespeare and the Jews*.

29. Luxon, *Literal Figures*, pp. 24–25. My next chapter addresses the presence and absence of Jewish bodies in Milton's prose.

30. Calvert, *The Blessed Jew*, pp. 2–3.

31. Prynne, *A Short Demurrer to the Jewes*, part 1.

32. These three figures undertook an animated debate, in print, over the significance of Jewish sects for contemporary Christianity. Serarius's *Trihaeresium* (1604) was followed quickly by Drusius's *De tribus Sectis Judaeorum* (1605) and Scaliger's *Elenchus Trihaeresii* (1605).

33. See Haller, *Foxe's Book of Martyrs*, pp. 164–65.

34. Haller, in *Foxe's Book of Martyrs*, 138, points out that Foxe was probably following the compilations of John Bale, Matthias Flacius Illyricus, and Robert Fabyan, who in turn had drawn upon Gildas, Bede, and Geoffrey of Monmouth. In contrast to their counterparts in the ecclesiastical establishment, Wyclif and the Lollards, followed by the nonconformists of the late sixteenth and early seventeenth centuries, and subsequently by Milton, attributed the decline of the Church to the age of Constantine and the establishment of an endowed state church. See below, chapter 2, for further discussion of Milton's rejection of this Foxian view of Church history.

35. For their useful correctives to Haller's influential study, see Olsen, *John Foxe and the Elizabethan Church*; and Bauckham, *Tudor Apocalypse*. Bernard Capp, "The Political Dimension of Apocalyptic Thought," Patrides and Wittreich, *The Apocalypse in English Renaissance Thought and Literature*, pp. 93–124, provides an indispensible overview of the major trends in early modern English apocalyptic writing.

36. See Worden's survey, "Providence and Politics."

37. Carter, *The Schismatick Stigmatized*, pp. 3–4.

38. Arthur H. Williamson argues that the advent of English patriotism is inseparable from the development of English philosemitism. "By the first decade of the 17th century, patriotism and philosemitism underwrote each other within the framework of the apocalypse. If the apocalypse articulated English patriotism, the Jews made plausible that form of the apocalypse." See "Latter Day Judah, Latter Day Israel: The Millennium, the Jews, and the British Future," Brecht et al., *Chiliasmus in Deutschland und England*, p. 153.

39. John Goodwin, Θεομαχια, or *The Grand Imprudence of Men Running the Hazard of Fighting Against God* (London, 1644), pp. 23–24, in Haller, *Tracts on Liberty*, 3:29–30.

40. *An Endevovr*, pp. 25–26. This text offers extensive arguments for a form of church government modeled in minute detail on the synagogue as understood from biblical and postbiblical literature.

41. See above, note 22.

42. Early modern biblical scholars would never have used the term *intertestamental*,

but they were aware of the distinctive qualities of the period of Jewish history between the closing of the canon of the Hebrew Bible and the life of Jesus; they made skilled used of available apocryphal literature to learn more about the period. What I have characterized as "Christian era Jewish precedent" refers both to the period immediately following Christ's life and the destruction of the Second Temple in 70 *c.e.* and the period following the Roman Empire's embrace of Christianity in the fourth century. Obviously, there are important differences, ones that are crucial for other aspects of my argument. For this portion of my analysis, however, what matters is that this final stage of Jewish precedent postdates Christ's advent.

43. Glassman, *Anti-Semitic Stereotypes with Jews*, 86–87.

44. See for instance, Katz, *Philo-Semitism*, chapter 1. To be sure, Katz cites these and many other examples to demonstrate the extensive dissemination of interest in Jews and Judaism in England in the first half of the seventeenth century. But, as he observes, with the exception of those "Judaizers" who explicitly returned to some or all Jewish practices, most interest in Jews, even and especially among those so-called philo-semites, was part of a larger—often millenarian—desire to convert the Jews to Christianity. Even most of James Shapiro's useful study of these questions hinges upon largely negative portrayals of Jews.

45. *An Endevovr*, p. 16.

46. I borrow this term as a way of identifying advocates of structure, and ritualized worship, including, but not limited to Roman Catholics and Anglicans, from Achsah Guibbory's study, *Ceremony and Community*.

47. Stollman, "Milton's Dichotomy," p. 108.

48. The volume includes tracts by Richard Hooker, Lancelot Andrewes, Martin Bucer, John Rainoldes, James Ussher, Edward Brerewood, John Dury, and Francis Mason.

49. *Certaine briefe treatises*, pp. 51–52.

50. For a useful study of this group of English apocalypticists, among whom were many of Milton's friends and acquaintances, see Capp, *The Fifth Monarchy Men*. Arthur Williamson observes that "the more deeply apocalyptic an individual's perspective, the more likely he possessed philosemitic attitudes; the more deeply 'Anglo-Catholic' an individual, the more suspicious of apocalypticism, the more anti-semitic." Williamson, "Latter Day Judah," p. 159. As we shall see below, Milton offers a rich test case of this observation, insofar as he is neither "Anglo-Catholic" nor especially comfortable with the fuller implications of apocalypticism, especially toward the end of his writing career.

51. Calvert, *The Blessed Jew*, pp. 24–25.

52. *An Endevovr*, p. 12.

53. On the English discussions of Jewish conversion, see Hill, "'Till the Conversion of the Jews'"; and Katz, *Philo-Semitism*, chapter 3; and Matar, "Milton and the Idea."

54. Matar, *Islam in Britain*, pp. 181–82. Matar's recognition of the Christian militarization of the Jewish role in history has important connections to the competing notions of political agency in midrash and *Paradise Lost* that I discuss in my final chapter.

55. Shapiro, *Shakespeare and the Jews*, pp. 167ff. Shapiro notes the tension between the popularity of conversion narratives and the doctrinal need to construct Jews as racially unassimilable, precisely so that Paul's apparent prophecy of the mass conversion of the Jews as a sign of the millennium could occur. On the legacy of this question of conversion in later periods, see Ragussis, *Figures of Conversion*. On the origins of the associations of race with Jewishness, see the first and last essays in Netanyahu, *Toward the Inquisition*, pp. 1–42, 183–201.

56. Fuller, *A Pisgah-sight of Palestine*, pp. 197–98.

57. Concerning the other side of the political and religious divide, Arthur Williamson has speculated that "much of the resistance to the readmission of the Jews derived from the horror experienced by the mainstream elites when they saw their own assumptions pressed to what seemed grotesque conclusions. The distress arose less from the gulf separating them from their radical opponents than from the seemingly disfiguring consequences of their *shared* assumptions." Williamson, "Latter Day Judah," p. 165.

58. On Brightman's transformation of Foxe's international outlook into one specifically centered on English providential history, see Christianson, *Reformers and Babylon*, pp. 40–41.

59. See Janel Mueller, "Milton on Heresy," Dobranski and Rumrich, *Milton and Heresy*, pp. 21–38.

60. The rhetorical equation of the English and the Jews in this condemnatory context occurs especially frequently in the wake of the execution of Charles I, when Royalists compare those Englishmen complicit with and responsible for the regicide to the Jews responsible for the crucifixion of Christ. See, for example, John Warner, *The Devilish Conspiracy, Hellish Treason, Heathenish Condemnation, and Damnable Murder, Committed and Executed by the Iewes Against the Anointed Lord* (London, 1648); Paul Knell, *Israel and England Paralleled* (London, 1648); Henry Leslie, *The Martyrdome of King Charles* (The Hague, 1649); John Allington, *The Grand Conspiracy of the Members against the Minde, of Iewes against their King* (London, 1653). In his study of Milton's *History of Britain*, Nicholas von Maltzahn attributes the simple providentialism found in this later text to Milton's uncritical parroting of his earlier sources. Von Maltzahn goes on to suggest, "The idea of a flawed national character is central to Milton's response to the

events of the 1640s. He becomes increasingly preoccupied with the elect within the nation, with the true Christians, rather than with the elect nation he had proclaimed in *Of Reformation* and *Areopagitica*." See von Maltzahn, *Milton's "History of Britain*," pp. 84 and 139. I think the flawed national character with which Milton becomes explicitly preoccupied in his later writings can be located *in potentia* even in *Of Reformation*. For further implications of Milton's self-marginalization, see chapter 2.

61. Stephen M. Fallon, "'Elect above the rest': Theology as Self-Representation in Milton," Dobranski and Rumrich, *Milton and Heresy*, pp. 99–100.

62. Don M. Wolfe has written on this absence in the context of Milton's intolerance for Catholicism. See his "Limits of Miltonic Toleration." See also Matar, "Milton and the Idea."

63. Matar, in his "Milton and the Idea," regards these factors as evidence of Milton's general agreement with those Independents and nonconformists who included the Restoration of the Jews as an essential element of salvation history. It seems to me, however, that the weight of these factors makes the relative absence of material addressing the contemporary status of Jews in Milton's writings that much more remarkable.

64. The full treatise extends for thirty-four pages in the Yale edition of Milton's prose.

65. Elizabeth Sauer has observed, "The supporters of Readmission sought to establish a historical continuity with the ancient Hebrews, but also to convert contemporary Jews; toleration involved, ultimately, an assimilation of difference." See her "Religious Toleration and Imperial Intolerance," Rajan and Sauer, *Milton and the Imperial Vision*, p. 220. I would like to thank Professor Sauer for sharing with me an earlier unpublished version of this essay.

66. In her essay Sauer connects the readmission debates and questions of religious toleration to the English conflict with Spain and subsequently to *Samson Agonistes*, which she reads as a text about alterity and toleration. "Like the war with Spain, the proposal for Readmission was intended to divert attention away from England's domestic strife" (p. 219). I think Milton's comment in the *Observations* may be read in a similar vein, especially since the conflict in Ireland was a function of England's ongoing imperial project there. Indeed, it may be more appropriate to the period of the Interregnum than to the period of the Restoration, when Milton is generally regarded to have written *Samson Agonistes*. By this point in Milton's career, questions of "Imperial Intolerance" are likely to have been less pressing. I explore the further implications of my argument for a reading of *Samson Agonistes* in the epilogue.

67. "Signum aliud huc referunt nonnulli vocationem universam non Iudaeorum solum, sed etiam Israelitarum." As I have indicated in my introduction, despite re-

cent attempts to call Milton's authorship of *De Doctrina* into question, I see no compelling reason to doubt its origins with the poet of *Paradise Lost, Paradise Regained*, and *Samson Agonistes*. Indeed, the similarity in affect between *De Doctrina*'s reference to Jewish conversion and that of *Paradise Regained* seems to be yet further evidence of the treatise's Miltonic provenance.

68. Kerrigan, *The Sacred Complex*, p. 216.

69. Martin Luther, "De Servo Arbitrio," Watson, *Luther and Erasmus: Free Will and Salvation*, p. 259. For an illuminating discussion of Luther's opinions on these matters, and a helpful analysis of his disputes with Erasmus, see Oberman's biography, *Luther*, pp. 211–20.

70. Calvin, *Institutes of the Christian Religion*, 3.xxiii.8. Calvin's articulation of the *docta ignorantia* derives originally from Augustine's *Letters*. A century before Calvin the phrase was used as the title for a well-known theological treatise on the knowledge of God by Nicolas of Cusa, *De docta ignorantia* (1440).

71. Ibid., 3.xxiii.2.

72. See Bouwsma, *John Calvin*, chapter 9.

73. Milton, *Areopagitica*, YP 2:515.

74. I do not wish to place too much emphasis on the uniqueness of Milton's case. My aim in this book is to reveal some cultural tendencies that suggest a hitherto hidden way in which Hebraism and Judaism have contributed to Western culture and religion. Milton's case is striking, but it is not by any means the only one.

75. See, for example, Regina Schwartz's *Remembering and Repeating*.

76. Mann, *The Bible as Read and Preached*.

2. "Taking Sanctuary Among the Jews": Milton and the Form of Jewish Precedent

1. Milton draws this connection between the body and the letter explicitly several pages into the treatise, describing how as the Priests "fixt onely upon the *Flesh*, . . . men came to scan the *Scriptures*, by the Letter," YP 1:522. In her rich analysis of Milton's first foray into the pamphleteering, Janel Mueller has discussed the predominance of bodily metaphors in *Of Reformation*'s depiction of the Church, both positively and negatively. See "Embodying Glory: The Apocalyptic Strain in Milton's *Of Reformation*," Loewenstein and Turner, *Politics, Poetics, and Hermeneutics in Milton's Prose*, 9–40.

2. See Kraeling, *The Old Testament Since the Reformation*, chapter 2. Luther's position regarding the Old Testament was even more extreme: "Leave Moses and his people together. They are a thing of the past and none of my business. I hear the word that

concerns me. We have the gospel." Ibid., p. 16. It does appear, however, that Milton's characterization of the Old Testament as older than Christianity is more consistent with Luther's view.

3. Carter, *The Schismatick Stigmatized*, p. 7.

4. Though there may be interesting homiletical reasons for connecting the passage from Exodus with Stephen's speech in Acts, the Septuagint's version cannot be the source. The Greek translation of Moses's lament concludes with the phrase, εγω δε αλογος ειμι, "I am without words" or "I am not eloquent."

5. The Greek word for "uncircumcision" here is ακροβυστια, which literally means "foreskin." The more common New Testament term for uncircumcised is απεριτμο-τοι, literally, "uncut."

6. On the transition from an earlier form of Christian Hebraica, which worked toward dismantling entrenched forms of political and religious domination, to its later incarnation, which helped to install new forms of prejudice, see Shoulson, "'Proprietie in this Hebrew Poesy.'"

7. William Walwyn, *The Compassionate Samaritane Vnbinding the Conscience, and powring Oyle into the wounds which have been made upon the Separation* (London, 1644), pp. 28–30, in Haller, *Tracts on Liberty*, 3:78–79.

8. The belief that English was closer to Hebrew than other European languages dates back at least to William Tyndale. See "Obedience of a Christian Man," pp. 148–49. By the mid-seventeenth century Hebrew's status as the Adamic language was being challenged from diverse groups and writers who offered other alternatives, most notably Chinese, whose characters were believed to constitute a less mediated form of representation than languages that depended on any alphabet. See Katz, *Philo-Semitism*, chapter 2; and Leonard, *Naming in Paradise*, especially pp. 1–22.

9. Pace James Shapiro's attempts at debunking the long-held view that Jews were absent from England since their expulsion in 1290, I think that even his interesting new evidence reinforces the myth—if not the reality—that Jews did not live in England for over 350 years. As Shapiro himself argues, often myths are of greater cultural and political importance than "reality."

10. Haller, *Foxe's Book of Martyrs*. Haller observes that "the endeavor initiated by the martyrs and exiles of Mary's reign to convert the English people to a religion based upon the reading of the Word in print became an inseparable part of the great folk movement of their age and nation" (p. 51). Arthur H. Williamson's recent and innovative work on early modern Scotland in the context of trends in philosemitism offers the provocative suggestion that the rhetoric of election stemming from this nexus of religious and political discourses was even more profound and influential in

Scotland, since, "unlike England and Lutheran Germany, Scotland formally covenanted with God, an event of Sinaitic intensity and, potentially, of Sinaitic significance for the latter days." See Williamson, "'A Pil for Pork-Eaters,'" p. 240. In this essay, and others, Williamson further suggests that Scottish religio-nationalist rhetoric, through this ideology of the covenant, "sacrilized confederation with others. It could provide the basis for the British State" (p. 243).

11. See chapter 1 for a more detailed account of Milton's ideas of national election.

12. In his introduction to *Areopagitica*, Ernest Sirluck, YP 2:169–70, accurately points out that while Milton's position in the antiprelatical tracts of 1640–42 anticipated the claims of many Independents in their disputes with the Presbyterians in the mid-1640s, i.e., that civil government should be adequately separated from matters of religion, Milton does not take the position in his tract against prepublication licensing that church and state should be separated. This is all the more remarkable since he does make this claim both before and after the writing of *Areopagitica*.

13. Milton was not the first to condemn the period following Constantine's conversion. The Scottish reformer, John Napier, in a thoroughgoing attack on Foxe's apocalyptic view of English history, portrayed Constantine as the great subverter of Christianity, having "subdued all the Christian churches" to Silvester I. John Napier, *A Plaine Discovery of the Whole Revelation of Saint John* (1593), p. 145, cited in Williamson, "Scotland, Antichrist, and the Invention of Great Britain," p. 42. As the above passage demonstrates, Milton read church history in much the same fashion, although it is crucial to bear in mind the essential difference between Napier, one of the foremost writers on the coming apocalypse, and Milton, who, halfheartedly at best, advocated an overtly millenarian reading of his contemporary historical moment, both before and, what is more crucial for the ensuing analysis, after the Restoration and the complete disappointment of his political and religious expectations. C. A. Patrides has shown that Milton's tentativeness with respect to the millennium only grew stronger, as he increasingly chose to focus on the spiritual aspects of a "paradise within . . . happier far" than any imminent apocalytical rip in the fabric of history. C. A. Patrides, "'Something like Prophetick strain': Apocalyptic Configurations in Milton," Patrides and Wittreich, *The Apocalypse in English Renaissance Thought and Literature*, pp. 207–239.

14. See chapter 1 for a more detailed explication of this comparison.

15. Paul Christianson has identified two basic apocalyptic traditions that have their roots in the early English Reformation, the imperial tradition, which stressed the role of magistrates (princes and/or parliaments), and the tradition of the "persecuted and oppressed," who lacked worldly prestige. Although these two strains of

apocalypticism occasionally, if paradoxically, worked in tandem with one another, in the case of Milton and many of his contemporaries, clearly the latter tradition took on greater weight. See Christianson, *Reformers and Babylon*, p. 11.

16. On the ongoing importance of the visible church for Milton's ecclesiology, see Honeygosky, *Milton's House of God*. Referring to Milton's later prose, Honeygosky asserts that its apparently inward and spiritual thrust "occurred alongside Milton's attention to that broader, spatially unconfined international group of saints who were ingrafted into Christ's Mystical Body as the Church" (p. 127).

17. The rhetoric of "root and branch" was common among Puritans, dating back at least to the beginning of the century.

18. See Katz, *Philo-Semitism*, chapter 1.

19. James Ussher, "The Originall of Bishops and Metropolitans Briefly laid down," *Certaine briefe treatises*, pp. 53–54.

20. Gillespie, *A Late Dialogue*, pp. 18–19.

21. Woods, "'That Freedom of Discussion,'" p. 15. On the related matter of the apparent tension between an idealized body of English believers and the historical reality of a largely unregenerate English populace, Michael Fixler has suggested that Milton adopted a strategy drawn directly out of ecclesiastical Calvinism, treating "the nation and the Lord's people as synonymous quantities, affirming as a right to which the whole nation was entitled what was essentially the liberty of the regenerate." See *Milton and the Kingdoms of God*, pp. 124ff.

22. John T. Shawcross's recent biography offers an exemplary discussion of the tensions between personal and cultural forces in the making of Milton's writings. See *John Milton*.

23. John Goodwin, Θεομαχια, or *The Grand Imprudence of Men Running the Hazard of Fighting Against God* (London, 1644), p. 45, in Haller, *Tracts on Liberty*, 3:51.

24. For an extraordinary analysis of the modern legacy of the Jew as outsider, see John Murray Cuddihy's provocative study, *The Ordeal of Civility*.

25. Shapiro, *Shakespeare and the Jews*, p. 179.

26. Mueller, "Embodying Glory," p. 34.

27. For this August 1666 exchange between Heimbach and Milton, see French, *The Life Records of John Milton*, 4:421–6.

28. Hall, *Episcopacie by Divine Right*, pp. 31–32.

29. Ibid., p. 94.

30. Ibid., pp. 94–95.

31. Prynne, *Lord Bishops None of the Lords Bishops*, chapter 7.

32. Burton, *A Vindication of Churches*, pp. 26–27, emphasis in original.

33. See also Paul's letter to the Galatians, chapter 3, especially vv. 6–16. For an important analysis of Paul's use of flesh and spirit in matters of national and religious identity, see Boyarin, *A Radical Jew*, especially chapters 3 and 4. My focus here is on the seventeenth-century legacy of Paul's notions of fleshly and spiritual identity—however much they may constitute a misreading of the epistles. On the question of typology, see chapters 2 and 5, this volume, as it pertains to the final books of *Paradise Lost*.

34. Daniel Boyarin's insistence that Paul does not reject the body in his version of dualism does not contradict my argument here, since the hermeneutic legacy of Paul's writings, especially after Calvin, manifests a fairly consistent dismissal of the carnal in favor of readings deemed "spiritual" and "typological." See Boyarin, *A Radical Jew*, pp. 59ff.

35. Mueller, in "Embodying Glory," asserts, "To impress on the English the potential for glory that lay within immediate reach of their own institutions, body imagery became the master Miltonic trope . . . in *Of Reformation*" (p. 25).

36. Like the biblical model he is clearly echoing, Milton elides the essential role played by woman in this process of procreation, "man . . . beget[s] man." See chapter 4 for a fuller discussion of the function of female (pro)creativity in biblical and Miltonic poesis.

37. I am following Daniel Boyarin's reading of Galatians, in which he cites David M. Henkin's unpublished paper, "Faith and Patricide: Paul, Judaism, and the Question of Paternity." See Boyarin, *A Radical Jew*, pp. 150–51.

38. Thomas Aquinas, *Summa Theologica*, ques. 99, art. 4, trans. Dominican Fathers, 22 vols. (London: Burns, Oates and Washburn, 1920–42), 8:105–7, cited in YP 1:764, n. 21.

39. Wolfe, "Limits of Miltonic Toleration," p. 846.

40. Andrewes, "A Summarie View of the Government both of the Old and New Testament," *Certaine briefe treatises*, p. 22.

41. Gillespie, *A Late Dialogue*, pp. 33–34.

42. *A Survey*, pp. 9–10. As he makes clear in *An Apology for Smectymnuus*, Milton believed that Joseph Hall was responsible for the pamphlet, although the attribution has never been fully substantiated. See YP 1:905–6.

43. Hall, *An Humble Remonstrance*, pp. 9–11.

44. Smectymnuus, *An Answer to a Book*, p. 8.

45. Ibid., p. 8.

46. Hall, *A Modest Confutation*, pp. 30–31.

47. This is a phrase commonly ascribed to James I at the Hampton Court Confer-

ence of 1604. It became a rallying cry for supporters of the episcopacy in the early 1640s and proved to be quite prophetic of the political turn of events that was to lead to the period of the Interregnum and the execution of the Charles I.

48. Jason Rosenblatt has definitively elucidated Milton's "Hebraic Monism" and his dependence on the rabbinic knowledge of John Selden in matters of marriage law. See *Torah and Law*, chapters 1 and 2.

49. Matt Goldish provides an account of the English interest in the Temple in early modern England. See his *Judaism in the Theology of Sir Isaac Newton*, pp. 86ff. He traces the remarkably intense interest to Hieronymo Prado (1547–1595) and Juan Bautista Villapando (1552–1608), Spanish Jesuits who collaborated on a commentary on the book of Ezekiel in which the sections on the prophet's Temple vision became a central focus.

50. For a historical reconstruction of Templo's biographical details and the fate of his models during and after his lifetime, see A. K. Offenberg, "Jacob Jehuda Leon (1602–1675) and his Model of the Temple," van den Berg and van der Wall, *Jewish-Christian Relations*, pp. 94–115. Offenberg rejects the accuracy of the claim that Henrietta Maria, wife to the future Charles II of England, purchased the model from Templo in 1643. That the Stuart family was impressed by Templo's work is beyond dispute, however, and directly pertains to the issue of the Temple's appeal to different religious and political affiliations.

51. See Goldish, *Judaism in the Theology of Sir Isaac Newton* and Richard H. Popkin, "Some Aspects of Jewish-Christian Theological Interchanges in Holland and England 1640–1700," van den Berg and van der Wall, *Jewish-Christian Relations*, especially pp. 7–9.

52. For one of the most refined versions of this kind of discussion in relation to Milton, see Christopher, *Milton and the Science of the Saints*.

53. Luxon, *Literal Figures*, p. 35. My understanding of typology draws heavily on Luxon's compelling discussion in the first several chapters of his book.

54. Ibid., pp. 39 and 26.

55. Ibid., p. 58.

56. See von Maltzahn, *Milton's History of Britain*, for an account of Milton's relation to the writing of history in the early modern period.

57. To my knowledge, the closest that any contemporary critic has come to noting this fraught aspect of England's self-identification as the elect nation is Steven N. Zwicker. In trying to explicate the Restoration's transition from biblical models to Roman ones, Zwicker suggests that the defeat of the Puritans led also to an undermining of the scriptural authority that was so often used during the Civil War and Interregnum. The Roman analogy, writes Zwicker, "provided a complex and power-

ful alternative to Elect Nation. It allowed men to replace zeal and chiliastic fervor with valor and prudence; it allowed them to contemplate English history as progressive empire without the trap of eschatology." "England, Israel, and the Triumph of Roman Virtue," Popkin, *Millenarianism and Messianism,* p. 48.

58. Goodwin, Θεομαχια, pp. 2–3, Haller, *Tracts on Liberty,* 3:8–9.

59. Boyarin, *Radical Jew,* p. 156.

60. I take up the further implications of connecting Milton's Arminianism with this Jewish return in chapter 5.

61. Henry Robinson, *Liberty of Conscience,* p. 55, Haller, *Tracts on Liberty,* 3:171.

62. Ibid., pp. 6–7, ibid. 3:122–23.

63. Robert Burton, *The Anatomy of Melancholy,* part 3, sec. 4, mem. 1, subs. 3 (Oxford: Henry Cripps), 1st ed., 1621, 6th ed., 1639–40.

64. Burton here cites Johann Buxtorf's *Synagoga Judaica,* sec. 4, one of the primary sources on Jewish practice for the uninitiated, but one that expressed its disdain for Jewish errors proudly and repeatedly.

65. Burton, *The Anatomy of Melancholy,* 3.4.1.3.

66. See Katz, *Philo-Semitism,* chapter 4; and Elliot Horowitz, " 'A Different Mode of Civility': Lancelot Addison on the Jews of Barbary," Wood, *Christianity and Judaism,* pp. 309–25.

67. For Menasseh's report see Wolf, *Menasseh Ben Israel's Mission.* See also Wolf's useful introduction to these crucial primary documents.

68. Cartari's manual, entitled *Le imagini colla sposizione degli dei degli antichi,* was first published in Venice in 1556 and was translated into all the European languages, including English in 1599 under the title *The Fountain of Ancient Fiction, wherein is lively depictured the images of the gods of the ancients.* Francis Bacon, in his *De sapienta veterum liber* (London, 1609) was one of many English humanists who made acknowledged use of Cartari's manual. See Seznec, *The Survival of the Pagan Gods,* pp. 241, 279–80, and 313.

69. Horowitz, " 'A Different Mode of Civility,' " p. 312.

70. See Jean Seznec's monumental study of the persistence of mythology within Christianity, *The Survival of the Pagan Gods.*

71. Huldreich Zwingli, *Christianae fidei brevis et clara expositio,* cited in Seznec, *The Survival of the Pagan Gods,* p. 23.

72. Augustine famously justified his use of Hellenistic materials by comparing it to the gold the Israelites took with them from Egypt that was used to build the Holy Tabernacle. See *On Christian Doctrine,* 1.40.

73. The locus classicus for discussions of *prisca sapientia* and *prisca theologia* is Yates, *Giordano Bruno and the Hermetic Tradition.* See Schmidt, "Perennial Philosophy" and "Prisca Theologia e Philosophia Perennis"; Walker, *The Ancient Theology;* and McKnight,

The Modern Age and the Recovery of Ancient Wisdom. A critical reason for the success of this view stems from the crucial role Hellenistic philosophy—whether it be a version of Platonism, or the product of Hellenized Jews like Philo and the seventy elders who produced the Septuagint—played in the earliest formulations of Christian thinking. In other words, to say that a pre-Christ Christian theology informs Platonic thinking is like saying Freud's Oedipus theories inform Shakespeare's *Hamlet.* Maybe they do and maybe they don't; at least part of the reason Freud's writings on Oedipus appear to work so well as a way of reading Hamlet, however, is that Freud was such an avid reader of Shakespeare and incorporated much of his thinking about the English playwright into the development of many of theories of psychoanalysis.

74. Smectymnuus, *An Answer,* p. 19.

75. On the Puritan departures from classical rhetoric, see Smith, *Perfection Proclaimed;* and Tuttle, "Biblical Reference."

76. Kranidas, "Words, Words, Words," p. 160.

77. In an argument with useful implications for my own reading, Michael Lieb has connected this passage to Milton's view of history: "History destroys. The only way to reclaim it, that is to transform destructive violence into generative violence, is to make sparagmos meaningful through a reconstituting of the form of Truth as pharmakos. Such is the function of Reformation history: its purpose is to re-form. As a result of this reformative process, that which has been destroyed is given new life." See *Milton and the Culture of Violence,* p. 21.

78. For a suggestive discussion of this tension, see Cooley, "Iconoclasm and Self-Definition"; and Cable, *Carnal Rhetoric.*

79. One of the unexpected effects of the most recent research in early modern Christian Hebraica has been to bring back, albeit indirectly, the possibility of a Kabbalistic influence on Milton's writings. When Denis Saurat suggested in 1925 that Milton was a dyed-in-the-wool Christian Kabbalist, he did so under the erroneous assumption that Milton and many of his contemporaries had direct access to, and avidly read, Jewish mystical texts either in their original languages or in undigested translations. We now know that the likelihood of this having transpired, both for practical and for theological reasons, is very slight. Nevertheless, it appears that elements of Kabbalah, or at least the Christian, Neoplatonic, Pythagorean version of Kabbalah, made their appearance in unacknowledged ways among the writings of the Italian humanists, with whom there can be no doubt that Milton had a great deal of familiarity. It seems reasonable to suggest, therefore, that while Milton may not have deliberately made use of the idea of *tzimtzum* (divine contraction) in his ac-

count of creation in book 7 of *Paradise Lost*, his perspective on the wisdom of the Ancients may have indeed been informed by this increasingly hybridized early modern Christian humanism. Moshe Idel has informed me that the image of the scattered body of Osiris found its way into various Jewish Kabbalistic texts, used most often as a figure for the *galut*, the Jewish exile. In this same vein, Margery Sokoloff has keenly observed that the image of the deity's body "scatter'd . . . to the four winds" resonates powerfully with the diasporic traits I have associated with Milton earlier in this chapter.

80. Allen, "Some Theories"; Seznec, *The Survival of the Pagan Gods*, p. 250. Seznec reminds us that this view was originally expressed in the writing of the Church fathers and Annius of Viterbo.

3. The Poetics of Accommodation: Theodicy and the Language of Kingship

1. See Rosenblatt's essential study of the Mosaic aspects of Milton's poem in *Torah and Law*. In his introduction and first chapter, Rosenblatt provides a useful analysis of earlier Pauline and Hebraic accounts of Milton's poem.

2. For an important example of this kind of reading, see Hughes, "The Filiations of Milton's Celestial Dialogue."

3. I am bracketing the controversial question of Milton's anti-Trinitarianism here. Whether Milton's sympathies were with the more "heretical" Arians, or whether he held a somewhat less heterodox subordinationist view of Christ is of less relevance to my analysis than that the Son and Father serve distinct narrative (and hence interpretive) functions in the poem.

4. See chapter 1.

5. See Stern, *Parables in Midrash*, pp. 77–79.

6. Ignaz Ziegler, *Die Königsgleichnisse des Midrasch* (Breslau, 1903), cited in Stern, *Parables in Midrash*, p. 19.

7. Ibid., p. 94.

8. Ibid., p. 96.

9. Fallon, *Divided Empire*, pp. 34–35.

10. Ross, *Milton's Royalism*.

11. Empson, *Milton's God*, p. 146.

12. Ryken, *The Apocalyptic Vision*, pp. 18–19, n. 17.

13. Davies, *Images of Kingship*.

14. Bennett, *Reviving Liberty*.

15. Fallon, *Divided Empire*, p. 36.

16. See Paul Ricoeur's remarkable discussion of the Hebraic understanding of law and sin as a function of evil "already there" in *The Symbolism of Evil*, pp. 250ff.

17. The Hebrew word for "image" in the passage from Genesis, *tzelem*, can also be translated as "shadow." The dual connotation here recalls the idea of the Earth as "the shadow of Heaven" in Raphael's book 5 discourse. It may be that Milton was playing with a similar ambiguity in English; the OED suggests that "shadow" had a number of competing meanings by the seventeenth century: (1) comparative darkness, i.e., a degenerated image, (2) an image cast by a body intercepting light, i.e., a projection, and (3) a portrait, in contrast to the original.

18. See Michael Lieb's provocative discussion of Milton's position within debates concerning divine passibility, "Reading God." Lieb coins the term *theopatheia* to connote Milton's conception of an intensification of divine passibility. He goes on to suggest that "the Son is a primary vehicle for the expression of *theopatheia*" (p. 234). As I argue below, I read the Celestial Dialogue in book 3 as temporarily having the reverse effect, evacuating the Son of any human emotions and forging an empathic connection between the Father and the poem's human readership.

19. Kenneth Borris shows how Satan's flight through the Cosmos on his way to Earth at the end of book 2 functions as an allegory, not only in its local context but also as a structural element of the poem generally. See "Allegory in *Paradise Lost*." This allegorical network frames the problem of a fallen epistemology through the recurring topos of controlled and uncontrolled flight, like the instance I have described here. Borris's view that this overriding allegory functions as a commentary on the limits of representation corresponds to my understanding of Milton's accommodative mode. Yet, whereas Borris focuses on limits, I wish to enlarge our understanding of the possibilities described by this accommodative mode.

20. Fragment 114, in Kahn, *The Art and Thought of Heraclitus*. Kahn reads the variety of meanings available in the symmetrical Greek somewhat differently, suggesting three possible interpretations: first, "man's own character, not some external power . . . assigns to him the quality of his life, his fortune for good of for ill"; second, the character of a man is "identified with the corresponding [constitutive] element [that makes up the cosmos] . . . [serving as] the physical explanation or psychophysical identity of the particular life in question, the elemental equivalent of a given moral or intellectual character"; third, for "select souls . . . it is the character of the man that determines his fate as *daimon*, as occupant or visitor in the highest region of mortality, the celestial terminus of the upward path" (p. 261). Heraclitus was also the author of "the earliest extant statement of systematic monism," εν παντα ειναι, "all things are one" (fragment 36, as interpreted by Kahn, ibid., p. 131). Thus, his state-

ment on man's divine ethos seems especially appropriate for characterizing the views of his fellow monist, John Milton.

21. As Kathleen Swaim has shown, accommodation is at once a closing and an opening, a builder of reader confidence and a provocation of inquiry. See "The Mimesis of Accommodation."

22. MacCallum, "Milton and the Figurative Interpretation," pp. 397–415. Any kind of theodicy, poetic or otherwise, would have been inconceivable to Milton had he not held this latter view, which rested on a deep-seated faith in the capacities (albeit limited) of human reason. As John Rumrich has pointed out, in this regard, at least, Milton's sympathies were more with Christian humanism than with reformed Christianity. See *Milton Unbound*, pp. 10–12. For a compelling analysis of Milton's defense of reason as parallel to Erasmus's opposition to Lutheran determinism, see Danielson, *Milton's Good God*, chapter 3.

23. This retention of images may also account for Milton's ambivalent iconoclasm. See Lana Cable's penetrating analysis in *Carnal Rhetoric*. I shall return to my own reading of these oft-noted parallels in the next chapter.

24. Benin, *The Footprints of God*, p. 134.

25. BT Shabbat 88b.

26. The Babylonian Talmud records R. Ishmael's interpretation a second time, in Tractate Sanhedrin 34a, but with several variations. First, instead of *nitchaleq* the verb formed used is *mitchaleq* (the difference being between the standard reflexive form used in Sanhedrin and a conflation of the passive and reflexive forms in Shabbat). Second, R. Ishmael concludes that the biblical image is there to teach that "each verse can be used for several purposes."

27. Medieval commentators on the Talmud were greatly troubled by R. Ishmael's strange interpretation. Rashi tries (counterfactually?) to insist that even in R. Ishmael's analogy of the analogy, the stone is broken by the hammer. He actually changes the verb form to *mitchaleq*, and reads the statement as "Just as the hammer shatters the stone into many splinters." The writers of the Tosafot, a commentary of several generations after Rashi, were aware of this misreading and struggled to make sense of it in a variety of inventive ways.

28. Seventy is a standard rabbinic figure for a number without real limits. A comparable rabbinic statement avers that there are seventy faces to the Torah.

29. Handelman, *The Slayers of Moses*, p. 204. I am not the first to puzzle over this analogy of the hammer and the stone. Susan Handelman and David Stern have debated the implications of this difficult passage, and Handelman has concluded, "The ambiguous relation of interpreter and text, hammer and rock, Rabbi and Scripture are all described here." Stern and Handelman, "Controversy," p. 90. Stern

insists that modern Hebrew grammar and rabbinic grammar are not equivalent and that any attempt (Handelman's or mine) to locate a complication in R. Ishmael's use of a reflexive verb form for the hammer is an anachronism. Stern does recognize a radical revision of the biblical verse in R. Ishmael's interpretation, whose "sole concern appears to be to provide a visual equivalent to the idea that a verse can have more than a single sense, though the image they provide actually emphasizes the durability and permanence of Scripture in comparison to the evanescence of the spark-like interpretations." But he seeks to diminish the possibility that there may be any covert reference to the midrashic method as that which achieves this splintering or sparking. (David Stern, "Controversy: Fragments of the Rock: Contemporary Literary Theory and the Study of Rabbinic Texts," *Prooftexts* 5 [1985] 102, n. 1.) Stern's reading of the talmudic lemma (and its scriptural occasion) seeks closure and total interpretive clarity. Yet whether multiplicity is a result of the Bible's own heteroglossia or a function of the midrashic hermeneutic's tendency to resist full closure as it continues to clash with Scripture, it seems to me that R. Ishmael's statement is *precisely* about the refusal of full resolution.

30. See Stocker's fine essay, "God in Theory," pp. 70–88; and Jasper, *The Study of Literature and Religion*, chapter 3, for extended discussions of the relation between language and theology.

31. Gardner, *A Reading of "Paradise Lost"*. Dennis Danielson has shown the specific operations of God's speech, and how it draws on Milton's Arminianism, in his *Milton's Good God*, especially chapters 3 and 5.

32. See, for instance, Samuel, "The Dialogue in Heaven"; and Low, "Milton's God."

33. Fish, *Surprised by Sin*, p. 75. The interpretive tactics I see Milton's poem endorsing are not only about discovering our own fallenness—being surprised by it—over and over again. Rather, I wish to argue for a more embattled reciprocal relationship between the reader and the text.

34. Empson's remark in his *Milton's God*, that "God is much at his worst here, in his first appearance" (p. 120) is still as provocative as ever.

35. Peter, *A Critique of "Paradise Lost,"* p. 12. Peter goes on to take Milton to task for combining in the Father the functions of legislator, judge, prosecutor, and legal apologist simultaneously, apparently forgetting that these were *precisely* the functions that God fulfilled for Milton and many of his contemporaries! The "heterogeneous complex of ingredients, part man, part spirit, part attested biblical Presence, and part dogma" (p. 15) for which Peter criticizes Milton very nearly captures the kind of rhetorical heterogeneity that I wish to interrogate in the epic. The most thorough and convincing response to these readings from a historical and theological stand-

point remains Danielson in his *Milton's Good God*. As convincing as Danielson's rejoinder may be from a strictly doctrinal perspective, it nevertheless fails to account for the persistently unsettling tonality of God's presentation in Milton's epic (to which Peter, in *A Critique of "Paradise Lost,"* and Empson, in *Milton's God*, were both responding in their discussions of the poem). My analysis seeks to restore a kind of debate and struggle that Danielson's argument tends to foreclose.

36. Michael Lieb has offered a similar argument in "The Dialogic Imagination" in his *The Sinews of Ulysses*, pp. 76–97.

37. See Danielson, *Milton's Good God*, p. 162, for example.

38. The *tanur shel akhnai* was an oven with a peculiar construction placing it in an ambiguous position relative to the ground and its surrounding environment.

39. BT Bava Metziah 59b. This rabbinic legend has been the subject of many recent analyses, including Handelman, *Slayers of Moses*, pp. 37–50; and Boyarin, *Intertextuality and the Reading of Midrash*, pp. 33–36.

40. See Stern, "Midrash and Indeterminacy," pp. 153–55, for an important corrective to the attempts by some critics to equate rabbinic interpretation with twentieth-century poststructuralism.

41. Boyarin, *Carnal Israel*, p. 28.

42. A sociology of Milton studies over the past half-century or so might place this approach within the frame of the diverse and shifting cultural backgrounds of successive generations of Milton scholars. One might speculate that, given the tendency to which I alluded at the beginning of this chapter of aligning the Son with Christianity's emphasis on mercy and the Father with Judaism's demand for law and justice, this way of reading the Celestial Dialogue manifests a latent Christian triumphalism. I leave such speculations to others for the time being. For a suggestive beginning to this kind of analysis, see Fish, "Transmuting the Lump."

43. Both statements are quoted from Peter, *A Critique of "Paradise Lost,",* p. 12.

44. Kathleen Swaim has observed a different kind of double accommodation in her article, "The Mimesis of Accommodation": "The double-natured Son is by merit and by birthright the Son of God; he is the agency both through which God enters into form and matter and through which these are transcended in the reunion with God. By birthright he fulfills God's creative purpose mediating downward from God to angels or men; by merit he will fulfill God's redemptive or transcendent purpose mediating upward from men or angels to God. These roles coincide with the double thrust of accommodation." (p. 466)

45. Georgia B. Christopher has suggested that the uneven development of God's character "measures the jagged course of the narrator's religious experience, which

goes from deep rebellion and hatred through clarity, understanding, admiration, and finally to familial love and intimacy. Each stage in the narrator's experiential journey is marked by a change in God's tone." See *Milton and the Science of the Saints*, p. 116.

46. This is Hughes's position in "The Filiations of Milton's Celestial Dialogue."

47. In her essay on Milton's first antiprelatical tract, *Of Reformation*, Janel Mueller argues that Milton's divergence from the tradition begun with Foxe's *Book of Martyrs* of celebrating Constantine as the prototype for all Christian monarchs is part of a larger apocalyptic project that reaffirms human agency and its crucial role in further religious reform. See "Embodying Glory," p. 24.

48. Taking up a related matter, John S. Tanner, in *Anxiety in Eden*, offers a useful discussion of Milton's (and Kierkegaard's) position regarding the origin in terms of the Pelagian-Augustinian controversy. He concludes that *Paradise Lost* allows that "neither the communal determinism of Augustinian inheritance nor the individual freedom of Pelagian imitation completely cancel the other out" (p. 60).

49. Nagel *The View from Nowhere*, pp. 117–18.

50. Ibid., p. 127.

51. For an illuminating discussion of the problems of agency as they grow out of the question of the unity of the subject, see Korsgaard, "Personal Identity and the Unity of Agency."

52. A further irony embedded at this moment may be found in the poem's recourse to a Dantean *allegoresis* at the same time that the veil—a standard trope for allegory—has been lifted from the eyes of Adam and Eve.

53. There is a long tradition in Milton studies of regarding Eve's speech as crucial to humanity's rehabilitation. See, for instance, E. M. W. Tillyard, "The Crisis of *Paradise Lost*," in his *Studies in Milton*, p. 43; Stein, *Answerable Style*, p. 118; Fish, *Surprised by Sin*, p. 273; Canfield, "Blessed Are the Merciful," pp. 42 and 45; and Yu, "Life in the Garden," p. 271. Elizabeth Sauer has also identified Eve's role in the restoration of human-divine dialogue. See *Barbarous Dissonance*, pp. 125–26. Joseph H. Summers has discussed Eve's typological mirroring of Christ's self-sacrifice in *The Muses Method*, pp. 177–78 and 183. Against this common view, Georgia Christopher has asserted that Adam's recovery in book 10 is accomplished by a metonymic invocation of the crucifixion. See her *Milton and the Science of the Saints*, pp. 163–64. While I am more sympathetic to the view held by the majority of scholars listed here, I think Christopher's reassertion of Christ's self-sacrifice is well worth considering. My own reading seeks to restore some elements of Eve's speech that tend to disappear when it is read entirely in relation to the crucifixion, typologically or otherwise.

54. See Alexander Altmann's essay, "The Gnostic Background," which argues it was under Gnostic influence that the rabbis conceived of the primordial man as a being

almost divine in character. These same Gnostic legends serve as the source for a number of later Christian representations of satanic opposition to mankind that, in turn, clearly exercised some influence on Milton's thinking in his construction of the revolt of the angels under Satan's leadership. Even if we assume the most stringent criteria for determining any possible rabbinic influence on Milton's thinking, therefore, we have indirectly chanced upon one possible historical explanation for some of the similarities between Milton and the rabbis. But this structural parallel obtains far greater interest in light of the common approach to theomachy in midrash and in Milton's poem. The plural verb form ascribed to God in Genesis 1:26 becomes a crucial site for Jewish-Christian disputes, when most Jewish exegetes work very hard to prove that "Let *us* make man" must not be construed as evidence for the Trinity or any other pluralized notion of the Godhead.

55. Stern, "*Imitatio Hominis,*" p. 168.

56. Stern, *Parables in Midrash,* p. 16.

57. Boyarin and Stern, "An Exchange on the Mashal," p. 272.

58. Hayman, "The Fall, Free Will," p. 19.

4. Imagining Desire: Divine and Human Creativity

1. Pirke Avot (Ethics of the Fathers) 1:1. The citation appears at the beginning an elaborate genealogy of rabbinic heritage; the 120-member Great Knesset, or Assembly, is the mythic first organization of rabbinic Judaism.

2. Schwartz, *Remembering and Repeating,* p. 49.

3. Claus Westermann, "Biblical Reflection on Creator-Creation," in Bernhard W. Anderson, ed., *Creation in the Old Testament* (Philadelphia: Fortress Press, 1984), 98.

4. Milton, *De Doctrina Christiana,* 1.vii, YP 6:305–6. Milton was probably familiar with Paul Fagius's statement in his *Exegesis Sive Expositio Dictionum Hebraica* where he gives two alternative definitions for the Hebrew *bara*: "Aliquid ex nihilo creare et ubi non ex puro nihilo, sed ex praejacente materia novum aliquid, eximium, egregium, praeclarum, magnificum, singulari Deo virtute & potentia factum, in lucem profertur." (To create something out of nothing and where it is not from pure nothingness, but rather something new from preexistent material, it is made by the distinguished, eminent, splendid, magnificent, and singular strength and power of God, and brought forth into light.)

It is noteworthy that the definition of *bara* is one of the very rare occasions in which Milton explicitly disagrees with Fagius, whom he cites as an authority on matters of theology and divorce. My analysis of Milton's poetic expectations assumes that this disagreement owes as much to the poet's understanding of literary creativity as it does to any specifically theological doctrines he holds.

5. Guillory, *Poetic Authority*, pp. 118–19. See also Adelman, "Creation and the Place," p. 54, for a similar analysis of the satanic implications of this version of Milton creativity.

6. Wittreich, *Visionary Poetics*, p. 31. See also Kerrigan, *The Prophetic Milton*.

7. Burke, *The Rhetoric of Religion*, p. 203.

8. Gallagher, "Creation in Genesis," p. 197.

9. Fishbane, *Biblical Interpretation in Ancient Israel*. See J. B. Soloveitchik's moving essay, "The Lonely Man of Faith," which stands as a particularly eloquent modern version of this sensitivity to the differences in Genesis 1 and 2. Soloveitchik explicitly rejects the documentary hypothesis in favor of a comprehensive (and subtle) unity in the biblical text. The Adam of Genesis 1 represents the conflict of humanity's desire for mastery of a universe from which it is largely alienated. The Adam of Genesis 2 is made aware of this alienation as a loss that may be remedied only through devotion to a larger, divine power in the form of covenant.

10. Low, "Milton's God," pp. 28–9.

11. Fish, *Surprised by Sin*, pp. 148 and 151.

12. The *OED* offers no earlier example of this word's use.

13. Rumrich, *Matter of Glory*, p. 3. For further meditations on the political implications of this reading of chaos and matter, see Rumrich's second book, *Milton Unbound*, especially chapter 6.

14. Rogers, *The Matter of Revolution*, pp. 115–16. Rogers associates this ambivalence regarding female generative power with the seventeenth-century controversy over vitalism and animist materialism, the most articulate elaboration of which may be found in Jean Baptise van Helmont's treatise, *Ortus Medicinae* (1648).

15. See Rogers, *The Matter of Revolution*, chapter 4, and Rumrich, *Milton Unbound*, chapter 5.

16. Rumrich, *Milton Unbound*, p. 102.

17. As Jason Rosenblatt has shown, while the dualism of metaphor and typology eventually come to dominate the poem's representational mode in the last books, the middle books of the epic are distinctively, even defiantly, monist in outlook. See his *Torah and Law*, chapters 2 and 3.

18. Members of the Milton-as-misogynist camp include Landy, "Kinship and the Role of Women"; Gilbert, "Patriarchal Poetry and Women Readers"; and Froula, "When Eve Reads Milton," pp. 321–47. The Milton-as-proto-feminist camp has produced an even wider range of spirited responses, including Lewalski, "Milton

and Women"; Webber, "The Politics of Poetry"; McColley, *Milton's Eve*; and Wittreich, *Feminist Milton*.

19. In her groundbreaking work on Eve's creation, Mary Nyquist has highlighted the central problem of source text (biblical and nonbiblical) for each of the three accounts. See "The Genesis of Gendered Subjectivity in the Divorce Tracts and in *Paradise Lost*," Nyquist and Ferguson, *Re-Membering Milton*, pp. 99–127. This essay is a condensed and revised version of Nyquist's "Gynesis, Genesis, Exegesis."

20. The best account of Milton's use of Ovid is DuRocher, *Milton and Ovid*. In describing his own version of this source text subordination, DuRocher writes, "Classical matter has its place in *Paradise Lost* when it points to a spiritual correlative that makes it true" (p. 83).

21. Heather James has provided a fascinating analysis of the mirroring that occurs between the biblical epic Adam and the classical romance Eve. James argues that "Eve becomes the narcissistic reflection of Adam. . . . God thus leads Eve out of the pagan discourse of narcissism to the threshold of the Biblical discourse of marriage which fulfills the Ovidian poetics." See her "Milton's Eve."

22. See especially Rosenblatt, *Torah and Law*, chapter 2. Fresch, in "The Hebraic Influence," pp. 181–99, writes of the "humanizing effect" that stems from the "psychological bond between man and woman [which is] seldom to be found in the remarks of any Christian theologians" (pp. 182 and 189). Fresch and others who have written on this matter tend to view Hebraic influence as something monolithic and static rather than diverse and fluid. Even more problematic for Fresch's own essay, though her analysis is meant to discuss Eve's creation, her remarks focus *exclusively* on Adam's account of this creation in book 8, without any reference to the first version of this creation in book 4.

23. Turner, *One Flesh*.

24. Given the Bible's ubiquitous concern with male lineage and inheritance, it is of more than passing significance that the task of naming the child often falls to the mother (or surrogate mother, in the cases of Rachel and Leah and the children of their respective maidservants).

25. Pardes, *Countertraditions*, pp. 44–48.

26. Pardes suggests that many of the "countertraditions" that she has recovered in her analysis of the Hebrew Bible are in fact traces of matriarchal polytheistic societies rejected by the innovation of Hebraic patriarchal monotheism: "Eve's naming-speech may be perceived as a trace from an earlier mythological phase in which mother goddesses were very much involved in the process of creation" (45).

27. Pardes, *Countertraditions*, p. 56.

28. Adelman, "Creation and the Place of the Poet," p. 64. Rumrich, citing Kerrigan's *The Sacred Complex*, describes Milton's sense of his blindness as a castration that makes him female and hence capable of being impregnated by inspiration to produce the poem. See Rumrich, *Milton Unbound*, pp. 100–1. Kerrigan and Rumrich both offer psychoanalytic models to account for Milton's creative impulses, suggesting that Milton's writings are charged with the anxieties that stem from his relations to his father (Kerrigan) or his mother (Rumrich).

29. John Shawcross, in "The Metaphor of Inspiration," has written persuasively about the sexual connotations implicit in the metaphor of inspiration. Shawcross has recognized the crossing of gender roles in this model of sexual intercourse, but sees it as producing anxiety about poetic incompletion, and not the process of anxiety and creativity itself: "The creational relationship between the Spirit of God (as male force but presented as female inspirer) and the poet (as female factor but presented in terms of dream psychology as male) [convey] . . . anxiety . . . for the poet himself, lest he not be inspired further by the Spirit" (81).

30. Adelman, "Creation and the Place of the Poet," p. 55. See also Kerrigan, *The Prophetic Milton*, which argues that the poem that issues forth from the invocations is itself "the divine spectacle . . . between the prophet and his source of inspiration. We watch the inspiring" (141).

31. John Guillory, in *Poetic Authority*, writes of these lines that "the subject has disappeared altogether . . . and Milton no longer needs to specify what mind is feeding upon what thoughts. Merely to have hesitated at this crossing . . . permits the influx of power that turns the invocation around" (p. 126). Guillory's reading of this enjambment as the key moment of transition in the invocation is a suggestive one, but I am inclined to read it as a resistance to resolution rather than as an initiation of closure.

32. Flinker, "Courting Urania," p. 86.

33. Ibid., p. 97.

34. Michael Fishbane has described the Elohist (and later, Priestly) elimination of the panerotic and pandivine ontology inherent in the worship of prebiblical Mesopotamian mother goddesses. See "Israel and the 'Mothers,'" *The Garments of Torah*, pp. 49–63.

35. See Quilligan, *Milton's Spenser*, pp. 219ff, for a consideration of the rejection of this form of sexuality in light of Milton's "fit audience. . . though few." In her "Milton's Eve," Heather James shows how Milton, in his prose tracts as well as in his poetry, exploited the reputation of the romance genre generally and Ovidian poetics in particular "for excessive narrative pleasure" (p. 121). Patricia Parker describes the associations made during the early modern period between the digressiveness of the

romance genre and the supposed garrulity and irrationality of women and the seductive power of female desire. See *Literary Fat Ladies*, pp. 10–11.

36. Virginia Woolf's characteristically mysterious pronouncement on Milton in *A Room of One's Own*, that he had "a dash too much of the male in [him]," comes to mind. "Too much of the male" seems to refer to the subordination of the "suggestive power" (Woolf's own term) of the classics to the "self-assertive virility" (again, Woolf's words) of the Bible. See *A Room of One's Own*, pp. 102–3.

37. For an importance analysis of the poem's various instances of self-authorship in light of the science and politics of Milton's age, see Rogers, *The Matter of Revolution*, chapter 4. Rogers sees the ambivalent treatment of this theme as a sign of Milton's own ambivalences regarding the proper mode of government, especially in the wake of the failed revolution and Restoration.

38. Jacques Lacan has suggested, "by clinging to the reference-point of him who looks at him in a mirror, the subject sees appearing, not his ego ideal, but his ideal ego, that point at which he desires to gratify himself in himself." *Four Fundamental Concepts of Psycho-Analysis*, p. 257.

39. Jason Rosenblatt has shown that the lyric epithalamium at 4.748–65 draws on pagan (Ovid, *Metamorphoses* 1.468), Hebraic (Gen. 1:28), and Christian (Eph. 5:31–2, Heb. 13:4) sources. See *Torah and Law*, p. 135.

40. See Claus Westermann's comments on this phrase in *Genesis: A Practical Commentary*, trans. David E. Green (Grand Rapids: Eerdman's, 1987), pp. 18–19. Although Harold Bloom insists that this monism originates with J—it is, he thinks, one of "her" greatest innovations—Michael Fishbane's comparison of Elohim and the mother goddesses suggests that this monism was actually characteristic of most Middle Eastern cults that presumed a divine immanence. Compare Bloom, *The Book of J*, p. 176, with Fishbane, "Israel and the 'Mothers,'" pp. 50–51.

41. In his useful study, Gary Anderson demonstrates that Jubilees' depiction of prelapsarian sex specifically occurs *before* Adam and Eve are brought into the Garden of Eden. Adam and Eve had to wait forty and eighty days respectively before they could enter the Garden. These number reflect the Levitical procedure for purification following childbirth; they suggest that despite its assertion of sexuality before the expulsion from Eden, the book of Jubilees nevertheless understood sex to be impure and corrupting. See Anderson, "The Garden of Eden."

42. Boyarin, *Carnal Israel*, p. 57.

43. Golda Werman's discussion of Genesis Rabbah 9:7 makes the common mistake of dehistoricizing the midrash, reading it as emblematic of the rabbinic viewpoint at all times and in all places. See Werman, *Milton and Midrash*, pp. 143–44. Given this view of rabbinic writing—not unique to Werman—it is easy understand the temp-

tation to characterize many of Milton's deviations from normative Protestant thinking as "Hebraic."

44. With the exception of the verb forms in the creation account and the noun
forms in the story of the flood, words built out of the *y, tz, r* stem are almost nonexistent in the Pentateuch. They occur most frequently in the prophets, especially
Isaiah, where they usually describe some notion of imagination or desire rather than
creation.

45. There is some discussion among medieval exegetes concerning the meaning of
ph'qidah. Rashi suggests that it is the moment when an angel identifies a drop of se-
men to be brought before God in order to determine what kind of life will be produced from it. He cites a passage from Babylonian Tractate Niddah 16b that names
this angel *Laylah* (also the Hebrew word for night): "He raises the drop [of sperm],
brings it before the Holy One Blessed be He, and says, 'Master of the Universe,
what will become of this drop? Will it be strong or weak, wise or stupid, rich or
poor?' He does not ask whether it will be wicked or good, as R. Haninah has said,
'Everything is in Heaven's hands, with the exception of the fear of Heaven.'" This
moment is distinct from formation [*yetzirah*], which marks the development of the
bones, sinews, and flesh, and gives the fetus an identifiably human shape. For brevi-
ty's sake, I have referred to this moment as conception, although the rabbinic understanding of sexual reproduction and ontogeny was certainly not as detailed as our
own.

46. Sir Ronald Syme, in his *Emperors and Biography*, devotes his entire fifth chapter to
the *"Nomen Antinonorum,"* describing the great political and cultural capital it commanded, the frequency and inaccuracy of its use, and hence its unreliability for establishing chronology. Modern scholars have generally agreed that the "Antoninus"
of the rabbinic stories is Caracalla, who visited Palestine in 199 and 215 *c.e.* See Strack
and Stemberger, *Introduction to the Talmud and Midrash*, p. 89. H. Freedman cites several
other less likely possibilities, including Marcus Aurelius and Severus Alexander, although the latter would require that the conversations be between Severus and R. Judah II, Rabbi's grandson. See *Midrash Rabbah*, ed. Freedman, 2:611, n. 2.

47. Luitpold Wallach's extensive discussion of these encounters, "The Colloquy of
Marcus Aurelius," is surprisingly unaware of the biblical precedents of Joseph,
Mordechai, and Daniel, three Israelite figures who play precisely this role of adviser
to a pagan king. He writes that the motif of the non-Jewish king who asks questions
of a Jewish sage "cannot be looked upon as essentially Jewish; it is rather typical of
Hellenistic literature" (261). Based on this erroneous assumption, along with several
other assertions concerning the parallels between these colloquies and the issues
raised in Stoic literature, Wallach concludes that the author of this portion of the

midrash, "in all probability a Hellenistic Jew capable of reading both Poseidonius and Marcus Aurelius, must have been stimulated by the record of the latter" (281). Wallach's far too rigid distinction between Hellenism and Hebraism is an example of precisely the kind of dichotomy that has led so many Milton scholars to jump to conclusions regarding competing Hebraic, Christian, and Hellenistic influences.

48. Jill Robbins discusses some of the hermeneutic implications of this fraught encounter in her fascinating *Prodigal Son/Elder Brother*. This dialogue's position at a transitional moment is also evidenced by the inconsistency between the two conclusions reached: though the soul must be created simultaneous with conception (a distinctively monist ontology), the evil inclination is not placed within an individual until birth (a more dualist anthropology).

49. Ephraim E. Urbach, in his influential *The Sages*, notes that "the dualist anthropological view was prevalent at the end of the Second-Temple epoch, before the time of R. Judah the Patriarch" (223). Urbach goes on to downplay the full extent of this rabbinic dualism, suggesting that "even those Sages who maintained the dualism 'body-soul' did not draw extremist inferences from it. Fundamentally, Talmud Judaism retained . . . the concept of the unity of body and soul" (250). While Urbach may be correct to see rabbinic dualism as less extreme than strict Platonism—and its heir, Pauline Christianity—I think he does not take sufficient note of the degree to which the rabbis altered their dualist views in response to the advent of a politically empowered Christianity.

50. Daniel Boyarin has argued that Paul's dualism, though it does favor the spirit above the flesh, does not completely denigrate the body since it its only through Christ's incarnation that redemption is achieved. Christ's body nevertheless does not partake of all aspects of the flesh, especially sexuality. See *A Radical Jew*, 59ff. Most of the early Church fathers, however, did not follow this nuanced dualism, adopting instead a more severe version.

51. BT Sanhedrin 91b. David Winston has recently argued that the distinction between rabbinic monism and Hellenic dualism is not as clear as has been suggested by Boyarin and others. Indeed, Winston perceives a correlation between the rabbinic body-soul synergy and Platonic conceptions of the daemon, particularly as detailed in the writing of Philo. See Winston, "Philo and the Rabbis." Though Winston's cavils deserve further consideration, I do not think they completely elide the differences between the rabbis, for whom the body is often depicted as open and grotesque, and the Platonists, for whom the body is idealized as closed and inviolate.

52. There is no fail-safe method for determining which of two alternative versions of the same rabbinic legend is the older one. The fact that this second version appears in the Babylonian Talmud, which was redacted at the end of the fifth and be-

ginning of the sixth century, a century after the redaction of Genesis Rabbah, would seem to support my conclusion. As I have suggested, however, I think that the nature of the changes is more compelling evidence than the location of the two versions.

53. Based upon a play on the words *chitah* (wheat) and *chet* (sin).

54. This is perhaps the oldest opinion, based largely upon the mythological idea that wine was the drink of the gods and hence forbidden to humanity.

55. Based upon yet another play on words, the etrog being derived from *ragag* (he desired).

56. See Yonah Frankel's discussion of this parable, *Darkhei ha-Aggadah*, pp. 342–45. As I have indicated in the previous chapter, David Stern's analysis of the parable of the king portrays this exegetical form as an important textual residue of rabbinic Judaism's encounter with Greek and Roman political authorities. See his *Parables in Midrash*. Even if the specific story of the prince's self-corruption is not Greek in origin, the use of the *mashal le-melekh* nevertheless marks this interpretive moment as one informed by the encounter between Hebraism and Hellenism. I was delighted to discover that in some of his most recent work David Stern has arrived at conclusions very similar to my own. In an essay published as part of a two-part special issue of *Poetics Today* devoted to "Hellenism and Hebraism Reconsidered: The Poetics of Cultural Exchange," Stern discusses the influence of the Greco-Roman romance narrative on rabbinic literature. Coining the term "deep Hellenization," Stern identifies the rabbinic erotic narrative as "a kind of myth or foundational story that helped explain [the Rabbis'] place in the pagan world and their uneasy relationship to that world; indeed, in its transformed shape, this narrative became for the Rabbis one through which they represented their understanding of cultural influence itself." See Stern's fascinating discussion of how the rabbinic opposition to Hellenization was often articulated via an assimilation of precisely that culture in his "The Captive Woman," pp. 91–127.

57. See Ginzburg, *Legends of the Jews*, 5:97, n. 70.

58. Milton, "Of Education." YP 2:366–67. Jason Rosenblatt has reminded me of a Christian version of this restoration in the belief that the Cross (the instrument of salvation) was made from the wood of the Tree of Knowledge (the vehicle of corruption).

59. J. L. Sharpe, "Prolegomena to the Establishment of the Critical Text of the Greek Apocalypse of Moses," Ph.D. diss., Duke University, 1969, part 1, p. 226. Cited in M. D. Johnson, "Introduction" to "Life of Adam and Eve," Charlesworth, *The Old Testament Pseudepigrapha*, 2:252.

60. The Latin text, chapters 12–17, also offers one of the earliest accounts of Satan's

rebellion and subsequent expulsion from Heaven. Some Milton scholars have offered the *Vita* as a source for many of the narrative details in *Paradise Lost*.

61. The narrative had earlier described how Adam and Eve had each been allotted portions (or domains) of plants and trees.

62. Johnson, "Life of Adam and Eve," Charlesworth, *The Old Testament Pseudepigrapha*, 2:281, emphasis added.

63. Virginia R. Mollenkott suggested almost twenty years ago that the Apocryphal texts (which she distinguishes from the Pseudepigrapha, of which the Apocalypse of Moses is a part), should be given greater attention as possible analogs to Milton's writings for their "union of Greek and Hebrew thought." Her own analysis, however, persists in the dichotomies that I am seeking to break down: "Milton is more careful than many Renaissance Christian humanists to distinguish between Hellenism and Hebraism, knowledge and wisdom/virtue, reason and faith." See "The Pervasive Influence of the Apocrypha," pp. 27 and 35–36.

64. See Nyquist, "Gynesis, Genesis, Exegesis," pp. 147–208, for a fascinating argument that ultimately identifies this voice as a secondary or derivative one issuing from heaven, equivalent to the Hebrew *bat qol*, literally translated as "daughter of the voice."

65. Alistair Fowler, ed., *Paradise Lost* (London: Longman, 1971), 4.474–75, p. 222, note.

66. Leonard, *Naming in Paradise*, pp. 38–39 and 43.

67. Gerard, *The Herball*, pp. 1331–32.

68. Svendsen, *Milton and Science*, 31–32. Henry Todd's expansive annotations on Milton's poem include a charming quotation from one of his own acquaintances, "a learned and ingenious Traveller, well-known to the literary world, Eyles Irwin, Esq.":

> A more poetical or just description of the *Bhur* or *Banian* tree cannot be imagined, than what had come from the pencil of the sublime bard. But, from the Portuguese name of this tree, he would seem to have been led into a mistake, and to confound it with the plantain, which, in all probability, from the magnitude and flexibility of its leaves, was applied by our first parents to the same purpose, as the Puliar cast now use it on the coast of *Malabar*. From the fruit, which resembles a fig in appearance, though not eatable, the first discoverers of India called the tree the *Figo*; as the service to which it is usually consecrated, induced the English to give it the appellation of *Banian*, or *sacred*. Its leaves are the smallest of the forest-kind, and not *broad as Amazonian targe*. While it becomes the duty of a traveller to correct the de-

scriptive passages of poetry, the true lovers of the divine art will agree with
him, that it would have been an irreparable loss to ther world, if the fancy of
Milton in the picture of the *Bhur*, had been restrained by the local knowledge
of his annotator.

Cited in Todd, *The Poetical Works of John Milton*, 5:106–7. The coda to Irwin's botanical
observation offers salutary advice to Milton's future readers. The analysis that follows seeks to uncover some of the less explicit ways in which the "fancy of Milton"
might have been "restrained"—*guided* may be a more appropriate term—by his own
literary and cultural milieu.

69. In his monumental collection, Louis Ginzberg writes that among the Church fa-
thers only Tertullian appears to have suggested the fig tree, cf. *Adversus Marcionem*, 2.2.
See Ginzburg, *Legends of the Jews*, 5:97, n. 70. Despite its wealth of erudition,
Ginzburg's collection is often too synthetic in its representation of rabbinic lore.
Since Ginzburg was also very often the source for many early critics interested in
Milton's Hebraisms, their failure to discern differing and evolving strains in rabbinic
Judaism probably originated at least partly in his work. Ginzburg was either unaware
of or uninterested in the non-Patristic Christian tradition of identifying the fig tree
as the Tree of Knowledge. As we have already seen, Bar Kepha was not the originator
of this identification, either. It is very likely he discovered it in the Apocalypse of
Moses (see my discussion of this version above). Between Bar Kepha and Becanus,
Peter Abelard (*Expositio in Genesim*) and Gregorius Barhebraeus (*Scholia on the Old Testament*) also identified the Tree of Knowledge as a fig tree. See Corcoran, *Milton's Paradise*, p. 24, n. 28.

70. Ralegh, *The History of the World*, pp. 138–39. The Amazonian shield cited from
Pliny also finds its way into Milton's passage.

71. Corcoran identifies the apple as the most popular choice among English writers,
citing Cornelius a Lapide who, in his *Commentaria in Pentateuchum Mosis*, claimed this
choice originated in the mistranslation of the generic term *malum*. See her *Milton's
Paradise*, p. 24, n. 28.

72. Patrides, "The Tree of Knowledge."

73. Fowler, *Paradise Lost*, p. 502, note.

74. Svendsen, *Milton and Science*, p. 135.

75. Guillory, "From the Superfluous," pp. 76–77.

76. Ibid. See also Sauer, *Barbarous Dissonance*, who writes that this passage functions
to import "the language of corruption and shame from the feminized East and the
New World" (pp. 122–23). For an extended discussion of the colonial aspects of this
and other passages, see Evans, *Milton's Imperial Epic*, especially chapter 4.

77. See, for example, Coffin, "Creation and the Self," pp. 4–5.

78. Ovid, *Metamorphoses*, 1.76–86. All subsequent quotations will be followed by line numbers in the body of the text.

79. Paul Ricoeur's remarkable discussion of the Hebraic imagination has contributed significantly to my understanding of some of the differences between a classical and biblical view of law and sin. See *The Symbolism of Evil*, pp. 250–51.

80. Hartman, "Adam on the Grass with Balsamum."

81. The midrash cites this verse in its conclusion to R. Samuel's homily, immediately following the passage I have quoted.

82. Another way of making this claim would be to put it in terms of Stanley Fish's fallen reader. Adam's prelude to his own story gives the reader grounds for expecting the ensuing narrative to bear greater similarity to his or her own experience than it actually does. The dynamics of instruction to which Fish has pointed operate as follows: with every interpretive decision the fallen reader, who will necessarily opt for the wrong choice, is reminded that the poem offers a nonfallen alternative. The didactics of book 8, in my view, offer a different model, in which Adam serves as the reader's surrogate, trying out forms of interpretation until he gets to one that works, i.e., until God grants his request for a mate.

83. I refer, of course, to the end of *Lycidas*: "Henceforth, thou art the Genius of the shore, / In thy large recompense, and shalt be good / To all that wander in that perilous flood."

84. Adelman, "Creation and the Place of the Poet," p. 59.

5. "So Shall the World Go On": Martyrdom, Interpretation, and History

1. Pecheux, "Abraham, Adam, and the Theme of Exile," pp. 365–66.

2. Broadbent calls the verse of these books "arthritic," in *Some Graver Subject*, p. 279. Martz defends the pessimistic vision of the final books as a means of preventing Adam from too easily accepting sin and death in *The Paradise Within*, p. 150. Fish regards the final books as the poem in miniature, "without the irregular movement and exquisite shading," in *Surprised by Sin*, p. 292. Entzminger has defended the final books for their depiction of the internalization of history in Adam, in "Michael's Options," pp. 197–98.

In a later essay, Stanley Fish argues that Lewis's condemnation of the last two books of *Paradise Lost* is an element of his *defense* of the poem against accusations of abstraction by F. R. Leavis and unacceptable religious views by T. S. Eliot. Fish goes on to show how responses to books 11 and 12 since Lewis reflect some of the prime shifts in literary critical discourse over the last forty years. See "Transmuting the Lump."

3. Lewis, *A Preface*, pp. 125–26.

4. In his innovative reading of Jesus's parable of the talents, Leslie Brisman has argued that Matthew's version (25:14–30) contains within it the possibility that God's most vocal condemnation is reserved for his most beloved suffering (third) servant, his chosen one(s), he who endures the wrath of his harsh taskmaster:

> Matthew's third servant . . . increases the I-thou contact with his lord, acknowledging the lord's threatening rather than promising aspect, but acknowledging also in the grammatically and epistemologically imperfect *gnosis*, "I knew thee" (*egnon se*), that relationship has, for him, priority even over benevolence. Fixation on the divine face, once there and, in the parousia, yet to return, casts into shadow the mercy that the absent divine face sometimes figures. For the servant, the lord's absence is devastating.

Brisman, "A Parable of Talent," p. 97. While Brisman's antithetical reading of this parable is certainly not the interpretation adopted by Jesus's audience in the gospel, nor does it find much expression within a normative Christian tradition, it offers a useful context for the phenomenology of suffering articulated by Jesus's most influential (mis)reader, Saul of Tarsus. I shall address this matter in greater detail below.

5. Alongside the question of their artistic merit, books 11 and 12 have typically raised the question of the status of history in a postlapsarian world. Recent criticism on these books reveals how ambiguous Milton's Restoration view of political agency has become. In his placing of these two books in the larger context of apocalyptic histories, Thomas Amorose has described a paradoxical engagement in and retreat from human agency. While the final books of the poem "trace a pattern of visionary figures who seem to rise above the historical narrative and participate as effective actors with God in shaping mankind's destiny," they also focus on "characters and events that will not have any ultimate historical significance." "Milton the Apocalyptic Historian," pp. 147–48. In her study of seventeenth-century historical paradigms, Achsah Guibbory has argued that Milton perceived history as cyclical but also understood it to be within human capacity to break from those cycles and force a progress into the future. *The Map of Time*, pp. 169–70. John Knott discovers a disjunction between Milton's portrayal of martyrdom in the prose tracts and in *Paradise Lost*. Whereas *Paradise Lost* adopts a more orthodox view of Christian martyrdom, the prose tracts praise "the combativeness of individual martyrs in the defense of truth"

rather than dwelling on their suffering. John L. Knott, "'Suffering for Truths Sake,' Milton and Martyrdom," Loewenstein and Turner, *Politics, Poetics, and Hermeneutics*, pp. 153–70. Marshall Grossman argues that "Milton's chiasmic reversal of the metaphor of authorship—through which an individual authors himself by acting out a story foreseen and revealed by God—marks *Paradise Lost* as the narrative expression of a sense of the historical self coming into being in Milton's time." *"Authors to Themselves,"* p. 5. Against this view, or perhaps as the other side of this plunge into historical narration, David Loewenstein has seen in Milton an anticipation of Joyce's Stephen Daedalus, wishing to awaken from the nightmare of history: "The just man of Michael's vision *would like* to be radically involved in the social order—to be an activist agent in the turbulent process of history—but instead finds himself radically alienated from the historical process itself. . . . The apocalyptic passages articulate Milton's powerful impulse to transcend, break through, and obliterate the historical process as a vicious pattern of decline." *Milton and the Drama of History*, pp. 103–4, 115.

Following the lead of Christopher Hill's ambitious study, *Milton and the English Revolution*, several critics have sought to attribute to the late Milton a persistent, albeit modified, belief in the historical role of humanity in its ongoing improvement. David Quint regards the late Milton as suspicious of any centralized state, regardless of its particular form. While not advocating a mere quietism, Milton's "inward turn to individual spirituality, even as it claims to subsume politics, appears to represent a turning away from the public spirit of Milton's controversialist prose." Milton's individualism thus becomes "an antithetical response to the very idea of the state." David Quint, "David's Census: Milton's Politics and *Paradise Regained*," Nyquist and Ferguson, *Re-Membering Milton*, pp. 129 and 142. Making more explicit the Foucauldian and Althusserian terms of Quint's analysis, Laura Lunger Knoppers suggests that Milton's late poetry struggles to resist spectacle and surveillance by retreating defiantly inward. *Historicizing Milton* p. 10.

6. Rosenblatt, *Torah and Law*, p. 234.

7. Yerushalmi, *Zakhor*, pp. 8–9.

8. Auerbach, "Odysseus' Scar," p. 12. Auerbach also discusses the historicity of the biblical narrative, compared to that of Homer's:

> The Biblical narrator, the Elohist, had to believe in the objective truth of the story of Abraham's sacrifice—the existence of the sacred ordinances of life rested upon the truth of this and similar stories. He had to believe in it passionately; or else he . . . had to be a conscious liar—no harmless liar like

Homer, who lied to give pleasure, but a political liar with a definite end in view, lying in the interest of a claim to absolute authority. (ibid., p. 14)

9. Yerushalmi, *Zakhor*, p. 17.

10. In his sustained response to Yerushalmi's reading of Jewish historiography—and its apparent absence—Amos Funkenstein has argued that the lack of a continuous record of political events from classical rabbinic and medieval Jewish writings should not be read as an absence of interest in or engagement with the idea of history. Funkenstein suggests that normative Judaism did "preserve a continuous and chronological record of legal innovations" in the ever expanding corpus of halakhic texts, which demands to be understood as a direct engagement with history in all its particularities. See *Perceptions of Jewish History*, pp. 16ff.

11. Neusner, *Judaism and Christianity*, p. 52.

12. Edward Tayler argues that Michael is sent to teach Adam to be a good biblical exegete, which cannot be done "merely by showing him pictures. Before Adam can accurately 'measure' the 'Race of Time,' before he can properly appreciate the movement and meaning of Christian history, he must be taught to read the 'mysterious terms of Scripture.'" See *Milton's Poetry*, p. 84.

13. Neusner, *Judaism in the Matrix of Christianity*, pp. 23–24.

14. Chilton and Neusner, *Trading Places*, p. 179.

15. Neusner, *Judaism in the Matrix of Christianity*, p. 136.

16. Yerushalmi, *Zakhor*, p. 20.

17. Although the Western Church regarded Hebrews as Pauline from the fourth century on, by the time of the Reformation Erasmus, Luther, Calvin, Melancthon, and others expressed doubts concerning its Pauline origins. Virtually all modern scholars agree that the letter cannot have been written by Paul, largely for the doctrinal differences discussed above. See Kümmel, *Introduction to the New Testament*, pp. 392–403.

18. Kümmel, *Introduction to the New Testament*, pp. 16–18.

19. Luxon, *Literal Figures*, p. 54. See my second chapter for a more detailed discussion of the relationship between this Reformation mode of reading and the parallels between English Puritanism and rabbinic Judaism.

20. For some readings of books 11 and 12 in traditional typological terms, see MacCallum, "Milton and Sacred History": "The dominant feature of [Milton's] typology is the Pauline and Augustinian emphasis on the men of faith as prefigurations of Christ" (p. 158); Burden, *The Logical Epic*: books 11 and 12 follow the doctrinal perception of Christian history as having "a beginning and an end, but no middle" (p. 180); and Fish, *Surprised by Sin*, which argues for a literary aspect to this typology: where

"history comes to be seen as one term in a Milton pseudo-simile, with eternity the other, and as we move through its spaces, the unity of the two terms is more and more apparent and the superficial differences less and less striking" (p. 310).

21. Rosenblatt, in *Torah and Law*, writes, "The Pisgah vision, equated with the law, becomes the 'glimpse,' 'sight,' and 'taste' of the gospel, and Moses' exclusion from the promised land signifies the inability of the law to bring humanity to the promised land" (p. 219). William Walker's attempt at denying the eschatological, teleological, or apocalyptic shape of typology is unconvincing, largely because what he reads as "one eternal omnitemporal shape" is inevitably the telos of Christ's salvation through sacrifice that bestows meaning on the history that precedes it. See "Typology and *Paradise Lost*," pp. 245–64.

22. Grossman, *"Authors to Themselves,"* p. 18.

23. BT Menachot 29b. As is true of virtually all rabbinic literature of this period, it is very difficult to determine with any accuracy the composition date of this story. If we rely upon the Talmud's attribution, then we have two potential *termini post quem*: Rav is believed to have died in 247 *c.e.* and R. Judah died in 299 *c.e.* In either case, the legend seems to have originated from a period prior to the ascendancy of Christianity within the Roman Empire.

24. Damrosch, *God's Plot and Man's Stories*, p. 117.

25. Leviticus Rabbah 22:1 (Acharei Moth).

26. Based on their reading of Scripture, the rabbis decreed that a man was required to recite the verses of Numbers 6:4–9, twice each day, in the morning and in the evening. These verses, known collectively as the Shema, from the first verse, "Hear, O Israel, the Lord our God, the Lord is One," were understood to signify the daily acceptance of the authority of the Kingdom of Heaven.

27. BT Berakhot 61b.

28. Solomon Zeitlin, "The Legend of the Ten Martyrs and Its Apocalyptic Origins," *Jewish Quarterly Review* n.s. 36 (1945–46), p. 8, repr. Zeitlin, *Solomon Zeitlin's Studies*, 2:165–80. David Stern adds that the legend of the ten martyrs is not to be taken as a hagiography: "As martyrology, it shares more in common with pagan and early Christian martyrological literature than it does with other kinds of rabbinic writings from the period." See Stern's introduction to his translation of *Midrash Eleh Ezkerah* in Stern and Mirsky, *Rabbinic Fantasies*, p. 144.

29. In the later liturgical poem, *Eleh Ezkerah*, God's reply to the objections of the ministering angels is even more fierce (and desperate?): "If I hear one more such cry, I will turn the world to void and desolation [*tohu va-vohu*]," a threat literally to reverse the act of creation.

30. I do not wish to oversimplify matters too much. The rabbis did not permanent-

ly retreat into their houses of study by the middle of the second century. Indeed, a new rabbinic aristocracy in the form of the Patriarchate and the Sanhedrin very quickly replaced the older priestly aristocracy. And rabbinic literature records numerous encounters between these new Jewish leaders and Roman political and military figures. See, for instance, my discussion of debates between Rabbi and Antoninus in chapter 4. Unlike the earlier ruling class, however, the rabbis needed to adopt a much more accommodating, nonaggressive mode of interaction with the world powers by which they found themselves surrounded. Internal political—as well as religious—questions continued to arise; affairs external to the Jewish community, however, receded far into the background.

31. Lamentations Rabbah 69:14; Dio Cassius cited in Feldman, *Jew and Gentile*, p. 580, n. 169.

32. Isaac and Oppenheimer, "The Revolt of Bar Kokhba."

33. Ibid., p. 49.

34. Zerubavel, *Recovered Roots*, p. 51.

35. Marks, *The Image of Bar Kokhba*, pp. 27–28.

36. Ibid., pp. 31 and 39.

37. Lamentations Rabbah 2:4.

38. See Virgil's *Aeneid*, 2.199–234: "et jam / bis medium amplexi, bis collo squamea circum / terga dati superant capite et cervicibus altis."

39. It is very specifically a Hellenic hubris and not a Hebraic chutzpah that this legend condemns.

40. David Biale has argued that as early as the destruction of the Kingdom of Israel in 722 *b.c.e.* Judean writers reformulated the terms of the biblical covenant with God depicted in the Pentateuch: "Defeat was the consequence not of divine desertion of Israel, but, quite the contrary, of God's love for His people." See *Power and Powerlessness*, pp. 31–32.

41. Lamentations Rabbah 2:4. For a slightly different version, see PT Ta'anit 4:8. Peter Schäfer has shown that these versions of Akiba's proclamation of Bar Kokhba as Messiah are the only sources in rabbinic literature in which the two historical figures are brought into direct contact with one another. He argues that there is no way firmly to establish that Akiba actually believed in the messianic nature of Bar Kokhba's activities. It remains the case, however, that the tradition of this connection was old enough that later redactors of rabbinic texts kept the association and even embellished it further. Since my concern here is less with the historical accuracy of the rabbinic accounts than with what kinds of (conflicted) values they embody, my argument does not depend on the validity of the claim. For further discussion of these historical matters see Schäfer, "Rabbi Aqiva and Bar Kokhba."

42. Marks, *The Image of Bar Kokhba*, p. 20. As Zerubavel points out, the nature of Bar Kokhba's legacy for over fourteen hundred years following his death is hinted at in how his name is reported. The glorifying name, Bar Kokhba, was preserved only by non-Jews, whereas Jewish sources used only the name Bar Koziva which, as the rabbi's interpretation suggests, was likely to carry negative connotations. See Zerubavel's fascinating discussion of the "recovery" of the Bar Kokhba legend as part of an emergent nationalist mythology that coincided with the establishment of the State of Israel in *Recovered Roots*.

43. See, for instance, Mishnah Sanhedrin 10: 3. Joseph Heinemann discerns no utopian or transcendent features to Akiba's messianism whatsoever. Heinemann, *Aggadoth ve-Toldotheyhen* [Rabbinic Legends and Their Origins], p. 108.

44. David Biale has argued that this disagreement between R. Akiba and R. Yochanan b. Tortha is part of a much larger pattern of repeated internal divisions within the Jewish (or Hebrew) community, between "nationalists" and "accommodationists." See *Power and Powerlessness*, chapter 1.

45. Depending on the date of origin of this legend, it may also be that Akiba's assertion of singularity responds to the Christian heresy of the Trinity. I suspect that this would only be a valid reading if the legend comes from at least a century after Akiba's actual execution, since in the early second-century Christian doctrine had not yet formulated a coherent Trinitarian theology and, more important, rabbinic Judaism did not yet view Christianity as a serious rival.

46. Boyarin, "Masada or Yavneh?" p. 315.

47. Boyarin, *Unheroic Conduct*, p. 116. Boyarin coins the term "femminization" to distinguish this rabbinic blurring of gender categories from one that suggests a tacit condemnation of a man who is "feminized."

48. Ibid., p. 114.

49. Alan Segal has observed that the Aramaic Targum to Isaiah—by most accounts, something of a hybrid document, having been compiled during the Tannaitic and Amoraic periods—maintains a surprising messianic interpretation where, against the literal meaning of Isaiah 53, the servant messiah makes all the enemies of God suffer. Segal concludes, "This is clearly a polemic against Christianity inserted into rabbinic commentary." *Rebecca's Children*, p. 190, n. 28. Bruce Chilton has countered that while this portion of the Targum clearly dates from a period closer to the destruction of the Temple and its aftermath, its polemic against Christianity is not as self-evident: "Although there is no reference to anything like the suffering of the Messiah . . . neither is there any attempt to claim the Messiah did not 'hand over' his soul to the death' (v. 12). Such an attempt would probably have been made if the purpose of the interpretation was to deny that the Messiah should die as Jesus had."

It would appear that such Christian claims were not in mind." *The Isaiah Targum*, p. 105, note. Whether Chilton or Segal is correct, it is noteworthy that this early rabbinic rendition of Isaiah 53 does include a number of overtly political and starkly nationalist sentiments. For the rabbis of this period, the suffering experienced by the servant was not to be ignored or endured patiently: "Then I will divide him *the plunder of many peoples*, and he shall divide the spoil, *the possessions of* strong *fortresses*; because he *handed over* his soul to the death, and *subjected the rebels to law*" (53:12, Chilton's translation of the Aramaic Targum; words in italics are those that have no counterpart in the Hebrew original). The view is a far cry from that expressed in the later homily of R. Huna, transmitted in BT Berakhot.

50. I take this date from Kümmel, *Introduction to the New Testament*, p. 311.

51. Most scholars agree that the letter could not have been written by Peter but may very well have been written by a member of the Petrine school living (temporarily, perhaps) in Rome ("the church that is at Babylon," 5:13) any time from 70 to 95 *c.e.* See Kümmel, *Introduction to the New Testament*, pp. 416–25.

52. Segal, *Rebecca's Children*, pp. 92–3.

53. Ibid., p. 94.

54. *Constitutions of the Holy Apostles*, 5.1.i, in Roberts and Donaldson, *The Ante-Nicene Fathers*, trans. Isaac Hall and John Napier, 7:438–39.

55. Tertullian, *Ad Martyras*, 3, in Roberts and Donaldson, *The Ante-Nicene Fathers*, trans. S. Thelwall, 3:694.

56. Ibid.

57. Tertullian, *Of Patience*, chapter 4, in Roberts and Donaldson, *The Ante-Nicene Fathers*, 3:708.

58. Ibid., p. 711.

59. Ibid.

60. Ambrose, *Duties of the Clergy*, chapter 5, par. 19, in Schaff and Wace, *Nicene and Post-Nicene Fathers*, trans. H. de Romestin, 10:46.

61. Calvin, *Institutes*, 3.viii.1.

62. Ibid., 3.viii.4, emphasis added.

63. I am following the convincing analysis of this portion of Calvin's thought by François Wendel, in his *Calvin*, pp. 248–52.

64. Luxon, *Literal Figures*, p. 54.

65. See Rosenblatt, *Torah and Law*, chapters 6 and 7.

66. See the important recent collection edited by Dobranski and Rumrich, *Milton and Heresy*. On Milton's Arminianism, see especially the essays by Thomas N. Corns and Stephen M. Fallon.

67. See especially Milton, *De Doctrina Christiana*, 1.xv, xvii, xix, and xx, YP 6:430–37, 453–60, 471–84.

68. Ibid., 2.iii, YP 6:662.

69. Ibid., 1.xxv, YP 6:506.

70. For a discussion of the salvific power of these two imitative gestures and its role in the theodicy of the epic, see chapter 3.

71. Hill, in *The Experience of Defeat*, writes, "There is no evidence that Milton ever adopted the post-1661 Quaker position of pacifism and abstention from politics. He did not shift his kingdom to another world" (p. 315).

72. Mary Ann Radzinowicz has also noted the contrast between Milton's 1660 prose tract and these lines in his later epic poem. She reads the poem's revision as evidence of an interpretive politics advocated by Milton after the Restoration that resists closure or the use of historical examples, biblical and nonbiblical alike, as coercive precedents. The poem corrects "the very concept of permanent and changeless political utopia" that the prose tract promised. Choosing *"not* the readiest way" in the poem is what produces the great Senate and ordained laws. Radzinowicz argues for a Miltonic politics of scriptural interpretation in which Michael's account functions as a reaffirmation of ethical behavior and religious and political liberty: "Scripture is history and not authority; no interpretation is coercive; no public policy comes with God's fiat behind it to overrule freedom." See "The Politics of *Paradise Lost*." Compare to Radzinowicz's earlier essay, " 'Man as a Probationer of Immortality,' " in which she wrote, "The lessons of time have a double burden. On the one hand they are ethical demonstrations from which moral truths are drawn to guide Adam and hence every man. On the other they are political and historical demonstrations from which political and historical laws are deduced. The great epic design is meant to reveal how the free will of the individual interacts with historical necessity" (p. 36).

73. In his reading of *Paradise Regained* Northrop Frye writes that Satan's fall in book 4 marks the final separation of gospel from law. "Judaism joins classical wisdom as part of the demonic illusion, as the centre of religion passes from the Temple Christ is standing on into the true Christian temple, the body of Christ above it." "The Typology of *Paradise Regained*," p. 237.

74. Milton, *Eikonoklastes*, YP 3:348–49. As Merritt Hughes observes in his note on the text, Milton would have been familiar with this episode from his readings in Josephus's *Wars of the Jews*.

75. Menasseh ben Israel, *The Hope of Israel* (1652), Wolf, *Menasseh ben Israel's Mission*, section 31, p. 38 [p. 48].

76. A number of essays in the recent collection edited by Rajan and Sauer, *Milton*

and the Imperial Vision, reveal Milton's intense ambivalence regarding the idea of empire. See especially Janel Mueller, "Dominions as Domesticity: Milton's Imperial God and the Experience of History," pp. 25–47. In addition to showing how *Paradise Lost* moves from "an imperial to a postimperial construction of the course of human history" (p. 26), Mueller suggests that *Paradise Regained*'s ending prior to Christ's Passion reveals Milton's "decisive rejection of imperialist formulations of spiritual victory and triumph, with their associated hypermasculinity" (p. 45).

77. Fixler, *Milton and the Kingdom of Gods*, pp. 225ff.

78. Regina Schwartz has argued that "Michael's use of typology is controlled, not so much by the expected vocabulary of finality, as by such key adverbs of deferral. When he waxes most typological . . . we would most expect to hear of completion. Instead, Milton uses typology in the last two books of his epic to frustrate, rather than fulfill our expectation of an end." See "From Shadowy Types to Shadowy Types: The Unendings of *Paradise Lost*," *Milton Studies* 24 (1988), p. 127.

79. Reuther, *Faith and Fratricide*, p. 245.

80. Slonimsky, "The Philosophy Implicit in the Midrash," p. 238.

81. Ricoeur, *Symbolism of Evil*, p. 251.

82. See not only 12.335–343, which obliquely recounts the first Temple's destruction, but also 1.490–505, which associates Belial with the corruption of the priests during the period of the First Temple, and 9.1119–21, where the epic voice connects the imminent exile from Eden with the Babylonian captivity lamented in Psalm 137. Jason Rosenblatt has shown how these last two references to the invasion of the Temple in Jerusalem are not only associated with the invasion and corruption of Eden but also with the Restoration of Charles II, that is, the invasion and corruption of England. See "Eden, Israel, England," pp. 59–60.

Epilogue: Toward Interpreting the Hebraism of Samson Agonistes

1. See the final chapter of Rosenblatt's *Torah and Law* (pp. 218–34) for an important comparison of Adam's vision with that of Moses.

2. Mekhilta de-Rabbi Simeon b. Yochai, Beshalach 17:14. For parallel midrashic statements, see also Sifre Deuteronomy 357, and Midrash Tannaim, Deuteronomy 34:1. All of these collections date from between the third and the fifth century *c.e.*.

3. Anne K. Krook has offered a persuasive account of the dialectical relationship between *Paradise Regained* and *Samson Agonistes*. See "The Hermeneutics of Opposition."

4. Despite attempts by William Riley Parker and others to propose a much earlier date for the composition of *Samson Agonistes*, I am in agreement with the majority of

scholars, Mary Ann Radzinowicz, Michael Lieb, and Joseph Wittreich among them, who favor the period between 1667 and 1670.

5. In an address to the British Academy in 1908, published posthumously a few years later, Sir Richard Jebb explicitly invoked the Arnoldian categories with which I began this book to argue for the Hebraic qualities of the drama. See *"Samson Agonistes and the Hellenic Drama."*

6. See Parker, *Milton's Debt to Greek Tragedy*; and Krouse, *Milton's Samson*. Parker's book begins with one of the most bizarre analogies I have ever encountered in literary criticism:

> The Samson of Milton's tragedy has a good Athenian stamp; his behaviour reminds us at times of Hercules or the aged Oedipus; but his background, let us remember, was Jewish. I mention this in order to raise the interesting question: what were Milton's "sources"? Is the answer, after all, too obvious to justify the question? Commentaries on *Samson Agonistes* for the past hundred and fifty years would seem to prove the contrary. The story of Samson's life is ostensibly taken from *The Book of Judges*, but scholars have nevertheless, with almost Nazi fervour, ransacked libraries in search of a different pedigree. (p. 3)

Written only a few years before the outbreak of World War II, just as the Nazi party was beginning the process of enacting its Final Solution, which in part depended on identifying even the most hidden of *Jewish* pedigrees, Parker's comparison seems simultaneously perverse and prophetic.

7. Fisch, *Jerusalem and Albion*, p. 140.

8. Ibid., p. 140.

9. Stollman, "Milton's Samson and the Jewish Tradition" and "Milton's Understanding of the 'Hebraic.'" For a critique of Stollman's rigid distinction between Hebraic and Judaic, see chapter 2.

10. Shapiro, "*Samson Agonistes* and the Hebraic Tradition"; and Muskin, "Milton's Understanding of Hebraism." Muskin subsequently published a portion of her dissertation as "'Wisdom by Adversity.'"

11. For a striking discussion of how the fact and figure of circumcision contribute to Milton's sense of self, especially in light of *Samson Agonistes*, see Lieb, "'A Thousand Fore-Skins.'"

12. PT Sotah 1:8.

13. Feldman, *Josephus's Interpretation of the Bible*, 461.

14. Todd, *The Poetical Works of John Milton*, 5:440–41. In his book on *Samson* Michael

Krouse also cites Josephus's version of the Samson story as a possible source for Milton. See *Milton's Samson*, pp. 32–33.

15. Feldman, *Josephus's Interpretation of the Bible*, pp. 471, 475, 489.

16. Joseph Wittreich's provocative and antithetical reading of Milton's closet drama, *Interpreting "Samson Agonistes,"* remains the most thorough analysis of the disquieting generic and theological aspects of the text. My thinking in this epilogue owes a great deal to Wittreich's approach.

17. Mekhilta de-Rabbi Ishmael, Beshalach, Tractate Shira, chapter 2.

18. See Boyarin, *Dying for God*, especially chapters 2 and 3.

19. Michael Lieb has recently offered a useful account of the parallels between God's irrational violence and Samson's in "'Our Living Dread.'" Concluding that "the theology of dread that distinguishes the drama is one in which deity is portrayed in its most archaic and terrifying form," Leib's analysis offers further evidence for my argument that the presence of anthropopathisms and the theodical reliance on imitatio Dei—in both *Paradise Lost* and *Samson Agonistes*—make for a more troubling account of God's justice than has often been acknowledged.

20. Leviticus Rabbah 8:2.

21. PT Sotah 1:8.

22. See my discussion of this passage in chapter 2.

23. PT Sotah 1:8.

24. BT Sotah 9b–10a.

25. As I have indicated, it remains difficult to determine the relative composition dates of rabbinic statements. It is equally difficult to determine whether R. Yosse and Rav ever knew of each other's remarks concerning Samson's sexuality. I offer these two polar opinions not so much to suggest any direct dispute between these rabbinic figures as to reinforce my previous assertions concerning the heterogeneity of rabbinic writings and to speculate on possible historic factors that might have contributed to these two divergent viewpoints.

26. BT Berakhot 12b.

27. It is striking that the Chorus of *Samson* invokes precisely the same verse from Psalms: "Unless there be who think not God at all: / If any be, they walk obscure; / For of such Doctrine never was there School, / But the heart of the Fool, / And no man therein Doctor but himself" (295–99).

28. Genesis Rabbah, Vilna ed., 98:14.

29. Genesis Rabbah, Albeck ed., 99:11.

30. Mark is silent on John's genealogy. Luke provides an extended narrative of John's birth in 1:5–80, in which Zechariah, John's father, is described as a priest and Elisa-

beth, John's mother, is "of the daughters of Aaron." John could thus not be of the tribe of Gad and therefore, according to the rabbinic view, cannot be Elijah.

31. Unfortunately, no English translation of *Christus Patiens* is currently available in print. I have made use of a translation by Alan Fishbone. I want to thank Professor Fishbone for allowing me to use his translation and Joseph Wittreich for calling my attention to it.

32. See, for example, Radzinowicz, *Toward Samson Agonistes,*" p. 284; Bennett, *Reviving Liberty,* pp. 120 and 124; and McLoone, "'True Religion' and Tragedy," pp. 5 and 16.

33. Genesis Rabbah, Albeck ed., 99:11.

Selected Bibliography

PRIMARY

An Endevovr after the Reconcilement of that Long Debated and Much Lamented Difference between the Godly Presbyterians, and Independents; about Church-Government. In a discourse touching the Iews Synagogues. London, 1648 [1647].

A Survey of that Foolish, Seditious, Scandalous, Prophane Libell, The Protestation Protested. London, 1641.

Augustine of Hippo. *The City of God.* Trans. Marcus Dods. New York: Modern Library, 1993.

—— *On Christian Doctrine.* Trans. D. W. Robertson Jr. Indianapolis: Bobbs-Merrill, 1958.

Bereshit Rabba [Hebrew]. Ed. J. Theodor and Ch. Albeck. 2d ed. 2 vols. Jerusalem: Wahrmann, 1965.

Burton, Henry. *A Vindication of Churches, Commonly Called Independent.* London, 1644.

Calvert, Thomas. *The Blessed Jew of Marocco.* York, 1648.

Calvin, John. *Commentaries.* Trans. and ed. Joseph Haroutunian. Philadelphia: Westminster, 1958.

—— *Institutes of the Christian Religion.* Trans. Ford Lewis Battles. London: Library of Christian Classics, 1961.

Carter, Richard. *The Schismatick Stigmatized.* London, 1641.

Certaine briefe treatises: written by diverse learned men, concerning the ancient and moderne government of the church: wherein both the primitive institution of episcopacie is maintained, and the lawfulnesse of the ordination of the Protestant ministers beyond the seas likewise defended. Oxford, 1641.

Fagius, Paul. *Exegesis Sive Expositio Dictionum Hebraica, Carum Literalis and Simplex, In Quator Capita Geneseos Studiosis Linguae Hebraicae.* 1542.

Foxe, John. *Actes and Monuments.* London, 1570.

French, J. Milton, ed. *The Life Records of John Milton.* 5 vols. New York: Gordian, 1949–58.

Fuller, Thomas. *A Pisgah-sight of Palestine and the Confines thereof, with the Historie of the Old and New Testament Acted thereon.* London, 1650.

Genesis Rabbah: The Judaic Commentary to the Book of Genesis. 3 vols. Trans. Jacob Neusner. Atlanta: Scholars, 1985.

Gerard, John. *The Herball or Generall Historie of Plants.* Amsterdam: Theatrum Orbis Terrarum, 1974 [1597].

Gillespie, George. *A Late Dialogue Betwixt a Civilian and a Divine Concerning the Present Condition of the Church of England.* London, 1644.

Hall, Joseph. *An Humble Remonstrance to the High Covrt of Parliament.* London, 1640.

—— *Episcopacie by Divine Right.* London, 1640.

—— *A Modest Confutation of A Slanderous and Scurrilous Libell, Entitvled, Animadversions Vpon the Remonstrants Defense against Smectymnuus.* London, 1642.

Haller, William, ed. *Tracts on Liberty in the Puritan Revolution, 1638–1647.* 3 vols. New York: Columbia University Press, 1934.

Lightfoot, John. *In Evangelium Sancti Mattaei Horae Hebraicae et Talmudicae.* Cambridge, 1658.

Midrash Rabbah [Hebrew]. Ed. Aryeh Mirkin. 11 vols. Tel Aviv: Yavneh, 1958–67.

Midrash Rabbah. 10 vols. Ed. and trans. H. Freedman and Maurice Simon. London: Soncino, 1977.

Milton, John. *The Works of John Milton.* Ed. Frank Patterson. 20 vols. New York: Columbia University Press, 1931–40.

—— *Complete Poems and Major Prose.* Ed. Merrit Y. Hughes. New York: MacMillan, 1957.

—— *Complete Prose Works of John Milton.* Ed. Don M. Wolfe. 8 vols. New Haven: Yale University Press, 1953–1982.

Ovid. *Metamorphoses.* Trans. Frank Justus Miller. Loeb Classical Library. Cambridge: Harvard University Press, 1916.

Pirke de Rabbi Eleizer (The Chapters of Rabbi Eliezer the Great). Trans. and ed. Gerald Fried-lander. New York: Hermon, 1965.

Pirkei D'Rabbi Eliezer [Hebrew]. Commentary by R. David Luria. Jerusalem, 1963.

Prynne, William. *Lord Bishops None of the Lords Bishops.* London, 1640.

—— *A Short Demurrer to the Jewes Long discontinued barred Remitter into England.* London, 1656.

Ralegh, Walter. *The History of the World.* Ed. C. A. Patrides. Philadelphia: Temple University Press, 1971 [1614].

Roberts, Alexander and James Donaldson, eds. *The Anti-Nicene Fathers: Translations of the Writings of the Fathers Down to A.D. 325.* 10 vols. Grand Rapids: Eerdmans, 1978–1979.

Schaff, Philip and Henry Wace, eds. *Nicene and Post-Nicene Fathers.* 2d series. 14 vols. Peabody, Mass.: Hendrickson, 1890.

Smectymnuus. *An Answer to a Book Entitvled, An Humble Remonstrance.* London, 1641.

Tyndale, William. "Obedience of a Christian Man." *Doctrinal Treatises and Introductions to Different Portions of the Holy Scripture.* Ed. Henry Walter. Parker Society. Vol. 42. Cambridge: Cambridge University Press, 1848.

Watson, Philip S., ed. and trans. *Luther and Erasmus: Free Will and Salvation.* Library of Christian Classics 17. Philadelphia: Westminster, 1969.

Wilkinson, Henry. *Miranda, Stupenda: or the Wonderful Mercies Which the Lord Hath Wrought for England.* London, 1646.

Wolf, Lucien. *Menasseh Ben Israel's Mission to Oliver Cromwell.* London: Macmillan, 1901.

SECONDARY

Adams, Robert M. *Ikon: John Milton and the Modern Critics.* Ithaca: Cornell University Press, 1955.

Adamson, J. H. "The War in Heaven: Milton's Version of the *Merkabah.*" *Journal of English and German Philology* 57 (1958): 690–705.

Adelman, Janet. "Creation and the Place of the Poet in *Paradise Lost.*" In L. L. Martz and Aubrey Williams, eds., *The Author in His Work: Essays on a Problem in Criticism,* 51–69. New Haven: Yale University Press, 1978.

Allen, D. C. "Milton and Rabbi Eleizer." *Modern Language Notes* 62 (1948): 262–63.

—— "Some Theories of the Growth and Origin of Language in Milton's Age." *Philological Quarterly* 28 (1949): 5–16.

Altmann, Alexander. "The Gnostic Backgrounds of the Rabbinic Adam Legends." *Jewish Quarterly Review* 35 (1944–45): 371–91.

Amorose, Thomas. "Milton the Apocalyptic Historian: Competing Genres in *Paradise Lost*, Books 11–12." *Milton Studies* 17 (1983): 141–62.

Anderson, Bernhard W. *Creation versus Chaos: The Reinterpretation of Mythical Symbolism in the Bible*. New York: Association, 1967.

Anderson, Gary. "The Garden of Eden and Sexuality in Early Judaism." In Howard Eilberg-Schwartz, ed., *People of the Body: Jews and Judaism from an Embodied Perspective*, 47–68. Albany: SUNY Press, 1992.

Arnold, Matthew. *Culture and Anarchy*. 1869. In A. Dwight Culler, ed., *Poetry and Criticism of Matthew Arnold*. Boston: Houghton Mifflin, 1961.

Auerbach, Erich. "Odysseus' Scar." *Mimesis: The Representation of Reality in Western Literature*, 3–23. Trans. Willard R. Trask. Princeton: Princeton University Press, 1974.

Baldwin, Edward Chauncy. "Some Extra-Biblical Semitic Influences Upon Milton's Story of the Fall of Man." *Journal of English and German Philology* 28 (1929): 366–401.

Bauckham, Richard. *Tudor Apocalypse: Sixteenth Century Apocalypticism, Millenarianism and the English Reformation*. Appleford: Sutton Courtenay Press, 1978.

Benin, Stephen D. *The Footprints of God: Divine Accommodation in Jewish and Christian Thought*. Albany: SUNY Press, 1993.

Bennett, Joan S. *Reviving Liberty: Radical Christian Humanism in Milton's Great Poems*. Cambridge: Harvard University Press, 1989.

Biale, David. *Power and Powerlessness in Jewish History*. New York: Schocken, 1986.

Bialik, Hayim Nahman. *Law and Legend or Halakah and Aggada.* Trans. Julius L. Siegel. New York: Block, 1923.

Bickerman, Elias. *The Jews in the Greek Age*. Cambridge: Harvard University Press, 1988.

Blau, Joseph Leon. *The Christian Interpretation of the Cabala in the Renaissance*. New York: Columbia Unversity Press, 1944.

Blessington, Francis C. "Autotheodicy: The Father as Orator in *Paradise Lost*." *Cithara* 14 (1975): 49–60.

Bloom, Harold. *The Book of J.* Trans. David Rosenberg. New York: Grove Weidenfeld, 1990.

Boman, Thorleif. *Hebrew Thought Compared with Greek*. New York: Norton, 1960.

Borris, Kenneth. "Allegory in *Paradise Lost*: Satan's Cosmic Journey." *Milton Studies* 26 (1990): 101–33.

Bouwsma, William J. *John Calvin: A Sixteenth-Century Portrait*. Oxford: Oxford University Press, 1988.

Box, G. H. "Hebrew Studies in the Reformation Period and After: Their Place and Influence." *The Legacy of Israel*, 315–75. Oxford: Clarendon Press, 1927.

Boyarin, Daniel. *Intertextuality and the Reading of Midrash*. Bloomington: Indiana University Press, 1990.

— *Carnal Israel: Reading Sex in Talmudic Culture*. Berkeley: University of California Press, 1993.

— *A Radical Jew: Paul and the Politics of Identity*. Berkeley: University of California Press, 1994.

— "Masada or Yavneh? Gender and the Arts of Jewish Resistance." In Jonathan Boyarin and Daniel Boyarin, eds., *Jews and Other Differences: The New Jewish Cultural Studies*. Minneapolis: University of Minnesota Press, 1997.

— *Unheroic Conduct: The Rise of Heterosexuality and the Invention of the Jewish Man*. Berkeley: University of California Press, 1997.

— *Dying for God: Martyrdom and the Making of Christianity and Judaism*. Stanford: Stanford University Press, 1999.

Boyarin, Daniel and David Stern. "An Exchange on the Mashal: Rhetoric and Interpretation—the Case of the Nimshal." *Prooftexts* 5 (1985): 269–80.

Brecht, Martin, Frederich de Boor, Klaus Deppermann, Ulrich Gäbler, Hartmut Lehmann, and Johannes Wallman, eds. *Chiliasmus in Deutschland und England im 17. Jahrhundert*. Göttingen: Vanderhoeck and Ruprecht, 1988.

Brisman, Leslie. *The Voice of Jacob: On the Composition of Genesis*. Bloomington: Indiana University Press, 1990.

— "A Parable of Talent." *Religion and the Arts* 1 (1996): 74–99.

Broadbent, J. B. *Some Graver Subject: An Essay on "Paradise Lost."* New York: Barnes and Noble, 1960.

Bruns, Gerald. "Midrash and Allegory." In Robert Alter and Frank Kermode, eds., *The Literary Guide to the Bible*, 625–46. London: Collins, 1987.

Budick, Sanford. *The Dividing Muse: Images of Sacred Disjunction in Milton's Poetry*. New Haven: Yale University Press, 1985.

Burden, Dennis H. *The Logical Epic: A Study of the Argument of "Paradise Lost."* Cambridge: Harvard University Press, 1967.

Burke, Kenneth. *The Rhetoric of Religion: Studies in Logology*. Berkeley: University of California Press, 1961.

Cable, Lana. *Carnal Rhetoric: Milton's Iconoclasm and the Poetics of Desire*. Durham: Duke University Press, 1995.

Campbell, Gordon. "Milton's Theological and Literary Treatments of the Creation." *Journal of Theological Studies*, n.s. 30 (1979): 128–37.

Campbell, Gordon, Thomas N. Corns, John K. Hale, David I. Holmes, and Fiona J. Tweedie. "The Provenance of *De Doctrina Christiana*." *Milton Quarterly* 31 (1997): 67–117.

Canfield, J. Douglas. "Blessed Are the Merciful: The Understanding of the Promise in *Paradise Lost.*" *Milton Quarterly* 7 (1973): 43–46.

Capp, B. S. *The Fifth Monarchy Men: A Study in Seventeenth-Century English Millenarianism.* London: Faber and Faber, 1972.

Charlesworth, James H., ed. *The Old Testament Pseudepigrapha.* 2 vols. Garden City, N.Y.: Doubleday, 1985.

Chilton, Bruce D. *The Isaiah Targum: Introduction, Translation, Apparatus, and Notes.* Wilmington, Del.: Michael Glazier, 1987.

Chilton, Bruce and Jacob Neusner. *Trading Places: The Intersecting Histories of Judaism and Christianity.* Cleveland: Pilgrim, 1996.

Christianson, Paul. *Reformers and Babylon: English Apocalyptic Visions from the Reformation to the Eve of the Civil War.* Toronto: University of Toronto Press, 1978.

Christopher, Georgia B. *Milton and the Science of the Saints.* Princeton: Princeton University Press, 1982.

Coffin, Charles Monroe. "Creation and the Self in *Paradise Lost.*" *English Literary History* 29 (1962): 1–18.

Collinson, Patrick. *From Iconoclasm to Iconophobia: The Cultural Impact of the Second English Reformation (Stenton Lecture, 1985).* Reading, 1986.

Conklin, George Newton. *Biblical Criticism and Heresy in Milton.* New York: King's Crown, 1949.

Cooley, Robert W. "Iconoclasm and Self-Definition in Milton's *Of Reformation.*" *Religion and Literature* 23 (1991): 23–36.

Corcoran, Mary Irma. *Milton's Paradise with Reference to the Hexameral Background.* Washington, D.C.: Catholic University of America Press, 1967 [1945].

Cuddihy, John Murray. *The Ordeal of Civility: Freud, Marx, Levi-Strauss, and the Jewish Struggle with Modernity.* Boston: Beacon, 1974.

Daiches, David. *The King James Version of the English Bible: An Account of the Development and Sources of the English Bible of 1611 with Special Reference to the Hebrew Tradition.* Chicago: University of Chicago Press, 1941.

Damrosch, Leopold, Jr. *God's Plot and Man's Stories: Studies in the Fictional Imagination from Milton to Fielding.* Chicago: University of Chicago Press, 1985.

Danielson, Dennis. *Milton's Good God: A Study in Literary Theodicy.* Cambridge: Cambridge Univeristy Press, 1982.

Daube, David. "Rabbinic Methods of Interpretation and Hellenistic Rhetoric." *Hebrew Union College Annual* 22 (1949): 239–64.

Davies, Stevie. *Images of Kingship in "Paradise Lost": Milton's Politics and Christian Liberty.* Columbia: University of Missouri Press, 1983.

Davis, Walter R. "The Languages of Accommodation and the Styles of *Paradise Lost.*" *Milton Studies* 18 (1983): 103–27.

Dobranski, Stephen B. and John P. Rumrich, eds. *Milton and Heresy.* Cambridge: Cambridge University Press, 1998.

DuRocher, Richard J. *Milton and Ovid.* Ithaca: Cornell University Press, 1985.

Eilberg-Schwartz, Howard. "The Problem of the Body for the People of the Book." In Howard Eilberg-Schwartz, ed., *People of the Body: Jews and Judaism from an Embodied Perspective,* 17–46. Albany: SUNY Press, 1992.

Empson, William. *Milton's God.* Cambridge: Harvard University Press, 1961.

Entzminger, Robert L. "Michael's Options and Milton's Poetry: *Paradise Lost* 11 and 12." *English Literary Renaissance* 8 (1978): 197–211.

Evans, J. M. *"Paradise Lost" and the Genesis Tradition.* Oxford: Clarendon, 1968.

— *Milton's Imperial Epic.* Ithaca: Cornell University Press, 1995.

Fallon, Robert Thomas. *Divided Empire: Milton's Political Imagery.* University Park: Pennsylvania State University Press, 1995.

Fallon, Stephen M. "Milton's Sin and Death: The Ontology of Allegory in *Paradise Lost.*" *English Literary Renaissance* 17 (1987): 329–50.

Feldman, Louis H. *Jew and Gentile in the Ancient World.* Princeton: Princeton University Press, 1993.

— *Josephus's Interpretation of the Bible.* Berkeley: University of California Press, 1998.

Fisch, Harold. *Jerusalem and Albion: The Hebraic Factor in Seventeenth-Century Literature.* London: Routledge and Kegan Paul, 1964.

— "Hebraic Styles and Motifs in *Paradise Lost.*" In Ronald D. Emma and John T. Shawcross, eds., *Language and Style in Milton,* 39–64. New York: Frederick Ungar, 1967.

Fish, Stanley. *Surprised by Sin: The Reader in "Paradise Lost."* Berkeley: University of California Press, 1967.

— "Transmuting the Lump: 'Paradise Lost,' 1942–1982." In Gary Saul Morson, ed., *Literature and History: Theoretical Problems and Russian Case Studies,* 33–56. Stanford: Stanford University Press, 1986.

Fishbane, Michael. *Biblical Interpretation of Ancient Israel.* Oxford: Clarendon, 1985.

— *The Garments of the Torah: Essays in Biblical Hermeneutics.* Bloomington: Indiana University Press, 1989.

— "'The Holy One Sits and Roars': Mythopoesis and the Midrashic Imagination." *Journal of Jewish Thought and Philosophy* 1 (1991): 1–21.

Fisher, Peter F. "Milton's Theodicy." *Journal of the History of Ideas* 17 (1958): 28–53.

Fishman, Sylvia Barack. *"Paradise Lost* as a Midrash on the Biblical Bride of God." In

Jacob Neusner, Ernest S. Frerichs, and Nahum M. Sarna, eds., *From Ancient Israel to Modern Judaism: Intellect in Quest of Understanding*, 87–103. Vol. 4. Atlanta: Scholars, 1989.

Fixler, Michael. *Milton and the Kingdoms of God*. Evanston: Northwestern University Press, 1964.

Fletcher, Harris F. *Milton's Semitic Studies and Some Manifestations of Them in His Poetry*. Chicago: University of Chicago Press, 1926.

—— *Milton's Rabbinical Readings*. Urbana: University of Illinois Press, 1930.

Flinker, Noam. "Courting Urania: The Narrator of *Paradise Lost* Invokes His Muse." In Julia M. Wlaker, ed., *Milton and the Idea of Woman*, 86–99. Urbana: University of Illinois Press, 1988.

Frankel, Yonah. *Darkhei ha-Aggadah veha-Midrash* [Hebrew]. 2 vols. Jerusalem: Masadah, 1991.

Fresch, Cheryl H. "The Hebraic Influence Upon the Creation of Eve in *Paradise Lost*." *Milton Studies* 13 (1979): 181–99.

—— " 'As the Rabbines Expound': Milton, Genesis, and the Rabbis." *Milton Studies* 15 (1981): 59–79.

Friedman, Jerome. "Sixteenth-Century Christian-Hebraica: Scripture and the Renaissance Myth of the Past." *Sixteenth-Century Journal* 11 (1980): 67–85.

—— *The Most Ancient Testimony: Sixteenth-Century Christian-Hebraica in the Age of Renaissance Nostalgia*. Athens: Ohio University Press, 1983.

Froula, Christine. "When Eve Reads Milton: Undoing the Canonical Economy." *Critical Inquiry* 10 (1983): 321–47.

Frye, Northrop. "The Typology of *Paradise Regained*." *Modern Philology* 53 (1956): 227–38.

Funkenstein, Amos. *Perceptions of Jewish History*. Berkeley: University of California Press, 1993.

Gallagher, Philip J. "Creation in Genesis and in *Paradise Lost*." *Milton Studies* 20 (1984): 163–204.

Gardner, Helen. *A Reading of "Paradise Lost."* Oxford: Oxford University Press, 1965.

Gilbert, Sandra. "Patriarchal Poetry and Women Readers: Reflections on Milton's Bogey." *PMLA* 93 (1978): 368–82.

Ginzberg, Louis. *The Legends of the Jews*. Trans. Henrietta Szold. 7 vols. Philadelphia: Jewish Publication Society, 1968.

Glassman, Bernard. *Anti-Semitic Stereotypes Without Jews: Images of the Jews in England, 1290–1700*. Detroit: Wayne State University Press, 1975.

Goldin, Judah. *Studies in Midrash and Related Literature*. Ed. Barry L. Eichler and Jeffrey H. Tigay. Philadelphia: Jewish Publication Society, 1988.

Goldish, Matt. *Judaism in the Theology of Sir Isaac Newton*. Dordrecht: Kluwer, 1998.

Gossman, Lionel. "Philhellinism and Antisemitism: Matthew Arnold and His German Models." *Comparative Literature* 46 (1994): 1–39.

Grossman, Marshall. *"Authors to Themselves": Milton and the Revelation of History*. Cambridge: Cambridge University Press, 1987.

Guibbory, Achsah. *The Map of Time: Seventeenth-Century English Literature and Ideas of Pattern in History*. Urbana: University of Illinois Press, 1986.

— *Ceremony and Community from Herbert to Milton: Literature, Religion, and Cultural Conflict in Seventeenth-Century England*. Cambridge: Cambridge University Press, 1998.

Guillory, John. *Poetic Authority: Spenser, Milton, and Literary History*. New York: Columbia University Press, 1983.

— "From the Superfluous to the Supernumerary: Reading Gender in *Paradise Lost*." In Elizabeth D. Harvey and Katherine Eisaman Maus, eds., *Soliciting Interpretation: Literary Theory and Seventeenth-Century English Poetry*, 61–88. Chicago: University of Chicago Press, 1990.

Halivni, David Weiss. "From Midrash to Mishnah: Theological Repercussions and Further Clarifications of 'Chate'u Yisrael.'" In Michael Fishbane, ed., *The Midrashic Imagination: Jewish Exegesis, Thought, and History*, 23–44. Albany: SUNY Press, 1993.

Haller, William. *Foxe's Book of Martyrs and the Elect Nation*. London: Trinity, 1963.

Hamilton, Gary D. "Milton's Defensive God: A Reappraisal." *Studies in Philology* 69 (1972): 87–100.

Handelman, Susan. *The Slayers of Moses: The Emergence of Rabbinic Interpretation in Modern Literary Theory*. Albany: SUNY Press, 1982.

Hartman, Geoffrey H. "Adam on the Grass with Balsamum." *Beyond Formalism: Literary Essays, 1958–70*, pp. 124–50. New Haven: Yale University Press, 1970.

— "Milton's Counterplot." *Beyond Formalism: Literary Essays, 1958–70*, 113–23. New Haven: Yale University Press, 1970.

— *Saving the Text: Literature, Derrida, Philosophy*. Baltimore: Johns Hopkins University Press, 1981.

Hartman, Geoffrey H. and Sanford Budick, eds. *Midrash and Literature*. New Haven: Yale University Press, 1986.

Häublein, Ernst. "Milton's Paraphrase of Genesis: A Stylistic Reading of *Paradise Lost*, Book 7." *Milton Studies* 7 (1975): 101–25.

Hayman, A. P. "Rabbinic Judaism and the Problem of Evil." *Scottish Journal of Theology* 29 (1976): 461–76.

— "The Fall, Free Will, and Human Responsibility in Rabbinic Judaism." *Scottish Journal of Theology* 37 (1984): 13–22.

Heinemann, Isaak. *Darkhei ha-Aggadah* [Hebrew]. Jerusalem: Hebrew University Press, 1970.

Heinemann, Joseph. *Aggadoth ve-Toldotheyhen* [Hebrew]. Jerusalem: Keter, 1974.

Hill, Christopher. *Milton and the English Revolution.* New York: Viking, 1977.

— *The Experience of Defeat: Milton and Some Contemporaries.* London: Faber and Faber, 1984.

— *Writing and Revolution in Seventeenth-Century England.* Brighton: Harvester, 1985.

— "'Till the Conversion of the Jews.'" *Religion and Politics in Seventeenth-Century England,* 269–300. Amherst: University of Massachusetts Press, 1986.

Hirshman, Marc. "The Greek Fathers and the Aggada on Ecclesiastes: Formats of Exegesis in Late Antiquity." *Hebrew Union College Annual* 59 (1988): 137–65.

Honeygosky, Stephen R. *Milton's House of God: The Invisible and Visible Church.* Columbia: University of Missouri Press, 1993.

Howard, Leon. "'The invention' of Milton's 'Great Argument': A Study of the Logic of 'God's Ways to Men.'" *Huntington Library Quarterly* 9 (1945–46): 149–73.

Hughes, Merritt Y. "The Filiations of Milton's Celestial Dialogue." *Ten Perspectives on Milton,* 104–35. New Haven: Yale University Press, 1965.

Hunter, W. B. "Further Definitions: Milton's Theological Vocabulary." In W. B. Hunter, C. A. Patrides, J. H. Adamson, eds., *Bright Essence: Studies in Milton's Theology,* 15–25. Salt Lake City: University of Utah Press, 1971.

— "The Provenance of the *Christian Doctrine.*" *Studies in English Literature* 32 (1992): 129–42.

Hunter, W. B. and Stevie Davies. "Milton's Urania: 'The Meaning, Not the Name I Call.'" In William B. Hunter, ed., *The Descent of Urania: Studies in Milton, 1946–1988,* 31–45. Lewisburg: Bucknell University Press, 1988.

Isaac, Benjamin and Aharon Oppenheimer. "The Revolt of Bar Kokhba: Ideology and Modern Scholarship." *Journal of Jewish Studies* 36 (1985): 33–60.

James, Heather. "Milton's Eve, the Romance Genre, and Ovid." *Comparative Literature* 45 (1993): 121–44.

Jasper, David. *The Study of Literature and Religion.* Minneapolis: Fortress, 1989.

Jebb, Richard. "*Samson Agonistes* and the Hellenic Drama." *Proceedings of the British Academy, 1907–8,* 341–48. London: Oxford University Press, 1910.

Kahn, Charles H. *The Art and Thought of Heraclitus: An Edition of the Fragments with Translation and Commentary.* Cambridge: Cambridge University Press, 1979.

Katchen, Aaron L. *Christian Hebraists and Dutch Rabbis.* Cambridge: Harvard University Press, 1984.

Katz, David S. *Philo-Semitism and the Readmission of the Jews to England, 1603–1655.* Oxford: Clarendon, 1982.

Kelley, Maurice. "The Theological Dogma of *Paradise Lost,* 3, 173–202." *PMLA* 52 (1937): 75–79.

— *This Great Argument: A Study of Milton's "De Doctrina Christiana" as a Gloss Upon "Paradise Lost."* Princeton: Princeton University Press, 1941.

Kerrigan, William. *The Prophetic Milton.* Charlottesville: University Press of Virginia, 1974.

— *The Sacred Complex: On the Psychogenesis of "Paradise Lost."* Cambridge: Harvard University Press, 1983.

Klein, Michael L. "The Translations of Anthropomorphisms and Anthropopathisms in the Targumim." *Supplements to Vetus Testamentum* 32 (1981): 162–77.

Knoppers, Laura Lunger. *Historicizing Milton: Spectacle, Power, and Poetry in Restoration England.* Athens: University of Georgia Press, 1994.

Korsgaard, Christine M. "Personal Identity and the Unity of Agency: A Kantian Response to Parfit." *Philosophy and Public Affairs* 18 (1989): 101–32.

Kraeling, Emil G. *The Old Testament Since the Reformation.* London: Lutterworth, 1955.

Kranidas, Thomas. "Words, Words, Words, and the Word: Milton's *Of Prelatical Episcopacy.*" *Milton Studies* 16 (1982): 153–66.

Krook, Anne K. "The Hermeneutics of Opposition in *Paradise Regained* and *Samson Agonistes.*" *Studies in English Literature* 36 (1995): 129–47.

Krouse, F. Michael. *Milton's Samson and the Christian Tradition.* Princeton: Princeton University Press, 1949.

Kümmel, Werner Georg. *Introduction to the New Testament.* Trans. Howard Clark Kee. Nashville: Abingdon, 1975.

Labriola, Albert C. "'God Speaks': Milton's Dialogue in Heaven and the Tradition of Divine Deliberation." *Cithara* 25 (1986): 5–30.

Lacan, Jacques. *Four Fundamental Concepts of Psycho-Analysis.* Ed. Jacques-Alain Miller. Trans. Alan Sheridan. New York: Norton, 1978.

Lamberton, Robert. *Homer the Theologian: Neoplatonist Allegorical Reading and the Growth of the Epic Tradition.* Berkeley: University of California Press, 1986.

Landy, Marcia. "Kinship and the Role of Women in *Paradise Lost.*" *Milton Studies* 4 (1972): 3–19.

Leonard, John. *Naming in Paradise: Milton and the Language of Adam and Eve.* Oxford: Clarendon, 1990.

Lewalski, Barbara Kiefer. "Milton and Women—Yet Once More." *Milton Studies* 6 (1974): 3–20.

—— "The Genres of *Paradise Lost*: Literary Genre as a Means of Accommodation." *Milton Studies* 17 (1983): 75–103.

—— *"Paradise Lost" and the Rhetoric of Literary Forms*. Princeton: Princeton University Press, 1985.

Lewalski, Barbara Kiefer, John T. Shawcross, and William B. Hunter. "Forum: Milton's *Christian Doctrine*." *Studies in English Literature* 32 (1992): 143–66.

Lewis, C. S. *A Preface to "Paradise Lost."* Oxford: Oxford University Press, 1942.

Lieb, Michael. *The Dialectics of Creation: Patterns of Birth and Regeneration in "Paradise Lost."* Amherst: University of Massachusetts Press, 1970.

—— "*Paradise Lost*, Book 3: The Dialogue in Heaven Reconsidered." *Renaissance Papers* (1974): 39–50.

—— "*Paradise Lost* and the Myth of Prohibition." *Milton Studies* 7 (1975): 233–65.

—— *Poetics of the Holy: A Reading of "Paradise Lost."* Chapel Hill: University of North Carolina Press, 1981.

—— "Milton's 'Dramatick Constitution': The Celestial Dialogue in *Paradise Lost*, Book 3." *Milton Studies* 23 (1987): 215–40.

—— *The Sinews of Ulysses: Form and Convention in Milton's Works*. Pittsburgh: Duquesne University Press, 1989.

—— "Reading God: Milton and the Anthropopathic Tradition," *Milton Studies* 25 (1990): 213–43.

—— *Milton and the Culture of Violence*. Ithaca: Cornell University Press, 1994.

—— "'Our Living Dread': The God of *Samson Agonistes*." *Milton Studies* 33 (1997): 3–25.

—— "'A Thousand Fore-Skins': Circumcision, Violence, and Selfhood in Milton." *Milton Studies* 38 (2000): 198–219.

Lieberman, Saul. *Hellenism in Jewish Palestine: Studies in the Literary Transmission, Beliefs, and Manners of Palestine in the First Century B.C.E. to the Fourth Century C.E.* New York: Jewish Theological Seminary Press, 1950.

Lieu, Judith, John North, and Tessa Rajak, eds. *The Jews Among Pagans and Christians in the Roman Empire*. London: Routledge, 1992.

Lloyd Jones, G. *The Discovery of Hebrew in Tudor England: A Third Language*. Manchester: Manchester University Press, 1983.

Loewenstein, David. *Milton and the Drama of History: Historical Vision, Iconoclasm, and the Literary Imagination*. Cambridge: Cambridge University Press, 1990.

Loewenstein, David and James Grantham Turner, eds. *Politics, Poetics, and Hermeneutics in Milton's Prose*. Cambridge: Cambridge University Press, 1990.

Lord. George, de F. "Milton's Dialogue with Omniscience in *Paradise Lost*." In Louis

L. Martz and Aubrey Williams, eds., *The Author in His Work: Essays on a Problem in Criticism*, 31–50. New Haven: Yale Universoty Press, 1978.

Low, Anthony. "Milton's God: Authority in *Paradise Lost*." *Milton Studies* 4 (1972): 19–38.

Luxon, Thomas. *Literal Figures: Puritan Allegory and the Reformation Crisis in Representation.* Chicago: University of Chicago Press, 1995.

MacCallum, Hugh. "Milton and Figurative Interpretation of the Bible." *University of Toronto Quarterly* 31 (1962): 397–415.

— "Milton and Sacred History: Books 11 and 12 of *Paradise Lost*." In Millar MacLure and F. W. Watt, eds., *Essays in English Literature from the Renaissance to the Victorian Age*, 149–68. Toronto: University of Toronto Press, 1964.

— "'Most Perfect Hero': The Role of the Son in Milton's Theodicy." In Balachandra Rajan, ed., *"Paradise Lost": A Tercentenary Tribute*, 79–105. Toronto: University of Toronto Press, 1969.

— *Milton and the Sons of God: The Divine Image in Milton's Epic Poetry.* Toronto: University of Toronto Press, 1986.

McColley, Diane Kelsey. *Milton's Eve.* Urbana: Univerity of Illinois Press, 1983.

McKnight, Stephen A. *The Modern Age and the Recovery of Ancient Wisdom: A Reconsideration of Historical Consciousness, 1450–1650.* Columbia: University of Missouri Press, 1991.

McLoone, George H. "'True Religion' and Tragedy: Milton's Insights in *Samson Agonistes*." *Mosaic* 28 (1995): 1–29.

Madsen, William G. *From Shadowy Types to Truth: Studies in Milton's Symbolism.* New Haven: Yale University Press, 1968.

Mann, Jacob. *The Bible as Read and Preached in the Old Synagogue.* Vol. 1. New York: Ktav, 1971.

Marks, Richard G. *The Image of Bar Kokhba in Traditional Jewish Literature: False Messiah and National Hero.* University Park: Penn State University Press, 1994.

Martz, L. L. *The Paradise Within: Studies in Vaughan, Traherne, and Milton.* New Haven: Yale Unversity Press, 1964.

— *Milton: Poet of Exile.* New Haven: Yale Unversity Press, 1980.

Matar, Nabil I. "Milton and the Idea of the Restoration of the Jews." *Studies in English Literature* 27 (1987): 109–24.

— *Islam in Britain, 1558–1685.* Cambridge: Cambridge University Press, 1998.

Mendelsohn, Leonard R. "Milton and the Rabbis: A Later Inquiry." *Studies in English Literature* 18 (1978): 125–35.

Mollenkott, Virginia R. "The Pervasive Influence of the Apocrypha in Milton's Thought and Art." In J. Max Patrick and Roger H. Sundell, eds., *Milton and the Art of Sacred Song*, 23–43. Madison: University of Wisconsin Press, 1979.

Muskin, Miriam. "Milton's Understanding of Hebraism and *Samson Agonistes.*" Ph.D. diss., Case Western Reserve University, 1977.

— "'Wisdom by Adversity': Davidic Traits in Milton's Samson." *Milton Studies* 14 (1980): 233–55.

Nagel, Thomas. *The View from Nowhere.* Oxford: Oxford University Press, 1989.

Netanyahu, Benzion. *Toward the Inquisition: Essays on Jewish and Converso History in Late Medieval Spain.* Ithaca: Cornell University Press, 1997.

Neusner, Jacob. "Genesis and Judaism: The Perspective of Genesis Rabbah." *Tradition* 22 (1987): 88–101.

— *Judaism and Christianity in the Age of Constantine: History, Messiah, Israel, and the Initial Confrontation.* Chicago: University of Chicago Press, 1987.

— *Judaism in the Matrix of Christianity.* Atlanta: Scholars, 1991.

Neusner, Jacob and Ernest S. Frerichs, eds. *"To See Ourselves as Others See Us": Christians, Jews, and "Others" in Late Antiquity.* Chico, Calif.: Scholars, 1985.

Newman, Louis Israel. *Jewish Influence on Christian Reform Movements.* New York: Columbia University Press, 1925.

Norbrook, David. *Poetry and Politics in the English Renaissance.* London: Routledge and Kegan Paul, 1984.

Nyquist, Mary. "Gynesis, Genesis, Exegesis, and the Formation of Milton's Eve." In Marjorie Garber, ed., *Cannibals, Witches, and Divorce: Estranging the Renaissance,* 147–208. Baltimore: Johns Hopkins University Press, 1987.

Nyquist, Mary and Margaret W. Ferguson, eds. *Re-Membering Milton: Essays on the Texts and Traditions.* New York: Methuen, 1987.

Oberman, Heiko A. *Luther: Man Between God and the Devil.* Trans. Eileen Walliser-Schwarzbart. New York: Image, 1989.

Olsen, Viggo Norskov. *John Foxe and the Elizabethan Church.* Berkeley: University of California Press, 1973.

Pardes, Ilana. *Countertraditions in the Bible: A Feminist Approach.* Cambridge: Harvard University Press, 1992.

Parish, John E. "Milton and an Anthropomorphic God." *Studies in Philology* 56 (1959): 619–25.

Parker, Patricia. *Literary Fat Ladies: Rhetoric, Gender, Property.* London: Methuen, 1987.

Parker, William Riley. *Milton's Debt to Greek Tragedy in "Samson Agonistes."* Baltimore: Johns Hopkins University Press, 1937.

Patrides, C. A. "The Tree of Knowledge in the Christian Tradition." *Studia Neophilologica* 34 (1962): 239–42.

— *"Paradise Lost* and the Theory of Accommodation." *Texas Studies in Language and Literature* 5 (1963): 58–63.

— *Milton and the Christian Tradition.* Oxford: Clarendon, 1966.

— "The Godhead in *Paradise Lost*: Dogma or Drama?" In W. B. Hunter, C. A. Patrides, J. H. Adamson, eds., *Bright Essence: Studies in Milton's Theology,* 71–77. Salt Lake City: University of Utah Press, 1971.

Patrides, C. A. and Joseph Wittreich, eds. *The Apocalypse in English Renaissance Thought and Literature.* Ithaca: Cornell University Press, 1984.

Pecheux, Mary Christopher. "Abraham, Adam, and the Theme of Exile in *Paradise Lost.*" *PMLA* 80 (1965): 365–71.

— "The Council Scenes in *Paradise Lost.*" In James H. Sims and Leland Ryken, eds., *Milton and the Scriptural Tradition: The Bible Into Poetry.* Columbia: University of Missouri Press, 1984.

Peter, John. *A Critique of "Paradise Lost."* New York: Archon, 1960.

Popkin, Richard H., ed. *Millenarianism and Messianism in English Literature and Thought, 1650–1800.* Leiden: Brill, 1988.

Preus, James S. *From Shadow to Promise: Old Testament Interpretation from Augustine to the Young Luther.* Cambridge: Belknap, 1969.

Quilligan, Maureen. *Milton's Spenser: The Politics of Reading.* Ithaca: Cornell University Press, 1983.

Radzinowicz, Mary Ann. "'Man as a Probationer of Immortality': *Paradise Lost* 11–12." In C. A. Patrides, ed., *Approaches to "Paradise Lost,"* 31–51. London: Edward Arnold, 1968.

— *Toward "Samson Agonistes": The Growth of Milton's Mind.* Princeton: Princeton University Press, 1978.

— "The Politics of *Paradise Lost.*" In Kevin Sharpe and Steven N. Zwicker, eds., *Politics of Discourse: The Literature and History of Seventeenth-Century England,* 204–29. Berkeley: University of California Press, 1987.

Ragussis, Michael. *Figures of Conversion: "The Jewish Question" and English National Identity.* Durham: Duke University Press, 1995.

Rajan, Balachandra. *"Paradise Lost" and the Seventeenth-Century Reader.* Ann Arbor: University of Michigan Press, 1967 [1947].

Rajan, Balachandra and Elizabeth Sauer, eds. *Milton and the Imperial Vision.* Pittsburgh: Duquesne University Press, 1999.

Reuther, Rosemary Radford. "Judaism and Christianity: Two Fourth-Century Religions." *Studies in Religion* 2 (1972–1973): 1–10.

— *Faith and Fratricide: The Theological Roots of Anti-Semitism.* New York: Seabury, 1974.

Richmond, Hugh M. *The Christian Revolutionary: John Milton.* Berkeley: University of California Press, 1974.

Ricoeur, Paul. *The Symbolism of Evil.* Trans. Emerson Buchanan. New York: Harper and Row, 1967.

Robbins, Jill. *Prodigal Son/Elder Brother: Interpretation and Alterity in Augustine, Petrarch, Kafka, Levinas.* Chicago: University of Chicago Press, 1991.

Rogers, John. *The Matter of Revolution: Science, Poetry, and Politics in the Age of Milton.* Ithaca: Cornell University Press, 1996.

Rosenblatt, Jason P. "Eden, Israel, England: Milton's Spiritual Geography." In John McVeagh, ed., *1660–1780: All Before Them.* Vol. 1. *English Literature and the Wider World.* Ed. Michael Cotsell. London: Ashfield, 1990.

— *Torah and Law in "Paradise Lost."* Princeton: Princeton University Press, 1994.

Rosenthal, E. I. J. "Rashi and the English Bible." *Bulletin of the John Rylands Library* 24 (1940): 138–67.

Rosenthal, Frank. "The Rise of Christian Hebraism in the Sixteenth Century." *Historia Judaica* 7 (1945): 167–91.

Ross, Malcom Mackenzie. *Milton's Royalism: A Study of the Conflict of Symbol and Idea in the Poems.* Ithaca: Cornell University Press, 1943.

Roth, Leon. "Hebraists and Non-Hebraists of the Seventeenth Century." *Journal of Semitic Studies* 6 (1961): 204–21.

Rumrich, John Peter. *Matter of Glory: A New Preface to "Paradise Lost."* Pittsburgh: University of Pittsburgh Press, 1987.

— *Milton Unbound: Controversy and Reinterpretation.* Cambridge: Cambridge University Press, 1996.

Ryken, Leland. *The Apocalyptic Vision in "Paradise Lost."* Ithaca: Cornell University Press, 1970.

Samuel, Irene. "The Dialogue in Heaven: A Reconsideration of *Paradise Lost,* III, 1–417." *PMLA* 72 (1957): 601–11.

Sauer, Elizabeth. *Barbarous Dissonance and Images of Voice in Milton's Epics.* Montreal: McGill-Queens University Press, 1996.

Saurat, Denis. *Milton: Man and Thinker.* London: Dent, 1925.

Schäfer, Peter. "Rabbi Aqiva and Bar Kokhba." In William Scott Green, ed., *Approaches to Ancient Judaism,* 2:113–30. Chico, Cal.: Scholars, 1980.

Schmidt, Charles B. "Perennial Philosophy: From Agostino to Steuco to Leibniz." *Journal of the History of Ideas* 27 (1966): 505–32.

— "Prisca Theologia e Philosophia Perennis: Due temi del Rinascimento italtiano e la loro fortuna." In Giovannagiola Tarugi, ed., *Il Pensiero del Rinascimento e il tempo nostro,* 211–36. Florence: Olschki, 1970.

Schwartz, Regina M. *Remembering and Repeating: On Milton's Theology and Poetics.* Chicago: University of Chicago Press, 1993.

Segal, Alan. *Rebecca's Children: Judaism and Christianity in the Roman World.* Cambridge: Harvard University Press, 1986.

Seznec, Jean. *The Survival of the Pagan Gods: The Mythological Tradition and Its Place in Renaissance Humanism and Art.* Trans. Barbara F. Sessions. New York: Harper, 1961.

Shapiro, James. *Shakespeare and the Jews.* New York: Columbia University Press, 1996.

Shapiro, Marta Berl. "*Samson Agonistes* and the Hebraic Tradition." Ph.D. diss., St. John University, 1974.

Shawcross, John T. "The Metaphor of Inspiration in *Paradise Lost.*" In Amadeus P. Fiore, ed., *Th'upright Heart and Pure,* 75–85. Pittsburgh: Duquesne University Press, 1967.

— *John Milton: The Self and the World.* Lexington: University of Kentucky Press, 1993.

Shinan, Avigdor and Yair Zakovitch. "Midrash on Scripture and Midrash Within Scripture." *Scripta Hierosolymitana* 31 (1986): 257–77.

Shoulson, Jeffrey S. "'Proprietie in This Hebrew Poesy': George Wither, Judaism, and the Formation of English National Identity." *Journal of English and Germanic Philology* 98 (1999): 353–72.

Sims, James H. "Milton, Literature as a Bible, and the Bible as Literature." In J. Max Patrick and Roger H. Sundell, eds., *Milton and the Art of Sacred Song.* Madison: University of Wisconsin Press, 1979.

Slonimsky, Henry. "The Philosophy Implicit in the Midrash." *Hebrew Union College Annual* 27 (1956): 235–90.

Smith, Nigel. *Perfection Proclaimed: Language and Literature in English Radical Religion, 1640–1660.* Oxford: Oxford University Press, 1989.

Soloveitchik, J. B. "The Lonely Man of Faith." *Tradition* 7 (1965): 5–67.

Stein, Arnold. *Answerable Style: Essays on "Paradise Lost."* Seattle: University of Washington Press, 1953.

Stern, David. "Rhetoric and Midrash: The Case of the Mashal." *Prooftexts* 1 (1981): 261–91.

— "Moses-cide: Midrash and Contemporary Literary Criticism." *Prooftexts* 4 (1984): 193–213.

— "The Rabbinic Parable: From Rhetoric to Poetics." *Studies in Biblical Literature Seminar Papers* 25 (1986): 631–43.

— "Midrash and Indeterminacy." *Critical Inquiry* 15 (1988): 132–61.

— *Parables in Midrash: Narrative and Exegesis in Rabbinic Literature.* Cambridge: Harvard University Press, 1991.

— "*Imitatio Hominis*: Anthropomorphism and the Character(s) of God in Rabbinic Literature." *Prooftexts* 12 (1992): 151–74.

— "The Captive Woman: Hellenization, Greco-Roman Erotic Narrative, and Rabbinic Literature." *Poetics Today* 19 (1998): 91–127.

Stern, David and Susan Handelman. "Controversy: Fragments of the Rock: Contemporary Literary Theory and the Study of Rabbinic Texts." *Prooftexts* 5 (1985): 75–103.

Stern, David and Mark Jay Mirsky, eds. *Rabbinic Fantasies: Imaginative Narratives from Classical Hebrew Literature*. New Haven: Yale University Press, 1990.

Stocker, Margarita. "God in Theory: Milton, Literature, and Theodicy." *Journal of Literature and Theology* 1 (1987): 70–88.

Stollman. Samuel S. "Milton's Samson and the Jewish Tradition." *Milton Studies* 3 (1971): 185–200.

— "Milton's Rabbinical Readings and Fletcher." *Milton Studies* 4 (1972): 195–215.

— "Milton's Understanding of the 'Hebraic' in *Samson Agonistes*." *Studies in Philology* 69 (1972): 334–47.

— "Milton's Dichotomy of 'Judaism' and 'Hebraism.'" *PMLA* 89 (1974): 105–12.

— "Satan, Sin, and Death: A Mosaic Trio." *Milton Studies* 22 (1986): 101–20.

Strack, H. L. and G. Stemberger. *Introduction to the Talmud and Midrash*. Trans. Markus Bockmuehl. Minneapolis: Fortress, 1992.

Summer, Joseph H. *The Muses Method*. Cambridge: Harvard University Press, 1962.

Svendsen, Kester. *Milton and Science*. Cambridge: Harvard University Press, 1956.

Swaim, Kathleen M. "The Mimesis of Accommodation in Book 3 of *Paradise Lost*." *Philological Quarterly* 63 (1984): 461–75.

Syme, Ronald. *Emperors and Biography: Studies in the Historia Augusta*. Oxford: Clarendon, 1971.

Tanner, John S. *Anxiety in Eden: A Kierkegaardian Reading of "Paradise Lost."* New York: Oxford University Press, 1992.

Tayler, Edward W. *Milton's Poetry: Its Development in Time*. Pittsburgh: Duquesne University Press, 1979.

Tillyard, E. M. W. *Studies in Milton*. New York: Macmillan, 1951.

Todd, Henry J., ed. *The Poetical Works of John Milton with Notes of Various Authors*. 2d ed. 7 vols. London, 1809.

Treip, Mindele Anne. *Allegorical Poetics and the Epic: The Renaissance Tradition to "Paradise Lost."* Lexington: University of Kentucky Press, 1994.

Turner, James Grantham. *One Flesh: Paradisal Marriage and Sexual Relations in the Age of Milton*. Oxford: Oxford University Press, 1987.

Tuttle, Elizabeth. "Biblical Reference in the Political Pamphlets of the Levellers and

Milton, 1638–1654." In David Armitage, Armand Himy, and Quentin Skinner, eds., *Milton and Republicanism*, 63–81. Cambridge: Cambridge University Press, 1995.

Urbach, Ephraim E. *The Sages: Their Concepts and Beliefs.* Trans. Israel Abrahams. Cambridge: Harvard University Press, 1979.

van den Berg, J. and Ernestine G. E. van der Wall, eds. *Jewish-Christian Relations in the Seventeenth Century.* Dordrecht: Kluwer, 1988.

von Maltzahn, Nicholas. *Milton's "History of Britain": Republican Historiography in the English Revolution.* Oxford: Clarendon, 1991.

Waldock, A. J. A. *"Paradise Lost" and Its Critics.* Cambridge: University Press, 1947.

Walker, D. P. *The Ancient Theology: Studies in Christian Platonism from the Fifteenth to the Eighteenth Century.* Ithaca: Cornell University Press, 1972.

Walker, William. "Typology and *Paradise Lost*, Books 11 and 12." *Milton Studies* 25 (1989): 245–64.

Wallach, Luitpold. "The Colloquy of Marcus Aurelius with the Patriarch Judah I." *Jewish Quarterly Review* n.s. 31 (1940/41): 259–86.

Webber, Joan Mallory. "The Politics of Poetry: Feminism and *Paradise Lost.*" *Milton Studies* 14 (1980): 3–24.

Wendel, François. *Calvin: Origins and Developments of His Religious Thought.* Trans. Philip Mairet. Durham: Labyrinth, 1987.

Werblowsky, R. J. Zwi. "Milton and the *Conjectura Cabbalistica.*" *Journal of the Warburg and Courtland Institutes* 18 (1955): 90–113.

Werman, Golda. *Milton and Midrash.* Washington, D. C.: Catholic University of America Press, 1995.

Westermann, Claus. *Genesis: An Introduction.* Trans. John J. Scullion. Minneapolis: Fortress, 1992.

White, Haydn. "The Rhetoric of Interpretation." *The Rhetoric of Interpretation and the Interpretation of Rhetoric.* Ed. Paul Hernadi. Durham: Duke University Press, 1989.

Williams, Arnold. *The Common Expositor.* Chapel Hill: University of North Carolina Press, 1948.

Williamson, Arthur H. "Scotland, Antichrist, and the Invention of Great Britain." In John Dwyer, Roger A. Mason, and Alexander Murdoch, eds., *New Perspectives on the Politics and Culture of Early Modern Scotland*, 34–58. Edinburgh: John Donald, 1982.

—— "'A Pil for Pork-Eaters': Ethnic Identity, Apocalyptic Promises, and the Strange Creation of the Judeo-Scots." In Raymond B. Waddington and Arthur H. Williamson, eds., *The Expulsion of the Jews: 1492 and After*, 237–51. New York: Garland, 1992.

Winston, David. "Philo and the Rabbis on Sex and the Body." *Poetics Today* 19 (1998): 41–62.

Wittreich, Joseph Anthony, Jr. *Visionary Poetics: Milton's Tradition and His Legacy.* San Marino: Huntington Library Press, 1979.

—— *Interpreting "Samson Agonistes."* Princeton: Princeton University Press, 1986.

—— *Feminist Milton.* Ithaca: Cornell University Press, 1987.

Wolfe, Don M. "Limits of Miltonic Toleration." *Journal of English and Germanic Philology* 60 (1961): 834–46.

Wood, Diana, ed. *Christianity and Judaism: Papers Read at the 1991 Summer Meeting and the 1992 Winter Meeting of the Ecclesiastical History Society.* London: Blackwell, 1992.

Woods, Susanne. "'That Freedom of Discussion Which I Loved': Italy and Milton's Cultural Self-Definition." In Mario Di Cesare, ed., *Milton in Italy: Contexts, Images, Contradictions,* 9–18. Binghamton: Medieval and Renaissance Texts and Studies, 1991.

Woolf, Virginia. *A Room of One's Own.* New York: Harcourt Brace Jovanovich, 1989 [1929].

Worden, Blair. "Providence and Politics in Cromwellian England." *Past and Present* 109 (1985): 55–99.

Yates, Frances A. *Giordano Bruno and the Hermetic Tradition.* London, 1964.

Yerushalmi, Yosef Hayim. *Zakhor: Jewish History and Jewish Memory.* Seattle: University of Washington Press, 1982.

Yu, Anthony C. "Life in the Garden: Freedom and the Image of God in *Paradise Lost.*" *Journal of Religion* 60 (1980): 247–71.

Zeitlin, Solomon. *Solomon Zeitlin's Studies in the Early History of Judaism.* 4 vols. New York: Ktav, 1973–1978.

Zerubavel, Yael. *Recovered Roots: Collective Memory and the Making of Israeli National Tradition.* Chicago: University of Chicago Press, 1995.

Index